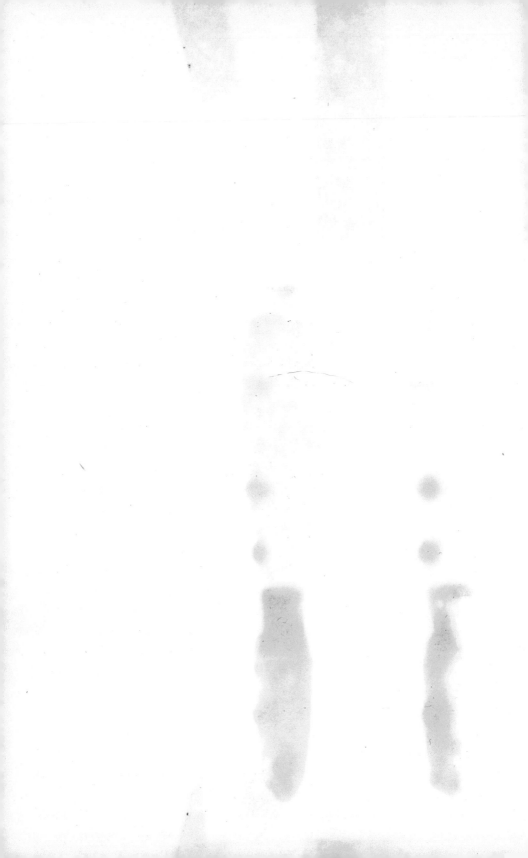

SCHOOL DESEGREGATION

Past, Present, and Future

PERSPECTIVES IN SOCIAL PSYCHOLOGY
A Series of Texts and Monographs • Edited by Elliot Aronson

A Continuation Order Plan is available for this series. A continuation order will bring delivery of each new volume immediately upon publication. Volumes are billed only upon actual shipment. For further information please contact the publisher.

SCHOOL DESEGREGATION

Past, Present, and Future

Edited by

Walter G. Stephan
New Mexico State University, Las Cruces

and

Joe R. Feagin
The University of Texas at Austin

PLENUM PRESS • NEW YORK AND LONDON

Library of Congress Cataloging in Publication Data

Main entry under title:

School desegregation.

(Perspectives in social psychology)
Includes index.
1. School integration—United States—Addresses, essays, lectures. I. Stephan,
Walter G. II. Feagin, Joe R.
LC214.2.S355   370.19'342   79-23436
ISBN 0-306-40378-1

© 1980 Plenum Press, New York
A Division of Plenum Publishing Corporation
227 West 17th Street, New York, N.Y. 10011

Printed in the United States of America

To Gordon W. Allport

Contributors

David J. Armor, The Rand Corporation, Santa Monica, California

Elizabeth G. Cohen, Center for Educational Research, School of Education, Stanford University, Stanford, California

Joe R. Feagin, Department of Sociology, University of Texas, Austin, Texas

Lino A. Graglia, University of Texas Law School, University of Texas, Austin, Texas

Andrew M. Greeley, Center for the Study of American Pluralism, National Opinion Research Center, Chicago, Illinois

Susan L. Greenblatt, Graduate School of Education, Harvard University, Cambridge, Massachusetts

Peter Iadicola, Program for Research in Integrated Multiethnic Education, University of California, Riverside, California

Jane R. Mercer, Program for Research in Integrated Multiethnic Education, University of California, Riverside, California

Norman Miller, Department of Psychology, University of Southern California, Los Angeles, California

Helen Moore, Program for Research in Integrated Multiethnic Education, University of California, Riverside, California

Gary Orfield, Department of Political Science, University of Illinois, Urbana, Illinois

Ray C. Rist, Youthwork National Policy Study, College of Human Ecology, Cornell University, Ithaca, New York

Walter G. Stephan, Department of Psychology, New Mexico State University, Las Cruces, New Mexico

Arthur L. Stinchcombe, National Opinion Research Center, Chicago, Illinois, and Department of Sociology, University of Arizona, Tucson, Arizona

D. Garth Taylor, National Opinion Research Center, and Department of Political Science, University of Chicago, Chicago, Illinois

Charles V. Willie, Graduate School of Education, Harvard University, Cambridge, Massachusetts

Mark G. Yudof, University of Texas Law School, University of Texas, Austin, Texas

Contents

3

The Serendipitous Effects of School Desegregation 51
Susan L. Greenblatt and Charles V. Willie

4

From Prohibiting Segregation to Requiring Integration:
      Developments in the Law of Race and the Schools
      since Brown 69
Lino A. Graglia

5

6

7

8

9

10

11

12

13

Historical Background of School Desegregation

A Brief Historical Overview of School Desegregation

WALTER G. STEPHAN

The desegregation of America's schools has been one of this country's most explosive social issues for more than a century. The origins of the present controversy over school desegregation extend deep into the American past. The foundation of this controversy rests on the relationship between the races. In order to grasp the complexities of the present situation, an understanding of the past is essential. For this reason, relevant aspects of the history of American race relations will be traced in this chapter. In this brief history, emphasis will be placed on the different patterns of race relations that evolved in the North and South. Special attention will be given to the evolution of segregation in education, early Supreme Court decisions relevant to desegregation, and to the contributions made by social scientists to the *Brown*[1] decision.

FROM SLAVERY TO EMANCIPATION

The most important historical antecedent of the present resistance to desegregation is the institution of slavery which was initiated following the arrival of the first Blacks to America in 1619. It has been argued that slavery was initially conceived as a temporary institution which was to function until the Blacks and Indians were converted to Christianity (Rose, 1944). Be this as it may, its economic function was to provide the plantation

---

[1] *Brown* v. *Board of Education*, 347 U.S. 483 (1954).

WALTER G. STEPHAN • Department of Psychology, New Mexico State University, Las Cruces, New Mexico 88003.

system with a stable resident labor supply. The concept of race developed within the context of this institution as a justification for the subordination of the labor force. The planters regarded the slaves as being from a biologically inferior group. The physical differences between the two groups were cited as the basis for this belief (Thompson, 1975).

Whites divested Blacks of their traditions and subordinated them. A natural consequence of these conditions was that negative traits generated by the plantation system came to be thought of as characteristics of Blacks. Blacks were forced to work under threat of punishment. According to John H. Franklin (1974), "the idleness and laziness of slaves . . . was inherent in a system of forced labor" (p. 144). Because their maintenance was provided for in the most minimal fashion, they were described as dirty or slovenly. And because they were permitted no education, they were regarded as ignorant. One of the cruelest legacies of slavery is that these stereotypical labels, that were a natural product of the contact between Blacks and Whites under the plantation system, would in time come to constitute the basis for discrimination against Blacks (Franklin, 1974; LeVine & Campbell, 1972).

The division that would evolve between the North and South in the treatment of Blacks became manifest at the time that the colonies declared themselves independent from Britain. Many of the northern states moved to eliminate slavery. Massachusetts abolished slavery in 1783, and Pennsylvania (1780), Connecticut (1784), and Rhode Island (1784) passed laws providing for the eventual abolition of slavery (Kluger, 1976). In deference to the South, the Constitution condoned slavery. Each slave was counted as three-fifths of a person for purposes of taxation and representation. Slaves, however, had no rights. In the words of James Madison:

> In being compelled to labor not for himself, but for a master; in being vendible by one master to another master; and in being subject at all times to being restrained in his liberty and chastised in his body, by the capricious will of another, the slave may appear to be degraded from the human rank and classed with those irrational animals, which fall under the legal denomination of property. (The Federalist, No. 54)

By 1794, every state in the Union had passed laws which banned the importation of slaves. The reason, in part, was that the institution of slavery was on the decline. Tobacco had depleted the soils of the southeastern states, and the demand for it was diminishing. By the turn of the century, however, cotton began to replace tobacco and this revived the plantation system. As the demand for cotton increased, the number of slaves increased correspondingly. There were less than 3,500 slaves in Mississippi in 1800, but by 1840 there were over 136,000 (Kluger, 1976). Franklin (1974) has summarized the causes of the revival of slavery as follows:

The Industrial Revolution in England, the invention of the cotton gin, the extension of slavery into the new territories, and the persistence of the slave trade into the nineteenth century all had the the effect of establishing slavery in the United States on a more permanent basis than ever before. (p. 110)

As long as slave labor continued to be imported from Africa, the planters took little interest in the education of their slaves beyond teaching them the skills required to maintain the plantation system. As imported labor became scarce, the planters began to rely on an indigenous source of labor, the children of slaves. These children required education of some kind, but formal education posed a threat to the system itself. As part of an increased repression directed toward Blacks during the early 1800s, the formal education of Blacks became illegal in nearly every slave state (Weinberg, 1977). In spite of these laws, a few schools for Blacks did exist in both the North and the South. However, the number of Blacks educated in these schools was never large. The usual solution to "educating" Blacks in the South was to provide them with a minimal vocational education. This solution is consistent with a universal pattern outlined by Edgar T. Thompson (1975):

In interracial societies the control of education is ordinarily vested in a racial oligarchy whose original purpose in yielding the privilege of education is to insure that the children of the laboring races will remain laborers. . . . This is an education designed not only to take racial differences into account, but to extend and perpetuate them as well. It is an education intended to discipline the classes that occupy the lower levels of the racial division of labor. (p. 158)

In the North, the public school movement was gathering momentum during the first half of the nineteenth century. In 1827, Massachusetts passed a law requiring the establishment of high schools in towns with populations of over 500 families (Atkinson & Moleska, 1975). Two factors provided the major impetus for the drive to achieve universal education. The first, stressed by educational reformers such as Thomas Jefferson, was that in a democracy power rests with the people. If a democratic nation is to be well governed, the general populace must be educated. The second factor was the influx of immigrants. Public education was an essential tool in transforming the children of immigrants into "good little" American citizens (Tyack, 1967).

Although antislavery sentiment was strong in the North before the Civil War, discrimination against free Blacks was widely practiced. They were not given the vote and were commonly denied access to public conveyances and other facilities. Among the free Blacks of the North, education was a privilege enjoyed by a small minority. Less than 7% of all free Blacks attended schools in 1860 (DuBois, 1935). There was little public education of any kind in the South prior to the Civil War and for some time following the war. According to W. E. B. DuBois (1935) most southern states did not even have school taxes during this period.

FROM THE CIVIL WAR TO WORLD WAR I

Race relations changed greatly after the Civil War. The formal basis for these changes was the Emancipation Proclamation of 1863 which freed the slaves in the Confederate States. Two years later the Thirteenth Amendment to the Constitution ratified and extended the abolition of slavery to all the states in the reunited union. In the South, the racist sentiment behind slavery was little diminished by its abolition. Immediately following the end of the war, "Black Codes" were enacted in many Southern states. These codes were designed to restrict the rights and freedom of movement of the newly freed slaves. Blacks could not hold office or vote and, in many southern states, stiff vagrancy laws were instituted (Gossett, 1965). Congress reacted to the Black Codes by passing a Civil Rights Act in 1866 and later wrote portions of this act into the Constitution as part of the Fourteenth Amendment in 1868. The Fourteenth Amendment read:

> No State shall make or enforce any law which shall abridge the privileges or immunities of citizens of the United States; nor shall any State deprive any person of life, liberty, or property without due process of law; nor deny any person within its jurisdiction the equal protection of the laws.

The right to an education, even a segregated one, was not guaranteed by the 1866 Civil Rights Act or the Fourteenth Amendment.

Congress had established the Freedman's Bureau before the end of the war and it was extended in 1866. Education for Blacks improved markedly during the brief existence of the Bureau (1865–1872). W. E. B. DuBois reported that, by 1870, the Freedman's Bureau had created 4,200 schools with nearly a quarter of a million pupils. Although this represented a significant increase from the prewar period, still less than 5% of the Black population was attending school. These schools were, of course, segregated (DuBois, 1935). Public education for Blacks was little better in the North than in the South. In 1871, the State Supreme Courts of Ohio and Indiana ruled that separate schools were legal—if they were equal (Gossett, 1965).

In 1867, Congress passed the Reconstruction Act which provided for the enfranchisement of Blacks and a limited disenfranchisement of Whites in the South. The right of Blacks to vote was subsequently ratified as part of the Fifteenth Amendment in 1868. The federal troops which had been in the South since the end of the war were removed in 1877 as a result of the Hayes–Tilden compromise. The removal of troops left the fate of Blacks in the hands of southern Whites.

Other changes of a less political nature were also occurring after the war. The rise of industrialization and the migration of Blacks to urban centers had a profound impact on race relations. Van den Berghe (1967) has characterized the changes occurring during this period as a transition from a paternalistic to a competitive orientation in race relations. With the fall of plantation agriculture, the traditional master–slave model of race relations gave way to a type of relationship in which Blacks and poor Whites competed for jobs. Relations between Blacks and Whites, which had previously been informal, paternalistic, and complementary, became formal, impersonal, and competitive. Threatened by equal status with Blacks, White supremacists moved to place Blacks in their former subordinate position.

Between 1890 and 1910, Blacks were effectively disenfranchised in every state in the South. The means employed included poll taxes, grandfather clauses, and literacy tests (Gossett, 1965); the use of which is evidence of the meager success of Reconstruction efforts to educate Blacks. Segregation on public conveyances was mandatory in many southern states. This direct challenge to the Fourteenth Amendment made its way to the Supreme Court in 1896 when Homer Plessy challenged the right of the East Louisiana Railway to place him in a segregated coach reserved for Blacks.[2] The decision of the court defined the legal framework of race relations for the next 58 years, until it was eventually reversed in *Brown* v. *The Board of Education*. In 1896, the court interpreted the Fourteenth Amendment as follows:

> The object of the amendment was undoubtedly to enforce the absolute equality of the two races before the law, but in the nature of things it could not have been intended to abolish distinctions based on color, or to enforce social, as distinguished from political equality, or a commingling of the two races upon terms unsatisfactory to either.... Laws permitting, or even requiring, separation in places where [the races] are liable to be brought into contact do not necessarily imply the inferiority of either race. . . .

In dissent, Justice Harlan wrote:

> The destinies of the two races, in this country, are indissolubly linked together, and the interests of both require that the common government of all shall not permit the seeds of race hate to be planted under sanction of law.

Thus, the doctrine of "separate but equal" became law.

The *Plessy* decision was used as a justification for the increasingly formal and legalized use of segregation in many aspects of social life in the South. Among the aspects of southern life where segregation took firm hold were public education, public transportation, hotels and restaurants, hospitals, housing, departments of the United States Government, and even the

---

[2] *Plessy v. Ferguson* 163 U.S. 537 (1896).

gallery of the United States Senate (Gossett, 1965). A little over a decade after *Plessy*, the Supreme Court, in *Berea College* v. *Kentucky* (1908),[3] upheld the right of the states to prohibit racial integration in the field of education (Kluger, 1976).

Black reaction to the growing repression directed toward them took a new form that was to have important implications for race relations. Led by W. E. B. DuBois, the Niagara Movement (1908) and then the National Association for Advancement of Colored People (NAACP–1910) were formed. Under DuBois's editorship, *The Crisis* provided Black America with an outlet for its new militancy. The NAACP also recognized the importance of using the law to challenge segregation, and in 1915 the NAACP hired its first lawyer (Kluger, 1976).

WORLD WAR I TO *BROWN*

Economic conditions in the South were deteriorating during the second decade of the twentieth century. The boll weevil ravaged king cotton, flooding was widespread, and unemployment was high. World War I opened up employment opportunities in the North, and this caused a vast migration of Blacks from the South. From 1915 to 1930, an estimated 1.5 million Blacks moved out of the South. Like many of the White ethnic groups, the Blacks were isolated in separate residential areas in northern cities. However, unlike many White ethnic groups, except perhaps the Jews, restrictive housing covenants were used to maintain this segregation. One implication of this segregation was that in the North, Blacks had educational facilities that were nearly as segregated as those of the South (Kluger, 1976).

In spite of the massive outmigration, the majority of Blacks (79%) continued to live in the South in 1930 (Bergman, 1969). As America was plunging into the depression, the national average per pupil expenditure was $99. In the South the average expenditure for White children was $44, but for Blacks it was only $13. The discrepancies were even larger in some southern states with large Black populations. In Georgia, the figures were $35 versus $6; and in Mississippi, $45 versus $5 (Thompson, 1974). The dual school system of the South was definitely separate and clearly unequal.

In 1930, Nathan Margold formulated a plan for the NAACP which outlined a legal strategy designed to eliminate school segregation. This plan was underwritten by a grant made a year earlier from the Garland Fund. It

---

[3] *Berea College* v. *Kentucky*, 211 U.S. 45 (1908).

was suggested that the NAACP sue for equal schools. It was expected that the suits would

> (a) make the cost of a dual school system so prohibitive as to speed the abolition of segregated schools; (b) serve as examples and give courage to Negroes to bring similar actions; (c) cause cases . . . to be appealed by local authorities, thus causing higher court decisions to cover wider territory; (d) focus as nothing else will public attention North and South upon vicious discrimination. (Kluger, 1976, p. 132)

Implicit in this statement of goals was a recognition of the symbolic value of challenging school segregation in the struggle to win equal rights for Blacks. The psychological effects of segregation were also being weighed by Blacks. In 1935, Charles Thompson, editor of the *Journal of Negro Education* wrote:

> I think most of us would agree that to *segregate* is to stigmatize. . . . For we all know that segregation is practically always initiated by Whites, and initiated on the basis that Negroes are inferior and undesirable. Thus, when Negroes allow themselves to be cajoled into accepting the status of the separate school, they do something to their personalities which is infinitely worse than any of the discomforts *some* of them *may* suffer in a mixed school. (p. 433)

This theme, elaborated upon by both White and Black social scientists, became a prominent part of the legal case against segregation.

The Margold plan advocated an attack on segregation which was to be based on the fact that the South had failed to provide equal facilities for Blacks. This plan, as modified by NAACP lawyer Charles Houston, was to be the blueprint for the battle against school segregation. The modification added by Houston was that desegregation should be pursued first at the highest levels of education, where it was likely to provoke the least resistance, and it should then be taken to progressively lower stages of the education process (Kluger, 1976). The need for clear strategies and centralized leadership was apparent from the fact that, before 1935, school segregation had been challenged in state courts 44 times and had been upheld in every case (Peterson, 1935).

The first case successfully pursued under the new plan was *Murray* v. *Maryland* (1936).[4] The court ruled that Maryland must admit Donald Murray to its law school because Maryland did not maintain a separate law school for Blacks. A similar ruling, also concerning law school admission, occurred in *Missouri ex rel. Gaines* v. *Canada* (1938).[5] These challenges to segregated education were posed within the framework of the separate but equal doctrine established in *Plessy*. The NAACP also argued cases on

[4] *Murray* v. *Maryland*, 182 A. 590 (1936); 169 Md. 478 (1937).
[5] *Missouri ex. rel. Gaines* v. *Canada*, 305 U.S. 337 (1938).

other fronts, seeking the right to vote, equal pay for Black and White teachers, equal employment opportunities, and an end to all-White juries and restrictive housing covenants (Kluger, 1976).

During the first half of the twentieth century, the pattern of race relations which emerged in the North differed sharply from the race relations of the South. Blalock (1967) has outlined three major differences between the types of discrimination practiced in the two sections of the country. The first consisted of restrictions on the political rights of minorities. In the South, disenfranchisement continued to be practiced to a greater degree than in the North. The second difference consisted of symbolic forms of segregation, notably those encoded in "Jim Crow" laws. This difference appears in the form of *de jure* school segregation in the South and *de facto* school segregation in the North. The third difference was the degree to which the dominant ideological system was threat-oriented. The activities of the Ku Klux Klan serve to illustrate the third difference. Blalock (1967) attributes these differences to the fact that Blacks constituted a greater threat to the power of the dominant group in the South than in the North.

By the midpoint in the century, race relations were beginning to change in both sections of the country. The attitude of the government, sensitive perhaps to the reenfranchised Black voters, began to soften. In 1941, Roosevelt banned discrimination in war-related industries, and, in 1948, Truman integrated the armed forces (Gossett, 1965). In the same year, the government filed an *Amicus* brief in the *Shelley* v. *Kraemer*[6] case, challenging restrictive housing covenants (Kluger, 1976).

Also in 1948, Thurgood Marshall, chief counsel for the NAACP, argued and won a third school segregation case. In his brief in *Sipuel* v. *Oklahoma State Board of Regents*,[7] Marshall argued that

> equality, even if the term be limited to a comparison of physical facilities, is and never can be achieved . . . the terms "separate" and "equal" can not be used conjunctively in a situation of this kind; there can be no separate equality.

In this brief, the works of social scientists were referenced regarding the deleterious effects of segregation. The court ruled that Oklahoma must establish a separate law school for Blacks. As a result of this decision, Oklahoma set up a law school with Ada Sipuel as the only student and assigned three teachers to instruct her. The court accepted this arrangement, but balked at a similar "school" created by the University of Texas in *Sweatt* v. *Painter* (1950).[8] The court ruled that the separate school for Blacks which Texas had established was not equal. The government also

---

[6] *Shelley* v. *Kraemer*, 334 U.S. I (1948).
[7] *Sipuel* v. *Oklahoma State Board of Regents*, 332 U.S. 631 (1948).
[8] *Sweatt* v. *Painter*, 339 U.S. 637 (1950).

filed an *Amicus* brief in this case and for the first time a prominent social scientist, Robert Redfield, testified for the plaintiff (Kluger, 1976).

In *McLaurin* v. *Oklahoma Board of Regents of Higher Education* (1950),[9] separation itself was the issue. As a result of a federal district court order, George McLaurin had been admitted to the graduate school at the University of Oklahoma. He was admitted on a segregated basis, which meant that he was required to sit in an anteroom outside of his classes and was given separate tables in the library and cafeteria. Thurgood Marshall argued that this segregation represented a "badge of inferiority." The restrictions placed on McLaurin were ordered struck down. On the strength of this decision, the NAACP decided that the time had come for an open challenge to segregation in public schools (Gossett, 1965; Kluger, 1976).

THE *BROWN* DECISION

This challenge, consisting of five separate cases which were ultimately joined together, is known as *Brown* v. *The Board of Education* (1954), and it merits a detailed examination. Each of the five cases was different but all posed the same basic issue. In all the cases it was argued that segregation itself violated the "equal protection under the laws" guaranteed by the Fourteenth Amendment. During the separate trials, the NAACP relied heavily on the testimony of social scientists to buttress its claim that separate schools were unequal. It is important to examine these arguments because they raise a number of questions which can be examined in the light of the data which have subsequently been gathered on the effects of desegregation.

Chronologically, the first case to challenge public school segregation was brought against the school system of Clarenden County, South Carolina. Three psychologists, Kenneth Clark, David Krech, and Helen Trager testified in this trial. Clark's testimony was based on the projective tests he had been administering to Blacks and Whites for over a decade. Clark had also given his tests to a small sample of Black students from the segregated schools of Clarenden County. In one report of these studies (Clark & Clark, 1952), he presented the responses of 253 Black children to a series of questions concerning their reactions to White and Black dolls. Part of his sample attended segregated schools in the South while the remainder attended integrated schools in the North. His results indicated that 67% of the children preferred to play with the White doll, 59% regarded the White doll as the "nice" one, 60% said the White doll was a nice color, and 59% said the Black doll "looks bad." Children from the

[9] *McLaurin* v. *Oklahoma Board of Regents of Higher Education*, 339 U.S. 637 (1950).

integrated northern schools chose the White doll more frequently in response to the first three questions and the Black doll less frequently with regard to the fourth question. When asked which doll looked like them, 33% of the children chose the White doll. Again, the children from the North chose the White doll more frequently than did the children from the South. Although these results appear to suggest that the children in the segregated schools were less rejecting of Blacks than the children in the integrated schools, Clark's interpretation was that "the Black children of the South were more adjusted to the feeling that they were not as good as Whites and . . . did not bother to use the device of denial" (Kluger, 1976, p. 356). In his testimony Clark stated:

> I have reached the conclusion from the examination of my own results and from an examination of the entire field that discrimination, prejudice and segregation have definitely detrimental effects on the personality development of the Negro child. The essence of this detrimental effect is a confusion in the child's concept of his own self-esteem—basic feelings of inferiority, conflict, confusion in his self-image, resentment, hostility toward himself, and hostility toward Whites. (Kluger, 1976, p. 353)

There are two important ideas in this statement, that the self-esteem of Blacks is low in segregated schools and that segregation leads Black children to be prejudiced toward Whites. Presumably desegregation should reduce this prejudice. It should be noted that although Clark's studies have been criticized (Cahn, 1955; Greenwald & Oppenheim, 1968; van den Haag, 1960), the pattern of results obtained by the Clarks has been widely replicated with the exception of some recent evidence (e.g., Datcher, Savage, & Checkosky, 1974; Hraba & Grant, 1970).

Clark also cited a study of social scientists by Deutscher and Chein (1948) which revealed that 90% felt that enforced segregation has "detrimental psychological effects on members of racial and religious groups which are segregated, even if equal facilities are provided," and 83% agreed that enforced segregation has "a detrimental effect on the group that enforced segregation even if that group provides equal facilities to the groups that are segregated." The results from these two questions also suggest that Blacks will have low self-esteem in segregated schools.

Krech testified:

> My opinion is that legal segregation of education is probably the single most important factor to wreak harmful effects on the emotional, physical, and financial status of the Negro child. . . . Legal segregation, because it is obvious to everyone, gives . . . environmental support for the belief that Negroes are in some way different from and inferior to White people, and that in turn, supports and strengthens beliefs of racial differences, or racial inferiority. (Kluger, 1976, p. 361)

Like Clark, Trager testified on the basis of the findings of her own empirical studies. In one study (Radke & Trager, 1950), she asked Black and White children from relatively segregated schools (90% or more of the students from one ethnic group) whether they liked a Black or a White doll best. The results indicated that the Black children preferred the White doll in 57% of the 90 cases, while the Whites preferred the White doll in 89% of the 152 cases. Trager testified that

> the Negro children, unlike White children, showed a tendency to expect rejection. . . . A child who expects to be rejected, who sees his group held in low-esteem, is not going to function well, is not going to be a fully developed child. . . . [If] we are to diminish the amount of hostility and fear that children of all groups have toward each other [the place to do it] is the school. (Kluger, 1976, p. 363)

In her reference to intergroup hostility, Trager appears to be suggesting that desegregation will reduce the prejudices of both Blacks and Whites.

In his summation, Thurgood Marshall argued that "there is no relief for the Negro children of Clarenden County except to be permitted to attend existing and superior White schools." Two of the three Federal District judges disagreed. The case was then appealed to the Supreme Court which remanded it to the District Court for re-argument. During this rehearing, Marshall argued that the Negro schools should be desegregated until such time as the facilities were equalized. When asked from the bench how this might be accomplished, Marshall responded, "It would be a problem of shifting some of the White children by district lines . . . and mixing them, or sharing the school equally. . . . They wouldn't all go to the White school" (Kluger, 1976, p. 533).

The second case to raise the issue of segregation was *Brown* v. *Board of Education of Topeka*. In Topeka, the secondary schools were integrated but the elementary schools were segregated. The major inequality that existed was that many Black children had to travel long distances, often by bus, to attend school. The real issue of the case and its relationship to psychological factors, became clear during the pre-trial hearing:

> JUDGE HUXMAN: . . . In other words, the issue is whether segregation itself, I presume, is not a denial of due process, irrespective of whether everything else is equal. Is that not your general contention?
>
> (NAACP lawyer Robert) CARTER: Yes, sir.
>
> JUDGE HUXMAN: Because of the effect it has upon the mind, upon the student, upon his outlook—I presume that would be your position.
>
> CARTER: That is absolutely correct, your Honor. (Kluger, 1976, p. 405)

In this trial, education professor Hugh Speer argued that one aspect of the inequality of segregated schools was that "colored children are denied the experience in school of associating with White children, who represent 90 percent of our national society in which these colored children must live." Psychologist Horace English testified that segregation had negative effects on learning:

If we din it into a person that he is incapable of learning, then he is less likely to be able to learn. . . . There is a tendency for us to live up to—or perhaps I should say down to—social expectations and to learn what people say we can learn, and legal segregation definitely depresses the Negro's expectancy and is therefore prejudicial to his learning. (Kluger, 1976, p. 415)

The ideas that Blacks in segregated schools achieve at lower levels than Whites and that ending legalized segregation would increase the achievement levels of Blacks are implicit in the argument.

As in the South Carolina case, the court ruled against the plaintiffs. But in an important concession, the court found that segregated schools were inevitably unequal:

Segregation of White and colored children in public schools has a detrimental effect upon the colored children. The impact is greater when it has the sanction of the law; for the policy of separating the races is usually interpreted as denoting the inferiority of the Negro group. A sense of inferiority affects the motivation of the child to learn. Segregation with the sanction of law, therefore, has a tendency to retard the educational and mental development of Negro children and to deprive them of some of the benefits they would receive in a racial[ly] integrated school system. (Kluger, 1976, p. 424)

Chief Justice Earl Warren quoted this finding of the lower court in rendering the 1954 decision in *Brown*.

In Delaware, the NAACP brought its case against two small school districts in which the physical facilities provided for Blacks and Whites were clearly unequal. Psychologists Otto Klineberg, George Kelly, Jerome Bruner, and Kenneth Clark, and psychiatrist Frederic Wertham appeared as expert witnesses. Klineberg testified that the learning abilities of Blacks and Whites were equal. Kelly testified that segregated education for Blacks placed a burden on them physically, in terms of the long distances involved in transporting them to school. Bruner said that segregation was psychologically damaging for Blacks because it produced frustration, apathy, and hostility in the Black school children. Clark again presented the results of the doll tests and Wertham said that "most of the Black children we have examined interpret segregation in one way and only one way—and that is they interpret it as punishment" (Kluger, 1976, p. 444). The court ruled that while separate schools may be constitutional, the schools for Blacks in Claymont and Hockessin were clearly not equal to those for Whites and, therefore, the Black plaintiffs should be admitted to the White schools. For the first time, a judge had ruled against segregation in public schools.

The fourth case in which social scientists served as expert witnesses for the NAACP was in *Davis v. County School Board of Prince Edward County, Virginia.*[10] The students of Moton High School went on strike in 1951 and

---

[10] *Davis v. County School Board of Prince Edward County, Virginia*, 103 Federal Supplement 337 (1952); 347 U.S. 483 (1954).

solicited the aid of the NAACP in obtaining equal facilities. In the trial, psychologist M. Brewster Smith presented a version of Myrdal's vicious circle thesis as it applied to segregation:

> The effects of segregation . . . help perpetuate the pattern of segregation and prejudice out of which these effects arise. . . . [S]egregation has widely ramifying consequences on the individual's motivation to learn. (Kluger, 1976, p. 491)

Psychologist Isidor Chein presented the results of the Deutscher and Chein (1948) survey of social scientists. Kenneth Clark traced the relationship between segregation and prejudice:

> Segregation is prejudice concretized in the society, and in my work with Negro youth and in my interviewing them, I find this is the way they interpret it: Segregation is a mist, like a wall, which society erects, of stone and steel—psychological stone and steel—constantly telling them that they are inferior and constantly telling them that they cannot escape prejudice. Prejudice is something inside people. Segregation is the objective expression of what these people have inside. (Kluger, 1976, p. 495)

On cross-examination Clark testified:

> I think it is the desire of the Negro to be a human being and to be treated as a human being without regard to skin color. He can only have pride in race—and a healthy and mature pride in race—when his own government does not constantly and continuously tell him, "Have no pride in race," by constantly segregating him. (Kluger, 1976, p. 498)

Thus, according to Clark, the end of segregation will establish a necessary precondition for a more positive ethnic identity among Blacks. Clark appears to be suggesting that ending segregation has this effect because it would deprive Whites of an institutionalized sanction for their prejudices and as a result would diminish White prejudice. Therefore, desegregation should have the effect of reversing the vicious circle.

The defense in the *Davis* trial also employed psychologists as expert witnesses. Henry Garrett testified that "provided you have equal facilities . . . the Negro student at the high school level will get a better education in a separate school than he will in mixed schools (Kluger, 1976, p. 503). The court apparently agreed and ordered the school system to equalize its facilities for Blacks with "diligence and dispatch."

The fifth case involved in *Brown* came from the District of Columbia. Howard Law School Dean, James Nabrit, argued the case solely on constitutional grounds:

> When the Fifth Amendment was adopted Negroes in the District of Columbia were slaves, not entitled to unsegregated schooling or to any schooling. Congress may have been right in thinking Negroes were not entitled to unsegregated schooling when the Fourteenth Amendment was adopted. But the question of what schooling was good enough to meet their constitutional rights 160 or 80 years ago is different from the question what schooling meets rights now. (Kluger, 1976, p. 522)

Nabrit's contention was that the Constitution was a flexible document meant to be interpreted in the light of the times. The District Court did not accept this argument and when the case was appealed to the Supreme Court it was joined to the others.

When these cases went before the Sureme Court for oral arguments, the lawyers for the NAACP cited three basic reasons why the court should eliminate segregated education. The first reason was based on the previous rulings in *Sweatt* and *McLaurin*. It was argued that segregation in the public schools was similar to segregation at the graduate level. In both instances segregation denied students the equal protection of the laws because it was injurious to the students. The second reason was that classifying students by race was not justifiable. For a classification between two groups to be justified it must be shown "(1) that there is a difference between the two, (2) . . . that the difference has a significance with the subject matter being legislated" (Friedman, 1969, p. 38). To substantiate this argument, Thurgood Marshall cited Robert Redfield's testimony that there were no differences between the races with respect to learning ability. In Marshall's words, "the third point was the broader point, that racial distinctions in and of themselves are invidious. I consider it as a three-pronged attack. Any of the three would be sufficient for reversal" (Friedman, 1969, p. 45).

In 1954, the Supreme Court struck down the "separate but equal" concept in public education. The decision, written by Chief Justice Earl Warren, read in part:

> Does segregation of children in public schools solely on the basis of race, even though the physical facilities and other "tangible" factors may be equal, deprive the children of the minority group of equal educational opportunities? We believe that it does . . . to separate Negro school children from others of similar age and qualifications solely because of their race generates a feeling of inferiority as to their status in the community that may affect their hearts and minds in a way unlikely ever to be undone. . . . We conclude that in the field of public education the doctrine "separate but equal" has no place. Separate educational facilities are inherently unequal.

Chief Justice Warren had accepted one of the primary contentions of the social scientists, whom he duly acknowledged in a footnote. Because of the "wide applicability of this decision," further arguments were requested on the issue of how to implement the court's decree.

THE IMPLEMENTATION OF THE *BROWN* DECISION

One year after *Brown* the court issued its decision concerning when integration was to be achieved. The court's deliberations show that the justices approached this question with extreme caution. Justice Frankfurter wrote his colleagues that "'Forthwith' would either be given a meaning short of immediacy or introduce a range of leeway to render it imprecise, and it would most certainly provoke resentment" (Baker, 1973, p. 47). The court did not order the earlier decision to be implemented forthwith nor did it attempt to devise a formula that could be applied to all segregated schools systems. Instead, its decision read:

> The judgments below . . . are reversed and the cases are remanded to the district courts to take such proceedings and enter such orders and decrees consistent with this opinion as are necessary and proper to admit the parties to these cases to public schools on a racially nondiscriminatory basis with all deliberate speed.

Thus, the *Brown* decisions set in motion a gradual process of desegregation, which was to be mediated by the courts. The decision left the enforcement of the decree largely in the hands of the offended party. Desegregation progressed primarily when lawsuits were brought or threatened against local school boards. These legal actions required organized militancy and money. This accounts, in part, for the minimal compliance with the court's decisions in the following decade. The other factor responsible for the minimal compliance, of course, was the continued opposition of Whites. One example of this opposition was the 1956 manifesto signed by 101 southern senators and congressmen which declared that integration as ordered by the court was "contrary to established law" (Bergman, 1969, p. 555). A variety of legal strategies were devised to avoid desegregation including tuition payments, the intervention of state governments to "maintain the peace," closing schools, and minimal but ineffective compliance (Edelman, 1973).

In the late 1950s, the civil rights movement began to dismantle the Jim Crow system of segregation. Most of the initial challenges attempted to destroy the symbols of segregation. The civil rights movement focused on sit-ins and freedom rides before attempts were made to increase voter registration among Blacks. Progress in school desegregation was slight. Ten years after the *Brown* decision, 99% of the nation's Black school children were still in segregated schools (Edelman, 1973). In 1964, the Supreme Court in *Griffin* v. *The County School Board of Prince Edward County*[11] commented, "there has been entirely too much deliberation and not enough speed."

The first Civil Rights Act since Reconstruction was passed by Congress in 1964. Title VI of the act was used by the government to cut off federal funds to local school districts which were not in compliance with the 1954 court decision. The attorney general was authorized by Title VI of the Civil

---

[11] *Griffin* v. *County School Board of Prince Edward County*, 377 U.S. 218 (1964).

Rights Act to "file suits for desegregation of public schools." The threat of a cut-off in federal funds could be effective only if there were funds to be cut off, and most funds did not come from the national government. However, with the passage in 1965 of the Elementary and Secondary Education Act, the amount of federal funding for public schools increased markedly and the threat of a cut-off became more meaningful (Edelman, 1973).

The 1960s saw an increase in militancy among Blacks and a continuation and acceleration of civil rights activities. Division within the Black community over political goals and methods of achieving them also increased during the decade. This division in the Black community was reflected in their attitudes toward desegregation. A 1969 national poll found that 78% of the nation's Blacks favored having their children attend school with White children (Pettigrew, Useem, Normand, & Smith, 1973), but National Urban League analyses of three national surveys in 1972 found that only 52% of the Blacks sampled favored busing (Hamilton, 1973).

At the time Title VI was put into effect, many school systems were offering students some freedom to choose where to attend school. As a desegregation policy, this concept was nearly a total failure. It required individual initiative by Black parents and students and typically placed Black students in hostile White environments. In the fall of 1966, only 14% of all Black school children attended predominantly White schools. The Department of Health, Education, and Welfare (HEW) issued guidelines for desegregation in 1968 that explicitly rejected "free choice" plans that did not eliminate vestiges of the dual school system. By the end of 1968, more than 200 fund terminations had been ordered under Title VI (Edelman, 1973).

Desegregation proceeded rapidly in the years 1965–1969, but the forms it took were often antithetical to achieving equal nondiscriminatory educational systems. Black schools were usually the ones that were closed and Black students were bused more often than Whites. The costs of desegregation also fell unequally on Black and White teachers and administrators. The National Education Association, in a brief filed in a Georgia desegregation suit, cited HEW statistics indicating that over 1,000 Black educators in five southern states lost their jobs between 1968 and 1971. During the same period, more than 5,000 White educators were hired. Blacks were being made to pay for the opportunity to attend desegregated schools (Sinowitz, 1973).

In the second decade after the *Brown* decision, considerably more desegregation occurred in the South than in the North. In the fall of 1972 a greater percentage of Black children in the South attended majority White schools (44%) than in the North (29%) (Pettigrew, 1975). The primary reason was that *de jure* segregation had been the subject of the initial decision and of most subsequent attempts to implement it. *De jure* segregation also proved easier to eliminate than *de facto* segregation, especially in the rural South. In addition, the migration of Whites to the suburbs and the concentration of Blacks in the inner cities of the North made desegregation more complex in the North than in the South.

Opposition to school desegregation became a political issue in the 1968 presidential election. The ghetto riots and the high levels of civil rights activism of the 1960s were creating a backlash among White voters. The election of Richard Nixon resulted in a marked slowdown in desegregation efforts. Government policy was gradually changed, delays were granted to school districts implementing desegregation, and infractions in implementing plans were overlooked. Nearly one-third of the 300 southern school districts that were required to take action on their desegregation plans in 1969 failed to do so (Edelman, 1973). In 1968, HEW had begun to review northern and western communities to determine if they were in compliance with school desegregation guidelines. In that year there were 28 reviews. Over the next five years there was a steady decline, and by 1974 no reviews were being conducted (Kluger, 1976).

DESEGREGATION IN THE 1970s AND BEYOND

This book is primarily concerned with desegregation in the 1970s and beyond. Because this is the focus of the book, in this section I would like to discuss the contents of the book in relation to the issues that confront people who are concerned with school desegregation and its effects. In order to put the *Brown* decision and its effects into perspective, several of the authors have focused primarily on the past. This first section of the book is devoted to three such chapters. Following my chapter, Joe Feagin traces the origin of the pressures to desegregate the schools. He finds two primary sources, one from the American ruling class which was concerned with the stability and legitimacy of the political-economic system and one from Black civil rights groups. Feagin also documents the spread of desegregation during the first quarter century after *Brown*. He gives particular emphasis to the slowdown in desegregation during the 1970s, and the reasons for this slowdown which he traces to a conservative trend in decisions by the Supreme Court, the growing opposition of the White middle class to desegregation, and ultimately, the limits placed on the possibility of desegregation by the segregated nature of American housing patterns.

Susan Greenblatt and Charles Willie analyze some of the unintended and unexpected effects of the *Brown* decision. The increased desire for justice among non-Black minority groups, the increased role of state governments in guaranteeing equal educational opportunities, a redefinition of the function of education and the implications of this redefinition for the teaching profession, school boards, and parents are among these effects.

A second group of authors has defined the problems and issues surrounding school desegregation in the present. The first two chapters in this section focus on the legal aspects of school desegregation. Lino Graglia discusses the Supreme Court's decisions from *Brown* to the present. He argues that only segregation, not racial separation, was declared illegal in *Brown*. The court, until the late 1960s, has favored desegregation as the solution to segregation, but in the late 1960s the court began to favor integration as a solution. Graglia argues that since integration requires the consideration of race in the assignment of students to schools, it violates the racially neutral requirements embodied in *Brown*. Mark Yudof, in his chapter, analyzes the bases for the court's decisions on desegregation. He outlines three principles which could serve to justify the court's positions. The first principle, which he labels the *nondiscrimination theory*, is based on the necessity to remedy the present and past wrongs caused by racial discrimination. The *political corruption theory* suggests that superficially neutral government policies, such as those by school boards, may be tainted by racial prejudice and, therefore, should be scrutinized by the court. The third principle, labeled the *group protection theory*, indicates that desegregation is needed to protect Blacks against the still powerful, historical forces that led to their isolation and oppression. He concludes that the trend of the court's recent decisions is consistent with a reliance on the principle of nondiscrimination.

The chapters on legal issues are followed by four chapters concerning race relations and public attitudes. Ray Rist's chapter is concerned with the aspects of desegregation that constitute problems and those that are not problematical. He suggests that a lack of support for integration is not a problem since support continues to be high, nor is busing the problem because millions of American school children have been bused for decades. Rist also notes that losses in White achievement levels cannot be a problem because they do not occur. From Rist's perspective, the important issues to be addressed are that Whites perceive that desegregation remedies have been randomly applied and result in no beneficial effects, that Whites are fleeing from America's cities, that the court's orders result in diminished local autonomy, and that Blacks no longer unanimously support school desegregation.

This last issue is taken up by Andrew Greeley in his chapter. After presenting national survey data documenting Rist's contention that support for integration is high, Greeley considers the positions that Blacks as an ethnic group might adopt with respect to the goals they hope to achieve through desegregation.

In their chapter, Arthur Stinchcombe and D. Garth Taylor provide information on school desegregation in Boston. Reinforcing Rist's suggestion that the perception of desegregation by the White community is at the heart of the school desegregation controversy, they discuss the reasons for the extreme reaction in Boston. In their view, the Boston case presents a conflict between two principles in which Americans commonly believe: that we should be governed by law and that we should have a choice in how we are governed. In Boston, Whites voiced their choice by electing a school board opposed to desegregation. Their choice was overturned by the federal judiciary which went against the "will of the people" in the name of the law. The White population was unwilling to accept a desegregation plan that, in their view, asked them to bear too great a burden of the costs of desegregation. Stinchcombe and Taylor present data indicating that the opposition to the plan was based more on the expectation that it would lower the quality of education than on racial prejudice.

The results of the Boston survey are consistent with those reported by David Armor for Los Angeles. Whites in Los Angeles also opposed desegregation, primarily because they believed it would have harmful effects and because it would destroy the neighborhood school. This opposition to desegregation has contributed to White flight in Los Angeles (discussed by Norman Miller) and in other cities. Armor also reports the results of a nationwide survey of urban areas affected by desegregation in his chapter. He finds that considerable White flight occurs in communities that have substantial minority populations (more than 20%) and where there are well-developed suburbs. His results also indicate that White flight increases as the number of Whites affected by desegregation increases. He documents the magnitude of the problem posed by the resegregation that faces many communities experiencing losses in White enrollment.

The social science brief on school segregation and residential segregation was written by a group of social scientists for attorneys representing minority group interests in the Dayton and Columbus school desegregation cases. This brief reviews social science knowledge on the role of racial discrimination in housing in the United States and the interrelationship between housing segregation and school segregation. The brief demonstrates the close relationship between publicly-created segregated schools and the public and private decisions which create housing segregation. Many homebuyers look at school zones before buying a house; realtors sell schools as well as homes. Data discussed illustrate how and why racially identifiable schools signal neglected schools to parents of all colors, and thus have a pervasive effect on perpetuating residential segregation.

The final section of the book is concerned with the problem of making desegregation work for the millions of American school children who are affected by it. Elizabeth Cohen begins her chapter by criticizing social scientists for failing to recognize the complexity of the factors affecting education in desegregated schools. The outcome of school desegregation depends on the process by which the school came to be desegregated, the power relations among the different groups in the school, and in the community and the authority structure in the school, as well as the nature of classroom interactions. She specifically criticizes innovative educational programs which fail to undercut status and achievement differences between groups. She outlines a technique for producing equal status treatment of minority students in desegregated classrooms. Based on her research on this technique, she then formulates a series of recommendations for how desegregation can be pursued most effectively.

In the following chapter, Jane Mercer, Peter Iadicola, and Helen Moore explore the explanations that have been offered for the finding that desegregation generally does not lead to substantial educational or interpersonal benefits. Three types of explanations have been offered, one based on deficiencies in minority students, a second rooted in deficiencies in minority families, and a third based on deficiencies in teachers. They present data from their own studies indicating that teachers are not racially biased in their evaluations of the social and intellectual competence of their students. Mercer *et al.* conclude their chapter by presenting an integrated status equalization model that incorporates Cohen's work and extends beyond it. This causal model includes contextual variables such as the racial balance and social class composition of the school, educational process variables such as the degree of competitiveness and use of multicultural programs and the influence of these factors on the amount of equal status contact, and on educational outcomes such as academic performance and self-esteem.

In the last chapter, Norman Miller outlines a set of principles concerning how desegregation plans should be implemented. He argues that desegregation programs must be educationally sound, that interracial contact should occur under circumstances that promote positive intergroup relations, and that desegregation plans should be formulated to develop and maintain community acceptance. Miller criticizes the idea that there is a transmission of positive attitudes toward achievement from majority to minority group students. This process rarely occurs because of the conditions in desegregated schools. He suggests that a lateral transmission of such values may occur in desegregated schools that employ some type of cooperative learning experience. Miller cautions that desegregation programs designed to meet one goal, such as increased academic achievement, may fail to meet other goals, such as promoting positive race relations.

REFERENCES

Atkinson, C., & Moleska, E. T. *The story of education.* Philadelphia: Chilton, 1975.
Baker, L. With all deliberate speed. *American Heritage,* 1973, *24,* 47.
Bergman, P. *The Negro in America.* New York: Harper & Row, 1969.
Blalock, H. M., Jr. *Toward a theory of minority-group relations.* New York: Wiley, 1967.
Cahn, E. Jurisprudence. *New York University Law Review,* 1955, *30,* 150–169.

Clark, K. B., & Clark, M. P. Racial identification and preference in Negro children. In *Readings in Social Psychology*. New York: Holt, 1952, pp. 551–560.

Datcher, E., Savage, J. E., Jr., & Checkosky, S. T. School type, grade, sex and race of experimenter as determinants of the racial preference and awareness in Black and White children. *Journal of Social and Behavioral Sciences*, 1974, *20*, 41–49.

Deutscher, M., & Chein, I. The psychological effects of enforced segregation: A survey of social science opinion. *The Journal of Psychology*, 1948, *26*, 259–287.

DuBois, W. E. B. *Black reconstruction*. New York: Russell & Russell, 1935.

Edelman, M. W. Southern school desegregation, 1954–1973: A judicial-political overview. *Annals of the American Academy*, 1973, *407*, 33.

Franklin, J. H. *From slavery to freedom* (4th ed.). Knopf: New York, 1974.

Friedman, L. (Ed.). *Argument*. New York: Chelsea, 1969.

Gittell, M. The political implications of "Milliken v. Bradley." In *Milliken v. Bradley: The implications for metropolitan desegregation*. U.S. Commission on Civil Rights: Washington, D.C., 1974.

Gossett, T. F. *Race: The history of an idea in America*. New York: Schocken, 1965.

Greenwald, H. J., & Oppenheim, D. B. Reported magnitude of self-misidentification among Negro children—Artifact? *Journal of Personality and Social Psychology*, 1968, *8*, 49–52.

Hamilton, C. V. The nationalist vs. the integrationist. In N. Mills (Ed.), *The great school bus controversy*. New York: Teachers College Press, 1973, pp. 297–310.

Hraba, J., & Grant, G. Black is beautiful: A re-examination of racial preference and identity. *Journal of Personality and Social Psychology*, 1970, *16*, 398–402.

Kluger, R. *Simple justice*. New York: Knopf, 1976.

LeVine, R. A., & Campbell, D. T. *Ethnocentrism: Theories of conflict, ethnic attitudes, and group behavior*. New York: Wiley, 1972.

Peterson, G. T. The present status of the Negro separate school as defined by court decisions. *Journal of Negro Education*, 1935, *4*, 351–374.

Pettigrew, T. F. The racial integration of the schools. In T. F. Pettigrew (Ed.), *Racial discrimination in the United States*. New York: Harper & Row, 1975.

Pettigrew, T. F., Useem, E. L., Normand, C., & Smith, M. S. Busing: A review of "the evidence." *The Public Interest*, 1973, *30*, 88–118.

Radke, M. J., & Trager, H. G. Children's perceptions of the social roles of Negroes and Whites. *The Journal of Psychology*, 1950, *29*, 3–33.

Rose, A. *The Negro in America: The condensed version of Gunnar Myrdal's An American Dilemma*. New York: Harper & Row, 1944.

Sinowitz, B. E. School integration and the teacher. *Today's Education*, 1973, *62*, 31–33.

Thompson, C. H. Court action the only reasonable alternative to remedy immediate abuses of separate Negro school. *Journal of Negro Education*, 1935, *4*, 433.

Thompson, E. T. *Plantation societies, race relations and the South: The regimentation of populations*. Durham, N. C.: Duke University Press, 1975.

Tyack, D. B. (Ed.). *Turning points in American educational history*. Waltham, Mass.: Blaisdell, 1967.

Van den Berghe, P. *Race and racism*. New York: Wiley, 1967.

Van den Haag, E. Social science testimony in the desegregation cases: A reply to professor Kenneth Clark. *Villanova Law Review*, 1960, *6*, 69–79.

Weinberg, M. *A chance to learn*. Cambridge: Cambridge University Press, 1977.

2

School Desegregation

A POLITICAL-ECONOMIC PERSPECTIVE

JOE R. FEAGIN

INTRODUCTION

In two short decades, desegregation has come swiftly to many American school systems. The 1954 desegregation decision, *Brown* v. *Board of Education*,[1] took White America by surprise. Very little change in segregation in the late 1950s following the *Brown* decision was followed in the 1960s by a large-scale blending of racial groups. Yet this snapshot of change must be supplemented with other facts about desegregation. Most changes came in the South. Corporate liberals and foundations were somehow tied to the changes in the 1960s. Clearly, Black civil rights pressure played a major role. The rapid changes of the 1964–1971 period were followed by a sharp halt in the expansion of desegregation. When desegregation became a court-ordered issue for northern systems, northern White protest against significant school desegregation pressured government to back off. Statistics-oriented debates centered on student mixing or achievement—with many former liberal White supporters, including social scientists, backing off from large-scale desegregation solutions. Comprehensive school desegregation—such as desegregating curriculum, tracking systems, and extracurricular activities—seemed to be forgotten as parochially focused debates grew in intensity. Moreover, even though schools were being desegregated for a short period, mostly in the South and border states, housing remained remarkably segregated.

[1] *Brown* v. *Board of Education*, 347 U.S. 483 (1954).

JOE R. FEAGIN • Department of Sociology, University of Texas, Austin, Texas 78712.

Even this cursory overview suggests a number of broad questions that are seldom systematically analyzed in the desegregation literature:

1. Where did the pressure for school desegregation come from?
2. Why has education been the cornerstone of desegregation strategy?
3. Why and how was the pressure successful in bringing government action for significant school desegregation in the 1960s?
4. What are the concrete results of school desegregation so far?
5. Why did White backlash pressure against school desegregation develop by the early 1970s, and why was it so effective?
6. What are the limits of the school desegregation approach as a strategy for liberating non-White America from institutionalized discrimination?

I will grapple with these fundamental questions, drawing on a range of historical and political-economic materials to illustrate how important it is to view school desegregation from a broader vantage point than is the case in most social science analysis.

The Cast of Characters

Before looking at fundamental questions, we should be clear about the major characters who play critical roles in the unfolding of the desegregation process. Even though the role and motivation of each group will become clearer as we proceed, we can identify them in advance: (1) rank-and-file non-White parents and children; (2) the non-White middle class, especially Black lawyers and other leaders; (3) distinct groups within the White ruling class, especially corporate capitalists, top managers, foundations, federal judges, liberal politicians in Congress, and top federal bureaucrats in the Department of Health, Education, and Welfare (HEW); and (4) rank-and-file White parents and children. The groups are listed roughly in order of their entry into the drama of school desegregation.

The struggle between non-White Americans and the White ruling class in this nation is complicated by the fact that less powerful White groups are also involved. White society is not monolithic, for within White America there are major, competing, economic classes. In trying to make sense out of what has happened to school desegregation in recent decades, one must distinguish a number of different factions which have shaped, or been affected by, school desegregation. United States society is stratified both by economic class and by race.

In the class system, Americans are sorted out into different positions in terms of the control they have over the means of production (machines, factories) and in terms of their supervisory control over other workers. Those dominant groups at the very top of the society—the two main groups of (1) capitalists/employers and (2) top managers/professionals/politicians—have the greatest control both over the means of production and over other workers. We will group these together as the "ruling class." This class is the wealthiest, measured in terms of income, real assets, housing, and access to education. Below this top class falls a broad class of workers consisting of better-off workers with some control over their working conditions and/or some control over other workers. Often called the "middle class," there is considerable diversity within this group, since it includes lower-level managers and professionals, small business owners, better-off sales and government workers, and skilled manual workers. In general, these workers have enough income to purchase the homes (and thus the schools) in the "suburban areas" in towns and cities. Below this middle-level group are two other classes: (1) There are the less well-off clerical, sales, and manual workers who have little control over the means of production, their working conditions, or over other employees. With limited incomes, these workers are often confined to housing and educational facilities within the central areas of our cities. (2) There is the subproletariat of poor manual workers, the chronically unemployed, the low-wage, full-time workers, the class least in control of the conditions both of workaday life and of home life.

The better-off, middle-level workers in urban areas are usually Whites whose economic conditions, so long as they are working, include a degree of affluence, a new car, and a modest home, though these have often been attained only in recent decades and with the aid of large bank mortgages. Better-quality schools are thereby assured. The class of less-well-off sales, clerical, and blue-collar workers includes a large number of "White ethnic" and non-White workers. These workers are limited by their incomes to less adequate housing, particularly central cities (and rural areas). In addition, the subproletariat of poor workers is heavily non-White and thus severely limited to the poorest housing in central cities. Lesser-quality schools are typically the lot of these latter two classes.

The American racial hierarchy complicates this stratification picture. Whites toward the top of the racial hierarchy have considerably greater power, wealth, income, and status than non-Whites at lower levels. Those Whites at middle levels are not as well-off as those at higher levels but they are better off than non-Whites as a group. Such non-White groups as Blacks, Chicanos, Native Americans, and Puerto Ricans find themselves concentrated in the two bottom classes in the economic class system, though a significant proportion has moved up to at least the lower rungs of the middle level. The relatively lower incomes of the majority of non-White families consign them to lesser-quality housing—and thus educational facilities. In addition, a large part of their problem is the discrimination institutionalized not only in formal and informal personnel practices but also in real estate practices and school board decisions. Even those non-White workers now in middle-level ranks have found that additional income does not translate into an ability to buy better-quality homes, and thus schools, in White suburban areas.

These race and class groups play central roles in the development of school desegregation and thus in the basic questions outlined previously, questions to which we will now turn.

THE QUEST FOR LEGITIMACY AND STABILITY

The Pressures for Change

Where did the struggle for school desegregation begin? Where did the pressure for concrete change come from? Why were schools a central concern in the civil rights strategy? These questions are not as simple as they first appear. One might say that the struggle began with Black parents who were discontented with the crude discrimination their children suffered in unequal or nonexistent public schools. Or one might say it began with a few educated Blacks and their liberal White friends who, joined together in the National Association for the Advancement of Colored People (NAACP), decided on the strategy to fight discrimination in the schools. Or one might say it began when the Supreme Court became more reform-oriented on race issues, when it became more willing to accept the argument that separate Black schools were nearly always unequal schools. This catch-all list does include some useful answers to the pressure question. But these answers do not dig deeply enough into race and class realities.

Ruling class concern for the stability of the political-economic system in the United States lies at the heart of an adequate answer. Black and other non-White civil rights activity brought a growing legitimation crisis to the United States as the 1950s became the 1960s. The desire of the ruling class for maintenance of political legitimacy in the face of challenge is a central reason for the success of reform. Government in a capitalistic system must facilitate the growth of profits, but it must also expend significant effort to maintain the political legitimacy of the system in the eyes of major interest groups in the general population. The capitalist state is caught between the two imperatives of political legitimation and capitalist profit accumulation (Wolfe, 1977). The history of this society is both a history of government-assisted capitalist expansion and a history of government concessions to previously excluded challenging groups seeking fuller participation in the major sectors of the society. Government must, first of all, keep the peace.

The threat of revolt by excluded peoples—such as Black Americans—pressures a government with a democratic political framework to take action and, sometimes, to expend money and effort for goals not in line with the immediate profit accumulation interests of the ruling class.

Black and other non-White pressures for broader societal participation were not the first or the last in the twentieth century, but they were critically important pressures bringing a legitimation crisis. Clearly, the concessions made to Black Americans would not have been made without civil rights organization and protest. In the area of school desegregation, the NAACP has been central in the fight for liberation. Led by middle-class Black and White professionals, groups like the NAACP have played a critical role in managing and chaneling the revolt of the largely working-class group of Black Americans. Partially co-opted by the ruling class—a point we will document later—middle-level Black leaders control the style (legal-educational) and pace (gradual at best) of social change, while anointing the principle of desegregation through law and order. Benefits to all Blacks do come from this type of change, but they can easily be overrated.

Originating in the early 1900s, the NAACP had grown by 1921 to over 400 local organizations and had won three court cases in the areas of voting, housing, and juries. At an early point, the NAACP became committed to a strategy of litigation; by the 1930s it was focusing on educational issues. At least since the 1880s, Black parents in numerous southern areas had petitioned the courts for greater educational equality. In 1885, Black parents in Arkansas petitioned successfully the state Supreme Court to compel their school district to establish a school for Black children, as they had for Whites. Similarly, between 1885 and World War I, the suits of Black parents brought some changes in schools in Richmond County, Georgia; Kernersville, North Carolina; Jasper County, Mississippi; Camden County, North Carolina; and Mayfield, Kentucky. By the 1930s, the NAACP began to coordinate efforts to equalize the salaries of Black and White teachers in the South. Under the direction of Charles H. Houston of the Howard University Law School, an attack was made on racial inequality in the professional and technical schools of the South (Bullock, 1970; Miller, 1966).

Between the 1930s and 1950s, NAACP lawyers won desegregation cases against the University of Maryland, University of Missouri, and University of Texas law schools. Nathan Margold was hired in the 1930s to look at an earlier memorandum prepared by the Garland Fund, which had proposed that court suits be brought to force racially equal public schools, the logic being that the South could not afford to equalize separate Black and White schools. Margold quoted this memo in his report, though he preferred a more direct attack on the unconstitutionality of public school segregation. In the late 1930s, the NAACP Legal Defense and Educational Fund (LDF) was created, and it became a major source of funds for school desegregation litigation (Greenberg, 1969, p. 178). However, it was not until 1949 that a legal attack was mounted on segregation at the primary and secondary levels affecting large numbers of rank-and-file Black Americans.

The NAACP strategy in the 1930–1950 period was grounded in the view that court suits requiring racist governments to finance separate and equal facilities would crack legal segregation. But by 1950, a more direct Constitution-oriented strategy was decided upon by Thurgood Marshall, Walter White, and other Black leaders (Bennett, 1965, p. 186–187). In 1950, 17 states required school segregation for White and Black pupils, and four other states permitted it locally. Washington, D.C. was segregated by order of Congress. Beginning in the early 1950s, a series of NAACP-supported court cases successfully demonstrated the intentional, institutionalized discrimination in primary and secondary education suffered by Black Americans throughout the nation. NAACP lawyers launched a legal crusade that touched segregation in the North as well as in the South. The NAACP and its LDF provided the legal aid for the parents of Black children challenging state segregation laws in the states of Kansas, South Carolina, Virginia, and Delaware—four cases specifically grouped together in the Supreme Court's *Brown* decision. Led by NAACP lawyers, Black parents won one of the most famous Supreme Court decisions. Yet there was massive White resistance in the southern states to implementing the *Brown* decision. By 1963, only 2% of southern Black children had seen school desegregation in southern areas.

One crucial problem was getting the federal government to implement Supreme Court decisions in a vigorous way. Ten years after the Supreme Court decision, neither presidents nor the Congress aggressively pursued desegregation. The ruling class tends to respond to legitimacy threats with the minimum reforms necessary. But then rank-and-file Black protest (in stores and streets) accelerated, and the 1964 Civil Rights Act was the first nonjudicial action explicitly recognizing school desegregation as governmental policy, by providing that governmental aid could be cut off to school districts unwilling to desegregate. The 1964 Civil Rights Act gave the Department of Justice some new powers to bring school desegregation cases. These changes enabled the NAACP–LDF to specialize in the cases it chose. A series of important Supreme Court cases gradually expanded the areas covered and the requirements for desegregation. In *Green* v. *New Kent County* (1968)[2] the court held that "freedom of choice" plans were not sufficient, that desegregation must actually take place. In *Swann* v. *Charlotte–Mecklenburg Board of Education* (1971)[3] the Court upheld large-

---

[2] *Green* v. *New Kent County School Board*, 391 U.S. 430 (1968).
[3] *Swann* v. *Charlottee-Mecklenburg Board of Education*, 402 U.S. 1 (1971).

scale busing and a racial-balance desegregation plan. The *Keyes* v. *School District No. 1, Denver, Colorado* (1973)[4] decision extended desegregation to northern school systems when intentional school board actions to segregate could be shown. This was a major victory for the LDF of the NAACP. This movement of cases to the North—and recurrent demonstration of the intentionally discriminatory actions of northern school board officials—shifted the focus of the NAACP action to segregationist policies in the nation as a whole (Orfield, 1978, p. 19). The next year, however, in *Milliken* v. *Bradley* (1974),[5] the Supreme Court upheld an order of school desegregation for the city of Detroit, but the same court excluded the suburban school systems from the court order on the grounds that they had not been shown to be involved in the unconstitutional segregation in Detroit.

Why Litigation and Why Education?

This brief chronicle of court cases in the uphill struggle of the civil rights movement for desegregated education points up additional questions. These are questions about why education became the cornerstone of the civil rights movement, why courts and litigation have been so central in civil rights activities, and how powerful Whites have been involved in the Black movement. Take litigation as an example. Why was it the central Black strategy until the 1960s? Some have suggested that a major reason why the NAACP pursued litigation was that it lacked the resources for large-scale legislative lobbying or nonviolent civil disobedience; the NAACP, in the beginning, barely had enough resources to tackle school desegregation in the courts (Morris, 1975, p. 215). More importantly, the law was believed by key Black leaders to be the appropriate major instrument for changing the inferior position of Black Americans in all economic classes. Less orderly action, such as sitting-in and demonstrating, was frowned upon by NAACP leaders, because "the founders and subsequent leaders of the NAACP were highly supportive of the political system and apparently reluctant to undertake any activity that appeared to threaten that system" (Morris, 1975, p. 215). The NAACP chose a strategy of court action because it relied increasingly on liberal White support, support which reflected the concern for stability and legitimacy in the White ruling class.

The emphasis on education is distinctively American and can be linked to our individualistic ethic and upward mobility ethic. To all Americans, Black and White, education has long been sold by the ruling class as *the* way to improve life conditions. "Education will set you free" is an idea that has been bought by rank-and-file Americans everywhere. Schools are

---

[4] *Keyes* v. *School District No. 1, Denver, Colorado*, 413 U.S. 189 (1973).
[5] *Milliken*, v. *Bradley*, 418 U.S. 717 (1974).

important because they are seen as major avenues of mobility by Black parents with less education than they want for their children. So strong has this sales effort—in the media and schools shaped by the ruling class—been that there is an almost religious faith among Black Americans in the value of education as the appropriate way of rising out of oppressive economic conditions. "In the late fifties and sixties, Blacks were only willing to have their children confront the jeering anti-integration mobs because education was so important to them" (Newman, 1978, p. 80). The NAACP was able to sustain its painfully slow legal struggle because of the commitment of rank-and-file Black parents to education. Black leaders were committed to education for obvious reasons. As Dye and Ziegler (1978, p. 345) put it:

> The educated blacks of the NAACP sought only the removal of legal barriers to equality of opportunity. Being educated, they regarded education as the key to success. NAACP leadership, being economically successful on the whole, was better accepted by white elites and thus was culturally at the periphery of the black community.

As we have previously noted, education was also chosen for strategical reasons, because the inequality and discrimination in public schools was so easy to demonstrate. Since the law of the land was "separate but equal," forcing the school systems to pay teachers equal salaries and to maintain Black and White schools of equal quality would mean an economic burden no state or local government could long stand. In addition, desegregation change was possible in the sphere of education, because government plays a more central role there than in other areas.

There are several reasons for the greater potential and actual effectiveness of civil rights action, including litigation, in the public sector of education. There is the reality of one school board responsible for the whole system, one agency to be sued rather than thousands, as in the case of housing or employment. Another reason is that there are greater legal and constitutional constraints on government actions than there are on private employer or realtor actions. The Fourteenth Amendment to the United States Constitution, which plainly states that a state government cannot "deny to any person within its jurisdiction the equal protection of the laws" and the Fifth Amendment which states that the federal government cannot deprive a person of "life, liberty, or property, without due process of law" set explicit limits (in theory at least) on that action. In the United States, political developments have forced constitutional changes that have institutionalized a broader array of rights in the government sphere than in the private economic market sector. Subordinate groups have greater opportunities to sue for changes in the government sphere. Decision-making action in the private sector is far more autocratic and hierarchical and far less subject to democratic influence than in the public sector. Lindbloom (1977, p. 334) has noted that capitalists and "property owners see democracy in government as less threatening by far than democracy in industry."

Corporate Liberals and Foundations

Liberal White support, including corporate and foundation support, has been important to the civil rights movement. The NAACP has long depended on some liberal White support, support encompassing individuals and a few organizations. While much NAACP financial support has come from its dues-paying, predominantly Black, membership, the NAACP has received substantial gifts and grants from White individuals and foundations. According to Lomax (1962, p. 181), it was only in the 1950s that Black contributions to the NAACP began to equal and exceed the contributions of liberal Whites. In the 1960s, much of the financing of the newer civil rights group also came from Whites.

Since the early 1900s, corporate liberalism and reformism, often expressed through tax-saving foundations, have been directed at maintaining legitimacy and stability in this society. Improving the quality of segregated education was a major concern for those few foundations which dealt with Black problems prior to the 1960s. For the dozen or more foundations dealing with Black problems before and during the 1960s, education "fits the conventional wisdom of philanthropy, which holds that nothing is more productive in the service of human welfare than investment in the education and training of human beings" (Nielsen, 1972, p. 358). Aid to segregated Black colleges was central to early, and limited, White foundation involvement in Black problems. For example, the General Education Board, established by John D. Rockefeller in 1902, has given millions of dollars to Black schools and colleges in the South. The Rosenwald Foundation built schools for Blacks throughout the South.

Racial segregation was not seen as a problem by most corporate liberals and foundations until the racial-political crises of the 1950s and 1960s. Beginning in the 1960s, the Rockefeller Brothers Fund supported the Southern Regional Council, whose activities included a consulting service for communities desegregating their schools. Helping the school desegregation cases become central to the Black civil rights effort, major grants were made to the NAACP's Legal Defense Fund by a few foundations. In the 1950s, the Ford Foundation made a number of grants to NAACP-LDF and to the Southern Regional Council (Nielsen, 1972, pp. 344–358). After the *Brown* decision, the Ford Foundation and the Rockefeller Brothers Fund "began to make a number of useful grants to Black organizations and institutions" (Nielsen, 1972, p. 344). Moreover, the Rockefeller Brothers Fund has repeatedly been able to aid civil rights leaders (Nielsen, 1972, p. 75).

Most major foundation grants did not come until the 1960s, and separate corporate contributions did not start coming in to civil rights coffers until the mid-1960s. By the mid-1960s, under the leadership of McGeorge Bundy, the Ford Foundation came to see that, in his words, "full equality for American Negroes is now the most urgent domestic concern of this country" and that the Foundation "must play its full part in this field." In this period, both the NAACP and the Urban League received grants of several hundred thousand dollars from the Ford Foundation. In 1967, the NAACP Legal Defense Fund received from Ford one million dollars for work on the rights of indigents (Allen, 1970, p. 71–76, 144). In 1966–1968, the Carnegie Corporation funded a voluntary school desegregation program in Boston, a research study by the National Opinion Research Center (NORC) on the politics of school desegregation in the North, and a grant to New York University to train Black civil rights lawyers. And the Rockefeller Foundation (not the same as the Rockefeller Brothers Fund) made grants to the NAACP in the mid-1960s (Nielsen, 1972, pp. 350–358). From 1964 to 1967, the dollar contributions of foundations for race-related problems went from $2.3 million to $26.7 million.

Political attacks on the foundations in the late 1960s, reflected in a tax reform bill tough on foundations, were captained by southern conservatives who resented grants for southern school desegregation and by northern and western conservatives who resented foundation support for militant Black ghetto organizations in their regions. Whitney Young, director of the Urban League, saw the congressional debates in 1969 as filled with racism. In his view, this tax reform bill was one "with a purpose as much to intimidate as to legislate, a bill designed to discourage foundations who have belatedly found the field of social reform to be one in which they might tenderly tread" (quoted in Nielsen, 1972, p. 18).

The involvement of some White foundations in selected civil rights organizations makes sense when one examines class origins. The NAACP arose in the boom period of monopoly capitalism and reflected the concerns of a small group of middle-level Black leaders afraid of racial violence. Allen argues that in the early 1900s such civil rights organizations were relatively weak and even then "coopted by the well-heeled white progressives" of the era. The NAACP was "born of compromise" and "faced a sharply uphill struggle in carrying their message to the country at large (Allen, 1974, pp. 270–272)." Black reformers in the NAACP have usually represented the small middle class in most Black communities. Historically, they have been co-opted, isolated, or repressed by Whites. Though rather modest, the White investment in middle-class-oriented Black organizations helped to strengthen these organizations and thus to channel protest into legal channels.

THE SUCCESS OF CIVIL RIGHTS PRESSURES

Legitimacy Effects

Why and how were civil rights groups, such as the NAACP, successful in bringing some significant changes in the wall of school segregation? We now have the answer to this basic question. At the center of an adequate answer is political legitimacy. Ruling class control of basic political institutions shapes them so that they operate to foster capitalistic priorities of capital and profit accumulation. Yet the democratic political traditions built into this society have included a deeper view, seeing rank-and-file citizens participate in and benefit from government. As Black and other non-White pressures for change grew, so did concern grow among reform-minded members of the ruling classes for the legitimacy and stability of the American system.

Concern with the perceived legitimacy of this capitalist state, moreover, extends to concern with the world image. It well may be that a contributing factor spurring elite concessions to Black demands included a strong concern for the image of the United States on the world scene. As early as December 1952, Secretary of State Dean Acheson gave the Supreme Court a statement declaring that "the continuation of racial discrimination is a source of constant embarrassment to this government . . . and it jeopardizes the effective maintenance of our moral leadership of the free and democratic nations of the world" (quoted in Bennett, 1965, pp. 187–188). In regard to the *Brown* decision, the United States attorney general suggested that school segregation should be struck down because it "furnishes grist for Communist propaganda mills (quoted in Franklin, 1974, p. 421)." In 1957, President Dwight Eisenhower made it clear that the crisis over school desegregation in Little Rock, Arkansas was in fact doing harm to the "prestige and influence, and indeed to the safety, of our nation and the world," and in the early 1960s, President John Kennedy also linked the struggle with the South over desegregation to the world-wide prestige of the United States (Wolfe, 1973, p. 45). Political legitimacy, in a very broad sense, was a central concern. Impressionistic evidence on world opinion, particularly in the increasingly powerful third world countries, indicates that these worries about our image were realistic, for racial troubles in the United States do make news headlines overseas. Thus, it seems quite likely that the peaceful progress made in school desegregation enhanced the world image, and thus the legitimacy, of the United States. This image, in turn, facilitates United States economic and political expansion abroad.

Much of the pressure for change and to preserve political legitimacy fell directly on the federal courts. The legitimacy of this system was being questioned, and the potential for militant, even revolutionary, non-White action was growing by the 1950s, so some authoritative group had to take action. The Supreme Court has a constitutional mandate to decide fundamental constitutional issues in suits brought before it. It has exercised this responsibility from the beginning, by making public policy in response to specific controversies brought before it. Often, the executive and legislative branches duck controversial issues, tossing them to the judiciary to decide. A paramount social control organization, the judiciary has a major responsibility for dealing with group clashes. Less the center of public attention, and far less democratic, the courts are better able to "take the heat" for making far-reaching decisions than are the executive and legislative branches. This seems to have been the situation in regard to the school desegregation controversy.

Within the ruling class, there are significant divisions of opinion on resolving protestors' threats to legitimacy. Some advocate repression alone, and others accent moderate reforms. After World War II, in regard to civil rights, the reform-oriented group in the ruling class seemed to be growing in strength. This group included a number of federal judges. The evidence for blatant, intentional discrimination in southern (later, northern) school systems was usually overwhelming. Judges have been faced with extensive evidence that school boards, such as the Boston School Committee, "have knowingly carried out a systematic program of segregation affecting all the city's students, teachers, and school facilities and have intentionally brought about and maintained a dual school system" (quoted in Caplan, 1976, p. 389). Responding favorably to court suits brought by Black parents with the NAACP and other civil rights lawyers, some judges at the district, circuit, and Supreme Court levels cooperated in the process of dismantling segregated schools. Some have noted that between the 1950s and the early 1970s the Supreme Court, headed by reform-minded Earl Warren, did come down on the side of the underdog far more often than the subsequent court, headed by Warren Burger, has since the early 1970s. It is true that the Warren Court tended to reflect the views of the more liberal wing of the ruling class, views supporting some expansion of basic rights to groups previously excluded. However, it should be noted that there was far more outside pressure from Blacks on the Warren Court than on the Burger Court, that the Burger Court was pressured by a "White backlash."

The federal courts were not alone in bringing school desegregation to some parts of the nation. Had it not been for a small subagency in one executive branch department, the Office of Civil Rights in the Department of Health, Education, and Welfare (HEW–OCR), the court orders requiring desegregation would have had less effect. At the time of its passage, many members of Congress apparently did not realize the importance of a provision in the 1964 Civil Rights Act which permits the cutting off of federal aid to school districts refusing to desegregate. Yet in the mid-1960s, HEW–OCR officials began to enforce this provision of the law. An important ingredient here was the 1965 Elementary and Secondary Education Act, which provided major federal funding for public school systems. Now there was more federal money to be stopped if school systems did not desegregate. OCR cut off, or threatened to cut off, federal aid to many (southern) school districts that defied court orders. Lodged in HEW in this period were some of the important reform-oriented liberals in the ruling class, such as John Gardner, who believed in the strategic value of a selective opening up the society for dissenting minorities.

This federal action probably reduced Black protest activity significantly. Whatever its benefits for Black children, the benefits to the ruling class in the form of increased racial stability and enhanced legitimacy were those sought and secured. Here was evidence of success in government action to meet a legitimation crisis.

The Immediate Impact of Desegregation

As a result of this federal court action and HEW–OCR reinforcement activity, very significant shifts in the segregation of Black children took place in the late 1960s. Many moved out of exclusively Black schools to better quality, predominantly White, schools. The following figures, percentages of Black students in predominantly White schools, indicate that by 1970 southern schools were more desegregated than northern schools:

	1968	1970	1972
South	18%	39%	44%
North/West	28	28	29

They also show very little change in school segregation in the North, and a slowing of change in the South. More recent 1974–1975 data show that these trends have continued. Only in the South does segregation continue its decline, though now at a snaillike pace. Moreover, the most successful desegregation in the United States has come in small- and medium-size school districts, especially in the South (Orfield, 1978, pp. 56–58). Since 1970, the increases in the proportion of Black children in desegregated schools have come much more slowly; the same is true for Hispanic children. The large-scale progress had come to an end. The growth of private, segregated "White academies" and parochial schools can now be seen throughout the nation.

The positive educational achievements of the school desegregation era have been lost sight of in much of the public and scholarly debate over pupil transportation ("busing"). Millions of Black children are no longer hidden away in a forgotten corner of towns and cities, but are daily rubbing elbows with the rank-and-file White children. Many Black children, bused to desegregated schools, have thus come in contact with White students and teachers for the first time on a significant scale. Many learn new skills for coping with White-controlled organizations in the outside world. The many minority children who do better in desegregated than in segregated settings may often do so because of the coping-with-racism techniques they have learned. The achievement tests which are central to most research assessments of the impact of school desegregation do not measure adequately a child's learning to cope better with a White-dominated environment or success in the outside world after school.

There is a widespread, but quite erroneous, notion that social science research has indicated that Black children do not gain in terms of achievement in desegregated schools, often coupled with the view that the old liberal idea that desegregation would bring greater equality in achievement has been proven to be mistaken by new data. However, this critique of desegregation has misread the data available. The best achievement studies in desegregated schools, those with careful (segregated school) controls, tend as a group to show modest but positive achievement gains for minority children in desegregated schools. This is often true only for certain grades and in regard to certain subjects. The average achievement seems to be modest, but positive on the whole (St. John, 1975, pp. 149–157). Clearly, more *comprehensive* desegregation than has yet been tried might well lead to even more positive results.

Two important features of the desegregated schooling process have been shown to shape the achievement gains of minority children: the length of desegregation and the scale of the desegregation. Numerous studies have shown "the best achievement gains for those who begin desegregation in kindergarten and the first grade" (Pettigrew, 1974, p. 59). Other studies have shown that Black children in schools which are 25–50% Black do better than those in schools that are less than 25% or over 50% Black. Apparently, in a 25–50% desegregated setting, Black students are numerous enough to play a significant role in the schools (Jencks & Brown, 1972).

Desegregation opponents often overlook the fact that in many cities, especially the large group of small- to medium-sized cities, a great deal of school desegregation can be done without "massive busing." With smaller Black enrollments or smaller districts, such school systems can desegregate much more easily than the larger ones. Yet many of these cities have as yet made little progress in desegregating their schools. Pettigrew (1974, p. 57) has commented on one city of this type as of mid-1974:

> Consider the schools of Des Moines, Iowa. Only 10 percent of the district's 42,000 pupils are Black. Yet this small percentage is highly concentrated in five elementary schools and one junior high which range from about 52 percent to 80 percent Black.

One final point. In spite of large-scale desegregation efforts, the United States continues to have many school systems with large numbers of segregated schools. Does this "separation" still mean "unequal?" Yes, there is considerable evidence that "separate" remains, more often than not, "unequal." Based on a national survey, the famous 1966 Coleman *et al.* report, *Equality of Educational Opportunity*, is often cited as though it demonstrated conclusively that the separate schools of segregated Blacks and Whites are basically *equal* in overall quality. However, the report (Coleman, Campbell, Hobson, McPartland, Mood, Weinfeld, & York, 1966, p. 37) itself argues that its own statistical survey, which in fact shows small but consistent quantitative differences favoring White schools (as a group) on many variables, understates the inequality in school quality:

> The child experiences his environment as a whole, while the statistical measures necessarily fragment it. Having a teacher without a college degree may indicate an element of disadvantage: but in the concrete situation, a school-child may be taught by a teacher who is not only without a college degree, but who has grown up and received his schooling in the local community, who has never been out of the State, who has a 10th grade vocabulary, and who shares the local community's attitudes. . . . The statistical examination of difference in school environments for minority and nonminority children will give an impression of lesser differences than actually exist . . . so that subsequent sections will probably tend to understate the actual disadvantage in school environment experienced by the average minority child compared to that experienced by the average majority child.

Note that surveys such as this one primarily research quantity issues—the presence, absence, number of certain school facilities. The quality of facilities is seldom measured. "This is true of the description of physical facilities such as laboratories, gymnasiums, and textbook availability, as well as features such as curriculum and specialized classes" (Hanushek & Kain, 1972, p. 121). Thus, the predominantly segregated schools of the North, and of the largest southern cities, still mean inferior-in-quality learning settings for minority children. Since the movement toward desegregation in the 1968–1972 period has slowed sharply in the South and come to a complete standstill in the North, segregated schools are the future for a majority of non-White children in the United States.

REACTION AND STAGNATION

By the early 1970s, the movement toward school desegregation had slowed considerably. What were the factors in this drama of sluggishness and retrogression? Most obvious perhaps was the direct intervention of President Richard Nixon to reduce pressures on local governments to desegregate. Nixon officials, especially Robert Finch and John Mitchell, weakened the federal pressure; friendly persuasion became the primary method of bringing compliance. Presidents Richard Nixon and Gerald Ford gave great comfort, in their public statements against "busing," to those fighting school desegregation everywhere. Even Congress played a role. Congress added anti-busing amendments to the fiscal 1976 HEW appropriations bill, among others. The more conservative, Nixon-packed Supreme Court began to back off of requiring comprehensive remedies for segregation. The more reform-oriented court under Earl Warren saw itself, however paternalistically, as protecting the downtrodden. Increasingly, the Burger Court sees itself as protecting dominant classes and groups, and their bureaucracies, from the threat of too much social change favoring the dispossessed. The recent shift in the Supreme Court away from increased school desegregation has been mirrored in shifts at the lower levels of the judiciary.

In effect, the *success* of the (Warren) Supreme Court in facing the legitimation crisis created by the Black civil rights movement could be seen in enhanced societal stability and governmental legitimacy brought by modest civil rights reforms, while the *success* of the (Burger) Supreme Court is to be seen in stopping the reforms once the Black-generated legitimation crisis passed and a new White backlash (rank-and-file) legitimation crisis surfaced. The social control crises faced by this capitalist state change as we pass from one period to the next.

Since the early 1950s, the law and the operation of courts have become more complex. Prior to the last few decades, few questioned any person's right to go to court and sue. Today, a growing number of court (and congressional) restrictions are curtailing the ability of persons to sue. Moreover, prior to World War II, there was greater simplicity; typically, there were bipolar lawsuits, with two parties involved.[6] The remedy required was relatively clearcut. Today we have a bureaucratic-corporate society with many large-scale institutions; individuals and groups of individuals now sue large organizations. Since World War II, federal courts have become involved with remedies that involve such organizations. Not only is the organization's past wrongful action an issue, but so is its probable future

---

[6] I am indebted to Mark Yudof for stimulating my thinking on many of the points in this paragraph.

action. The remedies become much more complicated and thus more controversial. More conservative justices, such as Supreme Court Judges Rehnquist and Powell, wish to roll back the federal courts to an earlier period
when both cases and probable remedies were much simpler. They can
handle remedies for one White police officer beating up a Black person, but
they prefer not to deal with situations where the court would have to
intervene into the less overt, but still discriminatory, institutional operations
of a police department, such as racially biased personnel tests. They wish to
restrict remedies to the extent of the proven damage or error, which often
means very limited remedies, as in the restriction of school desegregation to
only those areas of a given school system proven in a given case to be
directly implicated in intentional discrimination. They seem less capable of
dealing with the problem of bureaucratized racial discrimination which has
no clearcut individual villains.

There are several reasons for this movement backwards. One seems to
be old-fashioned ruling-class conservatism, the desire for a reduction in
government ("rights") intervention into the natural laws of societal operation, a strong preference for established elites and their institutional order
over dissenting challengers. Supreme Court justices vote for different
reasons in any given case, but it is clear that there has been a significant
shift in favor of those justices who distrust democratizing movements and
who trust the actions of local elites, rejecting "human rights" intervention in
most state and local matters.

The White Backlash

The waffling and backtracking by federal courts in school desegregation cases was stimulated, in part, by a ground swell of rank-and-file White
reaction in the larger society, a reaction which created a new legitimation
crisis. Opinion polls showed a huge majority of middle-level Whites opposed
to pupil transportation ("busing") beyond the nearest school as a means of
promoting school desegregation. But large-scale White protest, in the North
and West, did not appear until the late 1960s. Here we see rank-and-file
White actors coming to play an important part in the increasingly national
drama of desegregation. The impact of school desegregation varies from
class to class. The ruling class, with the resources to build up wealth in
houses, land, and stocks, includes very few non-White Americans. Most of
the American judges and top political officials who make school desegregation decisions have their roots firmly in this class. It is this upper 5% of the
population which has such economic power that it can choose suburban or
"exurban" housing and elite public or private schools to suit its class
interests; its ability to compete in the housing and educational markets is
such that it need not fear governmental intervention in regard either to

housing or schools. Yet, the top classes are not monolithic in their view of public policy. Fearing greater internal upheaval as a threat to internal and external legitimacy, the liberal wing of the ruling class responded to Black protest by taking some limited steps to end segregation. The attack on school segregation was not, from the first, intended to be a full-scale attack; it was inaugurated slowly on a case-by-case, issue-by issue basis by the courts, then administered in its most rigorous enforcement period more as a "police action" (HEW–OCR) aimed at "southern criminals" than as a positive action aimed at restructuring the racist system North and South. It was not a strategy for renewal of the society.

Moreover, the "price" for this limited—and typically resource-starved—school desegregation was not to be paid by the top classes but by rank-and-file Whites and non-Whites at the less powerful class levels. It is Whites at the middle levels who began to resist, rather strongly, the school desegregation imposed on them, primarily by White judges and politicians in the higher classes. In a sense, then, middle-level Whites are both privileged and denied. As a group, they are privileged vis-à-vis Blacks and most other non-Whites. They generally have better incomes and access to better housing and schools. Yet they are disadvantaged relative to Whites in the higher-level professional, managerial, and capitalist classes. "The upward and downward pushes pinch them between simultaneous threats. From above they are squeezed economically. From below they are pushed to make room for more competition over resources already squeezed from above" (Wellman, 1977, p. 227).

From the 1950s to the mid-1960s, school desegregation was not a personal matter for northern Whites or affluent southern Whites in the suburbs of larger cities. When school desegregation began to "threaten" their schools, they began to defend their own interests.[7] Neither racial hatred nor outraged bigotry was required. Many were simply protecting their advantages and privileges against the "invasion" of non-White outsiders. Even then, one should note, it was the less well-off Whites in cities who were most likely to be involved in the desegregation plans. School desegregation, to some extent, redistributes educational "wealth" from rank-and-file Whites to rank-and-file Blacks. In the first stages, it was southern and/or working class Whites; gradually, middle-level Whites became involved in desegregation plans, including some in northern and western cities. Not surprisingly, then, recent increases in White opposition to desegregation have come primarily from these middle-level White groups in the North and West and in the suburbs of the South.

Rank-and-file White fear that the quality of the schools has declined in recent decades is widespread. This links, in turn, to a fear that mobility and

---

[7] Of course, in the South desegregation plans in smaller cities and towns have long involved Whites at middle levels as well, but middle-level Whites in the North did not become directly involved until the late 1960s and early 1970s.

prosperity wil not come for their children. We have a nationwide "back-to-the basics" movement aimed at improving the quality of the presumably decaying schools. "Why can't Johnny read?" articles and discussions appear in the mass media. There is an increasing rejection of experimentation in the schools. And the recent revolt against property taxes in the 1970s has won widespread rank-and-file White support, even though over the long run it may mean larger classes for children and decaying physical facilities even for Whites. Then, on top of these other educational problems, comes the additional problem of school desegregation. For many White parents, it is simply too much. So they lash out at "busing" as a major cause of school troubles.

Concern for traditional White values also lies behind the opposition to large-scale school desegregation. For many Whites, a major threat in the pressure for school desegregation lies in a threat to the fundamental principle of individualism. Many Whites are "convinced that America does not recognize color, it only recognizes individual achievement" (Wellman, 1977, p. 229). Strategies aimed at institutional discrimination—such as large-scale school desegregation with busing and affirmative action in higher education—are rejected because they violate the "very basic belief that individuals can succeed if they try hard enough" (Wellman, 1977, p. 229). Thus, many Whites do not recognize that the problems of Black Americans *were* and *are group problems*. Those Whites who do recognize that group oppression requires group remedies are often not conscious of the living contradiction which is the White middle class, the contradiction seen in advantages which have come to them as a result of the oppression of Black Americans. Rather than suffer a significant loss in their own (often tenuous) privileges, the rank-and-file Whites precipitated a new legitimation crisis.

The reaction and stagnation of the Nixon–Ford (and even Carter) periods, thus, can be seen as a toughening in response to earlier success in meeting a Black-generated legitimacy crisis and (at the same time?) a new attempt to grapple with a rank-and-file White-generated legitimacy crisis. The dilemma of a government oriented toward maintaining stability and legitimacy is that a democratizing concession to maintain control starts a new series of social waves; like a pebble in a pond, the concession to Blacks in this regard created societal waves that backwash in the form of a legitimacy crisis triggered by rank-and-file Whites, those living contradictions who are both oppressors of Blacks and oppressed by the ruling class.

THE UNDERLYING SYSTEMIC PROBLEMS

We have suggested previously that the ruling class involvement in desegregation reform was reserved, that desegregation was never intended to be full-scale, comprehensive reform aimed at liberating Black Americans.

This restricted orientation is clearly illustrated in two basic systemic issues that occasionally surface in the discussion of desegregation: (1) comprehensive school desegregation, and (2) the housing context.

A few antiracist analysts have seen desegregation as a comprehensive strategem encompassing the entire school situation, from student and teacher desegregation to revision of curriculum and extracurricular activities, a strategy requiring, at a minimum, costly governmental catch-up programs. Yet even the sympathetic federal courts have generally not been willing to adopt a costly comprehensive approach. The desegregation brought by the federal judiciary has typically been more of "form" rather than of "content." White and non-White students have been mixed, often in one-way busing programs which move Black children into previously all-White schools. Taken as a whole, school desegregation has gone little beyond the mixing of Black and White children. Yet, perceptive supporters have argued that desegregation must be thorough-going and costly before one would expect consistently greater positive effects from desegregated education than for segregated education.

Today, segregation persists even within desegregated schools; classrooms are segregated by unnecessary ability grouping. The few desegregated school systems which have reduced ability grouping and increased team teaching have generally had better achievement results than those that desegregated and increased ability grouping (Pettigrew, 1974, p. 58). In high schools, differential vocational and college tracking systems often separate Black and White students. The teaching orientation in desegregated schools is frequently slanted toward a one-way acculturation of Black children into "White culture." Rist's (1978) study of classroom histories shows the extent of this widespread White-acculturation orientation in desegregated schools. Often, the administrative staff at desegregated schools remains predominantly White; sometimes, the teachers remain predominantly White in newly desegregated schools. These factors, taken together, indicate that *no* existing desegregated system has come close to being comprehensively desegregated. The heavy *cost* of a comprehensive program seems to be a major limiting factor.

In addition, there are substantial limits placed on the possibility of comprehensive school desegregation by the rigidly segregated housing patterns of most American towns and cities. Segregation in housing patterns is the result of decisions by powerful, as well as rank-and-file, Whites. Yet it is one seldom discussed in connection with school segregation either by elite politicians, the mass media, or scholars. The limited variety of housing choices available to non-White minority groups can be seen by their concentration and segregation in the nation's cities.[8] Using the Taeuber

---

[8] This section on housing draws heavily on Feagin and Feagin (1978, pp. 85–120).

scale for measuring residential segregation (0 = random distribution of all racial and ethnic groups; 100 = total segregation), one important study of 30 cities based on 1970 census data revealed White/non-White segregation scores ranging from 55 (San Francisco) to 93 (Dallas). This means that in Dallas, 93% of the non-White population would have to change their residence and redistribute themselves throughout the city in order to achieve no segregation (Marlin, 1973, pp. 17–18). Suburbs of cities still have relatively small Black populations; in 1970 only one suburban resident in twenty was Black, and even then was likely to reside in a disproportionately Black suburban area next to a central city ghetto.

In a famous footnote to the *Milliken* v. *Bradley* decision, which knocked down an attempt to implement metropolitan desegregation, Supreme Court Justice Potter Stewart argued that the state and suburban governments were not involved in the segregation of children in the Detroit area. According to Stewart, "no record has been made in this case showing that the racial composition of the Detroit school population or the residential patterns within Detroit and in the surrounding areas were in any significant measure caused by governmental activity. . . . " In his view, the heavily Black school population of Detroit was "caused by unknown and perhaps unknowable factors such as immigration, birth rates, economic changes, or cumulative acts of private racial fears."

Yet, as Pettigrew has put it, there are many things in social science which are "unknown and unknowable," but the "tight, unremitting containment of urban blacks over the past half-century within the bowels of American cities is not of them" (Pettigrew, 1974, p. 62). Direct government involvement in the recent past in intentional residential segregation is easy to demonstrate. Federal aid programs, including the Veternan's Administration (VA) and the Federal Housing Authority (FHA), have often come with the condition that racial discrimination in housing was to be perpetuated. Thus, most of the new housing built in the years 1935–1950 (11 million homes) was built with discrimination as a condition of federal aid. Abrams (1966) notes that in this period, "federal policy did more to entrench housing bias in American neighborhoods than any court could undo by a ruling" p. 517). The FHA and other branches of the Department of Housing and Urban Development (HUD) are among the most influential federal agencies shaping housing patterns. Guidelines for mortgage ratings were set down in the FHA's *Underwriting Manual* (1936) and were written with the advice of top elite members of the (White) National Association of Real Estate Boards. In early editions, the *Underwriting Manual* emphasized the importance of homogeneous neighborhoods, listing "the presence of incompatible racial elements" as a basis for assigning a low rating to, or for rejecting, a dwelling in a racially mixed area. Racially restrictive deeds were recommended. Subsequent editions of the *Manual* (1955) removed explicit mention of race, but still prescribed low ratings for houses in areas undergoing social change and for older homes. In effect, it continued to encourage racial discrimination.

Under pressure from powerful economic interests, local governments of towns and cities have used zoning powers to keep many neighborhoods racially homogeneous. Many suburban areas ringing the cities are self-governing, which means that most such areas are controlled by Whites, with no Blacks participating in the establishment of their goals or regulations. The objectives of the suburbs do not usually include the minority point of view. Moreover, in numerous towns and cities, zoning regulations have been intentionally established to exclude non-White families from certain residential areas. For example, in Black Jack, Missouri, a St. Louis suburb, the threat of a nonprofit sponsor building multifamily housing led to that area incorporating itself and banning multifamily housing under new laws. Other suburban areas have incorporated in order to keep minorities out.

Blatant, door-slamming discrimination against minority homeseekers seems to have given way to more subtle forms of discrimination in recent years, but blatant discrimination is still evident in the treatment of Black brokers, treatment that, in turn, affects minority homeseekers. Paralleling the dual housing market has developed a dual real estate industry. The direct discrimination that occurs when Black brokers are discouraged from membership in White firms and in local White boards prevents them from having access to real estate listings in White areas, a measure White realtors consider necessary in order to preserve the market for themselves. Moreover, a major research study in the Detroit metropolitan area by Diana Pearce (1976) found considerable subtlety in the character of housing discrimination directed against Black Americans by real estate people. One Black and one White couple, with similar economic backgrounds, were sent to the same 97 real estate brokers. Consistent differences along racial lines were found in financial advice, interpersonal treatment, houses shown, and time devoted to the couples. Massive housing segregation inevitably sets strict limits on the strategy for school desegregation. Certainly, comprehensive school desegregation would require comprehensive housing desegregation.

The fundamental reasons for the lack of comprehensive school desegregation have become clearer as we have proceeded. Further school desegregation does not occur, not because segregation is inefficient or because minority parents are tired of segregation, but because Whites at the middle and upper levels of the society oppose it. Comprehensive school desegregation has not occurred because the more powerful societal actors did not, and do not, wish it to occur. From a broad vantage point, patterns of discrimination interlock across political, economic, and educational sectors. For non-White Americans, race oppression is indeed interlocking. No one organizational complex stands alone, and the principle of cumulation insures that the negative impact of the web of racism is much greater than it would be if the only problem were discrimination in one organizational sector such as education.

CONCLUSION

School segregation is a small part of the web of individual and institutionalized discrimination in which Blacks and other non-Whites continue to find themselves. It has been the cornerstone of civil rights action. Yet, there are many Black Americans whose lives are only indirectly touched by what goes on in the schools, and race discrimination oppresses the lives of "those who have no intentions of attending school" (Lomax, 1962, p. 113). Attempts at school desegregation do not deal with the critical patterns of housing and employment discrimination facing Black families in this last quarter of the twentieth century.

Today, there is little White awareness of the massive *scale* of racial oppression that persists in this society. Currently, federal courts seem to be rejecting a conception of this society as fundamentally racist in its institutions. Discrimination is seen as the result of prejudice, of "private racial fears," rather than as patterned practices preserving White privileges. Many of today's White leaders, including major judges, hold a social theory which views racial inequality as on a sharp decline. Justice Byron White put it this way in his dissent from the Supreme Court's *Milliken* v. *Bradley* metropolitan desegregation decision: "Today's holding, I fear, is more a reflection of a perceived public mood that we have gone far enough in enforcing the Constitution's guarantee of equal justice than it is the product of neutral principles of law. In the short run, it may seem to be the easier course to allow our great metropolitan areas to be divided up each into two cities—but it is a course, I predict, our people will ultimately regret" (quoted in Pettigrew, 1974, p. 63). The "benign neglect" perspective has made its way throughout industry, business, and government.

Equality of opportunity remains the expressed verbal goal of many Whites, but the move away from large-scale desegregation has led to a renewed emphasis on separate-and-equal schools as the major goal in reforming racism in American education. A number of prominent scholars, lawyers, and social scientists, have given up on large-scale school desegregation and have argued for a reconsideration of "separate-and-equal." Opponents of "busing" often say that "busing" monies should be used to improve schools. One of the difficulties with the call for equalizing rather than desegregating is that no one is currently putting—or is likely to put—big money into the school-equalizing process. Indeed, many school systems are seeing *cutbacks* in their operating budgets. Hardpressed central cities, such as New York City, have seen their tax base drop as capitalists move South, seeking low taxes, no unions, and lower wages. Cities have been forced for financial reasons to lay off teachers, eliminate electives, and close out special programs. Class size increases. Cutbacks have occurred in Detroit, Chicago, Philadelphia, and many other cities. At the same time, wealth surrounds the troubled school systems, as Orfield (1978, pp. 195–196) notes:

> Each of the nation's largest cities faces its problems of segregation and poverty surrounded by some of the wealthiest metropolitan areas in the world, areas where there are many hundreds of empty classrooms, far more ample tax resources, large existing school bus systems, and lopsided majorities of white children.

This fact of urban life reveals the power of the rank-and-file Whites who created a backlash legitimation crisis for the ruling class.

The views of Black parents remain as the last major support for large-scale desegregation. Today the struggle for meaningful school desegregation is still animated by the firm belief of many Black parents that quality schools can come only with the resources that flow to White schools: "equally devoted and competent teachers, lab and library resources, and all those supporting services that make American education exceptional" (Newman, Amidei, Carter, Kruvant, Day, & Russell, 1978, p. 83).

The issue in the federal courts at the height of NAACP victories was the educational future of Black children, not the high unemployment, the employment problems, and the residential segregation faced by their families. Equality of opportunity was and is a central notion in the school debates (Aronson, 1978, p. 412). More fundamental, large-scale societal change—such as guaranteed jobs or the redistribution of wealth—violate the individualistic ideology, whereas equality of educational opportunity plans do not. The emphasis on equality of opportunity holds out a chance for success to the best placed members of minority groups. Focusing on the relatively small number of people who do "make it" takes the focus off the desperate reality of those many who do not. As Aronson (1978) notes, "It is simply daydreaming to hope that equalizing educational opportunity among children can undo the natural and normal effects of a social system" (p. 413). It seems clear that of all the major spheres of American life where even equal opportunity changes might have brought great benefits to Blacks—housing, employment, education—education could bring the least in the way of concrete material benefits.

The convenient focus on equal opportunity assumes that the basic institutions, on the whole, are proper and just, that is, do not require large-scale reform. Too much White liberalism in the ruling class of this society, as in regard to school desegregation, has been a temporary response to a Black-generated legitimacy crisis and has faded to tinkering when the crisis abated. Even in the reform period, what is White is assumed to be better because of an allegedly superior cultural heritage. Thus, Robert Allen (1974) suggests that racial integration is "a liberal reform version of cultural chauvenism, for it still assumed that integration of nonwhites would not challenge the foundations of American society" (p. 277). White institutions are not expected to change massively as a result of legitimacy reforms. The high unemployment and subemployment rates for Black Americans will not be cured simply by providing better, desegregated education. Black Americans already have significantly higher educational attainments than most white-collar (clerical, sales, or blue-collar) jobs actually require—a point too many concerned with education often forget. Large numbers of minority persons with high school educations cannot find decent-paying jobs. The enormous number of jobs required to put all those needing and deserving work will require large-scale intervention into the economy, thus bringing major institutional change. The institutionalized defense and protection of the existing (maldistributed) property and wealth maintains elite White domination over all America, but most heavily over non-White America. Thus, a deep attack on racial discrimination in education, housing, and employment must ultimately become a struggle with the basic capitalist social order. Consequently, the liberation of Black and other non-White Americans will require larger-scale societal change than yet attempted.

ACKNOWLEDGMENTS

I am greatly indebted to the critical comments of David Perry and Walter Stephan on an earlier draft of this chapter.

REFERENCES

Abrams, C. The housing problem and the Negro. In T. Parsons & K. Clark (Eds.), *The Negro American*. Boston: Houghton Mifflin, 1966.

Allen, R. L. *Black awakening in capitalist America*. Garden City, New York: Doubleday, 1970.

Allen, R. L. *Reluctant reformers*. Washington, D.C.: Howard University Press, 1974.

Aronson, R. Is busing the real issue? *Dissent*, 1978, *25*, 409–415.

Bennett, L. *Confrontation: Black and White*. Baltimore: Penguin, 1965.

Bullock, H. A. *A history of Negro education in the South*. New York: Praeger, 1970.

Caplan, M. Truth—and shame—about busing. *Dissent*, 1976, *23* 383–391.

Coleman, J. S., Campbell, E. Q., Hobson, C. J., McPartland, J., Mood, A. M., Weinfeld, F. D., & York, R. L. *Equality of educational opportunity*. Washington, D.C.: U.S. Government Printing Office, 1966.

Dye, T. R., & Zeigler, L. H. *The irony of democracy* (4th ed.) North Scituate, Mass.: Duxbury, 1978.

Feagin, J. R., & Feagin, C. B. *Discrimination American style: Institutional racism and sexism.* Englewood Cliffs, N.J.: Prentice-Hall, 1978.

Franklin, J. H. *From slavery to freedom* (4th ed.) New York: Knopf, 1974.

Friedman, L. M. *A history of American law.* New York: Simon & Schuster, 1973.

Greenberg, J. Race relations and the American law. In H. H. Horowitz & K. L. Karst (Eds.), *Law, lawyers and social change.* Indianapolis: Bobbs-Merrill, 1969.

Hanushek, E. A., & Kain, J. F. On the value of equality of educational opportunity as a guide for public policy. In F. Mosteller & D. P. Moynihan (Eds.), *On equality of educational opportunity.* New York: Random, 1972.

Jencks, C., & Brown, M. The effects of desegregation on student achievement. Unpublished manuscript, Harvard University, 1972.

Lindbloom, C. E. *Politics and markets.* New York: Basic, 1977.

Lomax, L. E. *The Negro revolt.* New York: Harper & Row, 1962.

Marlin, J. T. City housing. *Municipal performance report*, 1973, *I:* 17–18.

Miller, L. *The petitioners.* New York: Random, 1966.

Morris, M. D. *The politics of Black America.* New York: Harper & Row, 1975.

Newman, D. K., Amidei, N. J., Carter, B. L., Kruvant, W. J., Day, D., & Russell, J. S. *Protest, politics and prosperity: Black America and white institutions, 1940–1975.* New York: Pantheon, 1978.

Nielsen, W. A. *The big foundations.* New York: Columbia University Press, 1972.

Orfield, G. *Must we bus? Segregated schools and national policy.* Washington, D.C.: The Brookings Institute, 1978.

Pearce, D. *Black, White and many shades of gray: Real estate brokers and their practices.* Ph.D. Dissertation, University of Michigan, 1976.

Pettigrew, T. F. A sociological view of the post-Milliken era. In U.S. Commission on Civil Rights, *Milliken* v. *Bradley: The Implications for Metropolitan Desegregation*, Washington, D.C., 1974.

Rist, R. C. *The invisible children: School integration in American society.* Cambridge: Harvard University Press, 1978.

St. John, N. H. *School desegregation: Outcomes for children.* New York: Wiley, 1975.

U.S. Federal Housing Administration, Housing and Home Finance Agency, *Underwriting Manual*, Form No. 2049 (rev. ed.). Washington, D.C.: U.S. Government Printing Office, 1936, part 2, sec. 2, arts. 252, 228, 229.

U.S. Federal Housing Administration, Housing and Home Finance Agency, *Underwriting Manual*, Form No. 2049 (rev. ed.). Washington, D.C.: U.S. Government Printing Office, 1955, part 3, sec. 13, arts. 1301, 1320.

Wellman, D. T. *Portraits of White racism.* Cambridge: Cambridge University Press, 1977.

Wolfe, A. *The limits of legitimacy.* New York: Free Press, 1977.

Wolfe, A. *The seamy side of democracy.* New York: David McKay, 1973.

3

The Serendipitous Effects of School Desegregation

SUSAN L. GREENBLATT AND CHARLES V. WILLIE

INTRODUCTION

When the *Brown*[1] decision was first handed down in 1954, its intent was to provide educational opportunities for Black children equal to those provided for White children. Although many observers would contend that this goal has not yet been achieved, we believe the *Brown* decision has resulted both directly and indirectly in significant changes both within the educational institution and in other social institutions. Although some of the changes that resulted from *Brown* and the myriad of desegregation cases following *Brown* were clearly intended, others were not. We refer to these unintended changes as the "serendipitous" effects of school desegregation. It is the intent of this chapter to explore some of the serendipitous effects that have already occurred and to speculate on some others that we believe will occur in the future.

Most of the commentaries on school desegregation have focused on the negative consequences of this process. Since these have been treated adequately in this and other volumes, we will analyze some of the positive serendipitous effects.

The major issues we will examine include the role of minorities in bringing about social change for themselves and the society at large; the probable contributions of social class desegregation in overcoming isolation and other forms of inequality in public school systems; the role of the state government in assuming its constitutional obligations for guaranteeing

[1] *Brown* v. *Topeka Board of Education*, 347 U.S. 483 (1954).

SUSAN L. GREENBLATT AND CHARLES V. WILLIE • Graduate School of Education, Harvard University, Cambridge, Massachusetts 02138.

equal protection of the laws with reference to education for all children. Internal changes for the educational system that we will examine include the redefinition of the function of education in society, implications of this change for the teaching profession, the changing relationship between school board members and systems, and the role of parents and other citizens in public education.

MINORITIES AND SOCIAL CHANGE

Court-ordered racial desegregation of urban education during the decades of the 1950s, 1960s, and 1970s has shaken the foundations of this institution and has prepared it for future changes that are discussed in this chapter. The fact that these changes have resulted from litigation initiated by racial minorities is in accord with social science theory. Robert K. Merton (1968) has noted that "it is not infrequently the case that the nonconforming minority in a society represents the interests and ultimate values of the group more effectively than the conforming majority" (p. 421). One of the authors (Willie, 1976) has recently made a similar observation, that from the time of the founding of this nation, minorities have always done the dreaming. Dreamers, like most individuals, have some ideas that are beneficial and others that may be detrimental. Certainly, this characterized the dreamers who wrote the Constitution. Some were slave-holders, yet they realized that their wealth and special position in society would erode if a republic were not established that would make available participatory powers for the poor as well as for the wealthy.

Members of the Constitutional Convention were dreamers who believed it was possible to achieve a just society, notwithstanding the injustices of the eighteenth century. These dreamers were

> male and white, merchants and manufacturers, property and plantation owners. Most of the delegates to the Constitutional Convention were lawyers by profession, not farmers, artisans, black and brown people, or women. The delegates were the minority during the Revolutionary period; and they were dreamers. The dreamers then were unlike most of the people. Most of the people were poor. (Willie, 1976, p. 37)

Yet Daniel Patrick Moynihan, United States Senator, former counselor to the president of the United States, and one-time public administrator in the United States Labor Department said, "It is clearly a disadvantage for a minority group to be operating on one principle, while the great majority of the population, and the one with the most advantages to begin with, is operating on another" (1965, p. 29). Clearly, Moynihan did not understand the beneficial effects for the nation of minorities functioning as creative dissenters.

Despite the limited perspective of some of our most influential public administrators and policymakers, minorities have continued to support the basic values of this nation and have continued to push for appropriate changes that would bring unity to the goals and methods in our various institutional systems so that they would conform to the Constitution of the republic, as it has been interpreted by the courts.

For many years prior to the *Brown* decision, Blacks and particularly the National Association for the Advancement of Colored People (NAACP) had utilized the court system to pursue their constitutionally guaranteed rights. The *Brown* decision in 1954 and the Civil Rights Act of 1964 represented major victories for minority groups in gaining these rights. However, some states, such as Virginia, refused to comply with the *Brown* decision at the outset and implemented programs of massive resistance; many cities and their public school systems, such as Boston, intentionally manipulated school attendance zones and used other means to create and maintain a dual school system.

Thus, Blacks, other racial minorities, the NAACP, and the NAACP Legal Defense Fund found it necessary to return to the courts continuously to obtain orders on ways of dismantling these dual school systems. Racial minorities have been plaintiffs in school desegregation cases in cities of all sizes in all sections of the country. The NAACP's success in these suits has served as an example for other groups to emulate. Thus, for example, Mexican-Americans established the Mexican-American Legal Defense and Educational Fund (MALDEF) in 1968 (Salinas, 1973). MALDEF, presumably modeled after the NAACP Legal Defense Fund, has become actively involved in litigation that attempts to gain civil rights for Mexican-Americans.

The National Organization of Women (NOW) has also sponsored the development of a legal defense and educational fund. During the summer of 1978, nearly 100,000 persons—women and men—marched in Washington, D.C. in support of the proposed Equal Rights Amendment. This amendment is aimed at helping women to secure their rights. The 1978 march was called the "largest women's rights rally on record" (*Post-Standard*, 1978, p. 1) and the demonstration was obviously patterned after the march on Washington in 1963 that preceded passage of the Civil Rights Act of 1964.

Citizens who are not members of racial minorities have witnessed the success of the NAACP and efforts by other racial minorities and also have begun to utilize the court system to redress what they consider to be grievances of a race-related nature in public schools. For example, Allan Bakke brought suit against the Regents of the University of California,[2] contending that he, a White male, was unjustifiably denied admission to medical

---

[2] *University of California Regents* v. *Bakke*, 98 S. Ct. 2733 (1978).

school at the Davis campus of that university because of his race. The facts of the case are these:

> The Davis affirmative action program set aside 16 of 100 places in each entering class for minority students. Minority applicants could seek these places or the 84 in the regular admissions program. Bakke, who is white, could not compete for the 16. (Lewis, 1978, p. 4)

The U.S. Supreme Court, by a 5 to 4 majority opinion, found that Bakke had been the victim of racial discrimination and ordered that he be admitted to the medical school in accordance with requirements of the Civil Rights Act of 1964, which forbid discrimination "on the ground of race." The four Supreme Court justices who dissented in the *Bakke* college admissions case indicated that the 1964 Act was designed to help minorities and did not outlaw affirmative action programs. But a fifth justice, who also believed that the Civil Rights Act did not rule out affirmative action programs for minorities in educational institutions, agreed with four others that the Davis medical school program of the University of California for the recruitment of minorities "set up an unjustified racial classification."

According to the above analysis of the several opinions by Anthony Lewis of the *New York Times* (1978, p. 4), this reasoning resulted in the fifth vote that required Bakke's admission while at the same time endorsing the concept of affirmative action programs. The point to this discussion is that a White person in 1978 had his legal interest protected by a law against racial discrimination that was enacted in 1964 largely because of political pressure exerted by racial minorities. The *Bakke* action, and particularly the law on which the court decision was based, is an example of the Mertonian theory mentioned earlier.

Similarly, groups representing handicapped students have initiated court suits in order to obtain equal educational opportunities for their constituencies. The Pennsylvania Association for Retarded Children (PARC) brought suit against the Commonwealth of Pennsylvania contending that denial of public education for severely handicapped children was unconstitutional (Kirp, 1977, p. 130).[3] It is unlikely that *Bakke, PARC,* or the myriad of the other education cases brought to litigation would have occurred had the NAACP not set such a strong and successful precedent by winning a favorable decision in *Brown.*

The examples presented in this section illustrated how the Brown decision and the other federal cases involving school desegregation have had a wide range of effects for racial minorities as well as for Whites, women, and handicapped individuals.

---

[3] *Pennsylvania Association for Retarded Children v. Pennsylvania,* 343 Federal Supplement 279 (E.D. Pa. 1972) (consent decree).

SOCIAL CLASS DESEGREGATION

Desegregation in urban education has been the most visible institutional change that racial minorities have pressed upon this nation. They did this by refusing to conform to an educational system that had become progressively unequal in services rendered. If they had listened to Moynihan and ignored the tradition of creative dissent that has been the function of minorities in the past, the public schools in the United States would have become increasingly segregated and the method of universal education for the goal of enhancing informed participation in a republican form of government would have been displaced eventually by selective segregated education by race, social class, and other population categories. The racial minorities cut off this movement by their dissent, by ceasing to cooperate in their own oppression, and by taking their case against unequal education to the court for a judicial decision. Because the minorities won, the nation also won as desegregated public education continues to serve as a way of including all in public affairs, in contrast to segregated public education that tends to exclude some people.

By desegregating public education in the cities, the minorities have started a process that may be completed by the majority in the suburbs in the future. In the *Brown* v. *Board of Education* decision of 1954, the Supreme Court described an equitable educational process as one in which a student of one racial group is able "to engage in discussion and exchange views with other students." Obviously, racial segregation prohibits this kind of exchange between White, Black, and other minority students so that the court, therefore, declared it to be unlawful in public education. The same principle could be applied to social-class segregation of the school systems in the suburbs.

One of the most important outcomes of desegregated urban education may be the eventual breaking of the hold of the social-class system upon the schools. At the midpoint of the twentieth century, James B. Conant observed that "a caste system finds its clearest manifestation in an educational system" (1961, pp. 11–12). Sociologist A. B. Hollingshead, in his study of *Elmtown's Youth*, found that "upper class control tends to result in the manipulation of institutional functions in the interest of individuals and families who have wealth, prestige and power." He said that such manipulation "is justified always . . . as being in the interest of 'all the people.'" Hollingshead (1949) warned that the "acceptance of this view of the rank and file . . . will seriously hinder the development of any effective program designed to reorient the schools" (p. 452). More recently, Gary Orfield (1978) has noted, "Educational research suggests that the basic damage inflicted by segregated education comes not from racial concentration but from the concentration of children from poor families" (p. 69).

We predict that people who study carefully the racial desegregation movement in urban education will realize its potential educational benefits for all and will undertake efforts in the future to extend this important process to suburbs by dismantling social-class segregated schools. Integrated education by social class is the reform for the future and may be classified as an unintended consequence of the *Brown* decision that has required racially desegregated urban education today. Desegregated social-class education will be achieved by eliminating snob zoning laws in suburban communities that limit residents to affluent households only, by extending mass transportation systems so that automobiles are not required to go to and from work, by federal and state housing policies and programs that will make subsidized housing available in the suburbs as well as in the cities, and by making available extraordinary educational opportunities in cities for suburban residents, such as the opportunities afforded in magnet and special-purpose schools that are part of the desegregation plans in several cities.

We believe that cooperative educational programs between cities and suburbs may increase in number and, in some instances, may lead to metropolitan school systems. Currently, several metropolitan areas have cooperative programs where students from the city are transported to suburban schools for their education. In the future, students may be transported from suburbs to the city. Perhaps the best known example of the city-to-suburbs program is Metropolitan Council for Educational Opportunities (METCO) which transports inner-city Black students from Boston to suburban schools. Programs such as METCO serve as stepping-stones to other forms of cooperation between school systems in cities and suburbs.

Another issue that is likely to hasten planning and cooperation at the metropolitan community level is the increasing tendency for city jurisdictions to require city residency for public employees, including those who work in schools.

Some metropolitan school systems will result from court orders such as the Wilmington/Newcastle County, Delaware school system ordered in the *Evans v. Buchanan*[4] case. Other metropolitan school systems may be established voluntarily with both urban and suburban systems viewing the merger as a solution to educational and financial problems. With shrinking tax bases in the cities and a lack of cultural institutions in the suburbs, both types of systems will eventually agree that metropolitan consolidation or cooperation is of educational value.

To deal with the flight of affluent households—Black and White—from the central city, Richmond, Virginia, in the early 1970s annexed part of an

---

[4] *Evans v. Buchanan*, 152 Federal Supplement 886 (D. Del., 1957).

adjacent county so that it officially became part of that city. The addition by annexation of 35,000 to 40,000 suburban White persons to a city population in which Blacks were becoming a majority was for the purpose of increasing the vanishing political strength of affluent Whites in the urban area. The serendipitous effect of this action was to place more affluent persons within a common urban school system and, therefore, enable them "to engage in discussion and exchange views with other students" such as students from poor and working-class families who have been limited by residence largely to cities or rural areas. The exchange between students from affluent families and other social classes in Richmond would increase because of the court order to desegregate the public schools and develop a unitary school system.

Dade County, in Florida, perpetuated control of local government by Whites when the central city and the remainder of the county were consolidated into a common metropolitan government (Sloan & French, 1977). The unintended effect of this action made schools outside the central city available to the children of racial minorities and poor and working-class families. Thus, social class and racial desegregation in education was facilitated by the process of metropolitan government consolidation.

INCREASED ROLE OF THE STATE

In order to establish metropolitan school systems, in many states it may be necessary for state legislatures to pass enabling legislation. This will represent only one aspect of the increased role state government will play in the educational arena. With decreasing dependence on local property tax to finance public education, the state will have an increasing funding responsibility in the future. More state control will accompany more state financing.

The cases that were brought in anticipation of the *Brown* ruling required state government to equalize professional and higher education with reference to buildings, curricula, salaries of teachers, and other tangible factors.[5] As these cases laid a foundation for the *Brown* decision, so the *Brown* case has become a foundation for litigation with reference to other forms of state-sanctioned inequality.

State officials who recognize their increasing obligation to public education may realize that by taking the initiative, they may avoid a large number of court cases. Thus, the state administrators, working together with the legislators will have to deal with social-class school segregation and the inequalities inherent in it, if state income tax rather than local property tax

---

[5] *Sweatt* v. *Painter*, 339 U.S. 629 (1950); *McLaurin* v. *Oklahoma State Regents*, 339 U.S. 637 (1950).

emerges as the major source of finance for public schools. The application of the "equal protection of the laws" clause in the Constitution to the education of people of varying social classes, therefore, will be a serendipitous effect of the application of this clause to people of varying racial groups today. This will result from the increased responsibility of the state.

As evidence of the growing movement to overcome inequality because of social class or wealth, at least 18 state legislatures have acted to revise their methods of financing school systems to reduce disparities between richer and poorer districts (Kirp, 1977, p. 123).

Several examples of this increased role concerning school desegregation have already occurred. Wisconsin passed a statute to encourage voluntary urban–suburban cooperation in school desegregation by allocating $5 million for the school year 1976–1977, payable to schools receiving transfer students from outside their district who increase the racial and cultural integration of their student bodies (Epps, 1977, p. 18). In Illinois, similar legislation was proposed, although it has not been passed; the state school superintendent, however, has encouraged interdistrict cooperation for voluntary desegregation (Epps, 1977, p. 18). The METCO program of voluntary desegregation in Massachusetts is state funded. And, of course, to resist school desegregation in the past, Virginia threatened to cut off state funds for any local schools that planned to integrate Black and White children in a unitary system.

REDEFINITION OF EDUCATION

Institutional systems, including educational systems, tend to change as new concepts become a part of them and are implemented as existing members of the system assume new roles and as new clients with new needs are taken into the system. The presence of racial minority children in previously segregated White schools and the presence of low-income children in previously segregated affluent schools will change these institutions as they adapt to the needs of all their students—the Black, Brown, and White students and the lower-class, middle-class, and upper-class students. Likewise, the role and responsibility of children from Black and Brown families of varying class levels or poor and working-class families who were segregated previously will change in schools in which they are the majority; in such schools they must be compassionate toward a new White minority or a middle-class population that is subdominant in terms of numbers.

One change we predict may come about in school systems in the future, as a result of racial and social-class integration, is increased concern with intergroup relations, particularly relations between members of various racial and ethnic groups. In order for classrooms that have students from various levels of social class, as well as a variety of racial and ethnic groups, to provide a positive learning experience, it will be necessary to adapt the curriculum to include the study of values and norms that are found within subcultures. This change in the curriculum will provide students with a sociological understanding of the differences that exist among groups.

Behavior for the dominant role is different from that learned as a subdominant. To endure and overcome requires a different kind of adaptation than that called forth by compassion. The coming together of students with different existential histories, such as those manifested by racial minority and majority group members, will result in a broader definition of education to the benefit of all. Increasingly, education as defined by the dominant majority group in segregated schools has narrowed to that largely of learning verbal communication and calculation skills.

Another change in the definition of education has already begun to occur as a result of school desegregation. Court-ordered racial desegregation in public schools is beginning already to teach this generation of city students important information about constitutional law and corporate justice. Students are learning how the judicial system operates and the consequences of judicial findings from the school desegregation cases themselves. Students have learned that their school assignments may depend upon the judicial findings at various levels of the court system. Since the legal procedures have personal impact on their lives, students as well as parents have been eager to follow the outcomes of these court cases. In this process, students have gained knowledge that they otherwise most likely would not have gained.

The students in Richmond, Virginia now know that state-sanctioned massive resistance to a court order to desegregate will not result in changing the law. The students in Little Rock, Arkansas realized the futility of violence after the massive military response of the federal government. Similarly, students in Boston who initially responded to the court order by boycotting the schools and by acting in a violent manner have returned to integrated, peaceful schools.

Such learning, of course, is beneficial for affluent suburban students, too. But they may be denied this learning, while continuing to increase their verbal and mathematical knowledge, because of the social-class segregation that they now experience in school. Education in a setting of social-class segregation fosters attitudes of entitlement that are untempered by concerns about corporate justice. This kind of education is deficient.

There is some evidence that as a result of school desegregation, school administrators have already begun to reevaluate the education their schools offer. Speaking at a conference held at the National Institute of Education, E. Lutrell Bing, assistant superintendent of schools for Hillsborough County, Florida, noted that school desegregation had provided members of his school system with the opportunity to do several things that they would not otherwise have done. Bing said that desegregation had provided the impetus to evaluate the curriculum, study instruments used for assessment, study the entire education delivery system, and provide training for teachers, administrators, and support staff (Bing, 1977, p. 24–25).

IMPLICATIONS FOR THE TEACHING PROFESSION

More than two decades ago, Howard S. Becker (1952) documented the typical career patterns of public school teachers in Chicago. Becker found that many teachers began their careers in slum schools which contained mostly Black children. Many teachers in slum schools requested transfers to "better" schools when openings became available. What resulted from this process was a seniority system that placed the new, inexperienced teachers in the predominantly Black inner-city schools and the more experienced teachers in the predominantly White schools in middle-class areas.

This type of seniority system has been typical of large urban school systems across the country. For example, in Boston's public elementary schools for the academic year 1970–1971, schools that had from 90–100% Black students had faculties with an average of 5.67 years experience in the Boston school system, whereas schools with 0–10% Black students had faculties with an average of 13.53 years experience in the system (*Morgan* v. *Hennigan*).[6] It is only through the implementation of desegregation plans that teacher seniority systems such as the ones described here can be broken down so that all students receive instruction from a teaching staff of diversified professional experience. Many court-ordered desegregation plans have reassigned faculty on the basis of seniority as well as race to achieve a more equitable distribution of educational resources. Many court-ordered plans have recognized the value of racial diversity on the instructional staff and have required that school systems increase the proportion of minority members at all levels of the system. Pertinent examples are the Dallas and Boston desegregation plans.

A change in the definition of education will inevitably have consequences for the selection and training of teachers. Educational institutions that stress teaching social values including interracial cooperation will no longer be able to select teachers solely on the basis of scores on standardized mathematics and English tests. New ways of assessing the qualifications of applicants for teaching positions must be developed so that members of the teaching profession are competent to teach diverse student bodies. Teachers in classrooms with students of various socioeconomic

---

[6] *Morgan* v. *Hennigan*, 379 Federal Supplement 410 (D Mass., 1974).

levels, races, and ethnic groups must be able to assess the individual and social needs of the student body in ways that standardized tests cannot.

Such a change in the qualifications of teachers will necessitate a concomitant change in the field of higher education that prepares teachers and in methods of measuring professional competence. New ways of training teachers for diversified classrooms must be developed. Such courses must emphasize the dynamics of group processes and race relations as well as individual diagnostic skills.

Teachers and educational administrators must also learn how to deal with the highly political nature of their field. Thus, graduate schools of education must offer training in politics so that educators may cope with the multitude of demands that are forthcoming from mayors, city councilors, community organizations, and individual citizens, as well as from their students.

Lawrence Cremin contends that education should emulate the educational models of the legal and medical profession which teach a common body of knowledge to all their practitioners (Report on Education Research, 1978, p. 9). Such a structural change in higher education for teachers should incorporate the kinds of changes necessitated by the redefinition of education that we predict will occur. Educational research pertaining to optimal teaching methods for diversified classrooms is a requirement for the changes that have been stimulated by school desegregation.

The upgrading of training for teachers and the accountability the public is demanding of the public education system via its numerous court cases will result in increased prestige for the teaching profession. This increase in accountability will result in stronger codes of ethics for professional societies and more stringent enforcement of these codes by members of the profession as well as by the public.

Professional surveillance will also increase in educational research. An example of such has occurred already in the American Sociological Association (ASA). In 1976, the issue of James Coleman's role in advocating various public policies pertaining to school desegregation on the basis of his sociological studies came before the executive council of the ASA. The issue was whether or not there was abuse of professional responsibility in interpreting research data for policymaking purposes. While the executive council failed to take action for or against Coleman, the fact that the issue arose in the ASA indicated that research findings and their political use will be scrutinized increasingly by professional colleagues in the future.

The increased politicization of education through desegregation has made education a much more newsworthy topic. Publicity regarding schools and school systems is likely to appear almost every day in the news media of large urban communities. This increased attention to the field of public education probably will add to the prestige of the teaching profession.

Public scrutiny is bothersome but in the long run tends to promote honesty and prevent abuse.

CHANGING RELATIONS BETWEEN SCHOOL BOARD MEMBERS AND SUPERINTENDENTS

There are indications that the relationship between school superintendents and school board members are changing as a result of the school desegregation process.

In 1964, Norman Kerr wrote an article based on his observations of the school boards and superintendents in two suburban communities. Kerr's major finding was that the role of school boards is to approve what superintendents suggest and that the board members themselves are not likely to originate educational policy. According to Kerr, one of the reasons for the boards' failure to initiate policy was a relative absence of educational pressure groups in the community. The school boards' deference to superintendents in creating educational policy is indicative of the existence of a professional model of education. The superintendent has been trained as an educational administrator and, under this model, school board members allow the superintendent to carry out his or her duties as the acknowledged expert in the field.

Relationships between school boards and superintendents under desegregation have changed to more of a political model. In virtually all instances where court cases have been initiated, school board members have been named as defendants, and the superintendent has also been named in many cases. Furthermore, many local pressure groups have been established as a result of the school desegregation process, creating an atmosphere to which elected school board members must respond. Indeed, the method of electing school board members at-large often has changed as a result of school desegregation court cases. District or ward electoral units have resulted in more diversified school boards in terms of race and ethnicity. The end result is a greater attempt, on the part of the school board, to control educational issues and the superintendent in terms of the interests of their constituency. In many instances, superintendents have lost their positions because the school board felt that the superintendent's response to the desegregation issue was not in accordance with views held by their constituency. This process has revealed the truly political nature of the educational system, a fact that has often been denied by the school board candidates and educators alike.

An example of the process described above occurred in Boston following the court order to desegregate public schools that was implemented in the fall of 1974. Boston's school committee made clear from the outset that it was not going to do anything on its own to make implementation of the court order go smoothly; rather, it responded to the antidesegregation sentiment of a vocal and highly organized part of the community and appealed virtually all the judge's rulings. The school committee performed only those acts directly ordered by the court. The superintendent, on the other hand, was clearly willing to cooperate with the court. The superintendent had only one year left of a three-year contract when desegregation began. As a result of his cooperation with the court, he lost his position at the end of his contract.

The Boston school committee then selected a superintendent who had previously been an associate superintendent in the system. Evidently, the school committee believed that the new superintendent's loyalty to the Boston school system would result in her siding with the school committee's attempts to thwart the desegregation process. The new superintendent, however, was not only cooperative with the court, but she became the court-appointed receiver when control of South Boston High School (the scene of much antibusing protest and violence) was removed from the school committee. Thus, it was not surprising that the school committee also refused to reappoint this superintendent at the end of her three-year contract.

In Stockton, California, the superintendent who was appointed in 1966 attempted to desegregate the schools without a court order. At the outset, he relied on the traditional relationship he had had with the school board, where members served as a rubber stamp of approval for his actions. His attempts to desegregate resulted in the formation of local antibusing groups which threatened to gain control of the school board in the next election. The incumbent school board took a more active role on the desegregation issue than they had on other educational issues and rejected the superintendent's desegregation plan. As a result, the superintendent resigned from his position. The school board became increasingly active in policy-making over the years and eventually hired a superintendent who agreed that the board should be the policymaking body for the school system.

These two examples of increased control of education by school boards are indicative of a trend that seems to be occurring in many cities facing public school desegregation. More research is needed to learn the specific nature of the changing relationship and the new roles played by superintendents that enable them to be effective administrators.

INCREASED CITIZEN INTEREST AND PARTICIPATION IN EDUCATION

Court-ordered school desegregation has aroused a great deal of interest and concern on the part of parents. Although much of this concern has focused on attempts to overturn court orders to desegregate schools or to subvert the implementation of these plans, the arousal of parents' interest in the operation of public school systems has had an effect that goes beyond the issue of desegregation.

For example, in 1970, a group of parents in Erie, Pennsylvania, formed a coalition of Concerned Parents and Taxpayers in an attempt to eliminate the busing of school children to achieve racial desegregation. At its peak, the group claimed to have more than 2,500 members and an executive board of 25–30 persons. The group organized protests at school board meetings, supported candidates for the school board, and utilized the mass media to promulgate their viewpoint. Although it was not successful in eliminating busing, the group was still in existence in the summer of 1978. Concerned Parents and Taxpayers no longer attracts a membership in the thousands, but its original core of leadership continues to be involved in educational issues, to attend school board meetings, and to organize parents in order to present a united front to school administrators. The leadership core of this organization had not previously been actively involved in public school issues but became active as a result of the desegregation controversy.

Citizen participation in education also increased in Boston. The court-ordered plan for school desegregation in Boston included the establishment of parent advisory councils at each school in the city. Although the councils did not obtain the degree of parent participation hoped for concerning desegregation issues, the establishment of these councils provides an important mechanism available to parents when educational crises arise. Thus, when Roxbury High School, in the heart of Boston's Black community, was scheduled to be closed, parents in Roxbury utilized the council to successfully fight against its closing. Had this council not already been established, leaders of this fight would have had to spend much of their time establishing an organizational mechanism and probably would not have had enough time to present their case to keep the school open.

SUMMARY AND CONCLUSIONS

In the light of this discussion, we believe it is fair to call *Brown* the turning point in regard to obtaining equal rights for all oppressed groups as well as initiating reform within the educational system.

The *Brown* ruling recognized that minorities have a legitimate claim upon the educational resources of schools, and that discrimination in the allocation of these resources is unconstitutional. This action forced school systems to honor the "equal protection of the laws" clause of the Constitution and to abide by it not only for racial minorities but for other special populations. The children of diversified racial and cultural backgrounds who have encountered each other in school because of the desegregation require-ments of *Brown* have contributed to both anguish and enrichment within the school system. While the anguish has been painful, the enrichment has been pleasurable. Those who experience desegregation are beneficiaries of both, although the pain and anguish are discussed more frequently.

Racial desegregation of public school systems has revealed many benefits that may also be applicable to social class desegregation. If this reform does occur, the implications for society as a whole would be enormous. Metropolitan school systems and governments would be one likely concomitant development of social class desegregation of public schools, and housing and other facilities would also achieve greater desegregation.

The increased role of state government that has already accompanied racial desegregation will probably also accompany social class desegrega-tion. Equalization formulas for financing school systems and increased con-trol over items such as curricula and facilities will most likely be conse-quences of social class desegregation.

The redefinition of education may also follow from desegregation of education. Children will learn the sociological differences that various subcultures have experienced as part of the school curriculum. This change in the curriculum should have important implications for relations among various ethnic, racial, and social class groups.

The redefinition of education will require that teachers and administra-tors acquire different skills than they have learned in the past. For one thing, schools will become more political than they have been in the past, since parents are more deeply involved in education because of the court orders. Desegregation has resulted in the recognition that education should be political, with trade-offs and compromises between all sectors rather than a dictated course of study by the affluent or any other elite. Teachers, administrators, school board members, and parents must learn to be effec-tive negotiators to deal with education as a political issue.

Some of these changes have begun only recently, and it will probably take many years for their full impact to be felt. At the present, however, we believe that the effects of school desegregation on American society are much greater than anticipated when the school desegregation process first began. It is evident that school desegregation has served as the impetus for a wide variety of social change in our country.

REFERENCES

Becker, H. S. The career of the Chicago public school teacher. *American Journal of Sociology*, 1952, *57*(5), 470–477.

Bing, E. L. Metropolitan desegregation: How is it working today? A panel presentation. In National Institute of Education, *School desegregation in metropolitan areas: Choices and prospects*. Washington D.C.: U.S. Government Printing Office, 1977.

Conant, J. B. *Slums and suburbs*. New York: McGraw-Hill, 1961.

Epps, E. City and suburbs: Perspectives on interdistrict desegregation efforts. In National Institute of Education, *School desegregation in metropolitan areas: Choices and prospects*. Washington, D.C.: U.S. Government Printing Office, 1977, pp. 17–23.

Hollingshead, A. B. *Elmtown's youth*. New York: Wiley, 1949.

Kerr, N. The school board as an agency of legitimation. *Sociology of Education*, 1964, *38*, 34–59.

Kirp, D. L. Law, politics, and equal educational opportunity: The limits of judicial involvement. *Harvard Educational Review*, 1977, *47*(2), 117–137.

Lewis, A. Bakke decision avoided rigidity. *The News and Observer*, Raleigh, N.C., July 1, 1978.

Merton, R. *Social structure and social theory*. New York: Free Press, 1968, 421.

Moynihan, D. *The Negro family: A case for national action*. Washington, D.C.: U.S. Government Printing Office, 1965.

Orfield, G. *Must we bus? Segregated schools and national policy*. Washington, D.C.: The Brookings Institute, 1978, p. 69.

Post–Standard. 100,000 ERA supporters march—Largest women's rights rally on record. *Post-Standard*, Syracuse, New York, July 10, 1978.

Report on Education Research, 1978, *March 8*, 9.

Salinas, G. Mexican Americans v. the desegregation of schools in the southwest. In Erwin Flaxman (Ed.), *Educating the disadvantaged*. New York: AMS Press, 1973, 445–468.

Sloan, L., & French, R. M. Black rule in the urban South? In Charles Willie (Ed.), *Black/Brown/White relations*. New Brunswick, N.J.: Transaction Books, 1977, pp. 199–212.

Willie, C. V. The American dream: Illusion or reality? *Harvard Magazine*, 1976, *78*(11), 35–38.

Problems and Issues Concerning School Desegregation

From Prohibiting Segregation to Requiring Integration

DEVELOPMENTS IN THE LAW OF RACE AND THE SCHOOLS SINCE *BROWN*

LINO A. GRAGLIA

The Supreme Court's constitutional decisions on race and the schools merit study not only because of their intrinsic importance but even more so as a means of understanding the nature and source of constitutional law in general. They demonstrate, perhaps more clearly than the court's decisions in any other area, not only the trite and obvious fact that "the Constitution is what the Court says it is" and therefore does not restrain the court's power, but also the much less frequently noted fact that neither is the court restrained by any requirement of truth or logic in its written opinions.

The history of the law of race and the schools since *Brown*[1] is, in a word, the history of the Supreme Court's conversion of *Brown*'s prohibition of segregation into a requirement of integration—the conversion of the *prohibition* of all racial discrimination by government into a *requirement* of racial discrimination by government—without the court ever admitting, and with the court always denying, that any change had taken place. The court imposed the new requirement of integration in fact, by what it actually did, but always and only by insisting, nonetheless, that it was doing no more than continuing to enforce *Brown*'s prohibition of segregation. The requirement, that is, was imposed by fraud. This fact is important, not only to students of constitutional law, but to all persons interested in the law of race and the schools because it means that the requirement is very easy to limit or eliminate, and this process is apparently now taking place. No more is

---

[1] *Brown* v. *Board of Education of Topeka*, 347 U.S. 483 (1954). See Graglia, 1976.

LINO A. GRAGLIA • University of Texas Law School, University of Texas, Austin, Texas 78712.

necessary to end the new requirement than for the court simply to conform its actions to its words, to do in fact what it has always claimed to be doing: merely prohibiting all racial discrimination in the operation of public schools.

It is important to state at the outset how the words "segregation" and "desegregation" will be used in this discussion. In popular speech and most social science discussions the words "segregation" and "separation," and "desegregation" and "integration," are used interchangeably. In constitutional law, however, the distinction between these terms is crucial because the Supreme Court has never purported to prohibit racial separation as such but only segregation—school racial separation that is the result of official racial discrimination by school authorities—and, correspondingly, has never purported to require integration as such but only desegregation—the ending and undoing of unconstitutional segregation. One may argue, of course, that these distinctions should not be made and that, as a matter of social policy, all school racial separation should be prohibited, but an understanding of the constitutional law of this subject is not possible unless these distinctions are maintained and their importance is understood clearly.

THE PROHIBITION OF SEGREGATION

The issue in dispute today on the subject of race and the schools is not, of course, whether segregation is or should be prohibited, but whether integration is or should be required. The discussion, nonetheless, often begins with a question as to the "meaning" or "true holding" of *Brown*, as if the answer to this question will settle the present dispute. The meaning or holding of *Brown*, however, cannot seriously be in doubt: the states may not require the assignment of children to school according to race in order to keep the races apart. That was the only question before the court for decision in *Brown*, and therefore, in legal theory, all that the court could decide. The court obviously did not, and had no occasion to, consider whether integration—a greater degree of racial mixing than results from the prohibition of segregation—should be required. If such a requirement is desired today, it must be defended on its own merits; it cannot be derived from *Brown*.

Of course, it is not only the precise holding of a decision that is important but also the basic principle applied or established to support that holding. The principle that was understood to be the basis of *Brown* at the time and that, in any event, most easily justifies the holding of *Brown* is also easy to state. It is, as the court put it in *Bolling* v. *Sharpe*,[2] decided with

---

[2] *Bolling* v. *Sharpe*, 347 U.S. 197 (1954).

Brown and prohibiting segregation by the federal government in the District of Columbia, the "principle that the Constitution of the United States, in its present form, forbids, so far as civil and political rights are concerned, discrimination by the General Government or by the States against any citizen because of his race." Dispute as to the basis of *Brown* has arisen only because the court sought to avoid flatly overruling *Plessy* v. *Ferguson*[3] and later cases which upheld segregation, and attempted to show that school segregation could not be upheld even under the "separate but equal" doctrine of those cases because "separate educational facilities are inherently unequal." In an effort to support this factual assertion as to a matter on which it has no claim to expertise, the court stated, "whatever may have been the extent of psychological knowledge at the time of *Plessy*," "modern authority" showed that school segregation impedes "the educational and mental development of negro children." On the basis of this statement, proponents of compulsory integration have argued that it was not merely segregation but all school racial separation that the court held unconstitutional in *Brown*.

If the court's reference to "psychological knowledge" is to be taken as the basis of *Brown*, that decision had and has no solid basis, for it was not in fact established then, and it has not yet been established, that school segregation is in fact harmful to the education of Blacks (St. John, 1975). That this highly questionable statement by the court was not the basis of *Brown*, however, is shown, not only by the totally adequate basis stated by the court in *Bolling* v. *Sharpe* at the same time, but also by the fact that the Court thereafter prohibited segregation and racial discrimination, not only in education, but in all areas of public life (parks, beaches, auditoriums, buses, etc.) without offering any explanation other than citation of *Brown*.[4] As Thurgood Marshall argued for the NAACP in *Brown*, "the only thing the Court is dealing with . . . [is] whether or not race can be used. . . . What we want from the court is a striking down of race" (Friedman, 1969, p. 402). As a purely practical matter, the issue in the realities of the time was not whether the *Brown* decision required integration, but whether its prohibition of segregation and of all official racial discrimination would prevail, a question that remained in some doubt until Congress, in the 1964 Civil Rights Act, ratified and adopted *Brown*'s prohibition of all racial discrimination as a matter of national legislative policy. Far from supporting a requirement of integration, the principle that was the basis of *Brown*—a simple prohibition of all official racial discrimination—would invalidate the imposition of such a requirement. Indeed, perhaps the greatest obstacle to

---

[3] *Plessy* v. *Ferguson*, 163 U.S. 537 (1896).
[4] E.g., *Mayor of Baltimore* v. *Dawson*, 350 U.S. 877 (1955); *Holmes* v. *Atlanta*, 350 U.S. 879 (1955); *Gayle* v. *Browder*, 352 U.S. 903 (1956).

legally required integration is that the *Brown* principle would somehow have to be overcome.

The great doubt that existed at the time as to whether *Brown* would prevail is demonstrated by the fact that the court did not require that its decision be enforced. If the assignment of children to schools according to race in order to keep them apart is unconstitutional, the appropriate relief would seem simple and clear, that they be assigned on some basis other than race. The court in *Brown* found the question sufficiently difficult, however, to require that it be reargued the following year. In *Brown* II (1955) the court did state that the requirement was that children be assigned to school on a "racially nondiscriminatory basis," but it held that this did not have to be done at once, or even within any specified time, but only "with all deliberate speed."[5] There could be no doubt that this unprecedented permission for delay in the enforcement of a constitutional right was not required, as the court purported to believe, by administrative considerations; Washington, D.C. and some of the border states demonstrated this by ending segregation without even waiting for the *Brown* II decision. And if there could have been any doubt about this in 1955, there certainly could have been none three years later when the court, in *Cooper* v. *Aaron*[6] again refused to order the immediate implementation of *Brown*.

Brown II's permission for delay in ending segregation was unfortunate for many reasons. Besides denying all relief to the plaintiff school children involved—the enforcement of whose rights was, in legal theory, the court's only warrant for acting at all—it made the court appear vacillating and its decision tentative. Despite the court's declaration that "it should go without saying that the vitality" of the constitutional principles announced in *Brown* "cannot be allowed to yield simply because of disagreement with them," its action made clear that demonstrated disagreement would lead to at least the postponement of the ending of segregation. The most unfortunate effect of *Brown* II, however, was that it enormously confused and complicated the issue of just what school boards were required to do. For the relatively clear and simple issue of whether racial assignment had ended there was substituted the almost totally unmanageable issue of whether, in the circumstances of each case, the time for ending it had come and whether a partial ending would suffice. These questions were litigated in the lower courts, with virtually no guidance from the Supreme Court, for a decade. Instead of a requirement that segregation (racial assignment) be ended, the requirement became the production of a proposal for ending it gradually and eventually, and thus was born the "desegregation plan." The time for ending segregation did eventually come, but the requirement of producing a "desegregation plan" remained; only its function was changed, from a

---

[5] *Brown* v. *Board of Education of Topeka*, 349 U.S. 294 (1955).
[6] *Cooper* v. *Aaron*, 358 U.S. 8 (1958).

means of permitting delay in ending segregation to a means of requiring integration.

The most remarkable thing about what the Supreme Court did in regard to the segregation issue in *Brown*'s first decade is that it did so little. Except for its rebuke to Governor Faubus in 1958 in *Cooper* v. *Aaron*, the Court did not issue a single signed opinion on the issue until 1963 when it disallowed the granting of school transfers on a racial basis.[7] Its most significant action in this period was its *per curiam* (by the court, without a signed opinion) decision in *Shuttlesworth* v. *Birmingham Board of Education*[8] in 1958 upholding Alabama's pupil placement plan. By the late 1950s, pupil placement plans had become the South's standard response to *Brown*. Under these plans, children were to be assigned to schools according to a long list of vague, ostensibly nonracial criteria. In practice, they were simply initially assigned by race as before, and the plan became operative only upon a pupil's request for a transfer. The vagueness of the criteria and provisions for administrative and judicial appeals were usually sufficient to ensure that the applicant would sooner be graduated than transferred.

Although token integration took place under some states' plans, none took place under Alabama's, which, indeed, had explicit racial provisions designed to preclude integration. In *Shuttlesworth*, the court, nonetheless, affirmed a lower court's decision that the plan was "not unconstitutional on its face." The meaning of this decision seemed clear, and the sense of relief in the South was great and general. If Alabama had found the answer to *Brown*, the terrors of *Brown* had indeed been overstated. This nearly forgotten episode is worth recalling if only because of its relevance to the charge of the South's "defiance" of *Brown*, to which the court was later to refer repeatedly as a justification for its imposition of ever harsher requirements on the South. The South, there is no question, did not welcome *Brown*; many southern school boards, especially in majority Black school districts, believed that an integrated public school system could not be maintained—and events have not proved all of them wrong. They certainly would not and could not voluntarily go farther than the Supreme Court actually required them to go, and the Supreme Court, it seemed, did not require that they go very far.

The question of the time for ending segregation—which should have never been a question—was finally answered in 1964, ten years after *Brown*, when the court announced that "the time for mere 'deliberate speed' has run out."[9] The death knell for segregation came, however, not from the Supreme Court but from Congress with the enactment of the 1964 Civil Rights Act.[10] That act, the greatest piece of civil rights legislation in our his-

---

[7] *Goss* v. *Board of Education of Knoxville, Tennessee*, 373 U.S. 668 (1963).
[8] *Shuttlesworth* v. *Birmingham Board of Education*, 358 U.S. 101 (1958).
[9] *Griffin* v. *County School Board of Prince Edward County*, 377 U.S. 218 (1964).
[10] 42 U.S.C., §§1971, 2000a–h (1970).

tory, adopted *Brown*'s prohibition of racial discrimination as a matter of national legislative policy and extended it even to privately owned public accomodations. Title IV of the act authorized the attorney general to bring school desegregation suits, and most important, Title VI provided that institutions receiving federal funds, as all or nearly all public school systems do, may not discriminate racially.[11]

The 1964 act was vigorously opposed by representatives of the South, not on the ground that segregation and racial discrimination could be defended, but on the ground that in the hands of the administrative agencies and the courts, the act would somehow become a means of imposing a requirement of integration. The proponents of the act, led by Senator Hubert H. Humphrey, found this argument incredible, and took every means of assuring the opponents that their fears were totally unfounded. As Senator Humphrey put it, "This bill cannot be attacked on its merits. Instead, bogeymen and hobgoblins have been raised to frighten well-meaning Americans."[12] The proposed act, after all, its proponents pointed out, explicitly stated that "'desegregation' means the assignment of students to public schools and within such schools without regard to their race." In response to the opponents' continued objections, the proponents of the act willingly added to this definition, redundantly, that desegregation "shall not mean the assignment of students to public schools in order to overcome racial imbalance" and, again, that nothing in the act "shall empower any official or court of the United States to issue any order seeking to achieve a racial balance in any school by requiring the transportation of pupils or students from one school to another or one school district to another in order to achieve such racial balance" and, finally, that the act did not "prohibit classification and assignment for reasons other than race." The ultimate assurance that the opponents' fears were unfounded, the act's proponents insisted, was that a requirement of integration could not result from the act, even if Congress had not specifically and repeatedly precluded it, because such a requirement would be a requirement of racial discrimination and that, everyone believed, had been prohibited by *Brown*. As Senator Humphrey stated, "while the Constitution prohibits segregation, it does not require integration. The busing of children to achieve racial balance would be an act to effect the integration of schools. In fact, if the bill were to compel it, it would be a violation, because it would be handling the matter on a basis of race and we would be transporting children because of their race."[13]

---

[11] Pursuant to the Elementary and Secondary Education Act of 1965, funds exceeding half a billion dollars became available to the seventeen southern states that practiced segregation. U.S. Commission on Civil Rights, *Survey on School Desegregation in the Southern and Border States, 1965–66* (Wash., D.C., 1966).

[12] 110 Congressional Record 6545 (1964).

[13] 110 Congressional Record 12717 (1964).

The fears of the opponents of the act, nonetheless, soon proved to be well-founded. Despite the act's specific prohibitions and unambiguous legislative history, HEW's Office of Education (with the approval and urging of the Civil Rights Commission), purporting to enforce the act, required, under threat of cut off of federal funds, southern school districts to practice racial discrimination in order to increase integration. Despite the assertion of Senator Jacob Javits, a proponent of the act, that any government official who sought to require racial balance under the act "would be making a fool of himself" and would give an affected school district "an open and shut case" in the courts,[14] many courts, and especially the Court of Appeals for the Fifth Circuit, which has jurisdiction over most of the South, soon showed themselves as willing and eager to pervert the act as were HEW and the Civil Rights Commission.[15] Indeed, by not only upholding and enforcing HEW's abuse of the act but also raising the requirement of integration to a constitutional requirement, the courts removed the matter from the power of Congress to correct. A clearer example of administrative and judicial abuse of power and contempt for the will of Congress would not be possible to find.

The 1964 Civil Rights Act removed all doubt that the *Brown* revolution had succeeded; *Brown*'s prohibition of segregation was the effective law of the land, and the era of litigation on race and the schools should therefore have ended. It did not end only because a second revolution was attempted. Litigation continued, but its objective was no longer to end segregation but to compel integration. Although segregation had ended, school racial separation had not, and the long struggle to end racial discrimination, now successful beyond all expectation, came to seem too limited in its goal. The idea therefore arose to *require* the mixing of races in the schools by law, even though this meant moving from the prohibition of racial discrimination that had just been successfully established to a requirement that racial discrimination be practiced.

COMPULSORY INTEGRATION IN THE NAME OF "DESEGREGATION"

The move from prohibiting segregation to requiring integration began in the Supreme Court with *Green v. New Kent County, Virginia*.[16] Although *Green* is much less well known than *Brown*, and current disputes on race and the schools continue to be stated as if the *Brown* issue were still involved, it is *Green*, not *Brown*, that is the source of these disputes.

[14] 110 Congressional Record 12716-17 (1964).
[15] *United States v. Jefferson County Board of Education*, 372 F.2d 836 (1966), aff'd *en banc*, 380 F.2d 385 (1967), certiorari denied 389 U.S. 840 (1967).
[16] *Green v. New Kent County, Virginia*, 391 U.S. 430 (1968).

Green involved a small, predominantly Black (740 Blacks and 550 Whites) school district in rural Virginia with only two schools, one of which (Watkins) had been for Blacks and one (New Kent) for Whites. In 1965, the school board decided to allow all students to choose the school they wished to attend. Thirty-five Blacks chose the formerly White school in 1965, 111 in 1966, and 115 in 1967; no White student chose the formerly Black school. On suit by the NAACP challenging this situation, the district court found that there was no racial discrimination in any aspect of the school system's operation and, therefore, no constitutional violation. The Court of Appeals for the Fourth Circuit, sitting *en banc* (all judges participating) affirmed: "Since the plaintiffs here concede that their annual choice is unrestricted and unencumbered, we find in its existence no denial of any constitutional right not to be subjected to racial discrimination." The Constitution, it held, does not require "compulsive assignments to achieve a greater intermixture of the races."[17] Although it found no error in the factual findings of the lower courts, the Supreme Court reversed.

It is at least arguable that the Supreme Court in *Green* could have found unconstitutionality under *Brown* on several grounds. The court could have held that a school district may not allow freedom of choice in school selection immediately upon abandoning segregation, because the former racial identification of the schools would make them continue to appear to be for one race or the other. In effect, Blacks, at least, would be offered a choice on racial grounds between an all-Black and an integrated school. The court might also have found unconstitutionality on the ground that simple, ordinary neighborhood assignment would have, in the particular circumstances of the case, resulted in more integration and that freedom of choice could serve no purpose except to minimize integration—an act not explicable except in racial terms is an act of racial discrimination. (In answer to this, however, it is arguable that permitting freedom needs no other explanation and always provides its own justification.) Finally, dissallowing freedom of choice might have been justified as a "prophylactic" measure, on the ground that although no racial discrimination was found, freedom of choice provided opportunities for racial discrimination and such discrimination would be difficult to detect.

The court in *Green*, however, did not find unconstitutionality on any of these grounds. It did not hold that the lower courts erred in failing to find racial discrimination or, at least, extensive opportunities for racial discrimination. But neither did the court hold that *Brown* was not controlling and that, therefore, racial discrimination did not have to be found. On the contrary, the court insisted throughout that it was doing no more than enforcing *Brown*. The only issue, the court stated, was whether admission to

---

[17] 382 F.2d 338 (1967).

the schools was "on a nonracial basis," and the only requirement was "a unitary system in which racial discrimination has been eliminated root and branch." But racial discrimination, the lower courts found and the Supreme Court did not question, had been completely eliminated. On what basis, then, could a constitutional violation be found? The court stated:

> The New Kent School Board's "freedom-of-choice" plan cannot be accepted as a sufficient step to "effectuate a transition" to a unitary system. In three years of operation not a single white child has chosen to attend Watkins school and although 115 Negro children enrolled in New Kent school in 1967 (up from 35 in 1965 and 111 in 1966) 85% of the Negro children in the system still attend the all-Negro Watkins school. In other words, the school system remains a dual system.

The board, however, had not offered any "freedom of choice plan" as a step to "effectuate a transition" to a unitary system; the board had established a unitary system, a system in which, as the court purported to require, racial discrimination was eliminated. The defining characteristic of the "dual system" was, of course, not school racial separation or imbalance, but racial discrimination, and no such discrimination was found here. New Kent County's system was "dual" and unconstitutional, it appeared, not because it was racially discriminatory, but because it was not sufficiently racially mixed. Despite the court's insistence that it was enforcing *Brown*, the real requirement now was, not assignment on a nonracial basis, but a greater degree of integration than results from such assignment. The duty of the district court on remand, the court said, was only to see that "state-imposed segregation is completely removed," but the district court had found, and the Supreme Court did not dispute, that such segregation had already been removed, and the district court's real duty now was to see that integration is state-imposed. The board, the court also said, was "to convert promptly to a system without a 'white' school and a 'Negro' school but just schools," but the actual requirement was, not "just schools," but racially mixed schools, and racially mixed to a greater degree than resulted from ending segregation. With no other justification than that all racial discrimination must be eliminated, a requirement of racial discrimination was imposed.

Whether or not a constitutional requirement of integration can be defended, the court's deceitful method of imposing it in *Green* clearly cannot be. That such a requirement cannot be defended, however, is perhaps best shown by the very fact that it was imposed by deceit. By insisting that the only requirement was desegregation, as in *Brown*, and denying that there is a requirement of integration as such, the court obviated all need to defend a requirement of integration on its own merits, in terms of any constitutional principle or of any benefits that might possibly be achieved, and the court has never attempted such a defense. Another major advantage that the court obtained by claiming to be requiring only desegregation was that it thereby minimized the attention and concern of the North. An openly admitted requirement of integration would apply nationwide, while a requirement of only desegregation, the ending and undoing of unconstitutional segregation, would obviously apply only to the South, where there had been unconstitutional segregation. Outside the South, *Green* appeared to be what the court said it was, another attempt by the court, apparently "losing its patience," to enforce *Brown* in the face of the South's evasion and recalcitrance. And the South, in the view of the rest of the country at the time, undoubtedly deserved whatever the "conscience of the nation" was proposing to do to it. This divide-and-conquer strategy proved highly successful in forestalling effective antibusing legislation by Congress. The North's time for "desegregation" would come, but only in one or a few cities at a time and after much of the worst had been done to the South, with the result that unified opposition was never obtained. Further, by appearing to require only desegregation, the court appeared to require only what was required by Congress in the 1964 Civil Rights Act, though the court was, in fact, requiring precisely what Congress had taken great pains to make clear the act did not require.

The most important advantage of the court's claim that it (i.e., "the Constitution") required only desegregation (the "remedying" of unconstitutional segregation) and not simply integration was undoubtedly that it enabled the court to avoid the apparently insuperable obstacle of *Brown* itself. A constitutional requirement of integration does not necessarily involve the overruling of *Brown*. There is no purely logical difficulty in distinguishing between racial discrimination to separate the races and racial discrimination to mix them or in holding that though the Constitution prohibits the former it requires the latter. As a practical matter, however, such a holding was impossible. After so many years of emphatic and finally successful insistence that all racial discrimination by government is constitutionally prohibited, the court could not suddenly announce that racial discrimination is sometimes not only constitutionally permissible but constitutionally required. Purporting to require only desegregation had the double advantage for the court of not only avoiding the unappealing task of attempting to justify a constitutional requirement of racial discrimination to integrate on its merits but also of wrapping the court in the by-then impregnable mantle of *Brown*. The court could *require* racial discrimination and integration, by what it actually did, as long as it was willing to *say* that it was only continuing to *prohibit* racial discrimination and segregation. When you are supreme, the important thing is not what you do but what you say.

The only difficulty—but not a serious one for the court—with the court's "desegregation" rationale for compelling racial integration was that it did not comport with what the court was requiring in fact. Each succeeding case made it more obvious that the court was not in fact requiring desegregation, the undoing of racial separation caused by official racial discrimination, but was simply requiring integration as such, the undoing of all school racial separation regardless of how it was caused.

"DESEGREGATION" MEANS BUSING

Green made clear, despite the court's insistence to the contrary, that the ending of racial discrimination in the operation of school systems was no longer the constitutional requirement and that some degree of racial mixing greater than that resulting from ending racial discrimination was now required. Because the requirement was said to be only desegregation, not integration as such, it would seem that the requirement was to make the schools as racially mixed as they would have been except for past unconstitutional segregation. It was nonetheless apparent, in the context of the time, that the real goal was the dispersal of Black students as thinly as possible among White students and, particularly, to the extent it was possible, the elimination of majority Black schools. Green did not, however, specify the steps that would have to be taken to increase integration, the degree of integration that would have to be achieved, or the lesser degree, if any, that might suffice given the particular difficulties of an individual case. Freedom of choice and of transfer could be and were prohibited by the lower courts; the gerrymandering of school attendance zones, the closing of some majority Black schools, the "pairing" and "clustering" of majority Black with majority White schools, and the placement and sizing of new schools to increase integration could be and were required; but due to the residential racial concentration that exists everywhere in the nation and particularly in urban areas, where most Blacks now live, it soon became clear that majority Black schools could not be totally eliminated by these means. Nothing less would suffice than the selection of children according to race for transportation out of their neighborhoods and away from their neighborhood schools. It was difficult to believe, even after Green, that the court could or would go that far in the name of enforcing Brown. In 1971, however, the court did go that far in Swann v. Charlotte-Mecklenberg Board of Education,[18] a decision that historians may someday rank with Dred Scott[19] in terms of gratuitous infliction of injury on the country by the court in matters of race.

The factual situation in Swann, involving a major urban area and one of the nation's largest school systems, bears little resemblance to that of Green. North Carolina had been much less resistant than Virginia to ending segregation. By 1965, nonracial geographic assignment was in effect for all

[18] Swann v. Charlotte-Mecklenberg Board of Education, 402 U.S. 1 (1971).
[19] Dred Scott v. Sandford, 19 Howard 393 (1857).

schools in the countywide Charlotte-Mecklenberg school district. The constitutionality of the school system under *Brown* was certified by the district court in 1965 and by the Court of Appeals for the Fourth Circuit, sitting *en banc*, in 1966. *Green*, however, made apparent that compliance with *Brown* was no longer the constitutional requirement. The NAACP, therefore, instituted a new round of litigation, asking now, not that racial discrimination be ended, but that it be begun again, this time to increase racial mixing.

One of the most striking features of *Swann* is that, though the school board lost in each of the courts it came before, it lost each time for a different reason; the courts agreed that further racial mixing was required, but they did not agree on why it was required. The district court judge found that the school board had complied fully and in good faith with the court orders under which it was operating, but, he stated with a naive candor not to be found in the Supreme Court, "the rules of the game have changed" since *Brown*. He was shocked to learn, for the first time apparently, that Blacks performed academically at a far lower level than did Whites, and relying on the testimony of education "experts," he believed that a "dramatic improvement" in Black performance could be "produced" by putting Blacks in majority White schools.[20] Under the new "rules of the game," as the district judge understood them, "desegregation" meant, not the undoing of segregation, but simply the creation of majority White schools in order to improve academic performance by Blacks. Fortunately, the huge Charlotte-Mecklenberg school system as a whole was 71% White, and the district judge, therefore, ordered that each of the 107 schools in the district's 550 square mile area be made approximately 71% White. The cost of the transportation that would be required to achieve this was to the judge, as is typical in the make-believe world of constitutional law, "not a valid, legal reason for continued denial of constitutional rights."

The Fourth Circuit, by a split decision, affirmed the district court's decision—except that it would have required less busing of elementary school children—but it did so without adopting either the district court's basis of decision—the need to improve Black academic performance—or the putative basis of *Green*—the need to "dismantle the dual system." The Fourth Circuit, instead, adopted still a third rationale for requiring additional racial mixing: the existing school racial imbalance resulted from residential racial concentration that was the result of official racial discrimination in housing, and school racial integration is therefore constitutionally required and justified to overcome *that* discrimination.[21] This theory, of course, would have made compulsory school integration applicable not only

---

[20] 300 F.Supp. 1358 (1969); 306 F.Supp. 1291 (1969).
[21] 431 F.2d 138 (1970).

in the South but nationwide, a result by no means unacceptable to southerners at the time who believed that compulsory integration would not be ended unless it could be extended to the North.

On appeal by both parties, the Supreme Court reinstated the district court's decision in all respects. It did so, however, without accepting either the district court's or the Fourth Circuit's basis of decision, but by purporting to apply the *Green* theory that increased integration was required only in order to "dismantle the dual system." The court thus both avoided the potentially explosive question of the cause and cure for poor academic performance by Blacks and seemed to continue to confine the integration requirement to the South, the area that had had the dual system. Ordering integration under this theory, however, required the court to ignore or grossly misrepresent the facts of the case. Whatever might be said for the *Green* theory on the facts of *Green*, it was patently inapplicable to the facts of *Swann*. In *Swann* most, if not all, of the existing school racial separation was plainly the result, not of the former dual system, but, as in the North, of residential racial concentration. Many of the Charlotte-Mecklenberg schools that were predominantly Black in 1968, when this phase of the litigation began, were either schools that had been built after racial assignment had ended or schools that had been White schools under the dual system and had become predominantly Black as a result of the increase in the system's Black pupil population from 7,500 in 1954 to 24,000 in 1968. These predominantly Black schools were, therefore, indistinguishable from such schools in the North and West, and there was no basis for the claim that integration was required in order to remove the racial identification these schools acquired under the dual system. To require that these schools be made majority White was clearly not to require the undoing of segregation, the disestablishment of the dual system, but simply to require integration as such.

The extent to which the court misstated the facts of *Swann* is illustrated by the following explanation it gave for approving the district court's order:

> The predicate for the District Court's use of the 71%–29% ratio was twofold: first, its express finding, approved by the Court of Appeals and not challenged here, that a dual school system had been maintained by the school authorities at least until 1969; second, its finding, also approved by the Court of Appeals, that the school board had totally defaulted in its acknowledged duty to come forward with an acceptable plan of its own, notwithstanding the patient efforts of the District Judge who, on at least three occasions, urged the board to submit plans.

This statement is incorrect in almost every respect. The facts are, first, that the dual system had *not* been maintained until 1969 but had been abolished by at least 1965; the district court had so held in 1965, and this holding was affirmed by the Court of Appeals in 1966. Second, the school board had *not* "totally defaulted" in submitting a plan. The board had submitted a plan that would have resulted in a greater degree of integration than exists in almost any urban school system in the country, that would, for example, have eliminated every majority Black high school and every majority Black junior high school except one that had never been a Black segregated school. Third, the district court had *not* found that the school board had "totally defaulted," and the court of appeals, of course, had not approved of any such finding. Indeed, the two judges of the court of appeals who would have affirmed the district court's order in all respects complained that "the majority implies that the actions of this Board have been exemplary."

Similarly, the court stated that the district court's order was necessary in order "to accomplish the transfer of Negro students out of formerly segregated Negro schools and transfer of white students to formerly all-Negro schools." In fact, however, the transfers involving the high schools and junior high schools and some of those involving the elementary schools could *not* be justified on this basis; they were transfers of Blacks from, and of Whites to, schools that had never been Black segregated schools but that had either not been segregated schools or had been White segregated schools. The court's "objective," it stated, was to ensure that "school authorities exclude no pupil of a racial minority from any school, directly or indirectly, on account of race," but the order the court approved *required* that pupils of the minority race—and pupils of the majority race as well—be excluded from their neighborhood schools on account of their race. A requirement of racial exclusion was justified only by reiteration that all racial exclusion is prohibited. This justification must suffice because the court is subject to no review, but there is nothing that entitles it to respect. In the face of what it required in fact—racial assignment and busing to achieve near perfect racial balance in every school of a major school system spead out over a large area, part urban and part rural—the court's continued insistence that the only requirement was to "dismantle the dual system" and eliminate "all vestiges of state-imposed segregation" is simply ludicrous.

The court's treatment of the 1964 Civil Rights Act in *Swann* is equally shameful. The act, as already noted, explicit provides that "desegregation" means the assignment of children to school "without regard to their race" and does not mean assignment "to overcome racial imbalance." Assignment according to race in order to overcome racial imbalance was, of course, precisely what the court required in *Swann*. Although the court purported to do so pursuant to the Constitution and not the act, the act was clearly an embarrassment. The court, therefore, simply stated that "the legislative history" of the act "indicates that Congress was concerned" only with the "situation of so-called '*de facto* segregation,'" where racial imbalance exists in the schools but with no showing that this was brought about by discriminatory action of state authorities." This statement is, to put the matter as charitably as possible, totally without basis. Both the language of the act and its legislative history leave absolutely no room for doubt that Congress intended to provide the most complete assurance possible that the act would not become a means of requiring racial balance and, in particular, busing to increase racial balance. The repeated provisions of the act to this effect were inserted at the insistence of the representatives of the South to protect the schools of the South, not to preclude compulsory integration only in the "*de facto* segregation" situation of the North.

"DESEGREGATION" MOVES NORTH

The principal question after *Swann* was whether—or more realistically, when and how—the requirement of school racial balance would be extended to school systems outside the South, which were by this time, especially in major cities, even more racially imbalanced than those of the South. In 1972, in *Spencer* v. *Kugler*,[22] the court affirmed *per curiam*, with only Justice Douglas dissenting, the refusal of a district court to require integration in New Jersey because only "*de facto* segregation" (racial separation) had been found. It was obvious, nonetheless, that the racial mixing required in *Swann* could not be explained as "desegregation," and, therefore, that the requirement could not logically be confined to the South. The question was answered in 1973 when, in *Keyes* v. *School District No. 1, Denver, Colorado*,[23] the first "northern" case to reach the court, the court found the requirement applicable to Denver. The court, however, still could not bring itself to state openly that "the Constitution" now simply required integration, prohibited school racial separation or imbalance however caused. The only requirement, the court still insisted, was desegregation. How, then, one must wonder, could the requirement possibly be applied to Denver, where school racial segregation had always been explicitly prohibited by the Colorado Constitution? Incredibly, compulsory integration and busing in the name of desegregation came to Denver, not because Denver had ever required school segregation, but because—unlike New Jersey, to which the busing requirement had been found inapplicable only the year before—Denver had been extraordinarily committed to *increasing* school racial integration.

In 1962, six years before *Green*, the Denver school board, abandoning its policy of no racial discrimination in the operation of the school system, rejected a proposal for a new school building on the ground that the school would open, or soon become, majority Black. In 1964, the board adopted a

[22] *Spencer* v. *Kugler*, 404 U.S. 1027 (1972).
[23] *Keyes* v. *School District No. 1, Denver, Colorado*, 413 U.S. 189 (1973).

resolution requiring that in such decisions as the drawing of school boundaries and location of new schools, race be considered so as to increase integration. And, in 1967, the board resolved to build no new schools in the Park Hill section of northeast Denver, an area of increasing Black residential concentration. No new schools were thereafter built in the area, and Blacks in excess of the area's school capacity were assigned to majority White schools in other areas. Finally, in 1969, the board, in the ultimate demonstration of its commitment to integration, adopted resolutions requiring that the Park Hill schools be integrated by busing Black students out of the area and White students in. This, predictably, was too much for even the people of Denver, and they promptly elected new school board members who rescinded these resolutions before they could be put into effect. In the American system of government as it has developed since *Brown*, however, a victory at the polls remains a victory only as long as it is not disapproved by our judges, a function performed in some other systems by the military. On suit by proponents of busing for integration, a federal district court judge held the rescission unconstitutional on the paradoxical ground that means to increase integration, even though not constitutionally required, cannot, once adopted, constitutionally be repealed. He ordered that the Park Hill schools be integrated by busing as if the rescinded resolutions had been put into effect.

The Supreme Court in *Keyes* did not adopt the district judge's theory that voluntary measures to increase integration may not be halted—indeed, in a later case it explicitly rejected that theory.[24] As in *Swann*, the court, instead, simply ignored the district judge's actual basis of decision and pretended that he had found that the Denver school board had racially discriminated to separate the races, despite the district judge's explicit statement that he had *not* found racial discrimination apart from the rescission. The court thereupon in effect instructed the district judge that he had not gone far enough in ordering busing, that he should have ordered the elimination of majority Black schools not only in northeast Denver but also in central Denver, Denver's other area of Black residential concentration. The district judge could do this, the court said, by finding that the majority Black schools in central Denver were the result of the racial discrimination by the board supposedly found by the district judge in northeast Denver. The logical and factual defects in the Supreme Court's opinion include that (1) the district judge had *not* found racial discrimination by the school board in northeast Denver except on the basis of his invalid rescission theory; (2) such discrimination, even if it had been found, could not possibly have been the reason that the schools in central Denver were majority Black; those schools had been majority Black *prior* to the time that the

---

[24] *Dayton Board of Education* v. *Brinkman*, 433 U.S. 406 (1977).

schools in northeast Denver became majority Black; (3) far from having racially discriminated to separate the races, the Denver school board had voluntarily undertaken to increase racial mixing, and found itself in constitutional difficulty only because of those efforts; and (4) the existence of majority Black schools in central Denver was, in any event, obviously the result, not of racial discrimination by the board, but of residential patterns.

Despite the fact that the court virtually ordered citywide busing for racial balance, its *Keyes* opinion was something of a disappointment to proponents of compulsory integration. Because it was clear that segregation could not properly be found in Denver and, therefore, that desegregation could not properly be ordered, these proponents hoped that the court would use *Keyes* as the occasion to announce openly that the requirement was not merely desegregation, after all, but simply integration. The court refused to do this, however; the at least rhetorical advantages of the claim—no matter how obviously fictional—that it was still only enforcing *Brown*, prohibiting rather than requiring racial discrimination, were simply too great to be given up. The court, therefore, explicitly purported to retain the distinction between *de jure* and *de facto* segregation and to require only desegregation—the undoing of *de jure* segregation. At the same time, however, the court undertook to ensure that limiting the requirement to desegregation in name would present no significant impediment to requiring integration in fact wherever school racial imbalance exists.

A constitutional requirement of desegregation is distinguishable from, and much more limited than, a requirement of integration in that, first, it can have no application except where segregation—the product of official racial discrimination, the constitutional violation—has been found, and, second, it requires and justifies the undoing ("remedying") of *only* such segregation, not the undoing of whatever racial separation may happen to exist. In *Keyes*, however, by apparently approving the district judge's finding of a constitutional violation (without actually reviewing the issue), the court indicated that a finding of racial discrimination was not necessary in fact; by holding that "all-out desegregation" (systemwide racial balance) could be ordered by the district judge on the basis of the limited violation he supposedly found, the court made clear that the "remedy" need not be limited to the violations found. The "desegregation" required in *Keyes* was, therefore, different from a simple requirement of integration only in name. If a constitutional violation could be found, and systemwide busing for racial balance ordered in Denver, surely a violation could be found and busing could be ordered everywhere. *Keyes* thus appeared to be a complete victory for proponents of compulsory integration in everything but name. In fact, however, *Keyes* proved to be the high-water mark of the integration requirement in the Supreme Court. That the requirement was still said to be only "desegregation" was its Achilles' heel, for it meant that the court could abandon the requirement at any time by merely taking its own statement at face value and thereafter requiring only desegregation in fact as well as name.

"DESEGREGATION" THEORY APPLIED TO LIMIT BUSING

Milliken v. *Bradley*,[25] the Detroit case, decided by the Supreme Court in 1974, was the turning point. With that decision, the NAACP's almost continuous stream of victories in the Supreme Court on the issue of race and the schools became an almost continuous stream of defeats. As in *Keyes*, the district judge purported to find "*de jure* segregation" despite the absence of significant evidence of racial discrimination by school authorities and despite the obvious fact that the existence of predominantly Black schools was due to the great post-war growth of the Black population, the concomitant withdrawal of White students from the schools, and racially concentrated residential patterns. Indeed, Detroit, like Denver, had not only never segregated the races, but had for some time voluntarily taken steps to increase integration; for example, in 1970, the board refused to fill 240 school positions except with Blacks.

Again, as in *Keyes*, the court in *Milliken* did not review the district court's finding of a constitutional violation ("*de jure* segregation") in Detroit. Because the requirement is only "desegregation," however, finding a constitutional violation is only the first step to a court order requiring increased racial mixing. The next step is to determine the effect of the constitutional violation—the extent to which existing racial separation is the result of the violation—and to order racial mixing *only* to the extent necessary to undo ("remedy") that effect. The district judge in *Milliken*, however, had better observed what the Supreme Court had been doing than what it said it was doing. To him, therefore, "desegregation" meant—as it does to most noninitiates in constitutional law—simply the creation of racially balanced schools and, most important, the elimination of majority Black schools if possible. The elimination of majority Black schools, unfortunately, was no longer possible within the confines of the Detroit school system, which was by then (1970) 64% Black. The school districts surrounding Detroit, however, were virtually all White, and therefore, presented the judge ample material for achievement of his objective. There was no evidence that this interdistrict racial separation was the result of official racial discrimination, that is, that it was segregation, the essential prerequisite for a requirement of desegregation. Nonetheless, the district judge, operating under his very different understanding of what "desegregation" meant, ordered the consolidation of the Detroit school district and 53

[25] *Milliken* v. *Bradley*, 418 U.S. 717 (1974).

surrounding districts—which would have created a district of 1,952 square miles, half again, as the Supreme Court was to note, the size of Rhode Island—and that children be transported throughout this area so that no school would be more than approximately 25% Black.

Although the court did not review the validity of the district judge's finding of a constitutional violation in Detroit—letting that indefensible finding stand—it did review the validity of the district judge's "remedy," and held that the 54 district busing order was not "constitutionally justified or required" by the violation found. No more was necessary for reversal than for the court to note that it had never said that majority Black schools were constitutionally objectionable, even with majority White schools nearby; the constitutional requirement, after all, is not integration but desegregation, and the district judge was clearly mistaken in believing that "desegregation" meant the elimination of majority Blacks schools. As there had been no finding that the interdistrict racial separation constituted segregation, there could be no question of requiring interdistrict desegregation. Compulsory integration in the name of desegregation was thus shown to be no more than a house of cards, requiring only a breath of truth to be brought down.

This breath of truth has been maintained by the court in later decisions. In *Pasadena City Board of Education* v. *Spangler*[26] (1975), the court again reversed a district court busing order on the ground that the increased integration it sought to achieve could not be justified as desegregation. In 1970, the district court had purported to find racial discrimination and, therefore, "*de jure* segregation" in the Pasadena school system, and with no attempt to limit its order to undo the effect of this supposed violation, simply ordered that pupils be identified and transported according to race so that no Pasadena school would be majority Black. This order was carried out, but by 1973, because of population movements and the withdrawal of Whites from the school system that inevitably follows busing orders in districts with a large percentage of Blacks, several schools again became majority Black. Demonstrating his misunderstanding of the desegregation requirement—and, incidentally, his self-esteem—the district judge then announced that "at least during my lifetime there would be no majority of any minority in any school in Pasadena," and he therefore ordered another reassignment of pupils so that majority Black schools might be eliminated again.[27] Again, actually holding, not merely stating, that though the Constitution requires desegregation it does not require integration or the elimination of the majority Black schools, the Supreme Court found the district court's order not constitutionally authorized. Desegregation does not

[26] *Pasadena City Board of Education* v. *Spangler*, 427 U.S. 424 (1976).
[27] 375 F.Supp. 1304 (1974).

require the undoing of school racial separation that is caused "by factors for which the defendants could not be considered responsible," such as residential racial concentration. The district court "was not entitled . . . to ensure that the racial mix desired by the court was maintained in perpetuity."

In *Milliken* the court made explicit, for the first time, that since the Constitution requires desegregation but not integration as such, a district court, after finding a constitutional violation (racial discrimination), can order only as much racial mixing as would have existed except for the violation. The constitutional authority of the district court is only "to restore the victims of discriminatory conduct to the position they would have occupied in the absence of such conduct." In *Dayton Board of Education* v. *Brinkman*,[28] decided in 1977, the court was even more specific. The court first noted: "Dayton is a racially mixed community, and that many of its schools are either predominantly white or predominantly black. This fact without more, of course, does not offend the Constitution." It is only "action in the conduct of the business of the school board which was intended to, and did in fact, discriminate against minority pupils, teachers or staff" that offends the Constitution. And because desegregation means the undoing of unconstitutional segregation, the district court, having found a violation or violations,

> must determine how much incremental segregative effect these violations had on the racial distribution of the Dayton School population as presently constituted, when that distribution is compared to what it would have been in the absence of such constitutional violations. The remedy must be designed to redress that difference, and only if there has been a system wide impact may there be a systemwide remedy.

The court "realize[d] that this is a difficult task. Nonetheless," it said, "that is what the Constitution and our cases call for, and that is what must be done. . . ."

The court in *Dayton* thus strongly reemphasized that only racial discrimination by school authorities, not mere school racial separation, violates the Constitution. The real importance of the case, however, lies in the fact that the court made explicit for the first time that when such a violation is properly found, a court must specifically determine the amount of racial separation caused by that violation and then require the undoing of only that separation. Most current "desegregation" litigation turns on the application of this holding. Because almost none of the racial separation that exists in the schools today is the result of racial discrimination by school authorities, but is the result of residential racial concentration, the

---

[28] *Dayton Board of Education* v. *Brinkman*, 433 U.S. 406 (1977).

conscientious application of this holding by the lower federal courts would mean the virtual end of court-ordered integration and busing.

THE REQUIREMENT OF A RACIALLY DISCRIMINATORY "INTENT"

Milliken, Pasadena, and especially *Dayton* severely limit the requirement of court-ordered racial mixing by making clear that the "desegregation" or "remedy" justification for such compulsory mixing is to be taken seriously, that a court-ordered increase in integration cannot be justified, or even properly described, as "desegregation" unless it is limited in fact to undoing unconstitutional segregation. At the same time, in *Washington v. Davis,*[29] decided in 1976, the court also limited the requirement by making clear that the need to find unconstitutional segregation—without which there is no violation to "remedy"—is also to be taken seriously, that unconstitutional segregation is to be limited in fact to racial separation caused by racial discrimination by school authorities.

Finding racial discrimination and, therefore, unconstitutional segregation presented no problem, of course, in cases from the South, where, as in *Brown,* racial discrimination had been explicit. The problem arises in cases from the North and West where there had not been explicit racial discrimination but where school racial separation nonetheless exists. In these cases many lower courts, following what the court did, rather than what it said, in *Green, Swann,* and *Keyes,* either openly rejected the requirement of finding racial discrimination or recognized it in name only to reject it in fact by finding racial discrimination on the basis of the existence of racial separation. In *Washington v. Davis,* the court explicity held that the requirement is not to be obviated so easily.

In *Washington v. Davis,* a group of Black applicants for police officer positions in the District of Columbia challenged as racially discriminatory the police department's use of a written test of verbal ability in selecting candidates for such positions. The Court of Appeals for the District of Columbia held that the use of the test was racially discriminatory and therefore unconstitutional because it had the effect of disqualifying, proportionately, four times as many Blacks as Whites. The Supreme Court reversed, explicitly rejecting "the proposition that a law or other official act, without regard to whether it reflects a racially discriminatory purpose, is unconstitutional *solely* because it has a racially disproportionate impact." We have never held, the court said, "that a law, neutral on its face and serving ends otherwise within the power of government to pursue, is invalid

[29] *Washington v. Davis,* 426 U.S. 229 (1976).

under the Equal Protection Clause simply because it may affect a greater proportion of one race than of another." Indeed, the court had "difficulty understanding how a law establishing a racially neutral qualification for employment is nevertheless racially discriminatory and denies 'any person . . . equal protection of the laws' simply because a greater proportion of Negroes fail to qualify than members of other racial or ethnic groups."

Of particular importance in the present context, the court in *Washington* seemingly went out of its way to make explicit that its rejection of an "effects test" for finding racial discrimination is fully applicable to "desegregation" cases:

> The school desegregation cases have also adhered to the basic equal protection principle that the invidious quality of a law claimed to be racially discriminatory must ultimately be traced to a racially discriminatory purpose. That there are both predominantly black and predominantly white schools in a community is not alone violative of the Equal Protection Clause.

The court soon confirmed this by a series of *per curiam* decisions vacating and remanding for reconsideration in light of *Washington* v. *Davis* lower court decisions that had found racial discrimination and therefore unconstitutional segregation on the ground that school racial separation existed as a necessary result of the school board's use of neighborhood schools.[30]

All racial separation in the public schools is an effect of official action and can be avoided by different action. It is, typically, an effect of the use of neighborhood schools in a school district in which, as in all school districts, the races are not evenly distributed by residence, and it can always be avoided by abandoning neighborhood school assignment and substituting assignment according to race in order to increase integration. When an act, even though not explicitly racial, is not reasonably explicable except in terms of its racial effect, it is properly and necessarily considered an act of racial discrimination. The use of neighborhood schools, however, has many very substantial nonracial justifications, such as that it minimizes the costs and inconveniences of pupil transportation and facilitates parental supervision of the schools. To find unconstitutional segregation on the basis of the use of neighborhood schools is, therefore, not to condemn racial discrimination, but simply to condemn the resulting racial separation; it is to condemn the school board, not for practicing racial discrimination to separate the races, but for failing to practice racial discrimination to mix them. Since it is only segregation, however, not all racial separation, that the Constitution prohibits, a constitutional violation cannot be found, *Washington* v. *Davis*

---

[30] *Austin Independent School District* v. *United States*, 429 U.S. 990 (1976); *Brennan* v. *Armstrong*, 433 U.S. 672 (1977); *Metropolitan School District* v. *Buckley*, 429 U.S. 1068 (1977); *School District of Omaha* v. *United States*, 433 U.S. 667 (1977).

makes clear, on the basis of the use of neighborhood schools and the resulting racial separation.

Although *Washington* v. *Davis* holds that racial discrimination, the constitutional violation, may not be found on the basis of the racial impact of racially neutral acts that have substantial nonracial justification, it does not solve all problems of how racial discrimination may properly be found. The court said that a finding of racial discrimination requires a finding of a "racially discriminatory purpose," and quoting *Keyes*, that the "differentiating factor between *de jure* segregation and so-called *de facto* segregation . . . is *purpose* or *intent* to segregate." Here, as elsewhere in the law, however, a "purpose or intent" test for the validity of acts presents many difficulties. An inquiry into purpose or intent is clearly meaningful when the issue is whether the act in question was accidental or mistaken as distinguished from deliberate or knowing; it is not ordinarily meaningful when the act—such as the use of neighborhood schools—was undoubtedly deliberate and its objectionable effect—racial separation—was foreseeable or inevitable. The purpose or intent of a legally competent actor is usually determined in the law by the natural and foreseeable consequences of his act—which is to say, of course, that it is those consequences themselves, not any "subjective intent," that is the actual subject of inquiry. Indeed, it is difficult or impossible even to assign meaning to the concept of "subjective intent," especially when, as in most school cases, the act in question is the act of a group. If the suggested inquiry is whether the actor or actors "really desired" the necessary consequences of the act, the answer must be that they desired them enough knowingly to bring them about. It is not a defense to theft that the thief desires only to gain possession of an article, not to deprive its owner of possession. It is also difficult to understand why the law should be concerned with an actor's "subjective intent," even if it could be defined and determined, at least where the issue is the validity of the act, not the culpability of the actor. The objective harms and benefits of an act do not vary with the actor's appraisal of them. The validity of the use of neighborhood schools, for example, should not ordinarily depend on who the school board members happen to be.

When an act has only "good" (valued) effects, there is, of course, no reason to condemn it; when it has only "bad" (unwanted) effects, it can easily be condemned. A problem arises only when the issue is the permissibilty of an act that has both good and bad effects. This problem obviously cannot be resolved by asking which of the effects was "intended;" they were *both* intended in that they were both deliberately and knowingly brought about. The problem can only be resolved by asking whether the good effects justify the act despite its bad effects, and this necessarily requires making a value judgment. An inquiry into the "intent" of a deliberate and knowing act must, therefore, be understood as an invitation to offer justification by pointing out possible good effects so that a more informed value judgment may be made. The inquiry is conventionally phrased in terms of intent primarily to conceal the necessary value judgment, to make it appear that only a factual determination is involved. In legal and democratic theory, only the elected representatives of the people are authorized to make basic value judgments. A judge cannot openly announce that, for example, he is invalidating the use of neighborhood schools because he feels, on the whole, that their advantages are less valuable than the greater racial integration that could otherwise be obtained. A judge who happens to feel this way—and who is also convinced, as most judges are, that it is his feeling that should be determinative—will, therefore, announce, instead, that he has found racial discrimination—which, on the authority of *Brown*, judges *are* authorized to prohibit—on the basis of a "factual determination" that the school board "intended" to discriminate racially.

The "purpose or intent" test can, however, also perform another function. In some cases a judge may have no strong feeling as to how the value conflict involved should be resolved, and he may, therefore, be willing to accept the judgment of the officials who initially resolved the conflict, provided he is convinced that they at least recognized and considered the conflicting values involved. Suppose, for example, that a school board decides to build a new school on a particular site where, because of racial concentration in the surrounding neighborhood, it will be a one-race school, and that another site is available, the use of which would cause greater integration and which is not inferior to the first site except that its use would require school children to cross a busy major highway. It is conceivable that a judge might uphold the decision where other acts of the board or its predecessors showed that the people of the area place a very high value on avoiding having children cross highways, but might invalidate the decision in another case with similar circumstances except that the board's acts showed that it did not place a high value on this consideration. If the value of avoiding highways is not to be given substantial weight, the decision is inexplicable except in terms of its racial effects, and may, therefore, properly be considered an act of racial discrimination. A judge might, therefore, find racial discrimination in one case but not the other by simply accepting and adopting in each case the school board's apparent evaluation of the highway factor.

In actual cases, however, it must be emphasized, these issues are almost always much more complex and unclear than in the above highly simplified example. Judges should approach these issues today, it is submitted, with a strong presumption in favor of the school board's judgment and good faith. Such a presumption is justified because it appears that most school boards today are not opposed to integration and make most close judgments in favor of integration—even though it is not realistically within their power to overcome the effects of large areas of residential racial concentration. Perhaps more important, Blacks today, at least in urban areas are, happily, able and willing to make their voices heard and to protest effectively any school board decision that operates to separate the races where an alternative without that effect is reasonably available. Most Blacks favor integration but do not favor the abandonment of neighborhood schools and the busing that abandonment entails. Finally, strenuous judicial efforts to find racial discrimination seem unjustified in that the busing that usually follows such a finding has not been shown clearly to contribute importantly to any good objective and, by accelerating the departure of the middle class from public school systems, is often self-defeating even simply in terms of increasing racial mixing.

Despite the difficulties of the "purpose or intent" standard, *Washington* v. *Davis* leaves no doubt that racial discrimination, and therefore a constitutional violation, may not be found solely on the basis of a challenged act's racial effect. The court emphasized and illustrated this by the extraordinary step of explicitly disapproving a large number of lower court decisions, concerning public employment, public housing, zoning, urban removal, and municipal services, that had, openly or in effect, found a constitutional violation solely because of an act that had a different impact on Blacks as a class than on Whites as a class. In the "desegregation" context, *Washington* v. *Davis* makes clear that racial discrimination, and therefore segregation, cannot properly be found by simply finding racial separation resulting from the use of neighborhood schools; the court thereby reaffirmed and made meaningful the distinction between racial segregation, which is constitutionally prohibited, and racial separation, which is not. Because the racial separation that exists in the schools today is the result of residential racial concentration, not of racial discrimination by school authorities, the faithful application of *Washington* v. *Davis* by the lower courts on the constitutional violation issue would, like the faithful application of *Dayton* on the "remedy" issue, mean the virtual end of compulsory integration ("desegregation") and busing.

Many lower court judges, however, have shown themselves most unsympathetic to, and even defiant of, the Supreme Court's recent efforts to confine court-ordered racial mixing to actual desegregation.[31] These judges have evaded the holding of *Washington* v. *Davis* by simply exploiting the ambiguity of the "purpose or intent" test for finding racial discrimination. They have "reasoned" as follows: Not all school racial separation, but only segregation, the product of racial discrimination, is unconstitutional, and a

[31] E.g., *Austin Independent School District* v. *United States*, 564 F.2d 162 (1978).

finding of racial discrimination requires, according to *Washington* v. *Davis*, a finding of a racially discriminatory purpose or intent; in law, however, a person is assumed to intend the natural and foreseeable consequences of his acts, and racial separation is usually a natural and foreseeable consequence of the use of neighborhood schools; in using neighborhood schools the board, therefore, must have intended to separate the races, and the resulting racial separation is, therefore, unconstitutional segregation. The result of this purely circular process is, of course, not to meet but to eliminate the requirement of finding racial discrimination and to make racial separation itself unconstitutional in fact. These lower court judges, now long accustomed to applause for their intervention in the operation of school systems, will not be convinced easily that the day of compulsory integration and busing is over, that the constitutional requirement is now desegregation in fact and not, as in *Green*, *Swann*, and *Keyes*, just in name. Repeated and ever more specific insistence on this by the Supreme Court will almost certainly be required.

The central issue in the law of race in the schools today, therfore, is no longer whether school racial integration is, or is about to be, constitutionally required; the Supreme Court has now made clear that it is not. The issue, instead, is whether and when the lower courts will accept and apply the Supreme Court's more recent decisions, and whether the Supreme Court will continue to insist that they do so. If the Supreme Court does not continue to so insist, the country will continue to suffer the disastrous consequences of compulsory integration and busing—injury to school systems, cities, race relations, and the political process—until some extrajudicial means is finally found to bring compulsory integration and busing to an end.

For one with a lingering faith in democracy as, if not a good, at least the best form of government, the twenty-fifth anniversary of *Brown* is no cause for celebration. As important as *Brown* was for its actual holding, it has proved far more important because of the change it has brought about in popular perception of the role of the Supreme Court in our system of government. That the court could make so momentous a decision and that its decision could eventually come to prevail easily led to the belief, now widespread, that there is nothing that the court cannot or should not do. It was the very success and acceptance of *Brown* that led the court to essay the disastrous experiment of *Green*, to the almost incredible holding that government is constitutionally required to investigate and ascertain the race of school children and transport them out of their neighborhoods and away from their neighborhood schools in order to achieve school racial "balance." In other areas the new role of the court that followed from *Brown* led to such decisions as those severely restricting the power of the states to limit the availability of abortion, requiring the redistricting of federal and state legislatures, proscribing most controls on the dissemination of pornography, prohibiting religious observances in the schools, virtually abolishing capital punishment, and generally impeding the effective enforcement of the criminal law to the point that guilt has seemingly become the least relevant consideration. More specifically, it has led to such grotesqueries as that Oklahoma cannot prescribe a higher drinking age for men than for women,[32] California may not punish the parading of an obscenity in its courthouses,[33] and New York may not grant college scholarship aid to American citizens that it refuses to aliens.[34]

Constitutional law, since and as a result of *Brown*, has become little more than a ruse for government by unelected and virtually unremovable judges, which is bad enough because it is by judges and worse because it is by ruse. If it is, in fact, government by philosopher kings we now want, we must find a better means of selecting our philosophers, provide them with means of obtaining available knowledge relevant to their task, and not require that they operate by pretense. What we have achieved is not government by philosopher kings, but, much worse, government by a committee of lawyers with no claim to special knowledge or wisdom regarding the issues they decide.

There is little point in lamenting the apathy of the electorate when our present system of government leaves less and less for the elected to decide. *Brown* has indeed worked a revolution, but it is one counter to the truly revolutionary idea—that the people can be trusted to govern themselves—on which this nation was founded. The most fitting observance of the twenty-fifth anniversary of *Brown*, therefore, would be the adoption of a constitutional amendment, or at least effective legislation, returning, at least to some extent, the government of this nation to its people.

Note Added in Proof

In *Columbus Board of Education* v. *Penick*,[35] and *Dayton Board of Education* v. *Brinkman*,[36] decided after the above went to press, the Supreme Court executed another amazing change of direction on the compulsory integration issue. Although it continued to insist that the constitutional requirement remains only desegregation and not simply integration as such, the court again upheld lower court busing orders that cannot be explained except as holding that all school racial separation or "imbalance," however caused, is unconstitutional. The lower courts complied with neither the

---

[32] *Craig* U. *Boren* 429 U.S. 190 (1976).
[33] *Cohen* U. *California* 403 U.S. 15 (1971).
[34] *Nyquist* U. *Mauclet* 432 U.S. 1 (1977).
[35] *Columbus Board of Education* v. *Penick*, 99 S. Ct. 2941 (1979).
[36] *Dayton Board of Education* v. *Brinkman*, 99 S. Ct. 2971 (1979).

requirement of *Washington* v. *Davis*, that racial separation is not unconstitutional (*de jure* segregation) unless it is shown to be the result of "intentional" racial discrimination, nor with the requirement of the first *Dayton* case that the amount of racial mixing ordered (the "remedy") be limited to undoing the effects of the constitutional violation. The result of these latest Supreme Court decisions is to return the law to the position it was in at the time of *Keyes* and virtually to cancel all subsequent developments. In effect, it was the Supreme Court and not the lower courts that "blinked" in their confrontation. The result is also to make clear that if busing for school racial balance under the guise of desegregation is to be ended, it will have to be by legislative action.

REFERENCES

Friedman, L. (Ed.). *Argument*. New York: Chelsea, 1969.
Graglia, L. A. *Disaster by decree: The Supreme Court decisions on race and the schools*. Ithaca: Cornell University Press, 1976.
St. John, N. H. *School desegregation: Outcomes for children*. New York: Wiley, 1975.

5

Nondiscrimination and Beyond

THE SEARCH FOR PRINCIPLE IN SUPREME COURT DESEGREGATION DECISIONS[1]

MARK G. YUDOF

INTRODUCTION

A few years ago, J. Harvie Wilkinson (1974) wrote that *Brown v. Board of Education*[2] evoked a "certain nostalgia" for him, for *Brown* was "one of those last, great actions whose moral logic seemed so uncomplex and irrefutable, and whose opposition seemed so thoroughly extreme, rooted as it was in notions of racial hegemony and the constitutional premises of John C. Calhoun" (p. 133). This is a nostalgia that I share. *Brown* was premised on the notion that state statutes and constitutions that require the separation of White and Black children in the public schools are designed to and have the effect of stigmatizing Black Americans as inferior beings (Kluger, 1977). In the words of Charles Black (1960), "the social meaning of segregation is the putting of the Negro in a position of walled-off inferiority ... [and] such treatment is hurtful to human beings" (p. 427). Whatever the original understanding of the 14th Amendment, the antidiscrimination principle, embodying the ethical assertion that race-dependent government decisions should be disfavored, is a principle of wide moral appeal that properly informs the interpretation and application of the Equal Protection Clause of that Amendment (Brest, 1976).

---

[1] This chapter is a modified version of an earlier published work, School desegregation: Legal realism, reasoned elaboration, and social science research in the Supreme Court. *Law and Contemporary Problems.* Durham, N.C.: Duke University School of Law, 1979, *42*(4), 57–110. Reprinted by permission of the publisher.

[2] *Brown v. Topeka Board of Education*, 347 U.S. 483 (1954).

MARK G. YUDOF • University of Texas Law School, University of Texas, Austin, Texas 78712.

But if *Brown* stands for the proposition that school authorities may not assign students to public schools on the basis of their race to maintain a segregated school system, the simplicity of that principle is belied by the complexity of applying it in the circumstances currently facing federal judges. In the original challenges to the dual school system, discrimination was explicit and generally embodied in state law and regulations. Today, although segregated school systems are still common (Orfield, 1978), the question of racial motivation is more difficult to answer as school assignments are justified on the basis of neighborhood attendance zones, overcrowding, ability grouping, parental choice, and the like. The factual and legal issues confronting the Burger Court then are more subtle than those confronting its predecessor (Wilkinson, 1974):

> The point is not to prove that the Burger Court is more or less liberal on matters of race. It has always been clear that the core of the Warren tradition—the prohibition of state-imposed segregation in public education and facilities ... remains fairly intact. But those are not generally the questions that reach the Supreme Court today. Rarely, in fact, does the race issue not appear in the context of overt and easily detected prejudice or without legitimate considerations on the other side. (pp. 136–137)

The court must decide when apparently facially neutral policies that produce or maintain segregated schools should be assimilated, morally and legally, to the concept of racial discrimination (Goodman, 1972).

The vagaries of detecting purposeful discrimination in its more subtle forms are compounded by additional considerations. As J. R. and C. B. Feagin have noted (1978), past discrimination (separate schools for Blacks and Whites), or discrimination practiced in some other areas (e.g., housing and employment opportunities) may have some impact on apparently neutral present practices in education. For example, one may argue that past employment discrimination resulted in lower incomes for Black families, and therefore, even in the absence of discrimination by race in housing or education, most Blacks are unable to afford expensive suburban housing. Under such circumstances, the continued use of school district lines to separate suburban and urban children may have the effect of creating racial isolation—an effect traceable in part to past and related discrimination.

There may be different forms of "unintentional" discrimination (Feagin & Feagin, 1978). Frankly, this concept is quite troublesome to me; for any public measure (e.g., public transportation or the construction of public tennis courts) may have the effect of being to the advantage or disadvantage of some particular group as it is over- or underrepresented among the class of beneficiaries (Yudof, 1975). With many others, I believe that motive is a critical factor (Brest, 1971; Ely, 1970; Simon, 1978), albeit "institutional motive" is a perplexing concept. Perhaps the concept of unintentional discrimination makes more sense in the context of individuals seeking to maintain their socioeconomic status and their associations with other middle class people (Graglia, 1976). Thus, without any animus toward Blacks, a person may seek to retain his or her job security based on seniority or to send his or her children to a predominantly middle-class school—even though Blacks, a disproportionately poor group, may find it impossible to gain entry to such jobs and schools under what appear to be neutral and defensible rules for allocating benefits. That is, the rules operate against a background of a prior allocation of wealth and benefits, and thus, they reinforce the status quo. From such a perspective, the line between intentional and unintentional discrimination becomes exceedingly hard to draw; for one may know the racial consequences of one's action even though the purpose *per se* is not to discriminate against a racial minority.

The more subtle and complex notions of discrimination also begin to merge with another approach to racial justice. The historic focus in race relations and schooling in America has been on equality of opportunity or access (Yudof, 1973). Some see this as a form of myopia. Too much attention is paid to formal mechanisms of access and not enough is paid to equality of outcomes. In one of its variant forms, this version of equality looks to a random distribution of schooling and life success between the races, viewed as subgroups within the population (Yudof, 1973). Strong inferences of discrimination are perceived where people end up in an unequal position, notwithstanding the apparent neutrality of the rules by which people acquire schooling, income, and life success. This is more of a socialist, group concept of equality, pitting what Robert Paul Wolff (1978) calls "methodological collectivism" against "methodological individualism." Thus, there is increasing dissensus about equality objectives at the very same time that traditional discrimination becomes more difficult to identify.

As if these questions were not enough, the desegregation cases raise particularly acute problems of remedies. Courts generally have more flexibility and discretion in fashioning remedies than they do in determining constitutional rights and violations in the first instance, and in the desegregation cases the question of remedy has often been more difficult than the articulation of rights and violations. The traditional remedy would be relatively straightforward: Black youngsters who are denied admission to schools which they are otherwise qualified to attend must be admitted and the schools must refrain from racial discrimination in the future (Bickel, 1962, p. 247). As history demonstrates, however, state and local bodies were ingenious in the extreme in devising superficially neutral plans (pupil placement laws, ability grouping, freedom of choice) which were subterfuges for keeping the races separate in the public schools. This ultimately led the Supreme Court and the Department of Health, Education, and Welfare to impose quotas for racial balance in all or nearly all schools in a district

(Dunn, 1967); numbers became the most manageable way of policing school districts for compliance with the nondiscrimination regime. Hence, the notion of a "unitary" school system in which schools were not racially "identifiable"[3] gradually came to be seen in terms of the dispersion of Black children, primarily to predominantly White schools. Integration and desegregation came to be synonymous. But integration of large urban school districts requires both pupil transportation from their neighborhoods and the assignment of children based on their race (Orfield, 1978). As this occurred, politicians and scholars (Graglia, 1976) advanced pragmatic and principled arguments against the court's handiwork.

This chapter explores the competing principles that might serve to justify racial balance remedies in the light of prevailing constitutional principles, of requirements of craftsmanship for judicial opinions, and of the relevant social science research results. In this regard, I have identified three such principles. First, integration flows from the nondiscrimination principle in that it is necessary to remedy the present and past wrongs of racial discrimination (Lawrence, 1977), e.g., the public schools of a given area would have been integrated but for these wrongs (Dworkin, 1977). More expansively, it may mean that the public schools would have been integrated but for discrimination in public and private housing, school assignments, and employment (Dworkin, 1977; Orfield, 1978). Alternatively, integration is necessary to undo educational, stigmatic, or other injuries to Black children caused by segregation (Fiss, 1965). Second, racial balance is required because of the fear that government decisions will be corrupted by racial discrimination, however well hidden (Dworkin, 1977):

> In a community that has settled prejudice of one sort or another . . . the [political process] machine will inevitably break down because there is no way of excluding these preferences based on prejudice from affecting the process. If prejudicial preferences are counted, then the personal preferences of those against whom the prejudice is directed are not counted equally in the balance; they are discounted by the effect of the prejudice. . . . A constitutional right is created among other reasons for this reason: We know that there is a high antecedent probability that the political judgment reached about a particular matter will not fairly reflect the kind of preferences that rightly make up the general welfare, but will give influential expression to preferences based on prejudice. We create constitutional rights of one sort or another to guard against this. (pp. 28–29)

Third, concern for the welfare of Blacks as a group and an interpretive judgment as to their historic treatment (Fiss, 1976) lead to the conclusion that integration and not just nondiscrimination should be fostered by constitutional decisions under the Fourteenth Amendment (Fiss, 1965; Yudof, 1973).

[3] *Green* v. *New Kent County School Board*, 391 U.S. 430 (1968).

THE REMEDIAL THEORY

The theory that appears to dominate judicial discussions of remedy is that racially balanced schools are a necessary corrective for past acts of discrimination rooted in the dual schools system (Dworkin, 1977). In its strongest form, the hypothesis is "if there had not been *de jure* segregation in the past, there would now be *de facto* integration" (p. 27). A somewhat weaker version is the hypothesis that "past. . . *de jure* segregation may be presumed to be part of the causal chain that has produced (perhaps through its impact on residential housing patterns, perhaps in other ways) *de facto* segregation of today" (p. 27). The concept of remedy is superficially similar to that which permeates law: remedies should be designed to put the innocent parties (Black children) in the position that they would have occupied (integrated schools) but for the wrongful conduct (racial discrimination) of the defendants. The difficulty, as we shall see, is that such notions of backward-looking remedies in a well-defined, two-party contest do not readily apply to modern, public interest litigation where there are many parties; the remedy is forward-looking, and the remedy itself has broad public policy implications (Chayes, 1976).

In theory, the investigation and illumination of such causal links should be the stuff of social science since the constitutional questions have been formulated in instrumental (cause and effect) terms. But there are manifest problems with this causal theory. Whatever the theoretical scope of social science inquiry, the complexity of these causal links is such that it is unlikely that social science methodologies will ever allow the drawing of such causal inferences with a reasonable degree of confidence (Cohen & Weiss, 1977). Indeed, the evidence and research thus far accumulated suggests the implausibility of the "but for" theory (Wolf, 1977), albeit there is no consensus among researchers (Farley, 1975; Pettigrew, 1973). The reasons for segregated schools are complex, involving not only discrimination in schools, but socioeconomic isolation, choices to live among people of the same race, employment discrimination, preferences among public goods, and public and private housing discrimination (Wolf, 1977). The primacy of *de jure* discrimination in the segregated pattern of schools, or even its influence, is not at all clear.

The court's theory becomes more attenuated as Black children today are reassigned to integrated schools as a remedy for discrimination against past generations of Black students. One set of persons constitutes the class of victims of the discrimination, while another set constitutes the class of beneficiaries of the remedy. The school board that implements the court-ordered remedy may well be an entirely different board than the one that committed the original wrong. Moreover, the traditional theory of remedies assumes that the relief granted will bring about an improvement in the current situation created by the breach of a legal obligation, or the wronged party would be unlikely to seek legal redress. But the evidence that Blacks are better off in integrated schools (in academic, psychological, or other terms) is mixed (St. John, 1975; Stephan, 1978; Weinberg, 1977). Finally, the vindication of the constitutional interest is made to turn on the vagaries of empirical research, with all the attendant instability and difficulties that this imports into the law (Yudof, 1973).

A more expansive view of the theory, one not yet adopted by the majority of the Supreme Court, is that integration of the public schools is necessary, not simply because of past *de jure* discrimination in the public schools, but as a means of undoing the accumulated discrimination in the private and public sectors. The theory has particular appeal if government is held accountable not only for its own acts or racial discrimination but also for tolerating or permitting racial discrimination by private individuals and entities (Dimond, 1972). The predicate for the theory strikes me as sound: there is no denying the sorry and sordid history of discrimination practiced against Black people in virtually all aspects of political, social, and economic life (Woodward, 1974). But the difficulty is in moving from the predicate to the conclusion. Why should only school-related racial discrimination trigger the remedy of integration if it is simply one of many wrongs suffered by Blacks? More importantly, in what sense does school integration or dispersion of the races make up for employment or housing discrimination, discrimination in the enforcement of criminal laws, social ostracism, and the like? This theory is supportable only by the assumption that school integration leads to progress for Blacks in these other areas. This assumption, however, has the same deficiencies as the other instrumental approaches to the remedial theory.

Rephrasing the remedial theory in interpretive terms makes it more plausible: segregation in the public schools is stigmatizing and symbolic of a hostile attitude by powerful Whites against relatively powerless Blacks (Lawrence, 1977). The issue then is not one of causal relationships but one of the impact of the current patterns of racial isolation in public schools (Goodman, 1972). If integrated schools remove the stigma and symbols of inferiority, integration is a justifiable remedy for discrimination. However, unless it is assumed that White and Black Americans view all racial isolation as indicative of the racial inferiority of Blacks, a dubious proposition, even this noninstrumental refinement of the remedial theory poses difficulties. If there is no evidence that segregation is the result of racial prejudice, then why should racial separation be deemed harmful to Blacks (Simon, 1978)? Even if there has been official racial discrimination in the past, if there is little causal connection between that and present racial isolation, should such isolation be interpreted as injurious to Blacks? One might be able to construct a theory that adventitious segregation is more stigmatizing in a school district that previously practiced explicit discrimination (Goodman, 1972), but this strikes me as unsound (Goodman, 1972). Such reformulations of the remedial theory are bottomed either in notions of the corruption of the political process or of the affirmative value of integration for its own sake.

The weaknesses of the remedial theory are illustrated by the Supreme Court's decision in *Swann v. Charlotte-Mecklenburg Board of Education*.[4] In Charlotte-Mecklenburg there had been a long history of separation of the races in the public schools, but in 1965, the lower courts approved a plan based upon geographic zoning accompanied by a free transfer program. The school district had achieved a unitary school system, at least in terms of an official policy of nondiscrimination by race. Yet, in 1969, the matter was reopened because approximately two-thirds of the 21,000 Black students in the city of Charlotte attended schools which were 99% or more Black. Chief Justice Burger, in an enigmatic opinion that can be cited for virtually any proposition, emphasized that the court was laying down guidelines for lower courts and boards of education in remedying past discrimination: federal judicial power may be exercised "only on the basis of a constitutional violation," and "the nature of the violation determines the scope of the remedy."

While denying that racial balance in each school was required or desirable, the *Swann* court affirmed a wide-scale busing plan that largely accomplished that result. Why is this the appropriate remedy? What is the relationship between the old dual school system and present segregated residential patterns in Charlotte? Were the present policies tainted by racial prejudice? To what extent? If there were no present discrimination, how does integration for students attending Charlotte's schools today remedy injuries inflicted in the past upon their parents and grandparents? If the burden of disproving these propositions is placed on school boards, is this not tantamount to adopting a racial integration principle? Consider these remarks by Fiss (1971) on the *Swann* case:

> The net effect of *Charlotte-Mecklenburg* is to move school desegregation further along the continuum toward a result oriented approach. . . . [I]n retrospect, *Charlotte-Mecklenburg* will then be viewed . . . as a way station to the adoption of a general approach to school segregation which, by focusing on the segregated patterns themselves, is more responsive to the school segregation in the North.
>
> The forecast is based . . . on my view that the predominant concern of the Court in *Charlotte-Mecklenburg* is in fact the segregated pattern of student attendance, rather than the causal role played by past discriminatory practices. . . . The Court made no serious attempt either to determine or even speculate on the degree to which it contributes to present segregation. Nor did the Court

---

[4] *Swann v. Charlotte–Mecklenburg Board of Education*, 402 U.S. 1 (1971).

attempt to tailor the remedial order to the correction of that portion of the
segregation that might reasonably be attributable to past discrimination. The
Court moved from (a) the undisputed existence of past discrimination to (b) the
possibility or *likelihood* that the past discrimination played some *causal* role in
producing segregated patterns to (c) an order requiring the complete elimination
of those patterns. *The existence of past discrimination was thus used as a "trigger"—and not for a pistol, but for a cannon. Such a role cannot be defended
unless the primary concern of the Court is the segregated patterns themselves,
rather than the causal relation of past discrimination to them. The attention paid
to past discrimination can be viewed as an attempt by the Court to preserve the
continuity with* Brown *and to add a moral duality to its decision.* (pp. 704–705,
emphasis added)

Although the remedial approach preserves some continuity with *Brown*,
it has the effect of clouding the real issues. I believe that the elimination of
nearly all racial prejudice in American education policymaking—from school
site selection, faculty assignment, to student attendance boundaries—would
still leave substantial racial isolation in urban public schools, and that past
discrimination in public schools is a relatively small factor in present urban
segregation (Wolf, 1977). The essential problem is segregated housing
(Orfield, 1978), a problem attributable to wealth disparities between the races
(treated as groups), personal preferences, prejudice in the housing market,
and a host of other factors (Wolf, 1977). Thus, the present school segregation
situation is probably more a function of socioeconomic than racial tensions
(Graglia, 1976). Middle-class Whites do not want their children going to
school with poor Blacks: they fear physical violence, the decline of educational standards, and the lowering of achievement levels (pp. 266–270).
Whatever the merits of these perceptions, the question is simply not one of
the need to achieve racial balance to remedy past discrimination committed
by school authorities.

THE POLITICAL CORRUPTION THEORY

Dworkin (1977), wishing to avoid the causal relationship quagmire, justifies integration as a prophylactic device designed to overcome the high
probability that superficially race-neutral decisions that result in segregation
are the result of a corrupt process of government decisionmaking. The corruption flows from the interpretive judgment that Blacks have not made
such decisions for themselves and that racial prejudice remains rampant.
His view finds little support in judicial opinions. Perhaps the case that can
be most easily construed to support Dworkin is *Green v. County School
Board,*[5] the first Supreme Court opinion pointing toward an integration
rather than a nondiscrimination remedy.

[5] *Green v. New Kent County School Board*, 391 U.S. 430 (1968).

In *Green*, as in *Brown*, school authorities had explicitly assigned students to schools on the basis of their race. After these policies had been declared unconstitutional, the school board adopted (and the lower court approved) a so-called freedom of choice plan permitting Black and White parents to choose the schools that their children were to attend. Segregation was perpetuated, a result that was readily predictable when the plan was adopted. The schools remained racially identifiable in terms of faulty, staff, and student assignments. The Supreme Court held that, in the circumstances of the case, the plan was constitutionally insufficient to disestablish the dual school system. Interestingly enough, fairly drawn and compact neighborhood attendance zones for New Kent County's two schools would have led to substantial integration (Graglia, 1976). Only a fool would need to search the official records for evidence of racial prejudice under such circumstances. It seems obvious that public officials rejected more traditional geographic and perhaps other criteria for assigning pupils precisely because they believed that the freedom of choice approach would maintain segregation. This is an interpretive judgment, a characterization of behavior, not based upon proof of causation in the sense of objective evidence of a subjective intent to discriminate. Thus, in *Green* it is hardly hyperbolic to speak of the local board's decisions as being corrupted by racial prejudice. The freedom of choice plan would not have been adopted but for racial prejudice (Graglia, 1976), and the significance of racial prejudice in governmental decisionmaking itself constitutes a stigmatic harm to Blacks (Simon, 1978).

The difficulty with the corruption theory, even if one assumes that it accurately describes the pervasiveness of prejudice and the relative powerlessness of Blacks, lies in formulating the appropriate remedy. In *Green*, the court did not order the implementation of a neighborhood pupil assignment policy; rather, it dwelled on the idea of compelling school districts to adopt plans that promised to work—"working" apparently meaning that some substantial progress had to be made toward achieving a "unitary" school system, i.e., racial balance in the schools. The Court moved to an outcome remedy for a constitutional wrong rooted in the decisional process. Dworkin (1977), however, is prepared to defend such integration remedies even though he characterizes them as "arbitrary." Lest I misstate his argument, perhaps I should let him speak for himself:

> Suppose, however, that . . . prejudice has not lessened much and blacks do not have the kind of political power that would cancel any antecedent probability of corruption. What else would persuade us to disregard that probability in any particular case? Only one thing: the outcome. If the decision actually produced by the political process was of a sort itself to negate the change [*sic*] of corruption, then we could withdraw, for that case, the judgment that the process was too corrupt to allow it to continue.
>
> We must understand a court order to integrate, even an order based upon a mechanical formula that otherwise has no appeal, in the following way. The

order speaks to those in political power and says this: "If you refuse yourself to produce an outcome that negates the antecedent probability of corruption, then we must impose upon you such an outcome. The only decision that we can impose, given the nature of the problem, is a decision that requires integration on some formula that is evidently not corrupt even if it is just as evidently arbitrary."

If I am right, then objection to these decisions based on doubt about the various causal hypotheses I identified are misguided, because these decisions do not rest on causal hypotheses. They rest on interpretive theory. Until the background changes in one of the two ways I suggested—until our sense of prejudice abates or blacks have the political power to make decisions in question—until that happens, then integration is required as the only thing that can sustain the burden of proof rising from the antecedent probability of corruption. (p. 30)

What is baffling about Dworkin's theory is not its predicate but its conclusion. Although it is true that sometimes predominantly Black and integration-minded school boards have been charged with *de jure* segregation and held to a racial balance remedy, the notion that many school boards hide behind superficially neutral criteria, when they are actually influenced by racial prejudice, seems entirely plausible. If the observation is rephrased to argue that board members rarely assign a positive value to racial integration in making decisions, the observation is essentially irrefutable. There appears to be no rush to relieve overcrowding, to construct new schools and remodel old ones, or to determine neighborhood attendance zones or feeder patterns for junior and senior high schools in a manner likely to advance integration. But why should the failure to treat integration as a positive value injure Blacks? How is it stigmatizing? *Green* is far removed from this situation. There, the policies resulting in segregation would not have been adopted but for racial prejudice. Perhaps in such cases the "arbitrary" remedy of racial dispersion has some merit. It is a guarantee that racial prejudice is not at work, although it is also a guarantee that race will be taken into account. Even in these circumstances, however, the outcome remedy is not compelling. The harm could be undone by requiring school districts to adopt those racially neutral policies, such as the choice of school construction sites and the drawing of attendance zone boundaries that most advance racial integration. The corruption, and hence the stigma, could be relieved without mandating a race-conscious policy of racial balance as the remedy.

The more common fact pattern probably lies between the two extremes of failing to promote integration and of taking an action that would not have been taken but for racial prejudice. People and institutions act for many reasons and combinations of reasons, and racial prejudice may be only one factor (Simon, 1978):

An action that a court finds was in any significant way prompted by prejudice is definitionally insulting, and for this reason proof that the action was so prompted

> simultaneously establishes a dignitary harm. Whether the plaintiff should be granted relief with respect to other harms produced by such an action is a more complicated question. *The complication arises from the possibility that although racial prejudice did play some role, the governmental entity might have taken the same action even apart from prejudice.* (p. 1054)

If a neighborhood schools policy—resulting in segregation because of current residential patterns—would be the preferred policy, even if every trace of racial prejudice were magically eliminated, what justification is there for putting Black students in a "better" position than they would have occupied if there had been no racial prejudice (Simon, 1978)?

Dworkin assumes "that once an action is proven to have been affected—or even potentially affected—by racial prejudice, the question of whether the same action would have been taken apart from prejudice should be simply irrelevant" (p. 1059). But it is relevant to a remedy premised on the necessity of undoing the harm of racial prejudice. At best, plaintiffs should be entitled to the remedy of racial mixing to the extent that the other policy objectives are not impeded. Or school officials should be ordered to reconsider their other policies without reference to racial prejudice. The harm is the insult of taking racial prejudice into account, not the failure to achieve integration. What, then, is the justification for a court doing more, particularly if the evidence is sparse that segregation gives rise to significant cognitive and affective harms and if the policy choice is within the constitutional powers of the school board (pp. 1055–1059)?

THE GROUP PROTECTION THEORY

Dworkin, with this customary breadth of vision, attempted a tour de force in explaining and justifying modern desegregation decisions. He sought to vindicate a process interest through an outcome remedy, while declining to be taken in by a fragile instrumentalism. In this, he has not succeeded. All that is left is a theory based on the outcomes themselves; both constitutional wrong and remedy should be rooted in the failure to achieve integration. This theory is premised on the interpretive judgment that segregation itself is the evil and that integration is necessary to undo that evil (Yudof, 1973). Adherence to this theory is an extension of traditional equal protection analysis in race cases, an extension that a number of commentators (Brest, 1976; Simon, 1978) have found troubling. On the other hand, the theory does not rely on the instrumental premises of the remedial theory, such as the idea that segregated education impedes the achievement of Black youngsters (Fiss, 1965), but upon the interpretive judgment that affirmative values such as racial peace and equality between the races are not attainable so long as the races are physically separated in important private and public institutions (Yudof, 1973). In this sense, it is a judgment about history and about the government of society to which we should aspire. Separation—insularity—of Blacks has left them open to the full measure of White hostility (Yudof & Kirp, 1978). Integration of public schools is justified not because of prejudice against *individuals* but because of the need to protect a racial *group* against the historical forces that have isolated and hence oppressed it. Integration is part and parcel of the undoing of a caste system that consistently, over long periods of time, has disadvantaged Black Americans.

A group protection theory represents a wide departure from traditional legal concepts (Tribe, 1978, p. 993 n. 18). As Brest (1976) has noted:

[S]ome remedies for racial discrimination are triggered by disproportionate racial impact or treat persons according to membership in racial groups; but group membership is always a proxy for the individual's right not to be discriminated against. Similarly, remedies for race-specific harms recognize the sociological consequences of group identification and affiliation only to assure justice for individual members (p. 48)

Those who advocate the group protection theory, however, emphasize that the wrong becomes a group wrong once that group has occupied a position of subordination for an extended period of time (Fiss, 1976). Van Dyke (1975) perceives that such group rights fall at an "intermediate" level between the individual and the state" (p. 614). One difficulty is simply in squaring constitutional provisions, rooted in liberalism, with the group protection approach. Recall that the Fourteenth Amendment refers to citizens and persons, and not to particular groups (in contrast, for example, to a number of international human rights instruments) (Yudof, 1979). Even the Thirteenth Amendment, abolishing slavery, does not refer to any specific racial group. Another difficulty lies in the fact that most injuries occur to individuals—even though the racial group may function as a proxy for individuals (Brest, 1976). And if the group were injured, the natural remedy would lie in the direction of reestablishing the group and its culture (p. 52). The group protection theory, however, does not address the latter injury, and if it did, it might well lead to community-controlled Black schools rather than racial dispersion remedies (Bell, 1975, Gittell & Hevesi, 1969; Kirp, 1970).

I take it, then, that the group protection theory focuses less on the injury to the group than on a vision of what a just society would look like for individuals. In turn, this depends on one's evaluation of the permanency of the group and the prospect of integrating the group into a common society (Glazer, 1978):

If the state sets before itself the model that group membership is purely private, a shifting matter of personal choice and degree, something that may be weakened and dissolved in time as other identities take over, then to place an emphasis on group rights is to hamper this development, to change the course of the society, to make a statement to all its individuals and groups that people derive rights not only from a general citizenship but from another kind of citizenship within a group. . . .

If, on the other hand, the model a society has for itself, today and in the future, is that it is a confederation of groups, that group membership is central and permanent and that the divisions between groups are such that it is unrealistic to envisage these group identities weakening in time to be replaced by a common citizenship, then it must take the path of determining what the rights of each group shall be. (pp. 98–99)

The dangers, then, are two-fold. In some circumstances, an individual justice concept is simply naive, for it is silly to believe that deep-seated group conflicts can be resolved by resort to principles of equal individual opportunity (Kirp & Yudof, 1974b). The concept will not serve to ameliorate the conflict between Catholics and Protestants in Northern Ireland, Moslems and Christians in Lebanon, or perhaps Blacks and Whites in Rhodesia. On the other hand, explicit recognition of group rights runs the risk of making permanent those group conflicts, rendering social integration near impossible, and ignoring the individual's claim to justice. Group justice, in terms of social stability and other values, appears considerably less than ideal in operation in Belgium, Canada, Lebanon, India, and other nations which have embarked on a group protection course. The recognition of group rights has its own destructive tendencies, however pressing the needs that call for its adoption.

To some extent, group protection theory rests not only on vision but on facts or future facts: predictions about what America will be like under each of the competing principles. Are racial conflicts so deeply engrained that individual justice is a hopeless anachronism? Are Blacks a separate group, with their group identity outweighing their societal identity? Will they be so in the future? Even admitting a group protection principle, is racial dispersion consistent with that principle? And it is here that I perceive great dissensus in the United States (Wolff, 1978). In the present context, the Supreme Court has never explicitly adopted a group protection theory; for even justices sympathetic to such an approach tend to articulate their views in terms of a remedial theory. Perhaps the case that comes closest to adopting a group approach is *Keyes* v. *School District #1, Denver*.[6] *Keyes* was the first northern desegration case to reach the Supreme Court, and the majority, relying on a remedial theory similar to *Swann*, ordered the integration of the public schools of Denver. There are a number of interesting aspects of the case. The discrimination that allegedly occurred consisted of some relatively isolated events, nearly all of which fall into the category of purportedly racially neutral policies with segregative effects. Those

[6] *Keyes* v. *School District #1*, Denver, Colorado, 413 U.S. 189 (1973).

included the gerrymandering of attendance zones, the use of optional zones, the excessive use of mobile classrooms, and the construction of a new elementary school in the middle of one of the Black areas of Denver. Most of the evidence showed a pattern of failing to take action to alleviate segregation, rather than showing that the school system was pursuing an independent segregationist policy.

Denver never had set up or maintained a dual school system such as those so prevalent in the pre-*Brown* South and border states (Graglia, 1976). Perhaps the *Keyes* court concluded that the cumulative circumstances indicated that racial prejudice was a factor in the board's policy decisions. If so, this conclusion is questionable since the board then in power had passed three resolutions which sought "to desegregate the [predominantly Black] schools in the Park Hill area. . . . " (p. 168–169). Thus, corruption by racial prejudice could only have entered the picture when the electorate replaced the board majority that had adopted these resolutions and "the resolutions were rescinded [by the board] and replaced with a voluntary student transfer program"[7] that showed little promise of integrating the public schools of Denver. Yet, the court did not rely on the rescission of the earlier resolution and it is doubtful that it would have supported a systemwide racial balance remedy in any event.

The district court, which had based its findings of *de jure* segregation in the Park Hill area on the fact of the rescission, refused to hold that the substantial segregation in the core of Denver had been brought about by deliberate policies of segregation. The Supreme Court, nonetheless, held that there was a presumption that unlawful segregation in one portion of the district had a significant impact on other parts of the district, and that proof of unlawful segregative intent with respect to some acts created a presumption that other acts, perhaps unexceptionable in another context, were also motivated by some illicit, racially discriminatory motive. This, again, sounds like the corruption theory. The difficulty with the formula, apart from questions about its reliance on a finding of past *de jure* conduct (Graglia, 1976), is that the segregation in the core area preceded the allegedly unlawful acts in Park Hill, and therefore could not possibly have been caused by it (p. 182).

Despite the language of the opinion, *Keyes* can best be explained on the theory that school districts have an affirmative duty to integrate. Justices Douglas and Powell said as much in separate opinions. There simply was no competent proof of widespread discrimination in the record, unless the definition of discrimination is expanded to include all actions or failures to act that promote or reinforce existing segregated patterns. There certainly was little evidence connecting specific wrongful acts to the degree of segregation existing in Denver. The court simply speculated on these points,

[7] 303 F. Supp. 279, 287 (1970).

failed to rely on a significant body of research, and conveniently allocated the burden of persuasion to the alleged wrongdoer, the school district. Further, the court made no real effort to match the remedy with the wrong. It did not ask what the racial composition of Denver's schools would have been had the discriminatory acts not been committed. It did not adopt a remedy that would undo only that increment of segregation caused by the discriminatory acts. Without relying on any social science evidence, without articulating, elaborating, or defending a corruption or group protection theory, and without any real admission that it was going beyond *Brown*, the court implied that the equal protection clause of the Fourteenth Amendment mandates integration of the races in the public schools (Kirp & Yudof, 1974a).

Lower courts apparently had some difficulty interpreting the command of *Keyes*, some emphasizing what the Supreme Court had said and others emphasizing what it had done. The result was that vastly different standards for determining the existence of and the appropriate remedies for *de jure* segregation were applied by different federal judges in different parts of the country, though the trend was toward systemwide integration. Over the dissents of Justices White and Powell, the Supreme Court simply ignored this phenomenon by denying petitions for writs of certiorari in cases raising questions about these inconsistencies.[8]

DEVELOPMENTS SINCE *KEYES*: THE RETURN OF THE NONDISCRIMINATION PRINCIPLE?

The *Keyes* decision marked the high water point for racial balance remedies, whatever the theory to justify those remedies. Since *Keyes*, the court has declined to order a metropolitan remedy in Detroit,[9] placed limits on the duration of desegregation decrees (even if resegregation occurs due to demographic changes),[10] and given indications that it is returning to a non-discrimination approach.[11] The evidence does not point all in one direction[12] but the preliminary signs are there. *Dayton Board of Education v.*

[8] *Medley* v. *School Board*, 482 F. 2d 1061 (1973), *cert. denied*, 414 U.S. 1172 (1974) (White, J., and Powell, J., dissenting); *Goss* v. *Board of Education*, 482 F.2d 1044 (1973), *cert. denied*, 414 U.S. 1171 (1974) (White, J., and Powell, J., dissenting).

[9] *Milliken* v. *Bradley*, 418 U.S. 717 (1974).

[10] *Pasadena City Board of Education* v. *Spangler*, 427 U.S. 424 (1976).

[11] *Austin Independent School District* v. *United States*, 429 U.S. 990 (1976) (Powell, J., concurring); *Dayton Board of Education* v. *Brinkman*, 433 U.S. 406 (1977); *Brennan* v. *Armstrong*, 433 U.S. 672 (1977). Recently, the Supreme Court agreed to review desegregation cases arising from Columbus and Dayton, Ohio. *Dayton Board of Education* v. *Brinkman*, 47 *Law Week* 3463 (1979); *Columbus Board of Education* v. *Penick*, 47 *Law Week* 3463 (1979).

[12] *Evans* v. *Buchanan*, 434 U.S. 880 (1977).

Brinkman,[13] decided in 1977, indicates both the new direction of the court and the ambiguities surrounding it. *Brinkman* was decided by a unanimous court. (Justice Marshall did not participate.) Justice Rehnquist, an advocate of the basic nondiscrimination formula, wrote an opinion which managed to attract the votes of all the participating justices. Given the differences among the justices articulated in earlier cases, Justice Rehnquist's ability to muster a unanimous court is something of a tour de force. As is so often the case, however, such miracles are often a function of a patchwork of unintelligibility.

In *Brinkman*, the district court found only isolated instances of intentional discrimination by the Dayton school authorities. These consisted of some faculty segregation, the establishment of an all-Black central high school, and some evidence that a few of many optional attendance zones had the effect of increasing segregation in high schools. Beyond this, the facts were remarkably similar to *Keyes*. The district court found that the majority of Dayton schools were racially imbalanced, that neighborhoods were segregated in Dayton, and that the school board had failed to take affirmative action to alter attendance zones or otherwise act to alleviate the segregation. Further, a previous board of education has adopted resolutions "stating that it recognized its own fault in not taking affirmative action" to reduce segregation in Dayton. This resolution was repudiated by a subsequent board. The district court then concluded that the racially imbalanced schools, optional attendance zones, and recent Board action . . . are cumulatively in violation of the Equal Protection Clause." The judge ordered the elimination of optional attendance zones, the selection of new students for the high schools by a random process, and the racial balance of classified personnel in each of the system's schools. Unlike the district court order in *Keyes*, the order in *Brinkman* did not require systemwide reassignment of students.

After a series of reversals by the Court of Appeals for the Sixth Circuit, culminating in a 1976 direction to "adopt a systemwide plan for the 1976–1977 school year,"[14] the district court finally entered a systemwide racial balance remedy requiring

> that the racial distribution of each school in the district be brought within 15% of
> the 48%–52% black–white population ratio of Dayton. As finally formulated, the
> plan employed a variety of desegregation techniques, including the "pairing" of
> schools, the redefinition of attendance zones, and a variety of centralized pro-
> grams and "magnet-schools."[15]

The Supreme Court unanimously vacated and remanded the decision of the

[13] 433 U.S. 406 (1977).
[14] *Brinkman* v. *Gilligan*, 503 F.2d 684 (1974), 518 F.2d 853 (1975).
[15] *Dayton Board of Education* v. *Brinkman*, 433 U.S. at 408–409 (1977).

appellate court affirming the district court's plan. Read most narrowly, the opinion is addressed only to the issue of the proper role of appellate courts in reviewing decisions of federal district courts: the court of appeals erred in reversing the district court's original determination of the appropriate remedy without specifically declaring that the lower court had made erroneous findings of fact or had reached improper legal conclusions:

> On appeal, the task of a court of appeals is defined with relative clarity; it is confined by law and precedent, just as are those of the district courts and of this Court. If it concludes that the findings of the district court are clearly erroneous, it may reverse them under Fed. Rule Civ. Proc. 52(a). If it decides that the district court has misapprehended the law, it may accept the court's findings of fact but reverse its judgment because of legal error. Here, however, as we conceive the situation, the Court of Appeals did neither. It was vaguely dissatisfied with the limited character of the remedy which the district court had afforded plaintiffs, and proceeded to institute a far more sweeping one of its own, without in any way upsetting the district court's findings of fact or reversing its conclusions of law.[16]

This mode of analysis is extremely misleading, although no more misleading than past discussions of the equitable remedial powers of trial courts. Once again, the court has sought refuge in notions of process, trying to paper over fundamental divisions over appropriate equal protection principles. On a record virtually indistinguishable from *Keyes*, the *Brinkman* trial judge had declined to mandate racial dispersion as the necessary remedy, refusing to do precisely what the Supreme Court had ordered in *Swann* and *Keyes*. The court of appeals was saying, in effect, that the lower court had reached the wrong legal conclusion.

The Supreme Court, adhering to the principles recently enunciated in the Detroit metropolitan desegregation suit, questioned whether a system-wide remedy was commensurate with the alleged constitutional violations. In its view, resolution of this issue would require new findings with regard to other possible violations apparently not in the record, suggesting that the trial court, if necessary, could and perhaps should hold hearings to supplement the record. The net result was to invite the district court to make additional factual findings to support its remedy. By hiding behind this procedural facade, the justices may have insured that virtually indistinguishable forms of school segregation would result in different remedies at the discretion of trial judges, but avoided having to choose between competing principles of racial justice.

Beyond the narrow holding of *Brinkman*, the case is filled with dicta indicating a shift toward a more limited remedial standard. Whether the "swing" justices are in agreement with the dicta is not clear since only two of them wrote concurring opinions. Justice Rehnquist, for the court,

---

[16] *Dayton Board of Education* v. *Brinkman*, 433 U.S. at 417–418 (1977).

stressed the isolated nature of the instances of intentional discrimination. Clearly the mere existence of racial isolation cannot justify a systemwide racial balance remedy:

> [T]he Court of Appeals simply had no warrant in our cases for imposing the systemwide remedy which it apparently did. There had been no showing that such a remedy was necessary to "eliminate all vestiges of the state-imposed school segregation." It is clear from the findings of the District Court that Dayton is a racially mixed community, and that many of its schools are predominantly white or predominantly black. This fact without more, of course, does not offend the Constitution.[17]

Rehnquist accused the court of appeals of applying a "sort of 'fruit of the poisonous tree'" doctrine, only speculatively tying the three segregative acts found by the district court to the broad racial imbalance that exists in the Dayton schools. Yet such apparently tenuous connections were accepted by the courts in *Keyes* and *Swann*. If a majority of the justices agree with the *Brinkman* dicta, *Keyes* and *Swann* have been effectively overruled.

CONCLUSION

The unwillingness of both the Burger and Warren courts to confront openly the essential and unavoidable choice among the remedial, corruption, and group protection principles for resolving the school segregation cases has led to a variety of consequences, none of them good. By failing to be forthright, the court has compromised its integrity and capacity for moral leadership. There has also been a tremendous loss of certainty in the law, as the Burger and Warren courts dangle the same nondiscrimination and remedial principles to reach inconsistent results. The lack of predictability about a particular outcome imposes severe transaction costs as lower courts and school districts scramble to comprehend what they are required to do. And the existence of doubt leaves lower courts free to go their own way in factually indistinguishable cases.

Enormous damage has also been done to the cause of those who would opt for the group protection or corruption principles in lieu of remedial theories which simply will not suffice to support racial balance outcomes. It is as if the court, and many seriously misled commentators, are afraid to broach their principle to the public for fear of the adverse consequences that would follow. A principle which is not cogently articulated and elaborated in a reasoned fashion, but tucked away in the nuances of an opinion, reinforces the notion that the principle is not defensible at all. This permits those who disagree with the results of earlier cases moving the nation closer

---

[17] *Dayton Board of Education* v. *Brinkman*, 433 U.S. at 417 (1977).

to integration to rely on the precise language of the earlier opinions to reach contrary results.

Optimally, the court should be engaged in a dialogue with the various branches of government and the American people (Tribe, 1978, p. 13) about the meaning of racial justice in the public schools and the most appropriate means to achieve a shared goal of racial justice. The court's lack of candor in desegregation cases makes such a dialogue all but impossible. What should be a serious effort to identify and discuss values and aspirations in the language and traditions of the Constitution has deteriorated into a word game, with the opposing sides invoking the litany which best supports their position. Busing becomes the catchword when it is not the central issue. Class conflicts are enveloped in the language of race conflicts. Desegregation comes to mean integration. The phrase *unitary school districts* refers to districts in which each school is racially balanced. Discretion in fashioning remedies becomes a facade for indecision. Clarity and reason have given way to a debasement of language, and for much of this the Supreme Court must assume responsibility. Only a willingness to articulate and confront the alternative visions of racial justice will yield defensible desegregation decisions in the future.

REFERENCES

Bell, D. Waiting on the promise of *Brown*. *Law and Contemporary Problems*, 1975, *39*, 341–373.

Bickel, A. *The least dangerous branch: The Supreme Court at the bar of politics*. New York: Bobbs-Merrill, 1962.

Black, C. The lawfulness of the segregation decisions. *Yale Law Journal*, 1960, *69*, 421–430.

Brest, P. *Palmer* v. *Thompson*: An approach to the problem of unconstitutional legislative motive. *The Supreme Court Review*, 1971, 95–146.

Brest, P. Foreword. In defense of the antidiscrimination principle. *Harvard Law Review*, 1976, *90*, 1–54.

Chayes, A. The role of the judge in public law litigation. *Harvard Law Review*, 1976, *89*, 1281–1316.

Cohen, D., & Weiss, J. Social science and social policy: Schools and race. In R. C. Rist & R. J. Anson (Eds.), *Education, social science, and the judicial process*. New York: Teachers College Press, 1977.

Dimond, P. School segregation in the north: There is but one constitution. *Harvard Civil Rights–Civil Liberties Law Review*, 1972, *7*, 1–55.

Dunn, J. R. Title VI, the guidelines and school desegregation in the south. *Virginia Law Review*, 1967, *53*, 42–88.

Dworkin, R. Social sciences and constitutional rights—The consequences of uncertainty. In R. C. Rist & R. J. Anson (Eds.), *Education, social science, and the judicial process*. New York: Teachers College Press, 1977.

Ely, J. H. Legislative and administrative motivation in constitutional law. *Yale Law Journal*, 1970, *79*, 1205–1341.

Farley, R. Residential segregation and its implications for school integration. *Law and Contemporary Problems*, 1975, *39*, 164–193.

Feagin, J. R., & Feagin, C. B. *Discrimination American style: Institutional racism and sexism.* Englewood Cliffs, N.J.: Prentice-Hall, 1978.

Fiss, O. Racial imbalance in the public schools: The constitutional concepts. *Harvard Law Review,* 1965, *78,* 564–617.

Fiss, O. The *Charlotte–Mecklenburg* case: Its significance for northern school desegregation. *University of Chicago Law Review,* 1971, *38,* 697–709.

Fiss, O. Groups and the equal protection clause. *Philosophy & Public Affairs,* 1976, *5,* 107–177.

Gittell, M., & Hevesi, A. *The politics of urban education.* New York: Praeger, 1969.

Glazer, N. Individual rights against group rights. In E. Kamenka & A. Erh-Soon Tay (Eds.), *Human Rights.* London: Edward Arnold, 1978.

Goodman, F. De facto school segregation: A constitutional analysis. *California Law Review,* 1972, *60,* 275–437.

Graglia, L. *Disaster by decree: The Supreme Court decisions on race and the schools.* Ithaca, N.Y.: Cornell University Press, 1976.

Kirp, D. L. Community control, public policy, and the limits of law. *Michigan Law Review,* 1970, *68,* 1355–1388.

Kirp, D. L., & Yudof, M. G. *Educational policy and the law.* Berkeley: McCutchan, 1974. (a)

Kirp, D. L., & Yudof, M. G. *DeFunis* and beyond. *Change,* 1974, *6,* 22–26. (b)

Kluger, R. *Simple justice.* New York: Vintage, 1977.

Lawrence, C. Segregation "misunderstood": The *Milliken* decision revisited. *University of San Francisco Law Review,* 1977, *12,* 15–56.

Orfield, G. *Must we bus? Segregated schools and national policy.* Washington: The Brookings Institute, 1978.

Pettigrew, T. F. Attitudes on race and housing: A social-psychological view. In W. Hawley & V. Rock (Eds.), *Segregation in Residential Areas,* Washington, D.C.: National Academy of Science, 1973.

St. John, N. H. *School desegregation: Outcomes for children.* New York: Wiley, 1975.

Simon, L. G. Racially prejudiced governmental actions: A motivation theory of the constitutional ban against racial discrimination. *San Diego Law Review,* 1978, *15,* 1041–1130.

Stephan, W. G. School desegregation: An evaluation of predictions made in *Brown v. Board of Education. Psychological Bulletin,* 1978, *85,* 217–238.

Tribe, L. *American constitutional law.* Mineola, N.Y.: Foundation, 1978.

Van Dyke, V. Justice as fairness: For groups? *American Political Science Review,* 1975, *69,* 607–614.

Weinberg, M. *Minority students: A research appraisal.* Washington: National Institute of Education, U.S. Government Printing Office, 1977.

Wilkinson, J. H. *Serving justice.* New York: Charterhouse, 1974.

Wolf, E. P. Northern school desegregation and residential choice, *The Supreme Court Review,* 1977, 63–85.

Wolff, R. P. The concept of social injustice. In F. R. Dallmayr (Ed.), *From contract to community: Political theory at the crossroads.* New York: Marcel Dekker, 1978.

Woodward, C. V. *The strange career of Jim Crow.* New York: Oxford University Press, 1974.

Yudof, M. G. Equal educational opportunity and the courts. *Texas Law Review,* 1973, *51,* 411–504.

Yudof, M. G. Suspension and the expulsion of black students from the public schools: Academic capital punishment and the Constitution. *Law and Contemporary Problems,* 1975, *39,* 374–411.

Yudof, M. G. *International human rights and school desegregation in the United States.* Unpublished manuscript, UNESCO, 1979.

Yudof, M. G. & Kirp, D. L. *Paternalism and gender policy.* Unpublished manuscript, 1978.

6

On the Future of School Desegregation

A NEW AMERICAN DILEMMA?

RAY C. RIST

If interpreting history is fraught with difficulties, ambiguities, and subject to multiple interpretation, how much more likely are probes into the future like looking into a prism. Yet in the context of the twenty-fifth anniversary of the *Brown*[1] decision, it is important to assess not only what progress has been made toward racial equality but to look forward down the paths we are taking.

What makes this effort of particular import is the widespread notion among White Americans that the issue of Black advancement is now self-sustaining and needs no further assistance. Indeed, there are many in America who see the matter of racial equality in general and school desegregation in particular as passé. The view is that the nation's debt to Black Americans has been paid, and with interest. At the extreme, one hears of "reverse discrimination," and that "Whites have rights, too." It seems that many Whites believe that few, if any, institutional inequalities still exist between Blacks and Whites and that the inequalities that do exist can be attributed to motivation, personal character, or even genetic differences.

From the perspective of Black Americans, the 1970s must appear as a time of retrenchment, of a lack of momentum, and even of the loss of some of the hard-won gains from the 1960s. Be it the fracturing of the black/labor/liberal coalition, the findings in the *Bakke*[2] case, or the rulings

[1] *Brown* v. *Topeka Board of Education*, 347 U. S. 483 (1954).
[2] *University of California Regents* v. *Bakke*, 98 S. Ct. 2733 (1978).

RAY C. RIST • Youthwork National Policy Study, College of Human Ecology, Cornell University, Ithaca, New York 14853.

of federal judges that the Department of Health, Education, and Welfare has been guilty of intentional nonenforcement of the Civil Rights Act of 1964, the message has to be coming through that a White blacklash and a retreat from the civil rights convictions of the 1960s are in full swing. If the vision of those earlier years was, "We Shall Overcome," the present challenge could perhaps be characterized as "we shall hold our own."

AN AMERICAN DILEMMA

Thirty-five years have elapsed since the Carnegie Corporation commissioned Gunnar Myrdal, the Swedish social scientist, to investigate and record the conditions of the Black minority in America. His monumental book, *An American Dilemma: The Negro Problem and American Democracy* (1944), still stands as a benchmark for assessing progress toward racial equality and the fulfillment of the American creed. What makes Myrdal's book central to any discussion of American race relations is that he not only identified but brought into full relief the gap between the creed of equality and the fact of racial inequality. He chronicled the schism between our words and our deeds.

So indefensible was this contradiction, Myrdal noted, that it constituted an inherent flaw in the fabric of American democracy. It was a flaw Myrdal contended would become evermore intolerable to White Americans and thus lead inevitably to improvement in the lot of Black people. The movement toward equality was inexorable so long as the American creed retained its legitimacy. The driving wheel of change would be the moral conscience of White America.

Myrdal's analysis was little less than visionary. The period of 1938–1942, when Myrdal conducted his study is, on one scale, a mere 420 months ago, but on another it is light years ago.

Something of that time is captured by Newman, Amidei, Carter, Kruvant, Day, and Russell (1978) in their description of the early 1940s:

> Three out of four black Americans still lived in the South, but North or South, virtually the only jobs open to them were the most menial; over half of all black workers were employed in agriculture or personal service. How much education a black man or woman might have meant little; skilled jobs involving contact with white workers were simply not available. Such jobs as blacks could get paid scarcely human wages: long days at stoop labor sometimes brought $3.00 or less a week, sunup to sundown; domestic work little more. Black children went to schools that were open fewer days each year (to free them up for field word during picking seasons), and black adults could still expect to be beaten or fired from their jobs for attempting to register to vote. Ordinary life was conditioned by discrimination: separate parks, separate water fountains, separate sections of the bus or train. One wartime munitions factory in St. Louis went so far as to

build a separate factory for black workers; elsewhere, places that did hire black
secretaries or clerks hid them behind partitions.

"No colored need . apply." "Whites only." "Negroes served in back."
America had its own version of apartheid in those days. In the South the signs
were everywhere and a matter of law; in the North they were not common except
in want ads, and a matter of custom rather than law, but the effect was similar.
Black and white everywhere shared the same geographical space while living in
different worlds. Black accident victims would bleed to death before white hospitals would treat them. White restaurants would serve German prisoners-of-war
inside, while black American soldiers were made to stay, unfed, outside. . . . To
be black was tantamount to being marked for victimization. It is little wonder
that black people were often disabled, more often sick, more often dead in what
should have been the prime of life.

While Newman *et al.*'s book, with the advantage of hindsight, contends
that it was not White guilt but Black protest that provided the main catalyst
for change, there can be no dispute but that the United States has made great
strides toward an egalitarian society. Constitutionally, Blacks have voting
rights and equal access to public accommodations; discrimination in housing, employment, and education are all illegal. *Indeed, the entire, elaborate
panoply of legalized discrimination has been swept away.* This, perhaps
more than any other facet of the comparison between the America of
Myrdal's time and our own, is most profound.[3] At the very core of this
transformation in the legal basis to American race relations stands the
Brown v. *Board of Education* decision.

The impact of the *Brown* decision has been far wider than simply
school desegregation. Indeed, shortly after this decree, federal courts at all
levels were citing *Brown* in cases challenging official segregation. Against
segregated beaches in Baltimore, golf courses in Atlanta, and public housing
in Michigan and Missouri, *Brown* was cited to show that state-sanctioned
segregation had to be wiped out from the laws.[4] Kluger (1976, p.749) suggests how the *Brown* decision effected Black Americans:

Every colored American knew that *Brown* did not mean he would be invited to
lunch with the Rotary the following week. It meant something more basic and
more important. It meant that black rights had suddenly been redefined; black
bodies has suddenly been reborn under a new law. Blacks' value as human beings
had been changed overnight by the declaration of the nation's highest court. At a
stroke, the Justices had severed the remaining cords of *de facto* slavery. The
Negro could no longer be fastened with the status of official pariah.

---

[3] For a recent and remarkable study of the manner in which American laws have in the past
served to support and harden the racist attitudes of White Americans, cf. Higginbotham,
1978.

[4] This is not to suggest that in the years preceding *Brown* there was not an active effort to build
a legal challenge to *de jure* segregation. Indeed, the 1938 *Gaines* decision, the *Smith* v. *All-
wright* in 1944, and the 1946 *Morgan* decisions were but several of the suits used as part of a
building frontal attack on *Plessy*.

If the status as "official pariah" was suddenly eradicated, the status of Black Americans as social pariahs was more slowly and grudgingly removed. Indeed, the process continues yet today. Nevertheless, the fact that the legal system in the United States sought to root out all forms of sanctioned racial segregation has to stand as one of history's great and positive forms of societal exorcism.

Although *Brown* and following decisions, in and of themselves, did not resolve all the contradictions Myrdal described in his book, they did go far to set the nation on a new course. The Supreme Court proclaimed to the nation that the enforced separation of human beings by race was neither God's will nor the purpose of the Constitution, as amended after the Civil War. In plain language, the courts told the American people that segregation was wrong and they had now to find ways to eliminate it.

A NEW AMERICAN DILEMMA

Much has been done to alter the legally enforced segregation and degradation of Black Americans at the core of the American dilemma Myrdal described. The ends have been defined; what remains is the working out of the means. Indeed, this process of finding the means to eliminate racial segregation has created a new chapter in American race relations. It is, as it were, a new American dilemma, manifesting itself in such areas as housing, employment, and education.

Orfield (1978), notes that American opinion is bifurcated between the desire for school integration and a simultaneous resistance to implementing it. He states:

> It is hard to find a political leader who opposes integrated education and equally hard to find one who supports busing. Polls of white people across the country show strong support for educating black and white children in the same schools but strong opposition to the technique used to bring them together. Though the courts have found no other way to end unconstitutional segregation in the big cities, the public is not convinced and does not want to make a decision between segregation and busing.
>
> . . . If the federal courts are right and the choice between busing and segregated education is often unavoidable, one can only interpret the political rhetoric and public opinion polls in two ways. Either the consistently expressed preference for integration is meaningless and cynical or it represents genuine misunderstanding of what the courts have chosen and what the consequences of their decisions have been. (p. 102)

If it is true that White America wants a segregated and unequal society while it mouths platitudes of equality and integration, then our future is bleak. It will ligitimize the findings of the National Advisory Commission on Civil Disorders (1968), better known as the Kerner Commission, which stated "This is our basic conclusion: Our nation is moving towards two societies, one black, one white—separate and unequal. . . . Discrimination and segregation have long permeated much of American life; they now threaten the future of every American (p. 1). Although it is one thing to know these trends exist and persist, it is quite another to confirm these disparities and caste-like conditions as the vision for the future of the country.

If, on the other hand, the present political rhetoric and public opinion are manifestations of "genuine misunderstanding," then a different vision is possible. If the present dilemma is based on misinformation or errant interpretation (rather than on a racism so ingrained that the American creed will be mortgaged to sustain it), then perhaps we are not headed for the reincarnation of *Plessy* v. *Ferguson*.[5] The positive alternative is the continual affirmation of the ideals of "a nation conceived in liberty":

> Of the ideals that animated the American nation at its beginning, none was more radiant or honored than the inherent equality of mankind. There was dignity in all human flesh, Americans proclaimed, and all must have its chance to strive and to excel. All men were to be protected alike from the threat of rapacious neighbors and from the prying or coercive state. If it is a sin to aspire to conduct of a higher order than one may at the moment be capable of, then Americans surely sinned in profession that all men are created equal—and then acting otherwise. (Kluger, 1976, p. ix)

There is no denying the depth of racism in America or just how pervasive has been its influence on our national history. The biography of American society is permeated with a deep and abiding antipathy toward its Black citizens. Further, the present goal of White America seems to be one of how to right past wrongs without paying the price.[6] Yet there has been change. The legal sanctions undergirding segregation have been cast off, and there has prevailed within the Black community such determination, courage, and conviction not to submit to a racist society that the potential for a society much different from that suggested by *Plessy* is possible to foresee.

SORTING OUT THE ISSUES

In a world full of complexities, paradoxes, and absurdities, it is foolhardy and arrogant to make unequivocal statements. The interpretations

---

[5] *Plessy* v. *Ferguson*, 163 U. S. 537 (1896).

[6] The matter of not wishing to "pay the price" for social change may have its origins in the vested self-interests of White Americans. It is not so much that White people are unknowing of the suffering of Black people but that they do not want the redress of these sufferings to be done in a manner that would affect their own circumstances or those of their children and neighborhood. Consequently, the price of school desegregation impinges too directly on the self-interests of White America and they choose simply not to pay.

available on the multiple dimensions of school integration are uncounted. Nevertheless, some aspects of this process have begun to clarify themselves, and if clarity can replace misunderstanding, we can count it our gain (cf. Rist, 1978b).

What The Issue Is Not

1. The issue is not that there is a difference in the form or content of school segregation between the North and the South. The argument is frequently made, however, that while the South perpetuated *de jure* segregation, segregation in the North has been the result of private, *de facto* choices made by individuals. By implication, a constitutional mandate would eliminate publicly sanctioned and supported segregation found typically in the South, whereas no such mandate exists vis-à-vis the kind of segregation found in the North. It would appear that legal efforts to eradicate segregation end at the Mason–Dixon line.

The reality is that every standing court order related to school desegregation has been based on findings of *de jure* segregation whether in the North or the South.[7] In each instance, the courts have found that local school districts, and occasionally state educational agencies as well, have systematically carried out policies leading to or reinforcing racial segregation. The stance of the courts, embodied in a massive number of litigations since *Brown*, consistently maintains that there is no essential difference in the reasons for ordering systemwide desegregation in either northern or southern school districts.

2. The issue is not one of rejecting the principle of school desegregation. Indeed, most Americans say they believe in school desegregation. Orfield (1978) has written:

> Increasing support for integrated schools has been a clear pattern in successive studies of public opinion over the decades. Three decades of surveys by the National Opinion Research Center showed remarkable growth of a consensus supporting integrated schools between 1942 and 1970. (p. 108)

What makes this growing support of White Americans for school desegregation both remarkable and concrete is to place it in the context of the day-to-day realities of interracial schooling. Table I, compiled by Orfield from numerous data sources, documents the expressed tolerance of White parents for school desegregation according to the proportion of Black students. Southern and northern attitudes alike have steadily moderated. In 1975, 76% of northern and 62% of southern White parents had no objection

---

[7] It should be noted that when reference is made to *de jure* segregation, such segregation is not only the product of federal and state law, but also is the result of segregation brought about by public officials through, e.g., administrative regulations, formal memoranda from school boards, and complicity with other governmental agencies to sustain racial segregation.

Table I. Percentage of White Parents Objecting to Integrated
Education by Proportion of Black Students, Selected Years,
1959–1975

School level of Black enrollment	1959	1963	1965	1966	1969	1970	1973	1975
South								
Few	72	61	37	24	21	16	16	15
Half	83	78	68	49	46	43	36	38
Majority	86	86	78	62	64	69	69	61
North								
Few	7	10	7	6	7	6	6	3
Half	34	33	28	32	28	24	23	24
Majority	58	53	52	60	54	51	63	47

SOURCE: Orfield, 1978, p. 109.

to sending their children to schools where Black students constituted half the student body.

3. The issue is not "busing" *per se*. Of the nearly 42 million children in public elementary and secondary schools, more than 50% (21.8 million) of the students ride buses each day to school. Of all children who do ride buses, the National Institute of Education (1976, p. 4) suggests only 7% are bused for reasons related to school desegregation.

Busing is portrayed as an educational disaster, not helping minority children but harming middle-class children, creating conflict situations where none previously existed, increasing educational costs, and jeopardizing the health and safety of children. Yet, the evidence is clear that busing does not generate these anticipated outcomes.

Once the prejudicial assumptions regarding busing are set aside, it becomes apparent that the national furor over busing has little relation to either the available social science data or to the information gathered from hundreds of school districts where busing plans have been implemented. Surveys such as the 1973 study by the National Opinion Research Center of 555 recently desegregated southern school districts reported there was "no evidence that busing per se has any negative consequences" (Vol. 2, p. 118). The busing controversy seems to exist in spite of the information presently available. But if our general assessment of the new American dilemma is correct, it is predictable that busing has come to symbolize White resistance to actively pursuing school desegregation.

4. The issue is not that school desegregation hinders academic achievement for either minority or White children (cf. Stephan, 1978; pp. 228–232). On this point, there is near unanimity of opinion among researchers. As St. John (1975, p. 35) has noted:

> The longitudinal data from desegregating school systems . . . indicate *in every*
> *case* that racial mixture in the schools had no negative consequences for majority
> group pupils. In busing experiments in which selected central city children are
> transported to outlying communities the universal report also is no significant
> difference in achievement between children that do or do not receive bused
> pupils. (emphasis added)

St. John also notes several studies (pp. 157–162) of school desegregation
where White students make clear gains on academic achievement test
scores.

As for minority pupils experiencing school desegregation, the most
recent data comes from a 1977 Crain and Mahard (1978) survey of 73 studies
of the effect of desegregation on Black achievement. A majority of the studies
conclude that desegregation has a positive effect on Black achievement test
scores. Indeed, that impact is more likely to occur if desegregation begins in
the earliest grades, and effects are especially likely to be positive for first
graders.

5. Finally, there is the misperception that school desegregation is a
violent, disruptive process that emperils the safety of children and deeply
disrupts the social fabric of communities. The reality is that school
desegregation can and most frequently does go smoothly. From 1968 to
1971, hundreds of school districts in the South underwent court-ordered
school desegregation, and little was heard about them. Likewise in the
North, Wichita, Las Vegas, Stockton, Providence, Waukegan, Berkeley,
Riverside, Portland, Racine, Minneapolis, Ann Arbor, and many other
cities have desegregated their schools, mostly on a voluntary basis, and little
has been heard. A recent Justice Department report (1976) suggests that
school desegregation seldom produces increased school violence and that,
contrary to expectations, the desegregation process can even lower the level
of violence in a school system when it is specifically addressed as part of the
plan.

Orfield (1978, p. 127) summarizes:

> Although school violence is a serious national problem, there is little evidence to
> show either that desegregation causes it or that reverse busing puts white
> students in physical danger. Perhaps the national concern about violence, rein-
> forced by 1975 Senate hearings and white parents' fears of ghetto conditions
> after the riots of the 1960s, help explain an apprehension that does not appear to
> be related to the desegregation experience. There is no evidence to show that bus-
> ing plans are impractical because of physical danger to students in their new
> schools.

What the Issue Is

The overlappings and interdependencies among the various dimensions
of school desegregation are extensive. To isolate them and treat them indi-

vidually is a slight distortion of their reality, but it also does offer a means of focusing on the components as opposed to the college.

1. The issue is the apparent randomness of school desegregation efforts, leading some to believe that they have been unfairly singled out for attention by the courts or by the federal government. Litigation in school desegregation has been carried out case by case, city by city, with some cities confronting no litigation while others are in court or under court order for implementing desegregation plans. This checkerboard effect suggests a randomness to the process which is partially true, given that court-ordered school desegregation cannot occur in multiple municipalities at once under something akin to a class action suit. Such might have been possible in the early years of enforcement of civil rights legislation, when both the Justice Department and the Department of Health, Education, and Welfare were involved, but is now surely a thing of the past.

This matter of "fairness" raises the question of distributive justice. If the resolution of school desegregation in one city is, in fact (or even perceived to be), vastly different from that in another, doubts as to the equity, uniformity, and necessity of different remedies can be raised. If Atlanta is allowed to retain several all-Black schools, why must Boston eliminate each and every one? If the desegregation plan in Louisville leaves intact already integrated schools, why must those schools in Detroit be disrupted?

The moral force of the law exists only so long as its subjects believe they have been justly treated. When they do not, the willingness to comply diminishes. The sporadic nature of the desegregation process, coupled with the difficulty in comprehending the legal system, creates severe problems of credibility for the courts who order desegregation and the local school officials who must carry it out. The question of "Why us and not them?" is not easily answered.

2. The issue is that the continuing exodus of Whites from the cities to the suburbs has left many large cities increasingly, if not predominantly, populated by minority group residents. The consequence for school desegregation is that although it is possible to achieve racial balance in these districts, it will not be possible to put all children in predominantly Anglo schools. Indeed, for the five largest school districts in the nation—New York, Chicago, Los Angeles, Philadelphia, and Detroit—the combined Black and Hispanic student populations for the 1974–1975 school year ranged from 53% in Los Angeles to 74% in Detroit (cf. Rist, 1978a).

The question is whether *any* remedy would work to desegregate the central-city schools. The options appear to be several: involve the suburbs in the desegregation effort; desegregate portions of the city school system but not all; call any school that enrolls students of two or more racial groups "desegregated," regardless of their proportions; or do nothing. The latter

option is increasingly being espoused by those who believe school desegregation within the large city districts is now virtually impossible.

The barriers erected by the Supreme Court in its decision on *Milliken*
v. *Bradley*[8] make metropolitan solutions exceedingly remote. Yet, including
suburbs is seemingly the only mechanism presently available to eliminate
the segregation of tens of thousands of minority group students within
central city school districts. The longer present demographic trends
continue, the more difficult any solution will become. The present prospects
for desegregating the five largest systems, the systems which in 1974
enrolled 18% of all Black students and 22% of all Hispanic students, are
grim.

3. Resistance to federal intervention and control constitutes the third
issue. Court orders and, less frequently, DHEW regulations remove options
from local communities to effect their school systems in ways they choose
(Rist, 1976). Although such intervention clearly has been justified given the
stark examples of *de jure* segregation perpetrated in many communities,
there has not been support in many instances for the mandated changes.
Resistance grows out of a community's support for existing segregation or
out of a sense that outside intervention is an affront to the community, its
citizens, and school officials. Distrusting the motives of government
officials, local communities are offended by unknown persons from Washington who suggest that "pillars" of the community are law breakers.
(*Community* in this instance would refer to the White social and political
structure.)

Yet another dimension of the resistance to federal authority is that the
federal government does not speak with one voice. The positions of the
various branches tend to be obscure, ill-defined, and even contradictory.
One sector of the government condoning the status quo and endorsing anti-
busing legislation tends to undercut and remove legitimation from another
sector which is calling for change. When the executive and legislative
branches contradict each other, the issue is necessarily left in the lap of the
courts. The courts, however, are not the most advantageous place from
which to educate persons as to their legal and civic responsibilities (cf. Rist
& Anson, 1977).

4. The issue is a widespread perception in the White community that
school desegregation seldom if ever enhances the quality of the educational
experience and, instead, creates educational disaster zones. In spite of
efforts by the courts and education officials to develop creative and
imaginative integration plans, they have not been able to persuade communities that the new options promise more to the students than did the old. In

---

[8] *Milliken* v.*Bradley*, 418 U. S. 717 (1974).

short, school desegregation is viewed as a process producing increasing costs and decreasing benefits for the students.

At one level, this perception is correct, particularly where the desegregation effort involves only Black and White students of low socioeconomic status. An integration program that excludes middle-class Whites on the edge of the city and in the suburbs while involving only students from working class and poor backgrounds, is to involve a group of White students most threatened by racial change and least able to handle it. This is especially so if the program seeks to minimize busing and thus integrate Black and White schools within close proximity. The Boston desegregation effort should be instructive in this regard.

When choices are made to minimize busing and only integrate lower income students from adjacent, often hostile neighborhoods, there is an indirect effect that contributes still further to the instability of the school and the likelihood of conflict and disruption. If Whites in these neighborhoods are afraid that the school/neighborhood/community are no longer safe or stimulating for their children, they will move—and Black people will come in behind them to take up the available housing. The pattern of White flight and ghetto expansion in American urban areas for the past 20 years should suggest that minimal busing is not a reasonable solution to creating stable neighborhoods.

5. The issue is a growing ambivalence of the Black community to pursuing school desegregation. So long as it was clear that the overwhelming majority of the Black community desired an end to segregated education, there were many in the White community who would join in pursuing this goal. But with the growing demand in the 1960s for "community control" or the 1973 "Atlanta compromise," when the local branch of the NAACP dropped its demands for busing in exchange for over half of the administrative leadership positions in the school system, many White people have grown hesitant to pursue desegregation efforts. Their rationale is clear: if the victims no longer believe remedies are feasible and, indeed, their victimization can be turned to their own benefit through the control of segregated institutions, then why seek desegregation?

One manifestation of the diversity of opinion within the Black community has been reported in a 1974 Gallup poll (see Table II). A more recent poll, this by Harris in 1976, also suggests the differences within the Black community on matters of integration and busing (see Table III).

Although these data do not suggest that Black persons are antagonistic to school desegregation *per se* there is nevertheless something of the same manifestation noted earlier in this chapter—a willingness to support school desegregation in the abstract, but dramatically less support for the means to achieve it. With an absence of strong support for busing, the only

Table II. Public Attitudes toward Integration and Busing,
1974 (by percent)

Policy favored	All respondents	Black respondents
Integration, even with long-distance busing	6	18
Maximum integration with short-distance busing	16	14
Voluntary open enrollment and busing	20	25
Neighborhood schools	50	33
Don't know	8	10

SOURCE: Orfield, 1978, p. 116.

mechanism readily available to achieve school desegregation, both our moral will and political courage are muted. Indeed, there exists within the Black community sufficient difference of opinion to ensure that those who in the White community oppose busing will find some support in the Black community

FURTHER IMPLEMENTATION: A GLANCE FORWARD

Progress is being made in the desegregation of public schools in the South, but the picture is not so positive in the North and West. In fact, in some parts of these latter two regions, schools are becoming more intensely segregated. Recently published HEW data (cf. Center for National Policy Review, 1977) indicate, for example, that in 1970, 74% of all Black children in the public schools in Chicago were in schools with 99–100% minority

Table III. Attitudes toward Busing as Means of Racial
Desegregation, 1976 (by percent)

Question:	Do you favor or oppose busing children to schools outside their neighborhoods to achieve racial desegregation?	
	White	Black
Favor	9	38
Oppose	85	51
Not sure	6	
	($N = 1,671$, W $= 1,328$, B $= 289$)	

SOURCE: Harris Poll, July 13, 1976.

enrollment. In 1974, the comparable figure was 80%. In Los Angeles, the figures for the same years are 55 and 62%, respectively; for Detroit, 36 and 50%, respectively. It should be remembered that these data are for the extreme—99–100% minority enrollments. The same picture is emerging for Hispanic children. Nearly two-thirds of all Spanish-surnamed students in the New York City schools were in schools with 99–100% minority student enrollments. In fact, on a national average, Latino children are now as concentrated in schools with more than 70% minority enrollment as are Black students.

In spite of these increased concentrations in sectors of the country, the national average shows a decline in the levels of school segregation. Whether such a decline will continue depends upon several critical factors. First among these is the matter of how the courts and federal agencies define *de jure* segregation in areas where schools have never been segregated by law. Although there have been individual instances where desegregation efforts have been set back because of judicial rulings that schools are not required to alleviate racial imbalances they did not cause, the more general stance of the courts has been oriented differently. Desegregation has been ordered where school officials were able to maintain segregation by arbitrarily drawing attendance zones, by selectively erecting new schools, and by the assignment of Black teachers to Black schools. If the courts continue to see such action as having the *intent* to segregate, these actions will be remedied under current statutes governing *de jure* segregation.

A second factor concerns what remedies for segregation will be invoked by governmental agencies and courts. Even though such efforts as magnet schools, the pairing of schools, and the altering of attendance zones may mitigate segregation, the evidence is overwhelming that the greatest decreases in segregation have come in those districts where students were bused to achieve desegregation. There is little doubt but that if busing as a tool of desegregation is limited or banned, urban areas would revert to having largely segregated schools due to neighborhood patterns.

A third factor, and one related to the second, concerns the future for interdistrict desegregation. If the only required integration in many of our urban areas is that of within-district, present demographic trends will produce a thorough resegregation for hundreds of thousands of Black students. The reality is that within-district desegregation is simply not possible in many of our large cities. Although desegregation can continue to proceed apace in many of our medium and smaller cities and towns, it is increasingly possible in the larger areas only when initiated on a metropolitan basis.

The matter of school desegregation is likely to be with us for years to come. Despite substantial desegregation in southern and border states in recent years, more than half of the Black children in these areas are in majority Black schools. In the North and West, the figures are even higher. In these regions, more than 80% of all Black students are in majority Black schools. Similarly, in states where there is a sizable Hispano-American school population, less than half of these students attend majority White schools—and the proportion who do so is generally declining. That so much of the task still lies before us, coupled with the general perception that school desegregation has passed the point of even diminishing returns, suggests it is time for a reconsideration of the basic and underlying assumptions influencing the present approaches.

Such a period of reevaluation is necessary if the desegregation process is to proceed in such a manner as to maximize the probabilities that the ultimate goals of this major effort at social change will be achieved. And while most people sympathetic to these goals will have little quarrel with this admonition, in principle, the implications may be less widely accepted. Indeed, the new American dilemma suggests so long as the means to school desegregation continue to be thwarted, the goal remains an abstraction. The bottom line for this generation of Americans is that if they wish to desegregate the schools, there has to be busing. The refusal to accept this fact and to act on it means the nation will continue into the foreseeable future with racial isolation being the norm, not the exception.

In order to respond to those conditions that make school desegregation an "issue," remedies and new initiatives may well have to move in ways different than at present. Further, strategies that are at present frequently rejected out of hand, e.g., partial desegregation, the preservation of one-race schools, different strategies in different parts of the school district, may have to be reconsidered. Strategies of school desegregation, be they at the local, state, or federal levels, cannot proceed as if the schools existed in a political and cultural vacuum.

If there is indeed to be future school desegregation in the United States, the present pattern of sporadic efforts through the courts does not appear to be an effective instrument for doing so. The more the task of desegregation has fallen to the courts alone, the less systematic, comprehensive, and acceptable the process has become. This is not the fault of the courts. But possibly, just possibly, those who have defaulted will be sufficiently disenchanted with the current state of affairs to reenter the fray and seek new and sensible initiatives. What is lacking at present is not the expertise, not the accumulated wisdom of the past two decades, and not those with leadership skills to see the process through. Rather, what we face is the absence of political will.

REFERENCES

Center for National Policy Review. *Trends in Black school segregation, 1970–1974.* Washington, D.C.: Catholic University Law School, 1977.

Crain, R. L., & Mahard, R. E. School racial composition and black college attendance and achievement test performance. *Sociology of Education*, 1978 *51*(2), 81–100.

Higginbotham, A. L. *Race and the American legal process*. New York: Oxford University Press, 1978.

Kluger, R. *Simple justice*. New York: Knopf, 1976.

Myrdal, G. *An American dilemma: The Negro problem and modern democracy*. New York: Harper & Row, 1944.

National Advisory Commission on Civil Disorders. *Report of the National Advisory Commission on Civil Disorders*. Washington, D. C.: U.S. Government Printing Office, 1968.

National Institute of Education. *School desegregation in the 1970's: Problems and prospects*. Washington, D.C.: U.S. Government Printing Office, 1976.

National Opinion Research Center. *Southern schools: An evaluation of the effects of the emergency school assistance program and of school desegregation*. Chicago: National Opinion Research Center, 1973.

Newman, D. K., Amidei, N.J., Carter, B. L., Kruvant, W. J., Day, D., & Russell, J. S. *Protest, politics, and prosperity: Black Americans and white institutions, 1940–1975*. New York: Academic, 1978.

Orfield, G. *Must we bus? Segregated schools and national policy*. Washington, D.C.: The Brookings Institute, 1978.

Rist, R. C. School integration: Ideology, methodology, and national policy. *School Review*, 1976, *84*, no. 3 (May), 417–430.

Rist, R. C. *The invisible children: School integration in American society*. Canbridge, Mass.: Harvard University Press, 1978. (a)

Rist. R. C. School desegregation: Sorting out the issues and trends. *Civil Rights Digest*, 1978, *10*, no. 2 (Winter), 40–44.(b)

Rist, R. C., & Anson, R. J. *Education, social science and the judicial process*. New York: Columbia Teachers College Press, 1977.

St. John, N. H. *School desegregation: Outcomes for children*. New York: Wiley Interscience, 1975.

Stephan, W.G. School desegregation: An evaluation of predictions made in *Brown v. Board of Education*. *Psychological Bulletin*, 1978, *85*, 217–238.

United States Department of Justice. *Report of the Community Relations Service to Senators Edward Brooke and Jacob Javits*. Reprinted in Congressional Record, June 26, 1976.

7

School Desegregation and Ethnicity

ANDREW M. GREELEY

This chapter deals with two similar but somewhat unrelated subjects, the impact of desegregation on current relations between Blacks and "ethnics"—a term which usually means White, urban Catholics—and the much broader question of whether desegregation promotes ethnic pluralism or cultural assimilation.

The first task is relatively easy. Although the findings to be reported are "counterintuitive," they are still relatively straightforward. The second topic, however, is complex, intricate, and ambiguous, with both normative and ascriptive pitfalls, as well as a notable absence of empirical evidence. In the first section of the chapter I will report empirical findings; in the second section I will be engaging essentially in an enterprise of clarifying the questions, a risky and uncertain business at best.

A FUNNY THING HAPPENED ON THE WAY TO THE ETHNIC BACKLASH

The White ethnic backlash against desegregation has been so written about in the popular media as to have achieved a mythological significance to which mere empirical evidence can scarcely respond. However, the White ethnic backlash myth tells us far more about those who have created it than about the ethnics themselves. As long ago as five years, Nie, Currie, and Greeley (1974), could find no evidence of this White ethnic backlash; Greeley and Sheatsley (1971) recorded the same thing. Taylor, Sheatsley, and Greeley (1978) repeated the finding. The most recent article will be discussed here because it provides the longest, sustained monitoring of White ethnic response to desegregation.

ANDREW M. GREELEY • Center for the Study of American Pluralism, National Opinion Research Center, Chicago, Illinois 60637.

In 1963, Donald Treiman, then a staff member of the National Opinion Research Center (NORC), prepared a seven-item Guttman scale to measure attitudes toward integration. That scale (reduced to five items after 1972) was administered to national samples of Americans in 1963, 1970, 1972, and 1976. Support for school integration has gone up 20 percentage points, support for a Black friend having dinner with the family has gone up 22 percentage points, rejection of the right of Whites to keep Blacks out of a neighborhood has gone from 44 to 60 percentage points, and opposition to laws against interracial marriage has gone from 36 to 66 percentage points. The mean score on the Guttman scale has gone from 2.09 (which means in 1963, the average respondent only agreed with the first two items) to 3.17 in 1976 (which means the average respondent agreed with more than three items). Despite the enormous racial crises of the 1960s and the acrimonious controversy about busing and quota-integration in the 1970s, sympathy for racial integration has consistently increased. (There was an especially powerful leap between 1970 and 1972, see Table I). If there was a backlash, in other words, it was not detected by the NORC scale; in those years when a backlash would have been most likely, between the Cambodia–Kent State riots and the McGovern campaign, there was the biggest increase in support of racial integration.[1]

Similarly, the change between 1963 and 1976 went on at approximately the same rate in both the North and the South, although in the mysterious years between 1970 and 1972, the increase in support for racial integration was particularly strong in the South (Table II). There is a certain, almost glacial, implacability in the shift of the NORC integration scale. It continues to increase no matter what happens and to have the biggest increase precisely at that time when one might expect a backlash phenomenon.

What, then, about the so-called White ethnics? Has there been a special backlash among them, since they tend to live in the North and in cities where racial tensions are the highest?

No ethnic question was asked in the first of the four NORC integration monitoring studies, so one is forced to deal with changes between 1970 and 1976. However, Table III shows that far from being a backlash, the northern Catholic ethnic groups have all grown progressively more pro-integration between 1970 and 1976. Indeed, the Irish Catholics are second only to the Jews in their support of racial integration, and Irish, German, and Italian Catholics are more likely to support racial integration than Anglo-Saxon Protestants living in the North.

---

[1] For a discussion of the components of this change, see Taylor, Sheatsley, & Greeley (1978). It is sufficient to note here that by no means can all of the change be explained by cohort replacement. It is not merely that young people are more enlightened about race than older people.

Table I. Attitudes on Integration (Percentage Pro-Integration)

Item	1963	1970	1972	1976
"Do you think White students and Negro students should go to the same schools or to separate schools?" ("Same schools")	63	74	86	83
"How strongly would you object if a member of your family wanted to bring a Negro friend home to dinner?" ("Not at all")	49	63	70	71
"White people have a right to keep Negroes out of their neighborhoods if they want to, and Negroes should respect that right." ("Disagree slightly" or "Disagree strongly")	44	49	56	60
"Do you think there should be laws against marriages between Negroes and Whites?" ("No")	36	48	59	66
"Negroes shouldn't push themselves where they're not wanted." ("Disagree slightly" or "Disagree strongly")	27	16	22	28
$\overline{X}$	2.09	2.49	2.91	3.17
Δ/yr		.06	.21	.07

I would point particularly at the Irish Catholics, long considered by the conventional wisdom to be incorrigible racists. Their support for integration in 1976 is not only the highest of the gentile groups, but virtually identical with Jewish support for integration only four years previous. If this be backlash, American society should make the most of it.

In addition to its periodic monitoring of racial attitudes, NORC also conducts a general social survey each year, which asks "classic" questions enabling social scientists to measure change with items that have been asked in previous surveys. Three questions seem especially appropriate for the issue at hand: (1) the proportion of respondents who would not oppose their children going to a school that was half Black; (2) the proportion of respondents who would not oppose their children going to a school which

Table II. Pro-Integration Scale by Region

	1963	1970	1972	1976
Non-South	2.45	2.88	3.16	3.46
(change/year)		(.06)	(.14)	(.08)
South	1.11	1.47	2.17	2.46
(change/year)		(.05)	(.35)	(.07)

was mostly Black; and (3) the proportion of respondents who favored busing. The combination of the three questions is important. Many observers are inclined to discount the responses of parents who say they would not object to their children attending a half-Black or mostly-Black school because they are saying only what they think they are expected to say. However, one would expect that respondents might also feel some pressure to give favorable answers when asked questions about busing. The majority of Americans accept school integration, even school integration where most of the students are Black; but the majority reject busing (Table IV). The seeming inconsistency of these responses suggests that the respondents are likely to be telling something approximating the truth. (Stinchcombe, Heimer, Iliff, Scheppele, Smith, & Taylor, 1978, have demonstrated that there is no significant correlation between attitudes toward busing and attitudes toward any other measure of support for racial integration.)

The NORC General Social Survey has been conducted every year since 1972; and it is therefore possible to obtain not merely responses to a question with a very large case base but also to measure whether there has been any change in the response of a given ethnic group during the six years the study has been conducted. We observe in Table IV that more than three-quarters of all the ethnic groups in the country would not oppose their

Table III. Pro-Integration Scale by Ethnicity
(Non-South Only)

	1970	1972	1976
All northerners	2.88	3.16	3.46
(change/year)		(.14)	(.08)
Anglo-Saxon	2.80	3.18	3.37
(change/year)		(.19)	(.05)
German Protestant	2.81	2.70	3.08
(change/year)		(−.06)	(.10)
Scandinavian Protestant	2.82	2.98	3.55
(change/year)		(.08)	(.14)
Irish Catholic	3.06	3.46	3.59
(change/year)		(.20)	(.03)
German Catholic	2.97	3.18	3.44
(change/year)		(.11)	(.07)
Italian Catholic	2.65	3.14	3.43
(change/year)		(.25)	(.07)
Slavic Catholic	2.45	2.76	3.07
(change/year)		(.16)	(.08)
Jews	3.79	3.67	4.15
(change/year)		(−.06)	(.12)

Table IV. Ethnicity and School Integration

Ethnic group	Percentage would send children to half-Black school	Percentage would send children to mostly Black school	Percentage favor busing
British Protestant	78 (695)	50	8
Scandinavian Protestants	78 (226)	55	16
German Protestants	77 (741)	51	13
Irish Protestants	78 (267)	54	12
Other Protestants	76 (57)	52	11
Irish Catholics	77 (212)	61	10
German Catholics	79[a] (204)	54	17
Slavic Catholics	79 (195)	55	15
Italian Catholics	78 (202)	47	12
Jews	86 (140)	50	18
Hispanics	84 (195)	68	36
Blacks			53[b]

[a] A gamma with year of .21, significant at .001 level, indicating an increase in opposition to school integration.
[b] A gamma with year of .23, significant at .002, indicating a decline in support for busing.

children's attending a school that was more than half Black. Only among German Catholics has there been a statistically significant decline in the approval of such racial integration. (And German Catholics living in rural areas are the least likely to encounter racial problems in their environment of any other Catholic group.) More than half of all American ethnic groups studied (with the exception of 47% of the Italians) say they would not oppose attendance by their children in a school in which most of the students were Black. Sixty-eight percent of the Hispanic respondents and 61% of the Irish Catholic respondents would accept such a situation, making them the ethnic groups most likely to support such a form of school integration—both of them substantially ahead of the 50% of Jewish support. Even Slavic Catholics are 5% more likely to say they would accept such a form of school integration than Jewish respondents. Furthermore, there have been no significant changes in the response to this question since the NORC General Social Survey began in 1972.

Finally, only a minority of all the ethnic groups in the country approve of busing to achieve racial integration in the schools. Of the Hispanics, 36% support busing, making them the most likely to approve busing, but only 18% of American Jews support it, which makes them similar to German Catholics, Slavic Catholics, and Scandinavian Protestants. The only significant change in attitudes toward busing is among Blacks, where there has been a decline in support for busing, so that in the 1977 General Social Survey a bare majority of American Blacks approved of busing to achieve integration.

There is, then, no evidence of a White ethnic backlash from two large and continuous monitoring operations. Nor, as far as the present writer knows, has anyone ever found statistical evidence of such a backlash. Whence, then, comes the mythology of a White ethnic backlash?

Two explanations come to mind. First, the social and cultural elites of the country need someone to blame for America's racial problems. As a group which has never been liked by the elites, the Catholic ethnics make an excellent scapegoat, particularly since they are likely to share the central city area of the northern cities with Blacks. In other words, it is their neighborhoods, their schools, and their occupations which are the most likely to be the targets of various forms of desegregation efforts. Furthermore, given this propensity to scapegoat White ethnics, it is very easy for the mass media to reinforce the mythology. Protesting mothers in front of a school building can easily be goaded into giving into racial hatred in front of a television camera in order to see themselves on the 10:00 P.M. news. The cultural and social elites, secure in their high-walled university communities or their high-rise condominium fortresses watch the screen and shake their heads. Just what they expected—more White ethnic racists. Amazingly enough, even social scientists don't pause to wonder about the representativeness of the sample. What do the women who are not demonstrating think, those who represent the overwhelming majority of the students in the school? That there might be a bias in those who participate in such demonstrations and an even greater bias in those who are selected by television directors and cameramen for interviews and pictures is a possibility that even the most sophisticated university professors often do not consider.

I would submit that until further and more careful investigation is made of the phenomenon, the myth of the White ethnic racist backlash is a combination of stereotyping (and bigotry) in the nation's cultural, intellectual, and social elites and highly selective (and highly prejudiced) reporting by the mass media.

The data reported in this section are not new (save for that reported in Taylor *et al.*, 1978). They have made little dent in the armor of the myth in the past, and they are not likely to make much more impact in their present form. All we can do is to challenge the skeptical reader to examine his conscience as to why he needs to remain so skeptical in the face of what in any other subject would be considered enormously powerful evidence.

ACCULTURATION, ASSIMILATION, PLURALISM

As one tries to sort out the tangled threads that must be ordered if any unity is to be woven into this section of the chapter, one finds four critical questions: (1) What is the nature of the acculturation processes going on in American society? (2) How do these processes work among American Blacks? (3) Does desegregation facilitate or impede these processes? (4) Should Blacks seek assimilation or should they seek a relatively distinct Black subculture within the larger society?

To avoid the reader's disappointment at the outset, I should note that it is difficult, if not impossible, to provide a definitive answer to any of these questions.

I shall begin by laying out a number of different theories—perhaps only images—of assimilation in American society, relying heavily on a discussion that was originally presented in my book, *The American Catholic: A Social Portrait* (Greeley, 1977).

The literature on assimilation in America is immense. Some authors see the process as rapid, others see it as slow. Some think it desirable that ethnic differences be eliminated so that a "common culture" may emerge; others think that assimilation should be decelerated so that many different cultures may flourish under the American umbrella. Milton Gordon (1964) combines the two by distinguishing between "structural assimilation," in which ethnicity is no longer pertinent even to primary group formation, and "cultural assimilation" (or acculturation), in which cultural differences diminish but the propensity to choose primary group relationships from within one's own group persists. Gordon argues that the latter process is far advanced in American society, whereas the former proceeds much more slowly.

What all the assimilationist literature, popular and serious, sophisticated or simplistic, assumes is that the strain toward homogenization in modern industrial society is so great as to be virtually irresistible. The influences of the common school, the mass media, common political and social norms, and ethnic and religious intermarriage work toward the elimination of diversity in a society. Basic beliefs, socialization styles, personality characteristics, political participation, social attitudes, expectations of intimate role opposites, all tend toward a similarity that is differentiated only by social class. Social class is generally assumed to be a "rational" basis for differentiation, as opposed to differentiation based on religion and national origin, which are "irrational." Race was formerly an irrational focus for differentiation but is now rational.

The assimilation picture is pervasive in American society. The picture as stated in abstract categories of social science or the concrete categories of popular journalism is one of many different cultures merging into one common "American" culture. Only minor differences (such as special foods) persist. It is part of our popular folk wisdom as well as an important component of the repertory of pictures available to social science theorists. Politicians, television commentators, movie critics, social planners, and reform political candidates all take it for granted. The picture has been wedged into our individual and collective unconscious, and has achieved the status not merely of conventional wisdom but of common sense.

It is but a short step from being undiscussably *descriptive* for a picture to become *prescriptive*. The picture becomes not merely an ideal type, it becomes a norm. To untangle the strands of nativism, liberal optimism, vulgar Marxism, secular rationalism, and immigrant self-rejection that underpin the melting pot norm is a challenge to which practitioners of the sociology of knowledge might want to respond. Sociology is supposed to involve the questioning of assumptions, but few have asked whether there might be other ways of looking at the phenomenon of ethnic differentiation in American society besides the "official" assimilationist picture or the moderately revisionist version advanced by Milton Gordon.

Certain limitations of the assimilation–acculturation picture must be considered. It frequently turns out to be not particularly helpful in generating hypotheses or in ordering data. It is difficult to determine, for example, whether a set of findings shows a high or a low rate of acculturation. It also offers no insight into why there are, at present, some self-conscious attempts to create ethnic groups. In the Northeast, for example, there is a deliberate attempt to create a Spanish-speaking ethnic group. An American Indian group is struggling to emerge, and in Chicago there is even an effort, as yet rather ineffective, to create an Appalachian White ethnic group. Harold Cruse (1971) has also suggested that the Black power movement is essentially an attempt to create a Black ethnic group, a suggestion that Paul Metzger (1971) has echoed from a very different perspective. The political and social leaderships concerned with the creation of ethnic groups must have insights into how power is exercised in the United States that are quite foreign to the acculturation picture.[2]

Similarly, the acculturation perspective does not take into account the fact, noted by many historians, that ethnicity was perceived by the immi-

[2] Nathan Glazer (1954) has observed that the ethnic group came into existence in the United States. It might be a mistake to conclude that the self-conscious formation of an ethnic group is a new development in American society. One wonders what reason there is to think that the leaders of previous efforts at ethnic group construction were acting unself-consciously.

grants as a way of becoming American. The hyphen in the hyphenate American was a symbol of equality, not inequality. In an urban environment where everyone, including the native American, was a something-else-American, one had to be ethnic to find one's place on the map. Thomas Brown (1966) notes that the principal argument of the nineteenth and early twentieth-century Irish American nationalists who favored freedom for Ireland was that only when Ireland was a free and independent member of the family of nations would Irish-Americans be accepted by the native Americans as worthy of full-fledged American citizenship. And Victor Greene (1966) has demonstrated that support among Polish-Americans and Czech-Americans for the nationalist movements in their native countries during World War I came only after the United States entered that war. Such support for free Poland and the new Czech republic was, paradoxically, an exercise in American patriotism more than an expression of Polish or Czech patriotism.

More historical research is obviously required, but there is sufficient reason to state, at least as a tentative hypothesis, that the creation of ethnic groups in the United States was a way for the immigrant population to look at its present and future in America rather than at its past in the Old World. In a complex society of an "unstable pluralism" (Kammen, 1972) you had to be "something" if you were going to be "anybody." Such a view of social reality is obviously foreign to the acculturation picture.

Another problem with the acculturation picture is that it does not account for the self-conscious manipulation of ethnic symbols in American society, a manipulation which ought to be increasingly difficult and infrequent but which in the social reality around us does not seem to be difficult at all. Polish and Italian self-consciousness, for example, can easily be written off as a response to Black militancy. Yet it could also be argued that ethnic consciousness is merely a result of the fact that by accepting Black self-consciousness, the larger society legitimated public manipulation of ethnic symbols, which in prior years had been manipulated privately. A particularly interesting example is the appearance of tricolor bumper stickers on the cars of many Italian-Americans in the eastern United States. It is safe to assume that most of these self-conscious Italians came from southern Italy and Sicily, where until fairly recently, the tricolor represented the "foreign" domination of the Piemontese. The Sicilians came to the United States and discovered that they were Italian-Americans. Now they have discovered they are Italian, a process exactly the reverse of that suggested by using only the acculturation picture. It is, of course, a research question as to how widespread the response is to such symbol manipulation. One would presume that sociologists would abstain from dismissing it as an irrelevant and unimportant phenomenon until they have studied it in detail.

As an alternative and complementary perspective, I would suggest that

ethnic groups come into being in the United States and have a "natural history." The study of their genesis and history, free of the dogmatic assumption that their destiny is obliteration, can be useful in approaching both the
history and the sociology of ethnic differentiation in the United States.

One need not subscribe to Lévi-Strauss's view of the binary differentiating propensities of the structure of the human mind (indeed, I do
not subscribe to his view) to be aware that humans "code" reality by differentiation. As Gerald Suttles (1972) remarked, one creates neighborhoods
so that one may have a chart of the city and know where one is going to
encounter role-opposites whom one can reasonably trust. But the mental
chart that divides the city into many different neighborhoods is only one of
a considerable number of such charts that we carry around in our minds.
There are microstructure charts that divide the family into parents and
children, and children into boys and girls or "big kids" and "little kids," for
example. And there are macrostructure charts that divide the world or the
human race or the population of the nation into various categories. Such
categories enable us to engage in preliminary coding operations that help us
to move in a tentative fashion through the maze of potential relationships
that constitute human society. Even academics, proudly aloof from the
prejudices and biases of ordinary men, still code their own departments by
specialization and/or interaction networks, if not by cliques or factions. The
pertinent question is not whether such charts exist but rather which chart
will be imposed on what social phenomenon.[3] It is much like using overlays
that drop down over the blank figure of the human body to show first the
arterial system, the venous, nervous, and muscle systems, until finally the
picture is complete though incredibly complex.

For purposes of preliminary coding, such differentiation is not
necessarily binary, although there may be a basic binary division of
potential role relationships—those in which you can be reasonably trusting
and those in which you must be cautious about extending trust, for example.
Nor does differentiation need to be conflict producing. Although it is certainly true that most conflict flows from some form of differentiation, it is
not true that differentiation necessarily leads to conflict. Indeed, Rosemary
Harris (1972) has pointed out that even in Ulster most Catholics and most
Protestants are not in active conflict with each other, but rather live in conditions ranging from suspicious coexistence to reserved friendship.

It is a truism that there are no native Americans (except the Indians, of
course), but it is frequently overlooked just how recent this immigration was
for many American families. Indeed, in the middle 1960s, half the

---

[3] One of my colleagues observed that when she was growing up in Florida she thought of
herself as an American; when she went to Washington, D.C., she discovered she was Cuban;
and when she came to Chicago she was told she was "Spanish-speaking."

American Catholic adult population was either the first or second generation in this country. If one believes in the power of the mass media and the
common school to wipe the cultural and psychological slates clean in the
space of a few decades, the persistence of ethnicity will come as a surprise.
But if one believes in a certain inertial strength of cultural traits and family
memories, it is not at all surprising that collectivities which took their origin
in a very recent immigration experience persist.

Ethnicity reveals itself as a relatively safe form of differentiation. There
may be conflict and competition among the various ethnic groups, but the
conflict is rarely violent. Society has implicitly legitimated ethnic differentiation (if not required it) and has provided protocols and processes
whereby the potential conflict that could arise from such differentiation is
minimized. The immigrants never saw their claim to be hyphenated Americans as involving any danger of tearing apart the new society, which on the
whole was relatively benign to them. They may have been accused of being
un-American on occasion and, more often, suspected of not being American
enough, but they never realistically perceived themselves as a threat to the
relative peace and harmony of the society. Despite the fears of the advocates of a common culture and assimilation, ethnic differentiation was never
a serious threat to the social order.

No differentiation is without cost, but the price of ethnic differentiation
in American society is modest—if one is White. There are certain clubs,
buildings, and companies from which Jews are excluded, for example. The
psychological costs may be more severe. The emphasis on "respect" among
some of the current militant ethnic groups indicates how pressing they may
be for some people. Many ancestral memories had to be repressed (the Irish
have been particularly successful at this repression) for one to become
thoroughly American. But given the situations the immigrants left behind,
the costs of ethnic differentiation seemed relatively minor compared to the
benefits the new society was capable of bestowing on them, or, more
precisely, benefits that could be wrested from the host society if one was
prepared to join with one's own kind to create a more equal match.

The most striking aspect of American ethnic differentiation is that by
definition, ethnic boundaries are *supposed* to be permeable. In other countries, ethnicity is considered a method of finding oneself in a systematic way
as being "over against" the rest of society. Under such circumstances,
ethnic differentiation implies ethnic separation. But among White groups
(and the theory becomes a dilemma on the subject of non-White groups) in
the United States, ethnicity has never been primarily a means of separation,
much less isolation. As I noted earlier, the combined form denotes equality;
it is not a way of withdrawing from the rest of society so much as an institution for dealing oneself into it. The ethnic collectivity does indeed provide a
rationale for self-definition, and implicit in all self-definitions is some sort

of separation from those who do not share the same one. But ethnic self-definition in the United States is more concerned with defining oneself as part of the American society and not separate from it. Under such circumstances, ethnic group boundaries are permeable because the political and social culture has decreed that they ought to be and because they have been so structured.

It is also required by both the national, political, and social culture and by the implicit constitutional structure that membership in an ethnic collectivity be optional. One has the right, American society assumes, to be an ethnic if one wants to be, but one is under no obligation. In practice, of course, it is easier for some individuals to dispense with their ethnic identification than it is for others. Blacks, Chinese, Japanese, American Indians, to some extent Chicanos, and perhaps to a lesser extent Puerto Ricans and Cubans, would find it difficult to persuade other members of society that they are not part of the ethnic group to which they have been assigned. But in theory and to a considerable extent in practice, the ethnic collectivity is a community of "limited liability" (to lift a phrase from a different but related discussion), one of the many such communities of limited liability that are available to an American. Whether and when a person chooses so to identify himself in his own thinking is completely up to him, and, in theory though scarcely yet in practice, such decisions ought to be accepted by others. To return to the image of the overlay, the ethnic chart is available to be used or not, frequently or rarely, whenever one wishes to code the possible relationships that are available.

I shall recapitulate here by introducing a schematic chart. The reader must realize that sociologists are fond of such charts, and that we cheerfully concede that they are bare bones oversimplifications of reality. Nonetheless, as Otis Dudley Duncan (personal communication) has remarked, the most obvious use of such charts is that they force us to make explicit the implicit causal explanations that underlie our prose. They are designed to show the direction of influence on the culture systems of the immigrants through time and an increasing number of generations since immigration and experience in the common school.

Figure 1 schematizes the ethnicization perspective. It shows that the host and immigrants may have had something in common to begin with. Some of the Irish, for example, spoke English and understood something of the English political style of the eighteenth and nineteenth centuries. The other European groups were part of the broad western cultural inheritance. Under the influence of education, generation, and the experience in American society both at the time of immigration and subsequently, the common culture grows larger. Immigrants become more like the host, and the host may become somewhat more like the immigrants. Certain immigrant characteristics persist; in fact, under the impact of the experience of

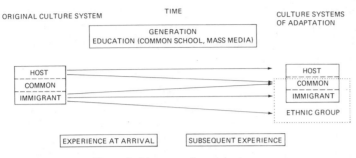

Figure 1. Ethnogenesis perspective.

American life, some traits become more rather than less distinctive. Certain aspects of the immigrant heritage are emphasized and developed in response to the challenge of American society. What appears at the end (the right-hand portion of Figure 1) is that the ethnic group has a cultural system that is a combination of traits shared with other groups and traits that are distinctive to its own group. For the ethnics, then, the mix of traits and the emphasis within the cultural system are different from those of their immigrant predecessors. They share more with the common culture than they did to begin with, but in some respects may also be more different from the descendants of the hosts than their ancestors were from their hosts. In principle, there is nothing to prevent testing of the various components of this perspective. In practice, however, an immense amount of social and historical research will be required. It is worth noting, incidentally, that although all the lines in Figure 1 are straight, in the reality this chart attempts to schematize, the lines might well be jagged. For example, if one considers the variable of ethnic consciousness as part of the original immigrant system of traits, that consciousness may well have waxed and waned through the years, moving away from the common culture, then toward it, and away again in zigzag fashion.

There are at least six different approaches to the study of ethnic diversity in the United States. (For this discussion I rely heavily on a report on a NORC study by Andrew Greeley, William McCready, and Gary Theisen, 1978.)

1. *Ideological.* The primary question of this approach is whether ethnicity is "a good thing." Should one even study it, since by studying it one tends to encourage it; and in a rationalist, universalistic society, distinctions based on origin are reactionary, regressive, chauvinistic, and even fascist. Orlando Patterson (1978) and Stein and Hill (1977) are the most articulate proponents of the proposition that ethnicity should not even be named among us (*ne nominatur inter vos*). Ethnic writers such as Richard Gambino (1974) and Michael Novak (1972) argued against Anglo-Saxon

Protestants (and Irish Catholic) oppression of ethnics and ethnic subcultural preferences in America. The former are horrified by ethnic diversity, the latter glory in it; neither side of this particular debate is notably encumbered by empirical evidence.

2. *Identity and identification.* The principal question in this approach focuses on the role of ethnicity in contemporary industrial society. It is most elegantly stated by Isaacs (1975) and Horowitz (1975). This approach explains the persistence of ethnicity as the result of a search for "basic group identity," "self-definition," or "social location." People identify with their ethnic group so they will know who they are in the midst of a society that is for the most part formal, bureaucratic, and ascriptive. Some empirical research has been done from this perspective, seeking to determine how important ethnic identification is as a means of self-definition in contemporary America and to what extent ethnic customs and practices that reinforce that self-definition are still important to Americans.

3. *Acculturation assimilation.* Milton Gordon (1964) introduced these terms into the discussion. *Acculturation* for Gordon consists of the immigrant group taking on the behavior patterns of the host society, and *assimilation* consists of the immigrant group losing its concern about maintaining its most intimate relationships (marriage and friendship) within the group boundaries. Gordon has suggested that in America assimilation proceeds at a much slower rate than acculturation. Those who are influenced by Gordon's approach attempt to define measures of assimilation and acculturation and compare progress on both. Thus, Alba (1976) has studied the increasing rates of ethnic exogamy and concluded that ethnicity is declining rapidly as an important factor in American life.

4. *Conflict.* This approach focuses on ethnic diversity as the axis of political competition and conflict in the industrial world. Glazer and Moynihan (1971) suggest that the ethnic collectivities in New York City are no longer bearers of separate cultural systems but are political interest groups. Much of the analysis done by political scientists and anthropologists in third world countries emphasizes conflict among various ethnic groups. Articles in Glazer and Moynihan (1975) by Kilson, Porter, das Gupta, Esman, and Mazuri, for example, discuss the various aspects of ethnic or racial-ethnic conflict in different nations. The primary question in this approach is which group dominates, which are dominated, and how the patterns of dominance and subservience are worked out. While such writers as Patterson (1978), Stein and Hill (1977), and, to some extent, Isaacs (1975), are concerned about the dangers in ethnic conflict, scholars using the conflict model of ethnicity typically assume that conflict is a given and try to determine who is conflicting with whom.

5. *Social class.* Early in the revival of interest in ethnic identity, there

were efforts by a number of writers (most notably Herbert Gans, 1962) to equate ethnicity with social class. More recently, others have suggested that although ethnicity is not the same as social class, ethnic stratification is a variety of class stratification. Just as humans can be stratified on such things as education, income, and social prestige, they can also be stratified as to whether they have membership in more prestigious or less prestigious ethnic groups. The primary question for those who use this research model is what the ethnic prestige ranking is and how that prestige ranking came to be.

6. *Subcultural persistence.* This approach, which has characterized much of the research done at the Center for the Study of American Pluralism at NORC, is concerned primarily with the persistence of ethnically linked attitudes and behaviors, regardless of such assimilationist influences and degree of ethnic self-identification.

It does not need to be observed, perhaps, that none of the six approaches is necessarily incompatible. Even though Orlando Patterson (1978) maintains that ethnicity should not be discussed, he is nevertheless prepared to discuss it, and once one concedes that ethnicity may be discussed, then issues of self-definition, acculturation, conflict, stratification, and subcultural persistence are pertinent. Those of us who focus on subcultural persistence, however, believe that our investigations begin where the other five approaches end. We have discovered that the persistence of some subcultural traits seem relatively independent of self-definition, are unaffected by acculturation and social class, and have nothing to do with political competition and conflict. In *Ethnicity in the United States* (Greeley, 1974) and "The Transmission of Cultural Heritages" (McCready & Greeley, 1975), it is reported that hypotheses fashioned from a knowledge of the Old World cultural heritages of immigrant groups are quite likely to be sustained when examined against data on attitudes and behaviors of the ethnic groups which have emerged from emigration from their old societies. If we know, for example, how the Irish and the Italians behaved in the old countries, we can be successful most of the time in predicting differences between them in the United States. Thus, we conclude that ethnic heritages seem to endure migration across the Atlantic Ocean. They are also apparently unlikely to be affected by education, generation in the United States, and ethnic self-consciousness. Certain ethnically-linked traits (religion, alcohol consumption, political behavior) seem to have remarkable durability despite assimilationist pressures.

This led us to suspect that Old World heritages, transformed to the New World, persist without any conscious intent on the part of "ethnics" because attitudes and behaviors are transmitted early in childhood. Ethnic subcultures, we have hypothesized, are socialization phenomena; that is, they are the result of behavior and attitude patterns transmitted from parent to child without any need for either to realize that these patterns are ethnically linked.

Our own research at the National Opinion Research Center has tended to concentrate on the last of the perspectives, in part because we fail to find much in the way of a significant decline in the correlations between ethnicity and attitudes and behavior under the impact of such assimilationist variables as generation in the United States, education, and self-defined importance of ethnicity. Our findings are available in a number of published and unpublished papers (Greeley, 1974, 1975a,b; Greeley et al., 1978; McCready, 1972). Briefly, we found remarkable durability among ethnic groups in family structure, political participation, and drinking attitudes and behaviors. These different subcultures persisted across three generations with little signs of being diminished by generation, education, proportion of own ethnic group in the neighborhood in which one lives (save for Jewish drinking, which increases as one moves into less Jewish neighborhoods), and even feelings of closeness to one's ethnic group and description of ethnicity as important in one's life. Finally, even ethnic exogamy does not seem to have a notable impact on drinking subcultures for either Irish Catholics or Jews. (There is only marginal incremental impact on drinking behavior, in other words, in having one parent from either an Irish or Jewish ethnic group.) Ethnic subcultures have a remarkable durability, apparently because they are acquired very early in life as part of a socialization process that is not perceived in any self-conscious way as being ethnic. Thus, for example, almost half the variation in the high score of Irish males on a problem drinking scale can be accounted for by family background variables; and the variation in the amount of alcohol consumed and in drinking problems among Jews, Irish and Italian Catholics, Swedish and English Protestants can be accounted for almost completely by a model which takes into account drinking in the family background, family structure, and Jewish religion. Ethnic subcultures, then, have extraordinary durability in the face of assimilation dynamics.

Nor is ethnic identification as unimportant to people as has been supposed. The majority of Irish, Italian, and Jewish respondents rank their ethnic background as either "extremely important" or "very important." The adolescent members of these ethnic groups are somewhat more likely to rate ethnic identity as important than are their parents. Italian Catholics are likely to say that they feel closer to members of their ethnic group than they do to coreligionists. Irish, however, are a few percentage points more likely to say that members of their religion are closer to them than members of their ethnic group; but still, fellow ethnics are very important to Irish Catholics after well over 100 years in the United States. This importance does not seem to be diminishing even among adolescents.

Thus, the NORC research shows that both unconscious transmission of ethnic subcultures and conscious ethnic identification are important aspects of American life. They do not seem to be diminishing in their importance even despite ethnic intermarriage. Kobrin and Goldscheider (1978) have arrived at fundamentally similar conclusions:

> What are the major conclusions that emerge from the analysis of these data? First and foremost, the evidence presented strongly supports the argument that ethnic pluralism is a continuing feature of community life in America. No analysis of family or mobility processes can be considered complete without attention to ethnic variations. To the extent that these fundamental social processes have implications for other social processes and for attitudes and values (that have not been considered in this study), the study of ethnic variation and changes increases in importance.
>
> The existence of ethnic variation in social processes does not however imply the absence of change. To the contrary. The cohort data showed clearly the multidimensionality of ethnic changes. Both the extent and pattern of ethnic change varies over time and differently among ethnic subpopulations and for the various processes analyzed. Hence, there are elements of continuity as well as change in ethnic variation that, over time, and in different social and economic contexts, result in changing forms of ethnic continuity and community structure. The changing nature of ethnicity cannot be viewed simply as an indication of the diminishing importance of the ethnic factor or of the "assimilation" of ethnic communities. Rather the manifestation of ethnicity changes as the broader society changes and new forms of ethnic identity and ethnic cohesiveness are emerging. (p. 226)

They also agree with the NORC conclusion that intermarriage does not eliminate the importance of the ethnic factor in American culture and society.

How does all this background on American ethnicity apply to Blacks? First of all, it should certainly be clear that Blacks have a common cultural heritage which they pass on from generation to generation—distinctive but not totally distinct from the culture of the rest of the society. It also should be obvious that Blacks do identify with their racial background and are likely to continue to do so. Finally, it should be beyond question that the degree of identification with their "ethnic" background varies greatly among Blacks. In these three senses, the Black segment of the American population can surely be considered an ethnic group.

But it is an ethnic group *sui generis*. First of all, Blacks do not have the option of becoming alienated from their own ethnic group. Even if one insists one is not Black and wants no part of Black identification, one will still be perceived as Black by the rest of the society. (To a lesser extent this lack of option to disaffiliate applies to other American groups—Chinese and Japanese, most notably, but also Jews and to a lesser extent Poles, Italians, and Irish.)

Second, the Black ethnic group is not merely a group constituted of assumed common national origin; it is also, like the Chinese and Japanese, a racial group. Race is not only a more visible manifestation of diversity than is nationality, it is also, generally speaking, at any rate, one that is more likely to lead to conflict.

Finally, the most important reason for saying that Blacks are an "ethnic group *sui generis*" is the obvious but never to be forgotten fact that Blacks are the only group which came to America in substantial numbers against their will as slaves (though many of their families were slaves before they left Africa). Since their forced immigration to America, Blacks were kept in involuntary servitude for many generations and for still more generations kept in involuntary oppression. Even today, many Blacks suffer from contemporary prejudice and from the residue of former prejudices. If most other American groups have been the victims of some form of racial, religious, or nationality oppression in the past, it is still true to say the Black oppression has been qualitatively different and that, therefore, Blacks are an ethnic group *sui generis*. The concept of ethnic groups can be applied to American Blacks only analogously.

There are two questions which must be addressed:

1. Is it useful for students of American group relationships to use the concept of ethnic groups when discussing Blacks? I would respond to that question by saying that it may well be useful and even necessary under some circumstances, but the students of group relationships must realize that the concept is applied only analogously to the Black segment of the population. Obviously, Blacks do have a common heritage, a common culture, and a common sense of group identity. To the extent that useful understanding may be obtained by using the *pluralism without fences* model, then it seems to me to be legitimate to use it.

I will confess that I have not used it in my research because, until recently, I have been afraid to. The issue of Black identity is too sensitive in American society for someone who is not Black to be anything but extremely cautious when addressing the matter. Recently, however, it has become possible to talk about such things again. Some of my work now begins to examine the transmission of subcultures across generation within the Black community.

2. The second question is whether Blacks should use the ethnic pluralism without fences model to think about themselves. This is, of course, a question for Blacks to answer. I suspect that since there is considerable diversity within the Black population, that some Blacks will answer it one way, others will answer it another way. Thus, Martin Kilson and Orlando Patterson at Harvard have vigorously and bravely argued against the rigid separatism of some of their Black nationalist colleagues.

Thomas Sowell, Black economist at the University of California, Los Angeles, and who is as distant as one can imagine from the Black nationalists at Harvard, explicitly accepts the model of a multiethnic society (Sowell, 1975). He dismisses the quota approach to racial integration as "the noble lie of our time," and explicitly accepts a multiethnic model of American society. He further points out that local Black organizations, including many chapters of the NAACP, have opposed the national NAACP's school desegregation suits and argues that those who are pushing desegregation are

> an organization fueled by money from affluent liberals whose own children are safely tucked away in private schools in a crusade run by men like Thurgood Marshall and Kenneth B. Clark, whose own children were also in private schools away from the storms they created for others. (p. 43)

Sowell continues:

> The very real educational problems of black children, and the early hopes that desegregation would solve them, provided the impetus and the support for a crusade that has now degenerated into a numerical fetish and a judicial unwillingness to lose face. What actually happens to black children, or white children, has been openly relegated to a secondary consideration in principle, and less than that in practice. (p. 43)

Black children, according to Sowell—sounding almost like Archbishop John Hughes when he founded the Roman Catholic schools—do not need to have White children present to be educated:

> As far back as 1939, the average IQ at Dunbar High School was 11 per cent above the national average—fifteen years before the Court declared this impossible. The counsel for the NAACP in that very case came from a similar quality all-black school in Baltimore. There are, and have been, other schools around the country where black children learned quite well without white children (or teachers) around, as well as other schools where each race failed to learn, with or without the presence of the other. The most cursory look at the history of all-Jewish or all-Oriental schools would have reduced the separate-is-inferior doctrine to a laughingstock instead of the revered "law of the land." (p. 43)

Sowell is critical of turning from integration to busing:

> However futile the various numerical approaches have been in their avowed goal of advancing minorities, their impact has been strongly felt in other ways. The message that comes through loud and clear is that minorities are losers who will never have anything unless someone gives it to them. The destructiveness of this message—on society in general and minority youth in particular—outweighs any trivial gains that may occur here and there. The falseness of the message is shown by the great economic achievements of minorities during the period of equal-rights-legislation before numerical goals and timetables muddled the waters. By and large, the numerical approach has achieved nothing, and has achieved it at great cost. (p. 43)

Finally, Sowell proves he is an ethnic pluralist in Arthur Mann's sense of pluralism without fences, because he also emphasizes the common humanity of Blacks and Whites:

> Underlying the attempt to move people around and treat them like chess pieces on a board is a profound contempt for other human beings. To ignore or resent people's resistance—on behalf of their children or their livelihoods—is to deny our common humanity. To persist dogmatically in pursuit of some abstract goal, without regard to how it is reached, is to despise freedom and reduce three-dimensional life to cardboard pictures of numerical results. The false practicality of results-oriented people ignores the fact that the ultimate results are in the minds and hearts of human beings. Once personal choice becomes a mere inconvenience to be brushed aside by bureaucrats or judges, something precious will have been lost by all people from all backgrounds. (p. 43)

The discussions between the Pattersons and the Sowells will have to be worked out inside the Black community, though I very much doubt that an "official" Black position will ever be achieved. Clearly, some Blacks, such as Patterson's adversaries, would advocate a mosaic or a pluralism with fences approach; other Blacks, such as Patterson, would advocate a melting-pot approach. But still other Blacks (I suspect a majority) would join with Sowell in advocating a pluralism without fences, or a mosaic with permeable boundaries approach.

We are finally able to come to the second of the two questions on which this paper is supposed to focus. Does school desegregation hinder or help the development of a pluralistic society?

If one adopts a melting-pot approach, then obviously the more school integration there is the better, because, although few would claim racial differences will go away in America in the near future, still, integration would certainly facilitate the process of the assimilation of Blacks into American society. Presumably, the slow but sure erosion of distinctive Black culture and identification would result. Indeed, the more desegregation the better. If one can break up Black schools, Black communities, Black organizations, then one is moving more and more toward the ideal of a melting-pot society. Mind you, the melting-pot ideal has not even been achieved for the Irish, who have been in America for well over a century-and-a-quarter; but if one has faith in the desirability and possibility of the melting-pot goal, then the destruction of all Black separatist institutions seems to be a legitimate goal.

If, however, one accepts a position of Black separatism, then one must logically be opposed to school desegregation (though since humans are not always logical, some Black separatists also support busing enthusiastically). Blacks must build up power and self-confidence within their own community and deal with the rest of the world from the strength that comes from their own common purpose. If Orlando Patterson is the Israel Zangwill of American Blacks (Zangwill was the author of the famous play, *The Melting Pot*), so the Black separatists play the same role as did Horace Kallen in his theory of cultural separatism. (Horace Kallen, a Jew like Zangwell, advocated separatism for each of the ethnic groups).

If one is like Thomas Sowell, a cautious ethnic pluralist, then one views desegregation with mixed emotions. It may be a good idea constitutionally and legally; it doesn't solve many educational problems. Black children don't need White children in their schools to do well. The ethnic tensions caused by a body-count approach to integration are dangerous in a pluralistic society. Since about half of the American Black population now opposes busing, Sowell seems to have the votes on his side.

A melting-pot approach to the American Black community seems ludicrous on the face of it. Also, American Blacks are simply not disposed to militant separatism. In a study done by the University of Michigan in 1968, more than nine out of ten blacks rejected the separatist approach. School desegregation, in other words, will not be rejected by most Blacks because it is a threat to their cultural identity; neither will it be advocated in a mindless, mathematical way because of an impossible dream of total assimilation. What counts for American Blacks is not mathematical integration but improvement of the quality of their children's education. In other words, until more data are gathered, it is not unfair to suggest, I think, that most American Blacks believe in pluralism without fences, as did William James, Charles William Eliot, Waclaw Kruszka, and most of the founding fathers of the republic. They simply want the fences that are around them to be taken down.

There are some costs to school desegregation, of course. In a school which is all or mostly Black, the class president, the student council president, the yearbook editors, the valedictorian, and the salutatorian will all be Black—as Catholics, Jews, and Asians found out. If its "your" school, you run it. It would also appear that in Chicago much of the younger civic, political, economic, and social leadership have attended the mostly Black Catholic inner-city schools. It also seems to be the truth that White Catholics who attended parochial schools are more successful economically and socially (with all pertinent background variables standardized) than Catholics who attended public schools. There are, it would seem, some advantages to segregation—but only when it is self-chosen and not that which is imposed by an oppressive outside society.

School integration, particularly according to a mathematical formula, may lead to a decline in these advantages. (Although obviously, there is virtually no empirical evidence to test these possibilities.)

How one views the impact of school desegregation on American racial/ethnic pluralism depends first of all on what one's norms are about the most desirable shape of that pluralism; second, it depends on what one perceives to have been the effects thus far of school desegregation. Until more data are in, the tentative conclusion of this chapter must be that (1) school desegregation has not created greater tensions between Blacks and other urban ethnic groups; and (2) it does not seem to be either a notable step forward toward the total assimilation of American Blacks or a notable impediment to the development of a culturally sophisticated and politically powerful Black ethnic group (*sui generis*) in American life.

I hate to say it after such a lengthy prelude, but school desegregation may not be very relevant at all to the future shape of American pluralism.

REFERENCES

Alba, R. D. Social assimilation among American Catholic nationality-origin groups. *American Sociological Review*, 1976, *41*, 1030–1046.

Brown, T. N. *Irish American nationalism, 1870–1890*. New York: Lippincott, 1966.

Cruse, H. *Crisis of the Negro intellectual*. New York: William Morrow & Company, 1971.

Gambino, R. *Blood of my blood: The dilemma of the Italian Americans*. New York: Doubleday, 1974.

Gans, H. *Urban villagers*. Glencoe, Ill.: Free Press, 1962.

Glazer, N. Ethnic groups in America. In M. Berger, T. Abel, & C. H. Page (Eds.), *Freedom and control in modern society*. New York: Van Nostrand, 1954, pp. 158–172.

Glazer, N., & Moynihan, D. P. *Beyond the melting pot* (2nd ed.). Cambridge, Mass.: M.I.T. University Press, 1971.

Glazer, N., & Moynihan, D. P. (Eds.). *Ethnicity: Theory and experience*. Cambridge, Mass.: Harvard University Press, 1975.

Gordon, M. *Assimilation in American life: The role of race, religion, and national origins*. New York: Oxford University Press, 1964.

Greeley, A. M. *American priests: A report of the National Opinion Research Center*. Prepared for the United States Catholic Conference. Chicago, Ill.: National Opinion Research Center, 1971.

Greeley, A. M. *Ethnicity in the United States: A preliminary reconnaissance*. New York: Wiley Interscience, 1974.

Greeley, A. M. Ethnicity and racial attitudes: The case of the Jews and the Poles. *American Journal of Sociology*, 1975, *80*(4), 909–933. (a)

Greeley, A. M. A model for ethnic political socialization. *American Journal of Political Science*, 1975, *19*(2), 187–206. (b)

Greeley, A. M. The American Catholic: A social portrait. New York: Basic, 1977.

Greeley, A. M., McCready, W., & Theisen, G. Explaining ethnic subcultures: The alcoholic example. Unpublished manuscript, 1978.

Greeley, A. M., & Sheatley, P. B. Attitudes toward racial integration: The South "catches up." In L. Rainwater (Ed.), *Social problems and public policy I. Inequality and justice*. Chicago: Aldine, 1971.

Greene, V. R. For God and country: The origins of Slavic Catholic self-consciousness in America. *Church History*, 1966, *35*, 446–460.

Harris, R. *Prejudice and tolerance in Ulster*. Totowa, N.J.: Rowman & Littlefield, 1972.

Horowitz, D. L. Ethnic identity. In N. Glazer & D. P. Moynihan (Eds.), *Ethnicity: Theory and experience*. Cambridge, Mass.: Harvard University Press, 1975, pp. 111–140.

Isaacs, H. Idols of the tribe. In N. Glazer & D. P. Moynihan (Eds.), *Ethnicity: Theory and experience*. Cambridge, Mass.: Harvard University Press, 1975, pp. 29–52.

Kammen, M. *People of paradox*. New York: Knopf, 1972.

Kobrin, F. E., & Goldscheider, C. *The ethnic factor in family structure and mobility*. Cambridge, Mass.: Ballinger, 1978.

McCready, W. Analysis of a three generational model of religious socialization. Paper presented at meeting of the Society for the Scientific Study of Religion, Chicago, October 1971.

McCready, W. C., & Greeley, A. M. The transmission of cultural heritages: The case of the Irish and Italians. In N. Glazer & D. P. Moynihan (Eds.), *Ethnicity: Theory and experience.* Cambridge, Mass.: Harvard University Press, 1975, pp. 209–235.

Metzger, L. P. American sociology and black assimilation: Conflicting perspectives. *American Journal of Sociology.* 1971, 76, 644–647.

Nie, N., Currie, B., & Greeley, A. M. Political attitudes among American ethnics: A study of perceptual distortion. In A. M. Greeley (Ed.), *Ethnicity in the United States: A preliminary reconnaissance.* New York: Wiley Interscience, 1974.

Novak, M. *The rise of the unmeltable ethnic.* New York: Macmillan, 1972.

Patterson, O. *Ethnic chauvinism: The reactionary impulse.* New York: Steing & Day, 1978.

Sowell, T. *Race and economics.* New York: McKay, 1975.

Stein, H. F., & Hill, R. F. The limits of ethnicity. *The American Scholar.* 1977, 46, 181–189.

Stinchcombe, A., Heimer, C., Iliff, R., Scheppele, K., Smith, T. W., & Taylor, D. G. Crime and punishment in public opinion. Chicago: National Opinion Research Center, 1977. (mimeo)

Suttles, G. D. *The social construction of communities.* Chicago: University of Chicago Press, 1972.

Taylor, D. G., Sheatsley, P. B., & Greeley, A. M. Attitudes toward racial integration. *Scientific American*, 1978, 238, 42–49.

Zangwill, I. *The melting pot* (2nd rev. ed.). New York: Macmillan, 1917.

8

On Democracy and School Integration

ARTHUR L. STINCHCOMBE
AND D. GARTH TAYLOR

INTRODUCTION

It is offensive to American ideals that a person, because of his or her birth, should be assigned to a slum school with antique facilities, an atmosphere of violence, a weak academic program, and a teaching force that has lost all hope. It is offensive whether the reason for the assignment is that the person is Black, or that the mother of the family must support four children without the help of the father, or that the family recently emigrated from a peasant background and speaks broken English. But it is also offensive if the reason for assignment to the slum school is to achieve racial balance, if being born in a suburb would have kept the student from being so assigned. The difference is that, in some circumstances, considerations of equal treatment may balance that offensiveness for the judiciary that must remedy the effects of segregation.

It is also offensive to American ideals that members of one race should be treated as social lepers, as contaminating whatever school they are in and turning it into a slum school. Any public act that implicitly or explicitly concedes to White people the right to treat Black people as a contamination, to be bottled up so as not to infect the student bodies of safely White

ARTHUR L. STINCHCOMBE • National Opinion Research Center, Chicago, Illinois 60637, and Department of Sociology, University of Arizona, Tucson, Arizona 85721. D. GARTH TAYLOR • National Opinion Research Center, and Department of Political Science, University of Chicago, Chicago, Illinois 60637. This research was supported by the National Institute of Education (Grant No. NIE G–76–003S) and by the resources of the National Opinion Research Center. Parts of the report were written while Taylor was a research associate at the Institute for Research on Poverty at the University of Wisconsin, Madison.

schools, is rightly seen as an intolerable exercise of racist sentiment. But it is nearly as offensive to use White children as merely a means, as an inoculation against racial insults, by substantially lengthening their school day by busing them for no apparent educational advantage to themselves, though the administrative, legal, and social benefits of busing may sometimes make such a policy judicially worthwhile.

However, these are substantive questions of how we ought to distribute educational resources, in a social and political context in which other students and the social environment of the school are seen as resources. Such issues address the debate on educational advantages distributed by the school system, raised by the Black parent's statement: "Sitting next to a White child is no guarantee that my child will learn, but it does guarantee that he will be taught" (Crain, 1968, p. 112). This was not the issue in Boston, and, in fact, Boston Black students had more White students sitting next to them *before* the controversy erupted than Black students in almost any other northern metropolitan area *after* court-ordered desegregation.

Instead, the controversy in Boston was about how we shall govern ourselves in a racially mixed society. Two of the principles involved were supported by almost everyone: equality under the law, and democracy. The court, as an authoritative source on equality under the law, imposed a policy that clearly was not what the representatives of the people, acting as the school committee, saw as the requirements of democracy. For, having found the school committee guilty of treating Black people differently, of consigning some of them by birth to ghetto schools, equality under the law required that Black people have remedies. The remedy proposed—busing to achieve racial balance—was unpopular in Boston, opposed by about 90% of the parents in six Boston neighborhoods (see the discussion of Table II, p. 176). When the requirements of equality under the law as interpreted by the courts run into 90% opposition, it is surprising not that there was community resistance, but that only after a couple of years the public was peacefully resigned to living with the court order.

Although we believe that some things can be done to reduce the intensity of the community conflict over desegregation by busing, the conflict reflects a deep dilemma in American government. Americans want to be governed by laws and not be deprived of equal protection under those laws, but they also want to be governed by people, and in a manner of their own choosing. When these two principles come into conflict, as they did in Boston, some weigh the rights of the school committee and "the people" more heavily than the rights of the court and "the establishment," valuing their own government and its policy higher than equal protection. Some choose differently—in large measure because they are aware that sometimes the courts have a duty and a right to go against the will of the people.

Under conditions of uncertainty and of civil disobedience by the leaders of "the people," this results in community conflict. Because the general value of conformity with the law is so well established in the United States, this community conflict is not very severe, and it disappears when it is clear that the court has won and will continue to win. Unless we want to be governed differently, there is no way to prevent community conflicts like that which took place in Boston. This is true because it is not actually a conflict over racial and school policy, but a conflict over a dilemma of a democratic government of laws.

The next four sections of this chapter will explore in much greater detail the issues we have just raised. Our ultimate goal is to explain the *way* that communities react to court-ordered busing to explain, in particular, why the reaction was so protracted and so violent in Boston. The next section of this chapter is an annotated chronology of the events surrounding Judge Garrity's court order—the event which precipitated the most recent Boston school desegregation controversy. The purpose of the chronology is to provide a common frame of reference for the theoretical discussions in the following sections. This kind of detailed presentation of the "facts" is required because the Boston busing conflict does not fit very well into the established theoretical frameworks social scientists have for understanding race relations or community politics.

The third section of the chapter analyzes the way the public perceives the costs and objectives of busing. Basically, we argue that the consensus among leaders and institutions which is the norm for most issues involving public sacrifice (in the sense of public expenditure) is lacking for school desegregation. Second, the costs of achieving school desegregation (by busing or by any nonvoluntary means) are unevenly borne in the White population. Third, the costs are new. Each of these circumstances produces greater conflict over busing and school desegregation than is the case for other "public costs" issues.

The fourth section of the chapter deals directly with the question of racism and opposition to busing. We conclude that the two attitudes are only weakly related. It is a serious misstatement to conclude that the explanation for the opposition to busing in Boston and in other American cities lies in White American racism. The factors which impel Americans to oppose busing are only weakly related to prejudice and stereotyped thinking. The protracted community conflict that sometimes occurs over busing is understood best in terms of the uncertainties and objections to the costs and benefits of busing and in terms of public attitudes toward the conflict between the rule of democracy (i.e., the voice of the people who oppose busing) and the rule of law (i.e., court-ordered desegregation). This conflict is analyzed in section five of this chapter. We find that the reason for the particularly explosive reaction in Boston, compared to other American cities, is that (1) school desegregation was seen by Bostonians as the continuation of a long-lasting struggle with the state legislature over local autonomy; (2) the community had divided on the school desegregation issue long before Garrity's decision; and (3) there was a protracted period of uncertainty as to whether or not there would be a court order implemented and, if so, which plan would ultimately be chosen. The legal and social conditions which made this uncertainty possible are analyzed.

THE EVENTS SURROUNDING THE COURT ORDER

This section contains the annotated chronology of the events surrounding Judge Garrity's decision in *Morgan v Hennigan*[1] on June 21, 1974. In constructing the time line, we have relied heavily on two sources: a special section of the *Boston Globe* of May 25, 1975, which provides a detailed summary of the events and personalities during this period; and the report of the United States Commission on Civil Rights (1975) which was based on a week of public hearings held during the summer after the implementation of Garrity's decision in order to document what happened during that period for the public record.

We have divided the historical period into five sections that correspond to the steps in the escalation of the controversy from a local problem in school board politics to a national issue rooted in constitutional principles. These stages are:

1. 1963–1970: State and local governments cope with the demands of the civil rights movement.
2. 1970–1973: The conflict widens to include federal authority and constitutional principles.
3. 1973–Summer 1974: The state plan is announced and the Garrity decision is heard.
4. Summer 1974–January 1975: Phase I begins and the community reacts.
5. January 1975–Summer 1975: The court plans Phase II and the school committee moves toward the threat of receivership.

1963–1970: State and Local Governments Cope with the Demands of the Civil Rights Movement

During this period, the patterns of community conflict over the Garrity decision are already apparent. The school desegregation issue was seen by Boston's populist minority (represented by Mrs. Hicks and others) as the

---

[1] *Morgan v Hennigan*, 370 F. Supp. 410 D. Mass. (1974).

most recent round in a battle with the state legislature over control of municipal government. The school committee tactics of litigation and delay became established several years before the NAACP suit which resulted in Garrity's order was even filed.

Feb. 19, 1964   Black students take part in the second boycott in one year of the Boston public schools as part of NAACP National School Boycott Day. The next day Owen Kiernan, commissioner of the state board of education, announced that a committee would be formed to study racial imbalance in the commonwealth and to conduct a racial census of the public schools.

March 1964   The report of the Advisory Committee to the Massachusetts State Commissioner of Education (the Kiernan Report) finds, using a criterion of half or more minority enrollment, that four commonwealth cities were maintaining a total of 55 imbalanced schools: Boston, 45; Springfield, 8; Cambridge, 1; and Medford, 1. The committee noted that "open enrollment alone cannot achieve school integration."

Aug. 6, 1965   The Boston School Committee passes a motion prohibiting busing as a means of relieving overcrowded school conditions.

Aug. 18, 1965   The Massachusetts Legislature enacts the Racial Imbalance Act (RIA), a law which included the most advanced school integration requirements of any major city in the nation. The law required local school committees to take affirmative action to eliminate racial imbalance using such techniques as redistricting, public reassignment, strategic placement of new schools, and busing. Strong sanctions were available for use against local school committees, the commissioner of education could refuse to certify all state school aid for that system. Nevertheless, the act was ineffective because it did not require integration of all-White schools; it prohibited involuntary busing; and its guidelines for compliance were vague, opening avenues for procrastination and evasion.

Beginning in 1966, the Boston School Committee sought, through litigation and legislation, to strike down the RIA. State legislators regularly introduced "repealers" of the RIA in each of its ten years of existence.

(See Levy, 1971, for a more detailed legislative history of the Racial Imbalance Act and for documentation of the factual claims of discrimination on which the law was based.)

April 1966   The State Board of Education determines that the Boston School Committee is in violation of the RIA; $6.3 million in educational aid is put in escrow.

August 1966   The Boston School Committee files suit with the Suffolk County Superior Court challenging the state board decision, and a second suit challenging the constitutionality of the RIA which is referred directly to the Massachusetts Supreme Court. Both suits fail. The school committee and the state board enter into negotiation and the following pattern of enforcement of the RIA is established for the next several years: each state board decision is litigated; all official actions come to a halt pending the outcome of the case; a compromise solution is arrived at wherein the amount of racial balance produced is relatively small.

(And again in November, 1971) Louise Day Hicks unsuccessfully campaigns against Kevin White for the mayorality on a platform of "removing the politics from city administration." By this she means that the city government has lost too much of its authority to the state legislature and to civil rights leaders.

The RIA and the recent legislative interference in the Boston schools were seen by a sizable element of the city population as the most recent manifestation of the tradition of "Boston bills" that were passed by the Massachusetts State Legislature to direct the actions of the Boston municipal government. Henry Parkman, writing in 1932, noted that because of the many laws which were passed and amendments which were made to the state constitution during the period of transition from Yankee to immigrant authority in the city's history:

> The State still retains control of many of the municipal activities of Boston. . . . The city . . . is forced to resort to the Legislature for the authority to borrow for many projects; . . . the Mayor is forced annually to present the Legislature a request for the authority to obtain sufficient revenue from taxation to carry out the activities of municipal departments, and the School Committee must obtain from the Legislature the necessary authority for funds for school building and administrative purposes; . . . the control and management of the police force is in the hands of a Commissioner appointed by the Governor; the Licensing Board is subject to gubernatorial appointment and on many boards and commissions, established from time to time, the State insists on representation. (p. 141)

Levy (1971) concludes that between 1930 and 1967 this pattern did not change very much. For instance, it was not until 1962 that the power to appoint the chief of police was restored to the city.

The theme of frustration and grass roots control in Boston politics has been analyzed by Handlin (1941) and Friedman (1973). An analysis of the 1959 mayoral election was conducted by Levin (1960) and a specific study of the appeal of Louise Day Hicks was conducted by Pettigrew, Ross, and Crawford (1966).

1970–1973: The Conflict Widens to Include Federal Authority and Constitutional Principles

This is a period of continued action by government agencies and Black groups which are trying to cope with the frustration and delay produced by the school committee's response to the demands of the civil rights movement. The school committee's response escalates slightly during this period to include outright noncooperation in situations where it could not be legally forced to provide assistance or information. During this period, there is a proliferation of proposals for desegregation, plans for desegregation, and lawsuits. In particular, the state board of education lawsuit and the NAACP lawsuit became enmeshed. The remedy for the NAACP lawsuit (Phase I) was the plan which had been arrived at during the state board of education lawsuit. This multiplicity eventually became a source of confusion as the various parties to the dispute claimed the legitimacy of the plan most to their liking.

1970	The Department of Justice Office of Civil Rights begins a review of the situation in the Boston public schools.
Fall 1971	The state board of education, in the most recent round of enforcement of the RIA (see August 1966) once again demands racial balance in the Boston public schools. Twenty-one million dollars is now withheld, the total will eventually become $50 million.
August 1971	The school committee, in order to meet the board of education requirements, votes for mandatory reassignment of students from Lee School to Fifield School.
Sept. 1971	The school committee reverses the Lee/Fifield policy. The state board of education withholds funds. The school committee sues in the Suffolk County Superior Court to recover the funds. The state board countersues on Fourteenth Amendment grounds, escalating the conflict to a constitutional issue. J. Harold Flannery, NAACP legal counsel, begins to develop a class action suit on constitutional grounds.
Nov. 1971	The federal executive branch becomes involved in Boston for the first time. The U.S. Department of Health, Education, and Welfare (HEW) writes a letter to the school board charging discrimination in certain educational programs. The letter is the first step in a process that would lead two years later to a finding of discrimination by HEW and a threat to cut off all federal education funds.
March 1972	The local chapter of the NAACP files suit (*Morgan v. Hennigan*) in the Federal District Court before Judge Arthur Garrity, alleging governmental discrimination in creating and maintaining a segregated public school system.
June 1972	On the basis of the Office of Civil Rights review (1970), HEW begins proceedings against the Boston School Committee. Ten million dollars in federal funds is at stake; by 1975 the total will be $13 million.
Fall 1972	Neil Sullivan, state commissioner of education, had been directed by the state board of education to draft a plan for achieving racial balance. The school committee had not cooperated in supplying information about the Boston school system. Sullivan now unveils his plan which leaves out large sections of the city.

Dec. 1972	The state superior court restores state aid to the Boston school system and directs the school committee to comply with the state board's revised version of the Sullivan plan which is to be announced.
Spring 1973	A federal administrative judge upholds the HEW suit on the basis of a dual school system.
June 1973	The state board of education, having found a number of Boston School Committee integration proposals unacceptable, presented its "Short Term Plan to Reduce Imbalance in the Boston Public Schools." The plan, designed solely to meet the limited requirements of the RIA, proposed to reduce the number of imbalanced schools from 61 to 42 by redistricting, reorganizing the grade structure, and by busing about 19,000 of the city's approximately 82,000 students to different schools. This plan was the Phase I plan under the Garrity court order.

1973–Summer 1974: The State Plan Is Announced and the Garrity Decision Is Heard

During this period the Racial Imbalance Act was repealed by the state legislature but then reinstated by the governor in a revised form which removed the compulsory aspects of compliance. The Racial Imbalance Act was the legal basis of the state board of education lawsuit. Garrity's ruling reasserted the state board of education's plan in its pre-weakened (i.e., in its compulsory) version. The success of the state-level strategy, however, fueled the hope that the remedy for the NAACP case would be found unconstitutional upon Supreme Court appeal. During this period the mayor made clear his low profile in supporting Garrity's decision and preparing the city for Phase I.

March 1974	The Boston School Department notified parents and students of new school assignments for September 1974, pursuant to the state's "Short Term Plan" (see June 1973). Plans were being made in a number of quarters to thwart the action of the state court. The governor and many state legislators promised to seek repeal or modifications of the RIA. Such action might negate the court-imposed plan.
Spring 1974	The mayor decided in the spring of 1974 to, in his words, "broker" the situation by acting as a mediator among the various factions in the conflict. He made it clear that he was against busing, that he had not created the state plan, that it was up to the superintendant to implement the court-ordered plan, and that he, as mayor, would provide police protection (*Boston Globe*, May 25, 1975).
	The mayor's public education effort consisted of a series of "coffees" in the homes of persons opposed to court-ordered transportation of pupils.
May 10, 1974	While the Supreme Judicial Court of Massachusetts upheld the constitutionality of the RIA, the state legislature now

votes to repeal it. Governor Sargent vetoed the repeal and submitted his own amendments to the act which were subsequently passed. The revised law removed the compulsory aspects of the original plan but guaranteed Blacks the chance to transfer from majority Black schools to White schools in other parts of the city.

June 21, 1974   Judge Garrity's decision reasserts the inevitability of the state plan (Phase I) after the weakening of the RIA (see May 10, 1974). Phase I left out Charlestown, East Boston, North End, Brighton, and much of West Roxbury. The decision left open the question of future revision of the state plan. Judge Garrity ordered the school committee to develop a full plan for all schools in Boston to begin in September 1975 (Phase II).

Summer 1974   One of the developments in the months prior to the opening of school in September 1974 was the consolidation of antibusing groups under an umbrella organization known as ROAR, an acronym for Restore Our Alienated Rights (see November 1967 and the discussion there of the meaning of "alienated rights" in Boston politics). Public officials who had become prominent opponents to forced busing during the past ten years were publicly associated with ROAR. ROAR meetings were held in the city council executive chamber or in the regular chambers when the meetings became too large.

Summer 1974–January 1975: Phase I Begins and the Community Reacts

The city had not prepared adequately for desegregation. Moreover, during this period the legal counsel for the Boston police suggested that the laws against trespassing on school property would not be enforced, the mayor of Boston suggested that school boycotts were legal, and the president of the United States said that he disagreed with the court order. Each of these statements lent legitimacy to the ideas that the laws need not be obeyed. Garrity's reaction is to escalate slowly the level of enforcement of Phase I, within the ambit of his legal possibilities.

July 1974   After Judge Garrity's decision, the Boston School Committee asked for and received permission to suggest modifications to the Phase I plan. The school committee's recommendations were to: (1) stay the order until a full citywide plan could be worked out; and (2) phase in segregation over two years, with the middle schools and high schools first, then the elementary schools. J. Harold Flannery, NAACP legal counsel, agreed with the second proposal but not the first, and on July 11 Judge Garrity invited the school committee to work out a plan.

July 28, 1974   The school committee votes to propose no alternatives.

Summer 1974   Prior to the opening of school in September 1974, attempts were made to provide training opportunities for faculty and administrative personnel. These attempts were thwarted by the nature of the collective bargaining agreement between teachers and the school system, difficulties involved in scheduling training sessions on short notice, and delays and unavailability of funding. The development of any overall school desegregation training plan was affected by HEW's freeze on Emergency School Assistance Act and other federal funds, which was brought about because of the federal district court finding of discrimination and which lasted until January 1975.

Sept. 5, 1974   Boston Police Patrolmen's Association legal counsel Frank Magee, in a press release and interview, instructs police that state laws on school trespassing do not require arrests and that court complaints would have to be sought against trespassers on public school property before they could be arrested. This was tantamount to announcing that trespassers would not be prosecuted.

Sept. 9, 1974   Mayor White appears on educational television in Boston with a lengthy address which includes the following statements:

> We are faced with the unpleasant task of implementing a court order. . . . The city has exhausted all legal avenues of appeal at a cost of in excess of a million dollars. . . . I'm for integration but against forced busing. They are not mutually exclusive. People who would boycott schools are asked to weigh the decision carefully, but it is their decision to make. Parents should attend open houses at schools before making a final decision to send or not to send students to school.
>
> The U.S. Commission on Civil Rights, in its report *Desegregating the Boston Public Schools* observed: "The mayor's position . . . strongly inferred that it was legitimate to boycott schools. It is not. Boycotting schools runs afoul of a panoply of state laws and can result in criminal prosecution.

Sept. 12, 1974   School opens. The Tactical Police Force is called to quell disturbances at South High. Most other schools show few incidents. Enrollment in the school system is down 10,000 from a possible enrollment of about 82,000. The boycott was participated in even in neighborhoods not involved in Phase I but where a citywide plan was expected. The average enrollment during the 1974–75 school year was about 60,000.

Sept. 22, 1974   State Senator Bulger, State Representative Flaherty, and Mrs. Hicks issue a Declaration of Clarification: There is resistance in South Boston because "it is against our children's interest to send them to school in crime infested Roxbury." (The statement was accompanied by charts showing neighborhood crime statistics.) "Routine, everyday violence ravages the black community (but is hidden from the public by a) conspiratorial press."

Oct. 2, 1974   After two weeks of boycott, White attendance had risen. On this day, however, a riot breaks out in the South Boston lunchroom, legitimating the fearful reaction White parents might have had about their children's schools. From this time on, at least 25 police are stationed inside South High and 300 outside.

Oct. 3, 1974   National Boycott Day, attendance is 41,800, the lowest it will ever be in the course of the conflict.

Oct. 7, 1974   A South Boston mob pulls Andre Yvon Jean-Louis from his car and beats him as well as beating the police who try to interfere.

Oct. 7, 1974   Mayor White asks Judge Garrity to assign federal marshals to Boston. He declared that he was able to maintain public safety and orderly implementation of the court's order in 90% of the city but that he could no longer guarantee the safety of the students in South Boston and Hyde Park high schools.

Oct. 8, 1974   Blacks in Roxbury stone White motorists. Mayor White bans all marches and demonstrations of any kind.

Oct. 9, 1974   President Ford enters the fray. In a press conference, he declares:

> The court decision in that case, in my judgment, was not the best solution to quality education in Boston. I have consistently opposed forced busing to achieve racial balance as a solution to quality education. And therefore I respectfully disagree with the Judge's order. . . . I hope and trust that it's not necessary to call in Federal officials or Federal law enforcement agencies. . . . The marshals, if my information is accurate, are under the jurisdiction of the court, not directly under my jurisdiction. . . . As far as I know, no specific request has come to me for any Federal involvement and therefore I'm not in a position to act under those circumstances.

Oct. 15, 1974   A White student is stabbed in Hyde Park High. The entire Tactical Police Force (125 men) is called in to restore order. Governor Sargent calls out the National Guard.

Oct. 31, 1974   Judge Garrity's final ruling on *Morgan* v. *Kerrigan* (the school committee appeal of *Morgan* v. *Hennigan*) sets in motion the citywide plan for fall 1975—Phase II.

Dec. 10, 1974   A White student is stabbed at South High. Boston School Superintendant Leary closes five schools in South Boston and Roxbury for two days.

Dec. 13, 1974   Judge Garrity orders a contingency plan for closing all the schools in South Boston and transferring the students.

Dec. 16, 1974   The school committee votes to defy Judge Garrity's order and not submit a Phase II plan (see Oct. 31, 1974).

Dec. 18, 1974   Judge Garrity threatens the school committee with receivership and civil contempt.

Dec. 19, 1974   A federal appeals court upholds Judge Garrity's decision. School Committee Chairman Kerrigan announces an appeal of both cases (see Oct. 31, 1974) to the Supreme Court.

Dec. 29, 1974   Mayor White, in a press release announces that the city will pay the costs of the Supreme Court appeal and says that

"citywide busing should not be imposed as long as widespread
boycotts and repeated disruptions are still blunting the success
of Phase I."

January 1975–Summer 1975: The Court Plans Phase II and the School Committee Moves toward the Threat of Receivership

Garrity's enforcement strategy included an escalation of the court's
authority into areas where community organizations and community leaders
would normally be expected to guide the public reaction. The court created
community organizations for overseeing the implementation of desegregation and created expert panels with community representation for preparing
plans for further change. Using the legal strategies available, the court also
stimulated the mayor to plan more comprehensively for the second year of
desegregation.

Jan. 7, 1975	The school committee proposes a totally voluntary plan for Phase II.
Jan. 8, 1975	South High reopens with 627 students, 500 police, and metal detectors at the doors. During the rest of the year there were, on average, 100 city and state police at South High each day and 85 at Hyde Park High.
Feb. 4, 1975	Judge Garrity announces a panel of four masters and two experts who will draw up the Phase II plan.
	State Congressman Richard Finnigan introduces legislation to repeal the RIA. The state law and the litigation based on it became moot when the federal court handed down its decision in *Morgan* v. *Hennigan*. In the Civil Rights Commission hearings, Finnigan agreed that "it wouldn't have any legal bearing (on the implications of the federal order). . . . I would say that the legislature in repealing the RIA, I would hope that the federal courts might take a second look at what is happening in the area of forced busing" (p. 158).
May 10, 1975	Garrity announces the final Phase II plan, which leaves out East Boston.
May 12, 1975	The U.S. Supreme Court refuses to hear the school committee appeal (see Dec. 19 and Dec. 29, 1974).
July 31, 1975	Mayor White submits to the Federal District Court "The City of Boston Safety and Police Utilization Plan" which, accord-ing to the U.S. Commission on Civil Rights report, contains many of the elements necessary for public safety in Boston during Phase II.
Aug. 1975	U.S. Commission on Civil Rights issues a report, *Desegregat-ing the Boston Public Schools: A Crisis in Civic Responsi-bility*, which contained the following language:

> We conclude that, on balance, substantial progress was
> made in Boston in 1974–1975 in the direction of upholding
> and implementing the constitutional rights of children and
> young people. We conclude further that the groundwork

has been laid for even more significant progress in this direction in the school year 1975–1976.

We have identified the fact that the Boston School Committee has consistently and persistently refused to accept the responsibility placed on them by the Constitution and the United States as defined by the Federal district court. . . . They have treated the court-ordered Phase I plan as an administrative problem for which the School Committee had only perfunctory responsibility. . . . We have taken note of the failure of the Mayor and other city officials to support unequivocally the Federal district court's finding of violation of the constitution by the Boston School Committee and the court's subsequent orders designed to bring the School Committee into conformity with the Constitution. . . . The School Committee did not view itself as having an affirmative duty to inform the public about desegregation planning. . . . As yet the mayor has not undertaken, in preparation for Phase II, a public education and information program comparable to his Phase I effort. . . . We have identified the failures on the part of leaders in many segments of the city's life to speak out in support of the constitutional and moral values which are an integral part of the court-ordered plan. . . . We recognize that the Federal government failed to provide the leadership that should have been provided in support of the court's decision. . . .

Therefore it is our recommendation that if the Boston School Committee persists in its refusal to take affirmative actions in support of the constitutional rights of the children and young people of Boston, the Federal district court should consider placing the Boston public school system in receivership. (v–viii, 39, 53, 56)

THE NATURE OF THE COSTS AND OBJECTIVES OF BUSING

In this section, we examine from a more theoretical point of view the reasons for the volatility of the busing issue in American cities. We argue that busing, or rather, mandatory school desegregation, is a social objective that is unevenly supported by the establishment leaders who are most interested in and most responsible for its achievement. Furthermore, the costs of achieving the social objective of school desegregation are borne unevenly by the White population. And, finally, the costs are new. Each of these characteristics makes busing different from other situations in which people are taxed or otherwise asked by their leaders to sacrifice for the common good.

Mixing races in school is an objective that serves only a few people's immediate short-run interests. Whenever free transfers out of ghetto schools are offered to the Black community, a small proportion of Black parents and students take advantage of them. The benefits of going to school with White students do not seem substantial enough to most Black people to be worth paying much, in money or in personal trouble, for. There is no evidence that very many White people actively seek out integrated neighborhoods and schools to improve the social education of their children. Furthermore, there is evidence that they usually object to any hint that their children will be sent to ghetto schools.

Table I shows the level of support for various proposals for alleviating racial imbalance in the public schools. The data are from surveys done in four northern cities and in one suburb of Boston. These results show that there are several different factors which people attend to in evaluating proposals for desegregation. If a plan is seen as voluntary, limited to older students, and/or transporting mainly Black students, then the plan will receive much greater support in White public opinion. Plans with these characteristics, of course, would not lead to great changes in the pattern of segregation. Other plans, which would have a greater effect on racial balance, are less popular. The range is from about 30% support (in the city) for metropolitanization and/or busing older children only to about 20% for mandatory programs at the elementary level. It is necessary to exercise particular caution in interpreting these figures, since the level of support shown for any plan is greatly influenced by the particular words which are used to describe the plan in the survey question. For instance, plans which "require transportation" are about 10% more popular than plans with "busing," all other things being equal.

Therefore, if positive investments in integration are in the public interest (in Boston, the agreement of the courts, the cardinal, the mayor, and the governor suggests that there are important reasons to believe investments in integration are worth the effort), they are to serve some long-run system goal rather than immediate interests. The benefits of desegregation, in other words, are systemwide. The costs, on the other hand, are local and, as we shall see, inequitably distributed. The lack of symmetry between the costs and objectives of busing makes it a highly volatile public issue, although there are other issues with a similar character.

A good many costs of doing business as a society are opposed to the short-run interests of most people. Foreign aid expenditures are investments in the collective welfare of the United States that are unpopular with the mass of ordinary people. Police budgets and expenditures for educating other people's children are local equivalents. Most of the time most of us consent to allowing people who are supposed to know what is in our collective interest–Congress and city councils, for example–decide how much these public goods ought to cost. While we all complain in April about the level of taxes, we regard paying for most public goods at a level decided to be best for us by our representatives as an inevitable cost of living in the United States.

To put the whole problem another way, most of the inevitable public functions mentioned above are passed by bipartisan agreement (except sometimes at the margin) in the houses of Congress, and the budgets of Democratic and Republican administrations look pretty much alike. If the public functions are local, then we find that the budgets of different cities are nearly equal (unless the state government takes over some local functions in a particular state), regardless of whether the city government is Democratic or Republican, has a mayor–council or a city manager, or employs at-large elections or ward elections. To a very large degree, the whole body of the elite are convinced that the functions of defense, police, and education are inevitable, and there is no real division between a populist and an establishment elite.

What makes the cost of doing something about the ghetto by busing children a distinctive kind of public cost issue is that few people really think it "simply has to be done." It does not have the sense of inevitability that national defense or paying firemen or even schooling itself has. We got by for a good many years without integration by transportation from one school district to another, and there is little evidence that very many individuals in either kind of school want to be bused. And, though many things are required by justice that nobody in particular wants, the evidence that *de facto* segregated schools are the most severe injustice visited on Black people is not very impressive.

There is little evidence that one school in the United States is much better than another, as far as pulling people out of poverty is concerned (Hauser, 1969; Jencks, 1972). Integrated schools may be slightly better for both Black and White people than either segregated White or segregated Black schools, once one controls for the input of students, but the difference is very small compared with the difference made by going from the average years in school of southern rural Black counties of a generation ago (or rural southern Italian and Polish averages of two generations ago) to urban American standards. What mainly determines how much people learn in school is how many years they stay there, not whether they attend a ghetto slum school or a suburban school. People who enter school somewhat behind in cultural accomplishments (and poor people on the average do) stay approximately equal distances behind throughout school, whether they go to predominantly White schools or predominantly Black schools. Those who enter somewhat ahead stay about equal distances ahead.

Thus, we cannot realistically make the argument that the only way to get Black people out of slums is to integrate schools—schools are crucial to the whole process, but unintegrated schools that taught mainly Jewish or Irish or Chinese students got people out of slums in previous generations.

Table I. Support for Alternative Desegregation Plans in Northern American Cities

Desegregation plan		Percent favoring desegregation, by city and race							
		Boston White	Suburb of Boston White	Louisville White	Louisville Black	Los Angeles White	Los Angeles Black	Milwaukee White	Milwaukee Black
1. Specialized schools, high quality programs open to everyone									
2. Open enrollment	(1)[a]	84	75	88	89				
3. Voluntary transfer, transportation paid by school system				82	74				
4. Magnet schools in Black areas	(3)	60	61						
5. Change school boundaries, keep busing at a minimum	(1) (3)	56 58	65 58						
6. Voluntary Specialized Learning Center, elementary grades, maximum 30 min bus ride						55	66		
7. Raise taxes to improve Black schools	(1)	38	28						
8. Bus a few Blacks to each White school	(1)	38	28						

9.	Divide the school district into smaller, autonomous systems					35	54
10.	Close schools in segregated areas, build new schools in border areas				37	73	
11.	Bus older children only	(1)	32	23			
12.	Metropolitanization	(1)	25	13			
		(3)	37	22			
		(4)	29	12			
		(5)	33				
13.	Merge city and suburban districts					27	52
14.	Bus Blacks only	(1)	26	12			
		(2)	16				
		(3)	25	27			
15.	Required attendance Specialized Learning Center, elementary grades, 30 min bus ride			—	21	60	
16.	Close Black schools, bus to White schools	(4)	14	12			

^a The numbers after the questions asked of the Boston residents indicate the time during the study when the question was asked. The calendar dates corresponding to each number are: (1) September 1973; (2) April 1974; (3) July 1974; (4) November 1974; and (5) July 1975. The results from Louisville, Los Angeles, and Milwaukee are from phone surveys of the adult population of the urban area. The results from Boston and the suburb of Boston are from samples of particular neighborhoods in these areas and are, therefore, not representative of the cities overall. The Boston data are from a panel study.

The argument instead has to be made on the ground of how we want to be governed. Do we want a government that allows school systems to treat children differently because of their race—specifically, that allows school systems to assign people to ghetto schools on the basis of their race? In Boston, the school committee was convicted of that. This occurred in spite of the fact that Boston had a higher proportion of Black children going to school in predominantly White schools than most other major cities. The offense, then, was not the gross amount of damage done to Black children by assignment to ghetto schools, but depriving Black children of equal protection under the law. What we want to do about busing is a much less serious question than whether we want to be governed in a discriminatory manner.

In addition to the uncertainty about the immediate educational and social needs served by busing, the establishment is not very well agreed on exactly what the consequences of busing will be. Only some cities need to be integrated (in the sense of mixing a large ghetto population and White students—of course it is easy in a suburb or a midwestern, small town to integrate those few Black people who ordinarily live there), and it is not a sufficiently important public purpose to cross into suburban jurisdictions to get it done. The establishment, then, is not willing to make a very good case for busing—only that not busing is illegal. And this means that part of the public leadership does not agree, and that the consensus among leaders we find on military budgets, for instance, is not found on busing. In sum, the first reason that busing is more volatile than other public costs issues is the uncertainty and high-level disagreement about the objectives of mandatory desegregation.

The second reason is that the costs that arise when a school system desegregates are inequitably borne. Through a series of judicial and legislative decisions, the ghetto has become a legal entity and the policy of subjecting Black children to ghetto conditions by any act of government is illegal. Because it is illegal to confine citizens to ghetto schools on the basis of race, Black parents and children have a grievance against the school system which does that, and that grievance will stand up in court. But what is distinctive about the nature of the decision is that, unlike the remedy for breach of contract, once the court finds a systematic pattern of discrimination by an organ of state authority, it is bound to remedy the complaint, not only for the complainant, but also for all people injured by the pattern of discrimination. Thus, an individual's legitimate grievance against the school committee results in the school committee's being required to figure out how to keep from subjecting Black children to ghetto conditions. But the specific form of the decision is usually that anything that one subjects Blacks to, one also has to subject Whites to.

The problem of desegregation then becomes redefined. It is now no longer that White people have to consent to having Black people in their schools—they are overwhelmingly willing to do that in Boston and elsewhere in the country. Taylor, Sheatsley, and Greeley (1978) and Taylor (1979) examine evidence on national norms for school integration and racial tolerance which supports this argument. Furthermore, we find that Bostonians are more liberal than the national norm for large northern cities on several of the survey questions which are usually used to measure racial prejudice. (This was also found by Schuman and Gruenberg, 1970, in their article comparing racial attitudes in different northern cities using the Kerner Commission data.) Our results for Boston are shown in Table II. Here we compare Boston with the national norm for northern standard metropolitan statistical areas (SMSAs) and also suburbs of northern SMSAs. Since there is a correlation between religion and racial liberalism in Boston (but not in the national population generally), results are shown separately for Protestants and Catholics. The basic finding is that on all but one question, the Bostonians in our sample are more racially liberal than is generally the case in large northern cities. The exception is one detailed question measuring tolerance for different amounts of Black–White integration. Over 50% did not object to a school that was half or more Black, but this was lower than the national norm for residents of large, northern cities.

The new problem caused by the court's decision is not that Whites are forced to agree to integrate their schools but that *certain White people have to pay the costs of abolishing the ghetto, by having their children mixed into the ghetto.* To minimize costs of transportation and to accomodate legal distinctions between central city and suburb, the people who are supposed to pay this cost are those who live near the ghetto inside the legal limits of the central city. This is, of course, no more than the cost that the system of segregation has imposed on middle-class Black people all along (children of middle-class Black people are much more likely to go to a ghetto school than are children of middle-class White people), but that does not change the perception of the White people—that they are being asked to pay a new cost of increased risks of crime and lowered educational quality in order to solve a social problem that is not their fault.

The result of the selective enforcement of transportation among school districts is that even if it is in the public interest, the costs of doing something about the ghetto fall very unevenly among White people. And the unevenness is greater than for such public goods as police or welfare costs: money can be transported into a ghetto school or into a city from across the country, but children have to be transported there from someplace nearby, and someplace within the same school board jurisdiction. So, not only are the costs of school desegregation poorly justified by the establishment, but

Table II. Racial Tolerance in Our Boston Sample and in Northern Cities Generally

| | Percentage giving the racially tolerant response | | | | |
| | Northern cities | | | Boston[c] | |
Racial tolerance questions[a]	Catholic	Protestant	Survey date	Catholic	Protestant
Dinner					
SMSA[b] central city	69	78	July 1975	79	82
suburb of SMSA	78	75			
Push					
SMSA central city	35	32	July 1975	51	61
suburb of SMSA	33	39			
Segregated neighborhood					
SMSA central city	60	63	Sept. 1973	86	95
suburb of SMSA	70	72			
Busing					
SMSA central city	10	10	Sept. 1973	9	20
suburb of SMSA	11	14	July 1974	7	22
			July 1975	5	26
School integration					
SMSA central city	26	24	Sept. 1973	52	38
suburb of SMSA	30	23			

[a] Question Wordings (racially tolerant responses used for analysis are italicized):
Dinner: "How strongly would you object if a member of your family wanted to bring a Black friend home to dinner? Would you object strongly, mildly, or *not at all*?"
Push: "Blacks should not push themselves where they are not wanted. *Disagree*."
Segregated neighborhood: "White people have the right to keep Blacks out of their neighborhood and Blacks should respect that right. *Disagree*."
Busing: "Do you favor or oppose busing both Black and White children to achieve racial balance? *Favor*"(Boston survey wording). "In general, do you favor or oppose the busing of Black and White children from one school district to another? *Favor*" (NORC wording).
School integration: "Would you yourself have any objection to sending your children to a school where more than 50 percent of the children are black? *No*."
[b] SMSA is the abbreviation for Standard Metropolitan Statistical Area. This is the unit used for statistical reporting of many different kinds of government data for urban areas.
[c] See the note to Table I on the representativeness of the Boston sample. The national data are pooled from the National Opinion Research Center General Social Surveys for 1972–1976.

these costs are unevenly borne. Of course, the costs of having to go to a ghetto school were unevenly borne before the busing decision as well. They were borne almost entirely by Black people, which is why the courts have held the pattern of racial segregation in schools to be unjust.

The third reason for the volatility of the issue is that the costs of desegregation by busing are new. In a democracy, any administration that imposes large new costs on the people, for instance a new sales tax or a rise in the income tax rate, is likely to be in trouble. The bipartisan agreement that we really need new tax revenues is often not enough to save the governor who signed the tax bill in the following election. Once the first governor has been kicked out by the public, though, the next governor who does not repeal the new tax has just as much responsibility for that tax before his Maker, but is not nearly as likely to lose the following election. New burdens rankle most.

So the costs of desegregation by busing are imposed with an uncertain purpose, they are unequally distributed, and they are new costs. A vacillating establishment, unequal privileges, and new taxes brought down the old regime in France—and these same factors provide fuel to be lit by sparks from the populist leadership in cities such as Boston where there is an alert and organized opposition to mandatory school desegregation.

RACIAL ATTITUDES AND OPPOSITION TO BUSING

The previous section of this chapter explained why people might question the legitimacy and equitability of busing. In the next section we will show the relation between these perceptions and actual opposition to the court. But first, we must explain why people's questions about the legitimacy and equitability of busing should not be interpreted as simple manifestations of racism.

Tables I and II showed that most people in Boston did not object to their children going to school with Black people, yet they did object to a program whose purpose was to mix ghetto populations in their schools. These results can help explain one of the surprising, nonintuitive results from survey studies of contemporary racial issues: busing attitudes are only weakly related to the traditional, psychological measures of racism or prejudice. Kelley (1974) found this with national data and our own analyses show the same for Boston during the time of the court order. Busing attitudes are, however related to people's perceptions that the new costs of integration by busing are inequitably allocated, illegitimately arrived at (illegitimately decided by the courts and the establishment), and pose personal threats to the personal well-being and academic achievement of one's children. For instance, people's attitudes about what will happen to test scores predicts very strongly how much opposition they will show to the court order.

We began the analysis which led to this complex theory by defining several measures of racial attitudes. One scale, which we will call *racial liberalism*, consists of three of the items from Table II: "segregated neighborhoods", "dinner", and "tolerance for school integration." This is a subset of the well-studied National Opinion Research Center (NORC) scale of attitudes toward racial integration (Taylor *et al.*, 1978). A second scale of racial attitudes measures White people's awareness of discrimination. Whites who are nonprejudiced agree with the propositions that: (1) discrimination hurts Black job chances; (2) Blacks have a worse chance of being able to attend good public schools; (3) discrimination hurts Black housing chances; and (4) Blacks do not receive equal educational opportunities. These items were first used in the Kerner Commission studies. We will call this the *discrimination awareness* scale.

These two scales are the "traditional" psychological measures of racism and prejudice in our analysis. They do not correlate consistently or highly with our dependent measures which are: (1) support for the school committee's defiant posture toward the court; (2) support for the boycott; and (3) "very strong" opposition to busing. Table III shows the relationships between the racial attitude scales and the dependent measures, controlling for religion, respondent's beliefs about the effect of desegregation on test scores and the respondent's position on neighborhood schools.

The traditional racial attitude scales do not correlate consistently or highly with the dependent measures. (The standard error for each coefficient is about .045 and so paths less than .08 or .09 should not be regarded as statistically significant.)

Table III. The Relation between Racial Liberalism, Discrimination Awareness, and Opposition to the Court and Busing in the Boston Sample[a]

Predictor variables[c]	Dependent variables[b]		
	Support school committee defiance	Support boycott	Very strongly oppose busing
Low racial liberalism	.05	.10	.02
Perceive low discrimination	.11	.04	.03
Catholic religion	.01	.13	.11
White scores will decline	.09	.11	.09
Strongly support neighborhood schools	.11	.09	.33

[a] The table shows the coefficients for three multiple regression equations predicting September 1973 levels of support for boycotts, support for school committee defiance and "very strong" opposition to busing as a function of racial liberalism, discrimination awareness, religion, beliefs about the effect of integration on White test scores, and support for neighborhood schools.

[b] All independent and dependent variables are scored as dichotomies. Therefore, coefficients may be read as partial percentage differences predicting the percent anti-integration on each of the dependent variables. For instance, controlling for the other predictor variables, those "high" on the racial liberalism scale were 5% more likely to support school committee defiance. The standard error for each slope in the table is about .045 and so this coefficient is not statistically significant. The intercept for each regression equation is not shown.

[c] Question wordings: Racial liberalism and Perceive discrimination: see text for discussion.
Test scores: "Research has shown that White student test scores often decrease when they attend desegregated schools. Agree."
Neighborhood schools: "Children should always go to school in their own neighborhood. Agree"
School committee defiance: "As a member of the school committee, would you encourage other members of the school committee to defy the court order?"
Boycott: "If you were a member of the Boston School Committee, how strongly would you favor or oppose school boycotts by White parents to protest change in the racial balance of White schools?"
Busing: (See Table II for wording of main question) "How strongly do you favor/oppose busing both Negro and White children from one school district to another to achieve racial balance? Very strongly, strongly, moderately, or just slightly."

However, the belief that test scores will decline does correlate consistently with opposition as does support for the principle of neighborhood schools. One possible interpretation of this pattern is that "test scores" and "neighborhood schools" are codewords for racism—issues which have been manufactured by opponents of the plan to channel racist sentiments into a political confrontation. If this interpretation is true, then the racial liberalism scale and the discrimination awareness scale should correlate highly with the "manufactured issues." This is not the case, however. Racial liberalism does not correlate with test score beliefs or with view toward neighborhood schools. Those who perceive discrimination are more likely to oppose neighborhood schools (which supports the codeword hypothesis) but they are slightly *more* likely to believe that integration lowers test scores (which contradicts the hypothesis). Thus, the pattern of relationships between these variables does not support the "codeword for racism" thesis and we are left with the conclusion that opposition to busing and to the court order do not correlate with measures of racism or prejudice but do correlate with beliefs about the negative effects of integration on one's children and on one's neighborhood schools.

This suggests that the perceived costs of integration are associated in their minds with the ghetto, and with ghetto schools, rather than with individual Black people. People think that ghetto schools are bad, and that this badness might be communicated to their schools under the busing program, and yet do not (or at least do not very often) think this badness is carried out by individual Black people. The people of Boston show sociological imagination in their view that the ghetto as a social institution has different effects on schools than the sum of the effects of individual Black people.

We can only speculate here on what this sociological imagination consists of, how people think that the school as a collectivity is undermined by ghetto forces. The core perceptions seem to have to do with two variables: academic standards and school discipline. The vision of the algebra class turned over instead to elementary arithmetic because most of the students are not ready for algebra, and the vision of a school terrorized by gangs of adolescents carrying guns and knives—these haunt the average nonghetto parent, White or Black. If the hours of homework assigned go down with an increase in the proportion Black in a school, if ghetto teachers are afraid to defend a student being bullied because they thought they saw the flash of a knife (which is, of course, when the bullied student most needs to be defended), if the curriculum is weighted down with nonintellectual subjects because much of the student body has low intellectual interest, then nonghetto parents think they are paying an undue cost for integration. Briefly, if ghetto students want to come into "our" schools and behave "our" way, the nonghetto parent thinks, we are glad "to give them a chance to overcome their background." But if "they" want to run the schools "their" way, with low homework requirements, with algebra classes turned over to arithmetic, and with strutting delinquents governing the playground, let them stay downtown.

This perception rests, in turn, on a perception of teachers and school administrators as generally weak, only rarely strong enough to overcome the slum environment and to create a well-run school with high standards in the ghetto. The heroes of the metropolitan press are ghetto principals who run a tight ship and push reading, writing, and arithmetic (and algebra) on all their students. If the general public thought that teachers and the principal created and controlled the social and academic environment of the schools, then they would not think test scores would go down with integration. They do not think teachers and principals can run ghetto schools, and they doubt that they can run a tight ship if the ghetto is mixed in with the rest of the school system.

It seems to us that a well-publicized plan to put special effort into obtaining school discipline, especially on playgrounds and in hallways, to monitor the academic standards of English and mathematics instruction, and to maintain an acceptable level of assigned homework, might mollify a good many of these fears. That is, if most of the "costs" of desegregation to White parents are mythical creations—semiparanoid worries about academic and discipline standards—then a systematic program to reduce those psychological costs might pay off. Further, it would probably reassure the more timid of the teaching and administrative staff, reinforce the authority of the principals in front of the students, and otherwise improve the authority position of the teaching and administrative staff. And this would not only help to reassure the public, but might also help integrated schools be better than segregated schools.

BOSTON'S CONFLICT BETWEEN DEMOCRACY AND SCHOOL INTEGRATION

We have analyzed some of the generic qualities of school desegregation which will make it a volatile issue in any city. We believe that three things about Boston further affected the amount of controversy over the decision there. First, Boston had a long history of conflict over integration, including a challenge for the mayorality (November 1967 entry in the chronology), passage and repeal of state guidelines on desegregation (which were essentially, because of the demography of Massachusetts, guidelines for how the Boston system should be conducted, see March, 1965), and previous involvement of the courts in affecting the outcome of the process.

Second, the leadership of the community was, in fact, divided. That is, the history of conflict both resulted from, and resulted in, a division in the city political and community leadership over the question of what attitude to show toward desegregation by court order. How far the division of leadership produced the history, and how far the history produced the fault lines splitting the leadership, cannot be determined directly from our data. What we can tell is that the fault line became a fracture during the controversy.

Third, there was an extended period of uncertainty about what would happen—or perhaps more exactly, an extended period in which people could pretend that the outcome was uncertain. Uncertainty is what makes news, makes opportunities to posture in the media, makes action make sense. The uncertainties in the situation were mainly that people were not sure *which* of the several plans under consideration was being implemented by Garrity's order (see March–June 1974), whether Garrity's action was illegal because of the repeal of the Racial Imbalance Act (May 10, 1974; February 14, 1975), whether the plan would ever be enforced effectively by the mayor or by the police (September 9, 1974), and whether the need to comply might be obviated by a successful Supreme Court appeal or by presidential intervention (October 9, 1974). Although the survey data show that most people were convinced throughout the controversy that the courts generally win these battles, and that they would probably win this one, there was no uniform community leadership that said, in effect, "We have to take this because we can't get out of it, so we might as well make it as easy on ourselves as possible."

These three features of the situation in Boston turned the issue of court-ordered desegregation into a question of how we shall be governed, a microcosm of a popular challenge to the constitutional order. For what the history of controversy, the division of leadership, and the uncertainty of the outcome all created was a historical stage on which people could make constitutional speeches at each other. The school committee could make speeches about how they, and not Judge Garrity, were elected to run the schools of Boston. And Judge Garrity could make speeches (render "opinions") about what the Constitution requires. This transforms the policy disagreement over whether busing children for the sake of integration is a good idea into a procedural argument in which the quarrel is about who gets to make the decision.

The problem with governing stably once the issue has escalated to this proportion is that the judiciary is badly set up for administering a school system, and in many ways badly set up even to make policy for a school system. Further, the fundamental illegitimacy of nondemocratic administration of a central function of local governments prevents the judiciary from taking over the function of running the school system. Finally, if the costs of fair treatment of the races in the school system can be minimized by people whose business it is to make wise decisions for school systems, busing will be both more legitimate and more socially effective. So, if the courts can force the school board to plan desegregation, many political benefits are to be expected.

Presumably, this is why the law is generally set up so that courts can order authorities in a given organization to follow the law, and only when they refuse can these authorities be deprived of their authority, and then only in that limited area of illegal behavior. Thus, one of the judicial theorems which underlies a busing conflict is that the court is required to assume that the school committee is a reasonable and law-abiding public body which will design a desegregation policy that will insure Black people's rights and minimize the educational and other costs of doing so. The evidence is that this assumption is usually right, that most people, most of the time, do what is right when the law is publicly and authoritatively pointed out to them and specific duties derived therefrom are laid on them by injunction.

The problem is that there is another definition of the duties of a school board, namely to be responsible to the people who have elected them. This is reinforced in Boston by the fact that the school committee is elected, and that political careers might be made using the school committee as a staging area. Perhaps the clearest sign of this dilemma is the behavior of the state legislature, which first passed a bill that required Boston to be just to Black students by not making them go to ghetto schools, and then, upon public outcry, especially in Boston itself, repealed that act (see the August 1965 and May 1974 entries in the chronology). The legislators wanted to live up to the ideals embodied in the Constitution, and yet be reelected. The court, in particular, was requiring the school committee to take a very substantial risk with their political futures for the sake of enforcing the Constitution. Not too surprisingly, the school committee chose instead to let the court enforce the Constitution, as the state legislature had chosen before them (August 1966 entry). The desegregation act of the state legislature is no doubt the right way to desegregate—by action of the politically responsible legislative body. But the court and the legislature have different relative weights on following the Constitution and on being reelected, and only the court's weighting system results in justice for Black people.

The legal theory that the school committee will be a reasonable, law-abiding public body, willing to sacrifice the legitimacy of democracy for the legitimacy of constitutional justice, is the ultimate source of the practical political uncertainty of whether or not the law will actually be implemented. There is nothing legally uncertain about whether the school committee has to produce a desegregation plan when so enjoined by the court. But, given the conflict between the judiciary and the establishment, on the one side, and the people, on the other, about what should be done, the legal certainty about the duty of the school committee cannot be translated into a practical certainty.

The theory of a reasonable school board is usually true even when the requirements of justice are as unpopular as they are in the busing controversy. However, that means that legal certainty about what the Constitution requires cannot be turned into practical certainty without the collection of legal evidence of irresponsibility and unreasonableness on the part of the school board such as the U.S. Civil Rights Commission hearings which recommended the possibility of receivership (August 1975).

The clearest evidence of unwillingness to obey the Constitution is, of course, mobilizing the people against the court's decision. When popularly elected bodies take that route—as did the Louisiana and Arkansas state legislatures—then the legal process of depriving them of their authority goes much faster than it does when they passively resist, take forever over each step, and appeal each ruling. In these particular circumstances, however, appealing to the public to defy the court produces an acute community controversy greatly increasing the cost of desegregation in terms of disruption of schooling, community bad will, and the erosion of the authority of the court.

The power of the southern civil rights movement was, in considerable measure, that it could produce community conflict on demand without violating any serious laws and without turning northern public opinion against the movement. Since community conflict was expensive for the real estate and business interests that ran most southern towns, the ability to create and to turn off community conflict on demand forced unwilling southern businessmen to negotiate for civil rights.

School boards are in a situation analogous to the civil rights movement in that they can produce community damage on demand against court-ordered transportation across school district lines for desegregation. This means that school boards have the same sorts of tools that the civil rights movement had to get their way against majority opposition. It must be remembered that the civil rights movement did attain its objectives in many southern communities even though the majority of "the people"—meaning, in this case, the politically relevant White people—were opposed to those objectives. Presumably, if desegregation by busing were made costly enough in enough communities by school board recalcitrance, some way would be found to reinterpret the Constitution. "The people" of the South managed to reinterpret the Constitution after Reconstruction so as to deprive Black people of their rights. The key is, of course, that school boards and the communities that elect them are not really willing to pay the costs of community conflict—they may not want busing, but they want violence and nationally publicized community conflict even less. That is why the legal assumption of reasonable, law-abiding school boards generally works.

No one in Boston urged that the people have no say in the public policies that apply to them, but many citizens were willing to endorse on a more limited scale the elite management of justice, even though it was against the will of the people. Our analyses found that many Bostonians who were opposed to busing were, in fact, in favor of the courts' having a distinctive role in the political system, and believed that sometimes the courts have to go against the people. The widespread adherence to this value of citizenship, i.e., consent that there should be some mechanism to put greater priority on system goals (like justice for Black people) against the will of the people if necessary, was clearly related to consent to the court order.

We tested this by constructing a scale of agreement with the court's duty to sometimes oppose the will of the people. This scale added together the number of times people agreed with the following propositions: (1) the courts have a duty to eliminate unlawful segregation; (2) the courts have the right to make decisions with which many people disagree; (3) Judge Garrity had the right to make his decision; (4) federal judges such as Garrity are qualified to draw up desegregation plans; and (5) school officials cannot legitimately delay compliance with a court order. This scale was divided into thirds of low, medium, and high "respect" for the court.

We found that those who agreed with busing were unlikely to take part in active opposition to the court, regardless of their level of respect for the court. But more importantly, for those who opposed busing (i.e., most Bostonians), agreeing with the court's right to disagree with the people (and to enforce its will) *substantially depressed* the tendency to boycott or advocate civil disobedience.

Table IV examines this result for those in our sample who were *opposed* to busing. The table shows the percentage of those people who supported the school boycott, controlling for the level of respect for the court. The effect is substantial and becomes greater as the conflict develops: those who agree with the right of the court to make unpopular decisions are much less likely to oppose the court's action even though they oppose the substance of the decision.

Table IV. Percentage Supporting Boycotts in September 1973, July 1974, and September 1974, by Degree of Respect for the Court, among Those Opposed to Busing Only

Respect for the court[a]	Percentage supporting school boycott		
	Sept. 1973	July 1974	Sept. 1974
High	31	33	40
Middle	41	64	58
Low	59	79	78

[a] Question wordings: Respect: See text for discussion. Boycott: See Table III.

Thus, Boston's conflict between democracy and school integration would have been much worse if a substantial proportion of the citizenry did not agree with the right of the court to oppose the popular will.

CONCLUSION

In sum, we do not believe that the question of busing created the conflict in Boston, though it is true that if the people had not been against busing they would not have been against the court decision. It was, instead, the busing question's being turned into a question of who is to run the schools that led to its being difficult to resolve. And that is why attitudes toward court authority, rather than attitudes toward Black people—prejudice or racism—were the central explanatory variable related to resistance to the court. If busing is a question of what we should do about the ghetto, not of whether we like Black people, it also becomes a problem of who has authority to make us pay the cost of doing something about the ghetto by integrating and busing children. In Boston, it was a controversy over who should decide and who should pay, embedded in a history of community conflict between different parts of the political leadership, in a situation of legal uncertainty.

ACKNOWLEDGMENTS

This report was based partly on research we undertook as investigators with J. Michael Ross on a project analyzing a five wave panel study of Boston residents' reactions to court-ordered desegregation. The initial work on the panel study and the supervision of the data collection were executed by Ross over a period of several years. We note here and also in our preliminary report on the project (Taylor & Stinchcombe, 1977) our acknowledgment of his patient attention to the details of such a large undertaking. The editors' comments on an earlier draft were extremely useful and are kindly acknowledged here.

REFERENCES

The Boston Globe, May 25, 1975.

Crain, R. L. *The politics of school desegregation.* Chicago: Aldine, 1968.

Friedman, D. J. *White militancy in Boston.* Lexington, Mass.: D.C. Heath, 1973.

Handlin, O. *Boston's immigrants.* New York: Atheneum, 1941.

Hauser, R. M. Schools and the stratification process. *American Journal of Sociology*, 1969, *74*, 587–611.

Jencks, C. *Inequality*. New York: Basic, 1972.

Kelley, J. The politics of school busing. *Public Opinion Quarterly*, 1974, *38*, 23–39.

Levy, F. *Northern schools and civil rights: The Racial Imbalance Act of Massachusetts*. Chicago: Markham, 1971.

Parkman, H. J. The city and the state. In E. Herlihy (Ed.), *Fifty years of Boston: A memorial volume issued in commemoration of the tercentenary of 1930*. Boston: Copyright Subcommittee on Memorial History of the Boston Tercentenary Committee, 1932.

Pettigrew, T. F., Ross, J. M., & Crawford, T. Negro neighbors—Banned in Boston. *Transaction*, 1966, September–October, *3*(6), 13–18.

Schuman, H., & Gruenberg, B. The impact of city on racial attitudes. *American Journal of Sociology*, 1970, *76*, 213–261.

Taylor, D. G., & Stinchcombe, A. L. *The Boston school desegregation controversy*. Chicago: National Opinion Research Center, 1977.

Taylor, D. G., Sheatsley, P., & Greeley, A. M. Attitudes toward racial integration. *Scientific American*, June 1978, *238*, 6, 42–49.

Taylor, D. G. Housing, neighborhoods and race relations: Recent survey evidence. *Annals of the American Academy of Political and Social Science*, January 1979, *441*, 26–40.

United States Commission on Civil Rights. *Desegregating the Boston schools*. Washington, D.C.: U.S. Commission on Civil Rights, August 1975.

9

White Flight and the Future of School Desegregation

DAVID J. ARMOR

Among the many debates that have raged over school busing, few have engaged social scientists with more intensity than the "White flight" debate. Although the White flight phenomenon has a long history in both public and social science discussions, it did not become a truly controversial issue in sociology until Coleman, Kelly, and Moore's (1975) well-publicized work on the subject, which concluded that school desegregation was a significant cause of declining White enrollments in public schools.

Shortly after Coleman *et al.*'s work appeared, three other major studies were published (or presented) which concluded, quite firmly, that Coleman's analysis was defective and that school desegregation has little or no effect on White flight. The first of these was a study by Reynolds Farley (1975), the second a study by Christine Rossell (1975–1976), and the third was a study by Thomas Pettigrew and Robert Green (1976). This latter study relied heavily on the Farley and Rossell data, supplemented by some original analyses.

Although this disagreement among social scientists has considerable academic interest, obviously the real significance of the White flight issue lies outside the profession. A great deal is at stake in this debate, with major policy decisions hinging upon its outcome. For decades, since the United States Supreme Court's historic *Brown*[1] decision, court-ordered school desegregation has been the keystone policy of the civil rights movement.

[1] *Brown* v. *Topeka Board of Education*, 347 U.S. 483 (1954).

DAVID J. ARMOR • The Rand Corporation, Santa Monica, California 90406. This essay is a substantially revised version of a paper presented at the American Sociological Association meetings in September 1978. The research for this paper has been sponsored in part by the San Diego and Los Angeles School Boards, and the Russell Sage Foundation.

Moreover, this policy has received considerable support from jurists, educators, and social scientists as the only feasible means for remedying the substantial racial and ethnic imbalance which exists in most large school districts throughout the country. It is no wonder, then, that the subject of court-induced White flight stirs strong emotions. If certain desegregation policies do cause White flight, and if the effect is strong enough to cause *re*segregation, then many desegregation advocates will be in the unfortunate position of promoting the very condition they seek to end.

One reason for the disagreement among these early studies is that they used somewhat different samples of school districts, and, therefore, they differed on the number of school districts which had implemented large-scale, court-ordered desegregation plans. After the initial furor, both Farley and Rossell expanded their data bases and refined their analysis techniques. As a result, they modified their original conclusions to some extent, finding more evidence for White flight due to desegregation than they had previously (Farley, 1977; Rossell, 1978). Interestingly, at this writing these newer studies had not been published, and as a result many persons are unaware that there is now less disagreement among social scientists on the *fact* of White flight when desegregation occurs.

Disagreement still exists, however, on many issues, especially on the size and duration of White flight in response to desegregation. Given the importance of the policy decisions involved, another investigation into the White flight phenomenon is warranted. This chapter reports findings from a new study that addresses a number of questions not fully answered by existing research.

First and foremost, what is the total magnitude of the White flight phenomenon in desegregating school districts? Assuming there is White flight, is it short-term or long-term? The term *White flight* will be applied to any loss of White students from a desegregating school district—whether by residential relocation, transferring to private schools, or residential avoidance—that can be reasonably attributed to desegregation itself. In order to determine the long-term effects of desegregation, it is argued that the unique demographic characteristics of a school district, especially declining White births and White outmigration, must be taken into account. The study introduces a demographic technique that allows comparison between actual White enrollment after desegregation and projected White enrollment, had desegregation not occurred, based on actual White births and outmigration rates for each district. For reasons that will become clear presently, the demographic analysis will focus on school districts that desegregate via court-ordered mandatory busing.

· Second, does White flight occur across-the-board in response to desegregation, or does the size of the effect depend upon various intervening conditions such as minority concentrations, the size of district, the availability of suburbs, or the type of desegregation? One of the most important policy questions in this regard is whether White flight occurs in metropolitan plans that, by including suburban districts, would appear to reduce opportunities for flight via relocation. Another important question is whether the *type* of desegregation plan—such as court-ordered, mandatory busing versus voluntary busing—affects the degree of White flight. It is reasonable to postulate that White flight will be strongest when White students are mandatorily reassigned to minority schools. Since existing research sheds light on some of these issues, the study shall begin with a review of the major studies by Coleman, Farley, and Rossell to find their points of convergence on conditions affecting the size of the White flight effect.

Third, if it is shown that under certain conditions desegregation does accelerate White flight to the point where resegregation is likely, then current desegregation policies should be reconsidered. In this regard it is contended that the *reasons* for White flight must be better understood in order to fashion more effective remedies. If, on the one hand, White flight is due mainly to racial prejudice and to opposition to integrated schools, then certain types of plans (e.g., voluntary) might be ruled out. On the other hand, if White flight is caused primarily by opposition to mandatory reassignment away from neighborhood schools, or "busing" as it is commonly called, then voluntary plans might prove ultimately more effective than mandatory plans, at least for intradistrict desegregation. Data from a special survey of parents in the Los Angeles school district will be introduced to examine the reasons for White support of or opposition to alternative desegregation plans.

Finally, the results of the White flight analysis and the Los Angeles survey will serve as the basis for a discussion of the future of school desegregation policy. One set of issues concerns the future of intradistrict desegregation, especially that ordered by courts. The higher federal courts have generally failed to consider resegregation as a feasibility factor when fashioning a desegregation remedy. If the ultimate goal of the courts is to reduce racial segregation, then the White flight problem should definitely be taken into account. A second set of issues revolves around metropolitan desegregation proposals, which are now the subject of a major policy debate. The future of metropolitan busing will probably be decided by the courts; however, the feasibility of such plans depends greatly on the White flight issue as well as the level of White opposition to mandatory busing. These and other issues will be discussed and the prospects for metropolitan plans will be evaluated.

THE COLEMAN AND FARLEY STUDIES

Coleman and Farley used a similar conceptual approach to study White flight, although their initial methods differed considerably. Basically, their approach is to analyze the relationship between changes in White enrollment and changes in a quantitative desegregation index for the same period.

In Coleman's approach the dependent variable is the annual change in White enrollment, from 1968 to 1973, and the independent variables are changes in desegregation,[2] the proportion of Black enrollment, district size, region (North versus South), and the extent of desegregation within the standard metropolitan statistical area (the SMSA). This latter variable measures the degree of concentration of Black students within the central city of a larger metropolitan area. Coleman then examines various linear regression models applied to the largest 21 central city school districts and the next 46 largest; he excluded countywide school districts. Coleman also tested various interactions between change in desegregation and proportion Black, region, and desegregation within the SMSA.

In Coleman's best model, the strongest and most consistent correlates of White loss are increases in desegregation, high segregation within the SMSA, and the interaction between desegregation change and proportion Black. SMSA segregation can probably be interpreted as a surrogate for the existence of White suburbs, since high segregation levels in an SMSA imply Black concentration in a central city district surrounded by largely White suburban districts. With this interpretation, then, Coleman's finding is that White loss is accelerated whenever desegregation occurs in large, central city school districts with a substantial proportion of Black enrollment, and this effect is enhanced whenever predominantly White suburbs exist around the district. He did not find any evidence for substantial long-term effects, although he admitted his analysis was not adequate for this test. Also, he found the effect strong in the South and much weaker in the North, but it must be emphasized that his latest data was for 1973, prior to the start of mandatory desegregation in many larger northern cities.

Farley's first analysis (Farley I, 1975) was based on 125 school districts for cities with over 100,000 population (excluding those districts with less than 3% Black). Like Coleman, he examined the changes in White enrollment from 1967–1972, and related it to change in a desegregation index (a different one than Coleman's).[3] But here the similarity ends.

Farley analyzed *total* change in White enrollment from 1967–1972 rather than year-to-year changes. Since Coleman found the largest White losses occurred in the first year following a significant desegregation action,

---

[2] The desegregation measure used is a relative exposure index which measures the average proportion of White students in schools attended by the average Black Student (Coleman *et al.*, 1975).

[3] The index of dissimilarity (Taueber & Taueber, 1965). It measures the percentage of Black students plus the percentage of White students who must be moved to attain perfect racial balance in each school.

longer time-intervals that include years where no actions occurred might weaken the relationship. More important, Farley did not experiment with more complex regression models, and, in particular, he did not test for the crucial interaction between desegregation and proportion Black. His main results showed only the bivariate relationship between White loss and desegregation change, separately for the North and for the South; in a footnote, he showed a three-variable regression using desegregation change and proportion Black. Perhaps not surprisingly, then, he did not find evidence to support Coleman's conclusion.

Farley's second analysis (Farley II, 1977) was quite different. Basically the same set of school districts were used as in Farley I, but enrollment data were added for 1973 and 1974. More crucial, however, he applied a regression model much like Coleman's to *annual* changes in White enrollment. He also added several variables not used by Coleman, including year, countywide district versus central-city district (Coleman analyzed only central-city districts), and average White enrollment change in the two years preceding desegregation.

With these modifications, Farley II comes to conclusions not unlike Coleman's. The highest correlates of White loss were found for proportion Black, change in desegregation, and the countywide variable (such that county districts have less loss than central-city districts), and the interactions between change in desegregation and percent Black, district size, and predesegregation White loss. In other words, according to Farley II, the effect of desegregation on White loss will be strongest in larger, central-city school districts that have a substantial proportion of Blacks and that show preexisting White enrollment declines.

Coleman found that, for a large central-city school district with White suburbs and 25% Black, a change of 20 points in his desegregation index is associated with an extra White loss of 8%; Farley II finds that, for a large central-city district with 30% Black enrollment, the incremental White loss associated with a 20 point change in his desegregation index is 6%. A rough idea of the meaning of a 20-point change in a desegregation index can be conveyed by a somewhat idealized example. For a highly segregated district with a 50–50 Black–White ratio overall, a 20-point change in either index would occur if the percent Black in each school moved 10 points closer to the district ratio.

Although it is encouraging that the Coleman and Farley II analyses show a convergence in conclusions, there are still many analytic difficulties and several unanswered questions. First, their common conceptual approach makes the assumption that only the *amount*, and not the *type* of desegregation makes a difference. If the reason for White flight is mandatory reassignment to nonneighborhood schools, rather than integrated schools *per se*, then changes in a desegregation index caused by voluntary transfers of minority students to predominantly White schools might not cause White losses. Moreover, it is possible that White flight will be diminished or nonexistent whenever desegregation—mandatory or voluntary—is supported by the community rather than being imposed by a court upon a protesting community.

A second and possibly more serious problem is that no attempt is made to model the basic demographic processes that are the primary causes of White losses in the *absence* of desegregation; namely, White outmigration to the suburbs and declining White birth rates. If large-scale desegregation causes White loss, and if the mechanism involves conscious choices of White families, then it would follow logically that some White losses—"anticipatory" White flight—would occur prior to the onset of desegregation. To measure such an effect, one must employ a demographic projection to compare actual and projected White losses prior to the implementation year. Such flight is missed entirely in Coleman's model and confounded with an independent variable in the Farley II model (average White loss for the previous two years).

Finally, neither analysis deals adequately with the issue of longer-term effects of desegregation, particularly for large-scale, court-ordered plans. The main reason, of course, is that the earlier works had data for only 1972 or 1973, and courts did not begin issuing large-scale desegregation orders until 1970 or 1971. Even 1974 is too early to determine long-term effects in the North, since many northern desegregation orders were not implemented until 1973 or 1974. Clearly, the full policy implications of White flight cannot be evaluated without knowing the longer-term effects of desegregation four or five years after it begins.

THE ROSSELL STUDIES

The original Rossell study (Rossell I, 1975) took a different conceptual approach for assessing the effects of desegregation on White flight. Observing that Coleman's analysis could not separate the effects of government-imposed desegregation from other types of desegregation, including changes in natural residential patterns, she adopted a quasi-experimental design. Her basic approach is to compare predesegregation rates of White loss with postdesegregation losses for school districts that implemented school desegregation plans, and then to compare differences, if any, to a group of control districts. The districts chosen for study comprised a nonrandom sample of 86 northern school districts (a subset of the National Opinion Research Corporation's Permanent Community Sample of 200 cities that were in the North and had at least 3,000 Black residents). The year of desegregation was established by means of a mail questionnaire sent to school district administrators.

Although Rossell I had a distinct advantage over the Coleman and Farley works by identifying government and court-ordered desegregation, a number of analysis problems hampered this first study, leading to the conclusion of no relationship between desegregation and White flight. First, the dependent variable used was not change in White enrollment but, rather, change in the *percent* White. This measure confounds the possibly different movements of two independent populations, Whites and Blacks. For example, the percent White will decline if Black enrollment is increasing while White enrollment is stable. After a desegregation action, if Black enrollment levels off and White enrollment starts declining, the percent White will continue to drop, thereby masking a significant shift in population movements. This phenomenon has actually occurred in a number of desegregation cases, including Boston.

Like Farley I, Rossell I enrollment data stopped in 1972, and no attempt was made to control for most of the significant factors identified by Coleman as intervening in the relationship between desegregation and White losses, such as proportion Black and existence of White suburbs, and no multivariate techniques were introduced to explore interactions among these potential correlates. Perhaps more important, no data were included for southern school districts, which were found by Coleman to yield larger White flight effects.

Finally, the effect of desegregation was evaluated for each district by comparing its rate of change (in percent White) before the year of desegregation to its rate of change after desegregation. But the year of desegregation was simply the year of the most significant action; if other desegregation actions occurred before the most significant one, such as a major court order or a partial desegregation plan, the predesegregation measure might already be influenced by White flight effects. For example, the year of desegregation chosen for San Francisco is 1971, when citywide, court-ordered busing began, but a major school board busing plan was adopted in 1969 and implemented in 1970, during which time substantial White losses occurred. As a result, San Francisco is not shown to have significant White flight in Rossell's studies.

Rossell II (1978) represents a major updating with more data and more extensive analyses. She included southern school districts, obtained enrollment data through 1975, corrected the measure of White loss, and analyzed the data with multiple regression techniques using models similar to those used by Coleman and Farley II. As did Coleman and Farley II, Rossell's new analysis also finds that desegregation leads to significant White flight under certain conditions.

The most important new finding in Rossell II involves an important variable not assessed in the Coleman and Farley studies. She measures not only the change in a desegregation index, but the percentage of White and Blacks *reassigned* by a desegregation plan (estimated by the percentage increase in Whites at Black schools and the percentage increase of Blacks at White schools).[4] Significantly, she finds that the amount of White reassignment is the critical determinant of White flight when desegregation occurs. Although Black reassignment is also correlated with White flight, once the White reassignment is taken into account, Black reassignment retains only a weak association with White flight.

Rossell II also finds that percent Black, the interaction between percent Black and White reassignment, being a southern district, and degree of SMSA segregation are significantly related to White flight in most models tested; these findings are consistent with those of Coleman and Farley II. On the other hand, Rossell II shows that unemployment rate, crime rate, and per pupil expenditures are not significantly related to White flight once other variables are controlled. Coleman and Farley II did not include these latter variables in their investigations.

Rossell II finds further that substantial White flight occurs only in the year in which significant desegregation occurs, and that in subsequent years White flight is negligible or nonexistent except in districts more than 35% Black. Since all districts with substantial Black and White reassignments are shown to reduce segregation significantly, she concludes that the net benefits of desegregation outweigh its net costs in White flight.

Although the correlational and regression methods used by Rossell II (as well as by Coleman and Farley II) may be adequate for testing a White flight effect during the year when mandatory busing or reassignment actually takes place, they are not adequate for testing the total magnitude and duration of White flight. To put the problem simply, these methods assume that White flight occurs only when busing or reassignment takes place, and not when other desegregation actions take place or in the years following the start of desegregation. If White flight does occur when busing starts, it makes sense to postulate that some White flight—albeit of smaller magnitude—will take place when a community becomes aware that mandatory busing is a possibility; for example, after a lawsuit is filed or after a court order. In fact, such events have frequently taken place during the early 1970s in school districts in Rossell II's "control" group, such as Grand Rapids, Michigan, Cincinnati and Cleveland, Ohio, Kansas City, Kansas, and Omaha, Nebraska. Some of these cities eventually started

---

[4] The percentage of students reassigned is based on those students who show up at schools to which they are reassigned. Thus, when White flight occurs, the percentage of White students actually reassigned is probably considerably higher.

mandatory busing and some did not. But the main point is that "threats" of busing can cause some degree of White flight, and since these events are not measured, the regression coefficients can be biased in the direction of predicting higher than normal White losses in the no-busing condition.

An extended example may help clarify the problem. Boston began its mandatory busing in the fall of 1974; the lawsuit was brought amid much controversy during the 1972–1973 school year. Between 1967 and 1972, Boston shows an annual White loss rate averaging between 2–3% a year. In the fall of 1973, following the federal lawsuit filing and several controversial orders from state courts concerning desegregation—some of which were accepted by the Boston school board in June 1973—the White loss climbed to 6.6%, twice as high as the preceding 5 year average. When busing started in 1974, the White loss rose to 15% and then to 20% in 1975 when a broader busing plan was implemented. Rossell II's best regression model predicts that if busing had not occurred in 1974, Boston's White loss rate would have been 6.9%. This hardly seems a reasonable predicted loss rate when its losses between 1970 and 1972 were half that figure. The reason the predicted figure is so high may be that many cities with about the same proportion Black as Boston experienced desegregation events—court actions, school board actions, local controversies—that produced some White flight in those years without actually experiencing mandatory busing. This is a reasonable explanation for Boston's sudden loss of 6.6% in the fall of 1973, the year prior to the start of its busing plan. Thus, the regression model finds Boston's excess loss in 1974 to be about 8%, but if the true White loss with no busing controversy would have been about 4%, then Boston's excess White loss that year is closer to 11%. This difference may not be significant for a single year, but over a four or five year period the difference can become quite substantial.

Another serious problem is that the regression model has no way of assessing the continuing White flight attributable to the rapidly increasing percent Black, which itself is caused by the White flight. This is an especially critical issue, since percent Black is shown to be the single most potent predictor of White losses with or without busing. White flight caused Boston's percent Black to climb 10 points between 1973 and 1975. Its predicted White loss without further busing in 1976 is thus 3% higher by virtue of the higher percent Black, even though this rapid change in percent Black is due mostly to White flight. If the normal White losses had led to an increase of only 4% Black during this period, the predicted increase in White loss would be only slightly more than 1%. The result of all this is that these regression models tend to underestimate the long-term impact of desegregation on White flight.

Rossell II recognizes these problems in part, and therefore includes a quasi-experimental analysis similar to that in Rossell I. This analysis is a district-by-district comparison of postdesegregation White loss rates with predesegregation rates. The advantage is that each city is allowed to have a unique White loss rate prior to desegregation, which serves as the baseline against which to assess its postdesegregation losses. Unfortunately, however, the analysis suffers from the same problem as Rossell I: the year of desegregation is chosen as the year of the most significant action, thereby allowing potential White flight accruing from other events to affect the pre-desegregation measure. Continuing with the example of Boston, she includes 1973 with the predesegregation White losses. By including this large White loss, a linear projection based on 1967–1973 losses leads to a predicted White loss of 5.5% in 1974 (without busing), and to a predicted White loss of 7.2% by 1978. If the 1973 loss is excluded, on the grounds that anticipated flight probably occurred, a linear projection of 1967–1972 losses leads to predicted White losses of 3.8 and 4.5% in 1974 and 1978, respectively. In other words, a forecast that counts the 1973 White loss as normal will nearly double the normal rate of White loss between 1974 and 1978.

Clearly, one must develop a method that not only allows each school district to have a unique normal White decline, but that can also establish a relatively long-term trend of normal demographic change against which the actual losses can be compared. Such a method must utilize the actual White birth and outmigration data unique to each school district. Only in this way can the total magnitude and duration of White flight be assessed.

There have been few other White flight studies of national scope besides the ones reviewed so far. For the most part they provide little additional information over and above the combined Coleman, Farley, and Rossell findings. A study by Pettigrew and Green (1976) does present some new analyses for the 21 largest cities, but their approach is basically the same as Farley I: they do not analyze year-to-year changes; they do not include critical interaction terms in their models; their data stops in 1973; and they do not identify and assess the impact of court-ordered desegregation. Not surprisingly, their results and conclusions are similar to those in Farley I and Rossell I.

A NEW STUDY

Given the latest works of Farley and Rossell, there seems to be substantial agreement on several critical points. First, the *fact* that White loss is associated with desegregation in some instances is not in dispute. Second, it is a conditional relationship: it occurs under some conditions but not others. Third, the effect is seen most clearly in the year that desegregation takes place, which in most cases is the first year of a plan's implementation except when a plan is implemented in several phases (as for Boston or Oklahoma City).

Although there is variation in the nature of the conditions cited by each investigation, some convergence is apparent when all three studies are compared. First, the effect appears to depend upon a substantial proportion of Black (or minority) students, perhaps on the order of 20–25%. Second, the effect appears strongest for central-city districts surrounded by accessible White suburbs (e.g., Boston) and weakest for large metropolitan school districts surrounded by minimally developed rural areas (e.g., Charlotte, North Carolina).

Finally, the effect appears strongest when there is a significant shift in the racial balance of schools, and primarily when White reassignment is involved in the shift. In the Coleman and Farley studies this shows up as a desegregation index change of 20 points or so, while in the Rossell study this corresponds to reassignment of at least 20% or so of Black students and at least 5% or so of the White students.

In the vast majority of cases, however, shifts on this order of magnitude occur rarely outside of court-ordered desegregation plans. In Coleman's list of the 70 largest central-city districts, 16 showed an annual change of 20 percentage points or more on his desegregation index, and only one was not involved in a court-ordered desegregation case (Wichita, Kansas, which was involved in a HEW mandate). Of the 86 Rossell II school districts, 27 showed a change in the index of dissimilarity of 20 points or more, but only 6 were not brought about by court order (Wichita and Tyler and Amarillo, Texas, which were involved in HEW mandates; and Berkeley and Riverside, California, and Ann Arbor, Michigan, which had school-board initiated plans). Perhaps more important, of the 13 Rossell II districts that showed at least 5% of White students reassigned—which she shows to be the strongest determinant of White flight—only Berkeley was not by court order.

It seems fairly clear, then, that while changes in desegregation indices are the empirical correlates of White losses, large White flight effects are generally brought about only through court orders.

Given this state of knowledge, the new study was designed to focus specifically on court-ordered desegregation cases in which mandatory reassignment (as opposed to voluntary transferring) takes place. Furthermore, the emphasis of the study is on certain questions not answered adequately by the existing research; namely, the magnitude, duration, and causes of White flight arising from court-ordered mandatory desegregation. In order to answer the first two questions with greater precision, we have employed demographic techniques to project school enrollments in the absence of desegregation.

The potential universe for the new study consisted of all school districts undergoing court-ordered mandatory desegregation (COMD) by 1975. *Mandatory* means a desegregation plan involving mandatory reassignment of students. Mandatory reassignment plans not due to court order and court-ordered voluntary plans will not be analyzed in detail. This is not a serious restriction since there are relatively few such cases.[5] Given the Coleman and Farley findings, the universe was further restricted to school districts enrolling over 20,000 students and having at least 10% minority enrollment in 1968, which is prior to the start of COMD cases.[6] These criteria yield 54 school districts.[7]

The detailed methods for assessing White flight effects have been presented elsewhere and will not be repeated here (Armor, 1978). It suffices to state that two different methods were used to assess White flight. The first involved all 54 districts and utilized a simple quasi-experimental design, where postdesegregation White losses are compared to losses prior to the first significant court order. The second and more precise demographic projection method was applied to those school districts which, according to the first analysis, have the greatest potential for White flight: 23 districts with over 20% minority which are surrounded by suburban development. The demographic projection method uses actual White births from 1950–1972 and cohort-retention rates from United States Census data (1950, 1960, and 1970) to project White loss due to declining White births and outmigration.[8] The advantage of the method is that the size of a birth cohort—which is the major determinant of *annual* shifts in a school population, as opposed to long-term trends—is determined five years before a given projectd school loss. This allows for an assessment of anticipatory White flight, since the projected loss rate is independent of significant court events which frequently take place in the one to three years prior to the start of a desegregation plan.

Finally, investigation of the causes of White flight will be aided by

---

[5] Rossell lists 8 board-initiated, citywide, mandatory plans all but one of which (Berkeley) had no White reassignment; none but Berkeley had significantly accelerated White losses. The author knows of only two court-ordered voluntary plans meeting the inclusion criteria after 1971: Dayton, Ohio, which was recently ordered to implement a mandatory plan in 1976, and San Diego which started a court-ordered voluntary plan in 1977.

[6] Most COMD cases occurred after *Swan* v. *Charlotte–Mecklenburg Board of Education* (402 U.S. 1), decided in 1971.

[7] Excluded from the present study are Stockton, California; Dayton, Ohio; Milwaukee, Wisconsin; and Omaha, Nebraska, whose court-ordered plans did not begin until 1976, and Charleston, South Carolina, for which complete data could not be obtained.

[8] The method assumes that White outmigration rates in the 1970s would be the same as in the 1960s, or that they would decrease by the same decrement that occurred between the 1950s and 1960s; the choice was dictated by the goodness-of-fit between projected and actual loss rates prior to desegregation.

results of a parent survey conducted in Los Angeles prior to implementation of its court-ordered desegregation plan.

RESULTS

Quasi-Experimental Analysis

One can get a broad picture of the White flight phenomenon through the crude "quasi-experimental" analysis applied to all 54 districts. First, the districts are grouped according to characteristics already known to be related to White losses; namely, the proportion of minority students, the availability of suburbs, and region.[9] To determine whether White flight exists, postdesegregation loss rates are compared to predesegregation loss rates and to analogous loss rates for a control group.

A summary of this analysis is shown in Table I. It is readily apparent that if there is a White flight effect, it appears most prominent among school districts that have over 20% minority and accessible suburbs. In these cases the northern postdesegregation White loss rate is three times the predesegregation rate, and double the rate in the control districts for the first two years after the start of desegregation. Moreover, the loss rates remain high, compared to both the pre-rate and the control district rate, three and four years after desegregation. No appreciable difference is found for northern and southern districts within this category; this differs from Coleman's results, which showed a stronger effect for southern districts. However, Coleman's data stopped prior to the start of court-ordered desegregation in many northern cities.

Districts that have substantial minority enrollments but less (or no) access to suburbs, all of which are southern countywide school districts, also appear to show an effect, but it is smaller in absolute terms and drops off rapidly in the third and fourth years. Actually, the rate of acceleration of White loss (from $-.8$ to -6.1) is greater than for the districts with suburbs, due mainly to the existence of several districts which were growing prior to the court order (e.g., Charlotte, North Carolina and Newport News, Virginia) and which stopped growing after desegregation. This raises the possibility that some White flight effects are manifested by the slowing down of White growth rather than the acceleration of White decline. In any event, from the point of view of providing desegregated education, such an effect has less policy relevance, since a relatively stable White population is all that is needed to maintain racially balanced schools.

[9] Size of district is controlled by confining the analysis to districts with over 20,000 enrollment. The amount of desegregation is not controlled, but since all are court-ordered plans, the amount of mandatory reassignment is substantial in all but a few cases.

Table I. Annual Enrollment Changes before and after Court-Ordered Mandatory Desegregation

Type of district	Average annual percentage change			
	Two-years pre-order	Two years post-start	3–4 years post-start	Number of districts
Over 20% minority, suburbs				
Northern White enrollment[a]	−3.6	−11.5	−8.4	9
Southern White enrollment[b]	−3.2	−11.6	−8.8	16
Minority enrollment	+3.6	−0.6	+0.8	25
Over 20% minority, no suburbs[c]				
White enrollment	−0.8	−6.0	−1.9	15
Minority enrollment	+1.7	+0.4	+0.4	15
10–20% minority[d]				
White enrollment	+1.0	−2.3	−2.5	5
Minority enrollment	+1.4	+2.0	+2.2	5
Florida districts[e]				
White enrollment	+2.4	+0.6	+1.6	9
Rossell nondesegregation districts[f]				
Northern White enrollment	−2.7	−5.0	−5.0	18

[a] See Table II for districts.
[b] Dallas, Houston, and Fort Worth, Texas; Atlanta, Georgia; Oklahoma City; Birmingham, Alabama; Little Rock, Arkansas; Memphis, Nashville, and Chattanooga, Tennessee; Norfolk, Richmond, and Roanoke, Virginia; Greensboro and Raleigh, North Carolina; Jackson, Mississippi.
[c] Mobile and Montgomery Counties, Alabama; Bibb, Chatham, Muscogee, and Richmond Counties, Georgia; Louisville–Jefferson County, Kentucky; Baton Rouge and Shreveport, Louisiana; Winston-Salem and Charlotte, North Carolina; Greenville, South Carolina (data for Charleston incomplete); Austin, Texas; Portsmouth and Newport News, Virginia.
[d] Minneapolis; Las Vegas; Tulsa; Lexington, Kentucky; Fulton County, Georgia.
[e] All are counties; Palm Beach, St. Petersburg, Pensacola, Daytona, Gainesville, Ft. Lauderdale, Miami, Jacksonville, and Tampa are the main cities in their respective county school districts.
Rossell northern "control" and "token plan" districts which reassigned no White students and less than 3% Black students and which had total enrollments over 20,000 with 20–60% minority in 1968. Pre-order is the average annual loss rates for 1969 and 1970 (prior to the start of most court-ordered mandatory desegregation); 1–2 years post–start is average loss for 1972 and 1973; 3–4 years post–start is average loss for 1974 and 1975. (See Armor, 1978, for list of districts.)

School districts with 10–20% minority have no significant White losses associated with COMD. The underlying reason undoubtedly has to do with the fact that relatively little reassignment of students—especially White students—is necessary in such cases, thereby minimizing the opposition by White parents. For example, before Minneapolis desegregated in 1973, no school was predominantly minority, and according to Rossell, only 7% of Black students and 1% of White students had to be reassigned to accomplish desegregation.

Finally, the Florida districts have been grouped together because they represent a distinctly different situation. All Florida districts were desegregated by a state court order between 1969 and 1971, and all are very large, countywide school districts. Thus, the White flight phenomenon can occur in Florida only if Whites leave (or do not move into) the state or if they enroll in private schools. This apparently has not happened to any great extent, and, therefore, the Florida group represents the only group where a majority of the school districts are still showing White enrollment gains well into the 1970s. These districts show clearly that the White flight phenomenon is conditional, with crucial dependence upon the environment surrounding the desegregating district.

In summary, the quasi-experimental analysis shows that the most serious White flight effects may occur in districts having substantial proportions of minorities, which require more extensive mandatory reassignment to accomplish desegregation, and in central-city districts with available suburbs, which offer the opportunity for convenient residential relocation. Districts with substantial minority populations but without developed suburbs—all of which are countywide or "metropolitan" districts—may have less White flight due to the inconvenience of relocation. The fact that there is some apparent White flight in these districts, especially in the first year or two, raises the possibility that private school transfers may well comprise a significant portion of White losses in metropolitan desegregation cases.

Demographic Analysis

Although the quasi-experimental method is suggestive, it is not definitive. The pre-court-order loss rates may be affected by anticipatory White flight, leading to an underestimate of the true magnitude of the effect. Conversely, demographic trends may be such that loss rates in the desegregating districts would be increasing even in the absence of desegregation; if so, the pre–post comparison would overstate the size of the effects, especially the long-term effects.

The demographic analysis can help alleviate these problems. We have applied demographic projections to those districts in the first category in Table I, which are the most likely candidates for White flight. These districts include all the important busing cases in large cities, including Dallas, Memphis, Denver, Boston, and San Francisco. The critical questions at issue here are the magnitude and duration of the effect, given a demographic projection of what school enrollments would have been without the desegregation activity.

Northern Districts

The average actual and projected White loss rates are shown for the nine northern districts in Figure 1. Prior to the filing of lawsuits in these districts, the average projected loss rate is nearly identical to the actual loss rate. But after the lawsuits were filed, prior to the start of desegregation, the actual loss rates are over one and one-half the projected loss rates, thereby offering evidence that anticipatory effects do occur.

The most substantial acceleration of White loss for these districts occurred in the first year of desegregation implementation, when the actual rate is nearly four times the projected rate. The actual rates of loss drop somewhat after the first year, but they remain between 1½–2½ times greater than projected loss rates up to four years after the start of busing. It would appear, then, that the magnitude and duration of the effect of court-ordered desegregation may have been underestimated by previous studies.

In order to demonstrate the impact of these accelerated loss rates, it might be helpful to give a hypothetical example. Consider a school district with 50,000 White students prior to the lawsuit, and assume that the loss rates in Figure 1 apply to six consecutive years following the filing year. At

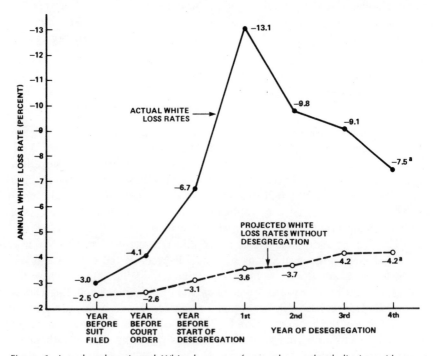

Figure 1. Actual and projected White loss rates for northern school districts with court-ordered mandatory desegregation (a = excludes Detroit).

the end of the six-year period the projected White loss would be about 10,000 students, whereas the actual White loss would be about 20,000. Therefore, the average long-term effect of the court intervention is to double the number of White students lost, over and above the losses due to demographic factors alone.

It is important to note that the projected loss rates do in fact rise in these districts, on the average, from 2.5 to 4.2% over the six to seven years spanning their desegregation periods. This reflects a combination of long-term declines in births and continuing White outmigration during the 1970s. Thus, a comparison of post- to predesegregation loss rates will probably overstate White flight effects, especially over the long run. However, neither the magnitude nor the pattern of these moderate demographic changes can begin to explain the dramatic increase in White loss rates during a desegregation controversy and after its implementation.

Another way to test the validity of these demographic projections is to compare them to other similar districts not experiencing desegregation. Figure 2 shows the projected rates for the northern desegregation cases compared to the actual loss rates of the 18 school districts from Rossell's northern nondesegregation group matched in size and percent minority.[10] The fit is fairly good, although the control districts show somewhat more variability with a decrease in loss rates followed by a steeper increase from 1971 to 1973 than the projected rates. However, the total losses explained by these two sets of rates shown in the upper portion of Figure 2 for a hypothetical population are nearly exact. Therefore, we conclude that the demographic projection method being used here yields realistic loss rates when compared to similar nondesegregating districts.

It might be worthwhile to examine the detailed results for one of these districts. Figure 3 shows the projected and actual White enrollment in Boston, which has been one of the most celebrated court-ordered cases. First of all, it is observed that the projected and actual loss rates for Boston are very close for the five-year period between 1967 and 1972. This is evidence that, for Boston, a projection method based on birth rates and net outmigration can account for virtually all the White losses during this period. But in 1973, after a lawsuit was filed and after considerable controversy over actions by the state board of education, the actual loss rate is −6.6 compared to a projected rate of −3.8. This is not a large difference,

[10] Prince Georges County is excluded from the desegregating districts because none of Rossell's districts had comparable growth rates during the late 1960s. It should also be noted that some of Rossell's districts, including Grand Rapids, Cleveland, Cincinnati, and Omaha were involved in court actions in the early 1970s, so that anticipatory White flight might be a partial cause of the rise from 1971 to 1973. In fact, it is hard to find any large school district with a substantial minority enrollment that has not been involved in some type of desegregation lawsuit.

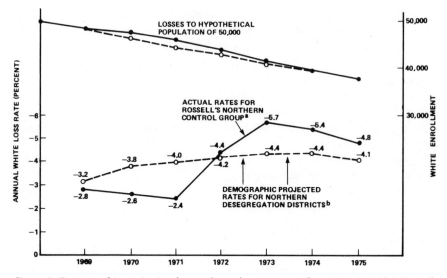

Figure 2. Demographic projection for northern desegregation districts compared to Rossell northern control group (a = districts having between 20–60% minority, and over 20,000 enrollment in 1968; b = excludes Prince Georges County).

but it does reflect some anticipatory behavior; any linear projection that includes the 1973 White enrollment for the predesegregation trend (such as Rossell's) would clearly overestimate the White losses in the absence of desegregation. The Boston plan was implemented in two phases, with Phase II involving more students than Phase I. When Phase I was implemented in 1974, the actual loss rate was nearly four times the projected rate; when

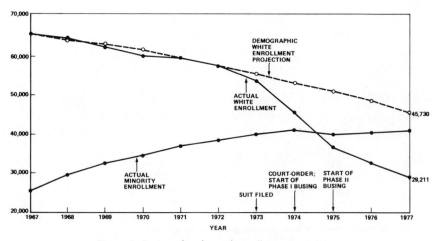

Figure 3. Projected and actual enrollment for Boston.

Phase II was implemented in 1975, the actual rate of loss jumped to over five times the projected rate. In the third year of implementation the loss rate was 10%, which is still more than twice the projected rate.

Before the desegregation action in Boston (1971), there were 57,000 White students, but by 1977 there were only 29,000. Of this total decline of 28,000, about 16,000 (or three-fifths) is attributable to desegregation activities. As a direct result of court-ordered busing, Boston became a majority Black school district in 1975. It is interesting to note, also, that minority enrollment stopped growing rather suddenly in 1975; although not shown on the graph, projected Black enrollment should have continued to grow slightly during this period. This suggests that Black flight—which has not been studied—may also be a phenomenon in court-ordered desegregation, although its magnitude is very small compared to White flight.

Southern Districts

The demographic projection method has also been applied to southern districts with over 20% minority and available suburbs.[11] The results are quite similar to those for the North, although the average effects are somewhat larger.

Figure 4 summarizes the actual and projected loss rates for 14 southern districts. Since nearly all these districts began desegregation in 1970 or 1971, the before-desegregation rates are given by year, with those districts which began desegregation in 1970 excluded from the 1970 averages. Interestingly, anticipatory effects seem weaker in the South; this may be due in part to the fact that these were the earliest cases, when the concept of mandatory busing was in its infancy; persons may have been less aware of what to expect.

The effects after busing started, however, are stronger than in the North, with the actual loss rates rising to over five times the projected rate in the first year of busing. In the second to fifth years of busing, the actual rate ranges from two to three times the projected rate. The elevation of the actual loss rate in the fourth year of desegregation is caused by major second-stage desegregation actions in three cities (Atlanta, Chattanooga, and Oklahoma City) which occurred coincidentally at this time.

It is noteworthy that, like the North, the projected loss rates do rise from the pre- to postdesegregation periods. The rates of White loss for the South are, however, smaller than for the North. This reflects the fact that most of these districts were gaining in school-age population in the 1950s, and outmigration levels in the 1960s were lower than in most northern cities.

[11] Richmond and Norfolk, Virginia could not be analyzed due to annexations which could not be disentangled from enrollment changes.

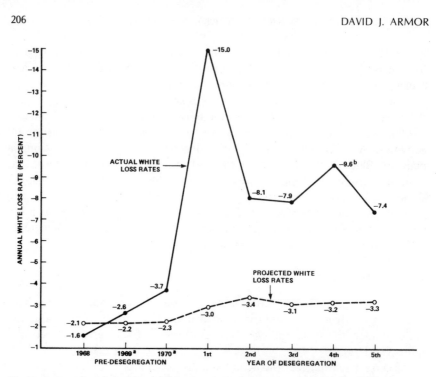

Figure 4. Actual and projected White loss rates for southern school districts with court-ordered mandatory desegregation (a = 1967 and 1968 for Oklahoma City, which started desegregation in 1969, and 1971 and 1972 for Memphis, which started in 1973; b = major desegregation actions in Oklahoma City, Chattanooga, and Atlanta).

Effects of Court Orders on Resegregation

The primary purpose of desegregation orders by courts has been to remedy illegal segregation existing within a school district. It has long been assumed by the courts that voluntary plans will not "work," in the sense of providing a sufficient degree of desegregation. Mandatory plans do, indeed, provide a greater amount of desegregation, at least initially. However, given the substantial accelerated White losses over a prolonged period, the possibility arises that mandatory plans ultimately fail because of resegregation. If so, the question arises whether voluntary plans might be more successful for intradistrict desegregation.

One of the difficulties in evaluating the extent of resegregation involves the definition of desegregation. If it means no more than ethnic or racial balance, then mandatory plans can always be successful, even if White flight causes a district's proportion White to drop to very low levels. As long as each school reflects the district ratio, even if the district is only 10% White, then a strict balance criteria would mean successful desegregation.

However, neither the courts nor social scientists have ever held to such a standard of desegregation; rather, most definitions embody the concept of substantial opportunities for contact between minority and majority students. Therefore, if the proportion of White students in a district drops too low, then the district as a whole becomes either segregated or imbalanced compared to the ethnic composition of a region as a whole. If this condition is undesirable for individual schools, then it is certainly undesirable for an entire school district. Accordingly, to study resegregation we adopt measures of desegregation that reflect the absolute proportion of White students within each school in a district.

Before turning to such desegregation indices, Table II shows the total losses of White students attributable to court orders, along with the effect this has had on the overall percent White. The long-term impact of court orders is massive in 15 out of 23 districts, accounting for over half of all White losses over periods of at least seven years. In larger districts, this translates into tens of thousands of students. In six other cases, the effects have been substantial, accounting for nearly a third of all White losses. Only Springfield, Massachusetts and Fort Worth, Texas, have experienced insignificant losses attributable to court orders.

Of those districts that were majority White prior to the start of mandatory busing, most are now predominantly minority or fast approaching that status. Of these cases, the *projected* percent White shows that many would still be majority White or close to 50–50 including Boston, Denver, Pasadena, Pontiac, Dallas, Houston, Little Rock, Jackson, and Chattanooga, if the court order had not occurred. Of those districts that were predominantly minority prior to the start of the court case, the accelerated White loss has contributed to transforming most of them into virtually minority isolated school districts, including Detroit, San Francisco, Memphis, and Atlanta.

Another way to evaluate the effect of court orders on resegregation is by means of a desegregation index. The index chosen for use here is called an absolute *exposure* index, which is the average percent White in schools attended by minority students (Coleman, Kelly, & Moore, 1975).[12] If all minority students were distributed in a completely random fashion throughout most urban regions of the United States, and all schools were desegregated, each school would be between 70 and 80% White, and thus each district would have an exposure index between 70 and 80.

Figure 5 shows the trends in the amount of desegregation in those four northern school districts that have "tipped" as a result of court orders. The

---

[12] The index of dissimilarity and Coleman's relative exposure indices are not appropriate for measuring desegregation as defined here, since they can attain "perfect" scores of 0 when all schools are racially balanced, regardless of the actual exposure of minority to majority students.

Table II. Long-Term Effects of Court-Ordered Desegregation on White Losses

District	Total White loss, before start to present[a]	Percentage of loss due to court orders[b]	Initial percentage White	Projected percentage White without court orders	Present percentage White
North					
Boston	30,179	55	62	53	42
Denver	23,615	52	60	55	47
Pasadena	11,087	30	63	44	36
Pontiac	6,146	59	66	56	49
Springfield, Mass.	5,721	16	60	58	56
Indianapolis	22,562	51	64	61	55
San Francisco	24,429	29	40	30	22
Detroit	50,328	60	31	26	16
Prince Georges	48,820	100[c]	80	72	56
South					
Dallas	47,880	52	61	49	39
Fort Worth	18,486	7	67	54	53
Houston	56,014	51	53	44	36
Oklahoma City	27,427	72	80	75	65
Little Rock	5,619	94	64	57	47
Jackson, Miss.	13,246	64	55	46	30
Greensboro, N.C.	5,908	52	68	63	58
Raleigh, N.C.	4,418	53	72	66	62
Roanoke, Va.	3,944	29	76	71	69
Chattanooga	8,114	44	52	46	33
Nashville	14,560	31	76	73	70
Memphis	40,882	54	47[d]	43	29
Birmingham	14,856	54	49	44	34
Atlanta	37,959	36	41	24	11

[a] In order to include anticipatory effects, "before start" means losses two years before actual implementation; "present" ranges from 1975 to 1977, depending on the districts; see Armor (1978) for detailed data.
[b] This is the excess White loss, over and above projected losses, expressed as a percentage of the first column.
[c] Prince Georges County's projected enrollment is larger than the initial enrollment.
[d] In 1967, prior to annexations.

most interesting case is Pasadena, which had an index value of 37 the year before court-ordered desegregation. The success of the court's mandatory plan is seen in the first year of busing, when the index rose to 53. But, influenced by White flight, the index dropped to 35 by 1977, two points less than it was before desegregation. Although there was considerable ethnic imbalance in Pasadena in 1969, on the average the amount of minority exposure to White students was higher then than today in spite of a massive busing program. The other three districts have not yet reached that point, but it is noteworthy that none of them have been able to maintain an index level over 50. In Boston, the White flight has been so massive that even when Phase II was implemented the index reached only 39, and it has dropped sharply to 35 during the past two years. In spite of the strong court actions in Boston, this low degree of minority and White contact makes it hard to claim that its schools are desegregated today. The major social and political upheaval experienced by Boston seems a high price to pay for raising the percent White in the average Black student's school by 10 points.

The trends in these four cities can be contrasted to San Diego, which has pursued a strictly voluntary plan. Although the percent White declined from 76% in 1968 to 64% in 1977, demographic projections reveal that there has been no significant White flight. During this time, the desegregation index has actually increased slightly, to a high of 46, due to a vigorous voluntary program. Under court orders this plan will be expanded over the next four years, and the index is projected to increase by several points by the early 1980s. Of course, some minority students are relatively isolated while others are in schools ranging from 60–80% White. But by avoiding White flight (so far), San Diego has managed to offer desegregated education to about half of its minority students.

It is frequently overlooked that mandatory busing increases the desegregation experience of the isolated minority student only by decreasing the desegregation of other minorities. Then, after ethnic balance is attained, desegregation is decreased for all minority students by White losses, which are accelerated by White flight. When the percent White drops below 50 for the district as a whole, none of the minority students are truly desegregated. By contrast, some voluntary plans have avoided White flight, thereby allowing these districts to maintain majority White schools. Under such conditions, a voluntary plan like San Diego's which desegregates a significant proportion of its minority students may well be considered more successful than a mandatory plan like Boston's in which no minority students are desegregated.

Although not all the districts studied here have experienced the same degree of White flight as Boston, it is noteworthy that only four districts in Table II are now over 60% White, thereby providing for a substantial degree of desegregation. Five others are between 50 and 60% White, but the rate of White loss in these districts is such that most will probably "tip" within a few years. Even now some of these districts (e.g., Fort Worth, Springfield, and Indianapolis) have desegregation indices below 50. It seems clear, then, that nearly all school districts meeting the percent minority and suburban access criteria have experienced sufficient court-induced White flight to be in clear danger of resegregating.

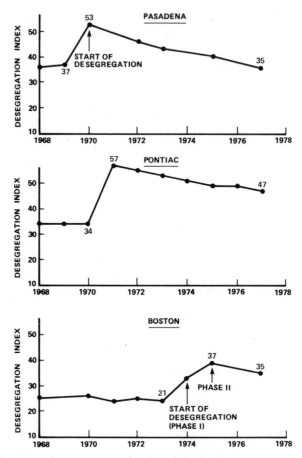

Figure 5. Changes in desegregation index for selected cities. (Desegregation index is the average percent White in schools attended by minority students.)

Metropolitan Plans: Jefferson County

The existence of White flight in central-city school districts has led some policy analysts to conclude that desegregation should be carried out on a metropolitan basis. A metropolitan plan combines central-city and suburban school districts and, if mandatory, exchanges inner-city minority students with suburban White students. Many advocates of mandatory metropolitan plans believe that eliminating the possibility of suburban relocation largely solves the White flight problem. Moreover, for those school districts that already have predominantly minority enrollments, a metropolitan plan of some type—either mandatory or voluntary—may be the only recourse for desegregation.

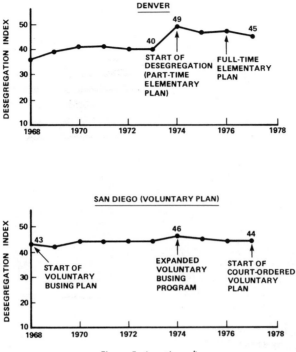

Figure 5. (continued)

Unfortunately, the evidence is not yet complete for evaluating White flight in metropolitan plans. The Jefferson County–Louisville desegregation plan is the only true mandatory metropolitan plan implemented by 1975. Although it is only a single case, nevertheless its outcome is of considerable interest for clues about metropolitan White flight.

The existence of a comprehensive study of enrollment trends in Jefferson County (Jefferson County Education Consortium, 1977), which documents both public and private White enrollment data from 1968 to 1977, can improve the projection analysis. The private school data enables a unique examination of the relationship between public and private school enrollments during court-ordered desegregation, an issue that may be especially important for metropolitan plans. Actual and projected White enrollments for Jefferson County are shown in Figure 6 (see Armor, 1978 for detailed data).

After some anticipatory White loss in 1974, there was a very substantial public school loss of 11.3% in 1975, when busing began, which is more than 3½ times the projected rate of 3%. The next two years, the actual loss rate was between 1½ to 2 times higher than the projected rate.

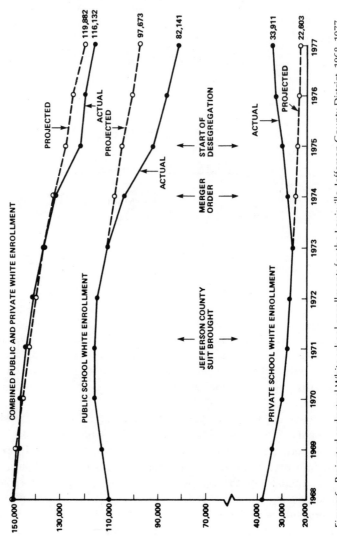

Figure 6. Projected and actual White school enrollments for the Louisville-Jefferson County District, 1968–1977.

Thus, the first-year White flight effect in Jefferson County is comparable to what we have found for central-city districts, but the longer-term effect is not quite as strong. This demonstrates that mandatory metropolitan plans can indeed have White flight, but perhaps with somewhat weaker long-term effects.

What is equally interesting about these results is the amount of flight due to relocation (or failure to move in) versus the amount due to transfers to private schools. By 1977, the excess White loss in Jefferson County public schools due to the court order was about 15,500 students. The excess increase in private schools, over and above their projected White enrollment, was about 11,000. Therefore, it appears that most of the White flight in Jefferson County is in the form of private school transfers; only about one-third of the loss is attributable to relocation.

These results reveal that significant White flight is possible in metropolitan plans, although, if Jefferson County is any indication, it may take the form of transfers to private schools. However, perhaps because of the expense and availability of private schools, the long-term White flight effects in metropolitan plans may be smaller than for central-city districts.

REASONS FOR WHITE FLIGHT

There is ample evidence in this and other studies that Whites do flee desegregation plans that mandatorily assign or bus students to schools outside their neighborhoods. One important remaining question, and one that has received scant attention by researchers, is why this flight occurs. This question must be answered, at least tentatively, before offering policy alternatives that could minimize White opposition to and flight from desegregation.

Some commentators have tended to view White flight as simply another form of old-fashioned racism (e.g., NAACP Legal Defense and Educational Fund, 1973). They frequently characterize the neighborhood school concept as an artificial issue, invented by White parents to cover prejudiced feelings against having their children attend integrated schools. The main evidence in support of this argument are the facts that a large fraction of Whites choose to live sufficiently far away from their school to require busing, without protest, and that large numbers—perhaps a majority—of minority parents are willing to be bused from their neighborhood schools to desegregated schools across town. And, of course, racists are frequently found among the louder protestors of mandatory busing.

Racism and prejudice are no doubt involved in White flight; however, there is much indirect evidence that argues against exclusive reliance on these factors. First, over the past 20 years or so there has been considerable improvement in racial and ethnic tolerance among Whites, manifested especially by increasing endorsement of school integration (Greeley & Sheatsley, 1971; Pettigrew, 1973). In spite of this trend, however, White opposition to mandatory busing has remained strong, long after its novelty waned and it became a commonplace policy among major American cities. Throughout the seventies, national surveys show that between 70 and 85% of Whites are opposed to busing for the purpose of desegregation, depending upon the survey; non-Whites tend to support it (AIPO, 1974, 1975; Weidman, 1975). Perhaps more significant, opposition to busing remains strong among White groups who have led the trend of increasing tolerance, including college graduates, younger parents, and those scoring low on traditional prejudice indices (Weidman, 1975).

Recognizing these facts, some have argued that Whites pay lip service to integration, which has now become a fashionable concept, but that the busing issue brings out their true inner feelings about racial integration of the schools. There is considerable behavioral evidence, however, that is incompatible with this interpretation. For example, many school districts such as San Diego have implemented minority-to-majority transfer programs which have caused many nearly all-White schools to enroll large fractions of minority students, and this has occurred without appreciable White flight (Armor, 1976). Likewise, the Rossell II study (1978) of 113 school districts shows that desegregation via increases in Black enrollment at White schools is not itself correlated with White flight once White reassignment is controlled.

This existing research evidence, although not conclusive, offers the strong suggestion that it is not school integration *per se* that Whites object to, but rather the method used to attain it. Most Whites may be willing to attend integrated schools, providing it occurs in schools they have already chosen for their children. It follows that it is not racial intolerance itself that causes all White flight, but something else about mandatory busing. Exactly what this "something else" is remains to be discovered.

Other analysts have noted a weak relationship between traditional racial prejudice and opposition to busing, and other explanations for anti-busing sentiments have been sought. One recent attempt to explain White opposition to busing involves the new concept of "symbolic racism" (McConahay & Hawley, 1977; Sears, Speer, & Hensler, 1976). *Symbolic racism* for Whites is defined by McConahay and Hawley as "the expression in terms of abstract, ideological symbols and symbolic behaviors of the feeling that blacks are violating cherished values and making illegitimate demands for changes in the status quo." Measuring symbolic racism with attitude items such as "blacks are getting too demanding" or "the government and news media have shown more respect to blacks than they deserve," they found in a Louisville–Jefferson County study that symbolic racism was far and away the strongest correlate of White opposition to busing; old-fashioned racism had only a weak relationship. Since they also found that self-interest variables such as having children in public schools or in the busing program were not related to busing opposition, McConahay and Hawley concluded:

> The low relationship of anti-busing attitudes to self-interest and its much higher relationship to racial and other symbolic issues is strong evidence that "busing" is a symbolic issue similar to the prohibition debates. . . . [They] argue as if they were concerned with harm to children or the family or the community or the nation, but only shout past one another because the debate is really over whose values will dominate public life and whose group will receive the con-commitment public interest. (p. 50)

The problem with this approach is that symbolic racism is not clearly distinct from the busing issue itself. In fact, given White opposition to mandatory busing in a community where the courts have ordered busing following a lawsuit brought by the NAACP, it may be logical to expect that Whites feel the government is being overly responsive to Black demands while ignoring White opinion. Anti-busing sentiments may be a cause of symbolic racism, as measured by these authors, rather than the other way around. If this is the case, we still do not have an explanation for White flight. It is not clear, either, whether racism is a justifiable term for these beliefs.

Moreover, these studies have measured only the behavioral aspects of self-interest, such as having children in public schools or having children being bused or being in an area where busing is threatened. Other aspects of self-interest, particularly beliefs about the consequences of busing or desegregation, are not assessed. If Whites believe busing is harmful, then is it not reasonable to expect them to oppose it whether or not they are exposed to it? In fact, the behavioral self-interest finding shows that anti-busing sentiment is not based on expediency alone, but must involve more general belief systems. Although McConahay and Hawley state the busing debate is not about harm to children or the family, their study does not include any direct assessment of beliefs about the benefits or harms of desegregation and busing.

The strong and consistent White opposition to busing in spite of increasing racial tolerance belies deeper and more complex issues, and indeed suggests that "cherished values" are being threatened differentially for Blacks and Whites. Just what these values are, and why they differ for Blacks and Whites, is not resolved by existing research. We therefore turn to the Los Angeles survey, which does shed some additional light on the dilemma.

The Los Angeles Survey

The Los Angeles survey was commissioned by the local school board for the purpose of evaluating parental reaction to alternative desegregation plans, including both voluntary and mandatory busing (Armor, 1977). The survey included questions about school integration in general, the reasons for supporting or opposing mandatory busing, and perceived benefits or harm accruing from desegregation. The survey sampled 1,805 persons with children in the Los Angeles public schools, including 639 Whites, 525 Blacks, 526 Mexican-Americans, and 115 other minority (mostly Asian). Telephone interviews were conducted by professional interviewers in the spring of 1977.[13]

Consistent with national surveys, the vast majority of Los Angeles Whites, 86%, were opposed to "busing children of all backgrounds—white, black, and Mexican-American to achieve school desegregation." In contrast, about two-thirds of Black parents were in favor, and, interestingly, a slight majority of Mexican-Americans, 53%, were also opposed to busing all groups.

On the other hand, a large majority of Whites, 72%, said they had no objection to their child attending a school with one-third to one-half Black or Mexican-American students, and 73% had no objection if a "considerable number of black and Mexican-American children were bused into [their] child's present school." It would appear that there is relatively little ethnic prejudice expressed toward integrated schools, at least in principle, and consequently, there is no substantial opposition to busing programs that bring minorities into White schools. Consistent with other studies, therefore, racially intolerant attitudes *per se* cannot explain the substantial opposition to "two-way" busing of all students, including Whites.

In order to explain the White support of desegregation, in principle, but opposition to two-way busing, the analysis turned to the respondents' beliefs in the effects of desegregation. The questionnaire contained six agree–disagree items concerning possible benefits or harms of desegregation: it would improve education for minorities, improve education for Whites, reduce racial prejudice, increase discipline problems, risk safety of students, and increase racial tensions. In general, a substantial majority of Whites disagreed with the benefit items and agreed with the harm items, whereas Blacks responded in the exact opposite direction, agreeing with beneficial effects and disagreeing with harmful effects. Mexican-American respondents showed yet a third pattern, agreeing with the benefit items

---

[13] The survey was supervised by staff from the Social Science Research Institute at UCLA, directed by Professor Howard Freeman. Mexican-American respondents who could not understand English adequately were interviewed by Spanish-speaking interviewers using a translated questionnaire. Sampling was disproportionate with respect to ethnicity.

(albeit by smaller majorities than for Blacks) but also agreeing with the harm items. These results suggest the possibility that support of or opposition to busing is explained not by ethnic prejudice, but rather by its perceived beneficial or harmful effects, or, at least by whether its benefits outweigh the perceived costs involved in abandoning neighborhood schools.

This thesis can be tested by first examining the relationships between perceived desegregation effects and opposition to busing or White flight for each ethnic group. Perceived desegregation effects are measured by combining the six belief items into a single scale and collapsing so that persons who agree with most of the harm items and disagree with most of the benefit items are designated as perceiving harmful effects, and persons with the opposite pattern are classified as perceiving beneficial effects. Others are classified as perceiving mixed effects, since they anticipate both harmful and beneficial consequences.

The impact of perceived desegregation effects on opposition to busing is shown Table III. In general, the explanatory power of one's belief in the virtues or drawbacks of desegregation is quite significant, particularly at the extremes. A large majority of those who believe that desegregation is more harmful than beneficial are opposed to busing, regardless of race or ethnicity. Likewise, most of those who believe the effects are beneficial are not opposed, except for Whites—where only 51% are opposed. Among those who believe effects are mixed, race plays a more important role, with

Table III. Percent Opposed to Two-Way Busing by Perceived Desegregation Effect and Ethnicity[a]

| Race or ethnicity | Perceived desegregation effect[b] | | | |
	Harmful	Mixed	Beneficial	Totals
Black	74	37	18	32
(N)	(35)	(263)	(226)	(524)
Mexican-American	84	47	34	53
(N)	(114)	(319)	(92)	(525)
White	97	82	51	86
(N)	(345)	(219)	(74)	(638)
Other	91	59	33	66
(N)	(35)	(59)	(21)	(115)

[a] Opposed to two-way busing means opposition to "busing children of all backgrounds—White, Black, Mexican-American—to achieve school desegregation."
[b] Based on a 6-item summated Likert scale indicating beliefs that desegregation will give better education for minorities, better education for Whites, lead to more discipline problems, reduce racial prejudice, increase racial tensions, or risk children's safety. After reverse-scoring appropriate items, mean scale scores were rounded and collapsed so that "harmful" includes persons on the agree side of the negative items and the disagree side of the positive items; likewise for "beneficial."

only 37% of Blacks opposing busing compared to 82% of Whites. It is possible that racial prejudice explains some of the differences which exist after perceived effects are removed, particularly for those who perceive mixed effects.

The joint impact of prejudice and perceived desegregation effects on White opposition to busing is shown in Table IV. For our purposes, school prejudice exists when Whites state they would object to their child attending a school with one-third to one-half Black or Mexican American students. In order to help clarify the role of school prejudice, the table also shows the percentage of Whites opposed to busing "a considerable number" of minority students into their child's present school.

The results in Table IV show that school prejudice does not explain the strong White opposition to mandatory busing, regardless of one's perception of the effect of desegregation. Among Whites not objecting to integrated schools, the percentage opposing busing of all groups resembles those shown in Table III. In a further tabulation controlling for education, even college graduates without school prejudice showed about the same rates of opposition. Among 37 persons with some college or higher education who do not object to integrated schools and who do believe in beneficial effects, 50% are still opposed to two-way busing. These data suggest that

Table IV. Percentage of Los Angeles White Parents Opposed to Minority-Only Busing or Two-Way Busing for Desegregation, by Ethnic School Prejudice and Perceived Desegregation Effects

School prejudice	Perceived desegregation effect		
	Harmful	Mixed	Beneficial
Objection to child attending school with ⅓ or ½ minority students[a]			
Opposed to:			
Two-way busing	98	85	38
Minority-only busing[b]	57	44	0
(N)	(113)	(48)	(8)
No objection			
Opposed to:			
Two-way busing	96	82	52
Minority-only busing	24	15	3
(N)	(212)	(164)	(65)

[a] Minorities were either Black or Mexican-American students; "Don't know" responses to either ⅓ or ½ minority are treated as prejudiced responses.
[b] "If a considerable number of Black and Mexican-American children were bused into your child's present school, would you object or not object?" The percentage opposed includes a small number who answered "don't know."

although perceived effects explain a good part of the opposition to mandatory busing, racial intolerance and education offer little additional explanatory power. Of course, we still have to explain why mandatory busing is unpopular among Whites who, from all other signs, should be its strongest supporters.

One possibility is that the measure of school prejudice is not an adequate criteria for racial intolerance. This interpretation appears to be ruled out by the opinions on minority-only busing also shown in Table IV. Generally, persons without school prejudice are not opposed to minority students being bused into their own school, particularly those who do not believe desegregation is harmful. However, among those with school prejudice, slightly over 50% are opposed to this policy. The school prejudice indicator does discriminate among supporters or opponents of one-way busing, as one would expect for a valid measure of racial prejudice, but not among supporters or opponents of two-way busing of all groups.

To understand more fully reasons for opposing two-way busing, we can turn to a question which asked parents their reasons for opposition. Among Whites who opposed two-way busing, the majority (54%) said that children should attend their neighborhood schools, or they gave specific reasons closely tied to the neighborhood school concept: their child would be too far away, would lose too much time, or would lose existing friendships. Even Whites perceiving beneficial effects—but who were opposed to busing—showed a similar rate of belief in neighborhood schools. More important, a 60% majority of Mexican-Americans who were opposed to total busing also cited the neighborhood school concept, and 47% of Blacks who opposed total busing did likewise. Among all ethnic groups, no other reason or set of reasons came close to matching the importance of the neighborhood school concept for opposing busing. It seems quite clear, then, that the neighborhood school concept is a fairly fundamental and widespread belief, and not one held exclusively by Whites to mask racial intolerance.

So far the analysis has considered opposition to busing as an attitudinal measure. How does this relate to the reasons for White flight? The Los Angeles survey includes questions asking parents what they would do if their child was mandatorily reassigned to another "good" school up to 45 minutes away located in three different areas—White, Black, and Mexican-American—for periods ranging from 9–10 weeks up to 2 years. They could respond whether they would "go along with it" or not, and if not, whether they would withdraw their children from the Los Angeles schools by moving to another district, transferring to private schools, or keeping their children out of school for this period. Of those Whites saying they would withdraw, about two-thirds cited transfer to private schools, and one-third cited move out of district. Only 3% cited the boycott method.

The White withdrawal rates and the relative impact of perceived effects and school prejudice are shown in Table V. As for opposition to two-way busing, White withdrawal is the majority response for all groups, regardless of perceived effect or prejudice, except for Whites with no school prejudice and who believe the effects are largely beneficial. Even for this group, over 40% say they would withdraw their child. Generally the effect of school prejudice, controlling for perceived desegregation effect, is to raise White withdrawal rates by about 10–15%, while the effect of believing desegregation is harmful (rather than beneficial), controlling for school prejudice, is to raise the withdrawal rate by 20–25%. Notice that withdrawal rates are not affected by the ethnicity of neighborhood bused into; this gives further credence to the conclusion that ethnic intolerance is not the major reason for White flight. Even though intolerance has some effect, the perceived benefits or harms of desegregation is a much stronger correlate.

The results of the Los Angeles survey are suggestive of a fairly complex dynamic to explain White flight. Basically, belief in the neighborhood school appears to be a fairly important component. However, it would be a mistake to put the whole burden on neighborhood schools. White flight originates not from commitment to neighborhood schools alone, but from the *combined* result of believing in neighborhood schools and in *not* believing desegregation is beneficial for minority children or their own children. Busing asks Whites to give up a valued policy, the neighborhood school, in return for an experience that is perceived to be either harmful or at least not

Table V. Percentage of White Parents Who State They Would Withdraw Child from Los Angeles Schools if Mandatorily Bused, by Ethnic Prejudice and Perceived Desegregation Effects[a]

School prejudice	Perceived desegregation effect		
	Harmful	Mixed	Beneficial
Objection to child attending school with ⅓ or ½ minority students			
If bused to White area	82	63	62
If bused to Black area	85	71	62
(N)	(113)	(48)	(8)
No objection			
If bused to White area	69	56	45
If bused to Black area	70	60	43
(N)	(212)	(164)	(65)

[a] Bused up to 45 minutes each way, for up to 2 years; withdrawal includes moving out of district, transfer to private schools, or boycott. Results for busing to Mexican-American neighborhoods are similar.

beneficial. Obviously, the existence of widespread nondesegregation busing shows that many Whites are willing to abandon the neighborhood school in favor of options they perceive as being more important, such as living in a more rural environment or sending their child to a distant school with a unique educational program. This latter reason is why magnet schools have worked in many school districts. Moreover, since Black parents as a group do believe desegregation is beneficial, most are willing to give up the neighborhood school.

White parents, on the other hand, have not yet been convinced that desegregation is sufficiently beneficial to justify abandoning the neighborhood school. As a sign that these are not weakly-held beliefs, when Whites are compelled to leave their neighborhood school in a busing program, many simply withdraw from the district as soon as they can bear the cost.

THE FUTURE OF SCHOOL DESEGREGATION

The findings of Coleman, the latest Farley and Rossell studies, and the present study all agree on one important fact: Desegregation can cause accelerated White flight, particularly in larger school districts with substantial minority enrollments (over 20% or so) and in districts with accessible White suburbs. This conclusion is robust, based on a concensus from four different studies employing different conceptual and analytic strategies.

Rossell's latest study and the present study clarify certain aspects of the White flight effect. The effect tends to happen only when significant numbers of students are mandatorily reassigned (or bused), and especially when White students are reassigned to formerly minority schools. This situation develops mostly in court-ordered cases, although there are several mandatory HEW-ordered plans and at least one case of a community-initiated mandatory plan.[14] Therefore court-ordered mandatory plans, rather than desegregation *per se*, have been the primary causes of accelerated White flight in desegregating school districts. Voluntary busing plans such as that adopted by San Diego do not appear to have any significant effect on White flight.

Using demographic projection methods, the present study offers further information about White flight induced by court-ordered desegregation. The effect is strongest in the first year of desegregation, with average White losses accelerating by factors of 2 to 4 in most cases. But the projections also show that many districts suffer anticipatory White losses, usually

---

[14] Berkeley, California is the only city meeting our size and percent minority criteria which voluntarily implemented a comprehensive two-way busing plan by 1975, the cut-off date for this study. Seattle, Washington became the second city to do so in the fall of 1978.

between the initial legal activities and the actual start of desegregation. More important, the method also shows that in most districts the accelerated White losses last for prolonged periods up to four or five years or more. Sometimes these longer-term effects are boosted by subsequent court actions taken to broaden desegregation.

The longer-term effects are stronger in larger, central-city school districts that have ample two-way busing, available suburbs, and higher minority concentrations. In some of these cases, the court action seems to have altered permanently the rate of White decline in the public schools.

It is important to stress that not all White losses are attributable to the court actions. Many districts, especially those in the larger urban areas, would have experienced substantial White declines during the 1970s without the court orders. Most of these "natural" declines are due to a demographic transition characterized by declining White births combined with increasing central-city White outmigration rates. Nonetheless, the extra White losses caused by court-ordered mandatory desegregation are very substantial, in most cases amounting to over half of all White losses over periods of six to eight years.

White flight appears to be insignificant in most Florida districts and in districts with small concentrations of minority students. The latter cases are apparently explained by the relatively minor dislocation necessary for desegregating relatively small numbers of minority students. In other countywide districts without suburbs—which might be considered "metropolitan"—court orders have induced White flight, but the effect may not be long-term like that in central-city districts. According to the Louisville–Jefferson County experience, the reason may have to do with cost and availability of private schools, which logically forms the primary avenue for White flight in metropolitan plans. Of course, should the supply of private schools be increased, as it might with tuition tax credits or with property tax cuts such as those occuring in California, metropolitan plans could rival intradistrict plans in White flight.

Having provided further evidence that court-ordered desegregation does cause White flight, and that under certain conditions the effect is very substantial, it must be conceded that the present study will probably not end the debate. All projection studies must make assumptions, and although the assumptions adopted here seem reasonable, they can be challenged. Moreover, at least one recent study using different methods has argued that long-term effects are rare (Rossell, 1978). As a result, it is likely that there will be continuing argument, not over the existence of court-induced White flight, but over its full magnitude.

Nonetheless, this argument should not be allowed to obscure the central policy issue. Most of the school districts studied here are losing Whites at a rapid rate. Part of the cause may be demographic, but the court action only increases the rate of loss and the risk of resegregation. For persons who sincerely desire to increase the total amount of integration, this risk has to be disturbing. At precisely a time when policies are needed to halt or reverse the normal White declines in urban areas, we have instead court actions which are exacerbating the condition. Although the effects may be relatively small in some cases, in other cases they are large. In either case, they seem inappropriate during an era when most urban experts are urgently seeking ways to attract Whites back into cities. Clearly, other remedies for school desegregation should be considered.

One alternative, of course, is to abandon "induced" school desegregation policies entirely, and let school desegregation take place naturally by housing choices of White and minority families. Given the failure to document definitive and meaningful educational and social benefits from induced school desegregation policies (Armor, 1972; St. John, 1975), we may eventually discover that natural desegregation is the wisest policy.

However, given current knowledge about housing segregation, which appears to be increasing in many metropolitan areas, many educational policymakers will not be content with the amount of desegregation arising naturally from neighborhood school assignments. Accordingly, for many policymakers there are only two meaningful alternatives: expanded voluntary plans, either on an intradistrict or metropolitan basis, or mandatory metropolitan plans.

In evaluating the relative merits of these two options, it is essential to take into account the reasons for White flight. Contrary to the suggestions of some policy commentators, the Los Angeles survey results are not consistent with the thesis that opposition to busing and White flight are latent forms of prejudice and racism. Of course, prejudice and racism do exist, and persons with such attitudes are among the first to flee a desegregation program. But racism as an explanatory factor is not alone sufficient to account for the fact that the vast majority of Whites accept desegregated schools when brought about by voluntary methods but reject them when their children are mandatorily bused or reassigned to schools outside their neighborhoods.

The primary reason for White flight appears to be a commitment to the neighborhood school concept coupled with a lack of confidence in desegregation benefits. The resulting strong White opposition to mandatory busing makes it unlikely that legislative bodies, whether state or federal, will enact mandatory metropolitan desegregation. Realistically, the only hope for mandatory metropolitan plans rests upon further court action. Before federal courts can order metropolitan remedies, however, they must show that state actions or suburban school districts have had a direct and substantial effect on the central city's school segregation. At present, this has been found for Wilmington, Delaware and may yet be found for

Indianapolis, both for quite special reasons.[15] As was true for Detroit, however, it will be difficult to show such connections in most cities. The NAACP and the ACLU are pursuing metropolitan remedies in Cincinnati and Atlanta on the grounds of government-caused housing segregation, but it is an open question whether federal courts will agree with this allegation.

An important exception may be California, whose school desegregation cases are being handled in state courts under a state Supreme Court edict that all school segregation is unconstitutional regardless of its causes. There is nothing in the logic of the state court's holdings that would preclude a judge from ordering a metropolitan remedy. Given the strong majority opposition to busing, however, and the inevitable legal and political battles that will ensue, it is unclear whether any court will try to do so. For example, if any school district needs a metropolitan remedy it is Los Angeles, where the Anglo losses under busing are likely to turn Los Angeles into a minority-isolated district by 1980 or so, where few minority children will attend desegregated schools (Armor, 1977).[16] Yet, the court allowed an intradistrict plan to start in 1978 and has given no indication it will expand it into a metropolitan plan.

Even if courts do order metropolitan mandatory desegregation, there is no guarantee of success. It is true that some of the early countywide plans in the South, and Florida in particular, have managed to keep White flight to a minimum. But the recent experience of Jefferson County, Kentucky, shows that White flight can occur in a metropolitan plan, albeit via transfers to private schools. The current dissatisfactions with public education coupled with growing pressure for California-style property tax cuts could lead to an upturn in private school resources. Property tax cuts can accelerate the trend with a two-pronged affect: they make it harder for public schools to deliver services, while at the same time increasing a family's ability to pay for private schooling. Tuition tax credits now being considered by Congress will have a similar effect. In this context, a court order of metropolitan busing could deliver a devastating blow to public education.

If the courts fail to order metropolitan desegregation, then voluntary plans will be the only remaining alternative, possibly on a metropolitan

---

[15] Wilmington's metropolitan remedy was imposed because of a state law which specifically prevented the largely Black Wilmington school district from annexing suburban districts. Indianapolis may get a metropolitan remedy because of state actions that created a metropolitan local government but which kept the school district intact. The Louisville–Jefferson County merger was first ordered by an appellate court but was actually implemented by the state board of education after the Supreme Court disapproved the appellate order.

[16] A study done by the author (Armor, 1977) for the Los Angeles Board predicted an 18–22% loss during the first year of large-scale busing. The actual loss in 1978 following implementation of a limited plan for grades 4–8 was 16%, which was twice the "normal" loss rate of 8% based on demographic projections.

basis if state or federal funds become available. Although voluntary plans are widely believed to be ineffective, we have shown that San Diego's voluntary plan has maintained a substantial degree of desegregation, surpassing the amount of desegregation offered by the celebrated mandatory plans in Pasadena, Denver, and Boston. Although we cannot generalize from the success of a single city, the fact remains that in recent times the voluntary approach has not led to the intense controversy observed in mandatory busing cases. Perhaps we have not given voluntary methods a fair trial. If other school districts can duplicate San Diego's experience, voluntary plans would provide desegregation for a large fraction of minority students, perhaps for those who could benefit most.

Most important, a voluntary program eliminates the inevitable social costs of programs that are forced upon an unwilling and protesting public. Aside from the direct costs in the form of White flight, it is quite possible that mandatory busing has already added to the erosion of confidence in public education. Indeed, recent Gallup polls show that integration/busing is named as the number two problem facing public education (AIPO, 1978). Given this climate of opinion, voluntary desegregation programs not only offer more enrollment stability; they may offer hope for stopping this unfortunate decline in support for the public schools.

ACKNOWLEDGMENTS

I am indebted to J. Michael Ross, Christine Rossell, Kevin McCarthy, Reynolds Farley, and Walter Stephan for helpful comments on earlier versions of this paper. Research assistance was provided by Donna Schwarzbach.

REFERENCES

American Institute of Public Opinion (AIPO), *The Gallup Opinion Index*. Princeton, N.J.: November 1974; May, 1975; February, 1978.
Armor, D. J. Segregation and desegregation in the San Diego Schools. Unpublished manuscript, December 1976..
Armor, D.J. Offer of proof in reference to the testimony of David J. Armor. in *Crawford v. Board of Education of the City of Los Angeles*. Superior Court of the State of California for the County of Los Angeles, No. C822 854, June 6, 1977, Exhibit C.
Armor, D. J. *White flight, demographic transition, and the future of school desegregation*. The Rand Corporation, August 1978.
Coleman, J. S., Kelly, S. D., & Moore, J. A., *Trends in school segregation, 1968–73*, An Urban Institute Paper, UI 722-03-01, August 1975.
Farley, R. *School integration and white flight*. Population Studies Center, University of Michigan, 1225 South University Avenue, Ann Arbor, Michigan, August 1975.
Farley, R., & Wurdock, C. *Can governmental policies integrate public schools?* Population

Studies Center, The University of Michigan, 1225 South University Avenue, Ann Arbor, Michigan, March 1977.

Greeley, A. M., & Sheatsley, P. B. Attitudes toward racial integration. *Scientific American*, December, 1971, *225*.

Jefferson County Education Consortium. *The impact of court-ordered desegregation on student enrollment and residential patterns in the Jefferson County, Kentucky, public school district: An interim report.* Louisville, Kentucky, 1977.

McConahay, J. B., & Hawley, W. P. Is it the buses or the blacks? Department of Psychology, Duke University, 1977.

NAACP Legal Defense and Educational Fund. It's not the distance, it's the Niggers. In N. Mills (Ed.), *The great school bus controversy.* New York: Teachers' College Press, Columbia University, 1973.

Pettigrew, T. F. Attitudes on race and housing: A social-psychological view. In W. Hawley & V. Rock (Eds.), *Segregation in residential areas.* Washington, D.C.: National Academy of Science, 1973.

Pettigrew, T. F., & Green, R. L. *School desegregation in large cities: A critique of the Coleman 'White Flight' thesis.* Harvard Educational Review, *46*, no. 1, February 1976.

Rossell, C. H. School desegregation and white flight. *Political Science Quarterly*, 1975–76, *90* 675–695.

Rossell, C. H. *Assessing the unintended impacts of public policy: School desegregation and resegregation.* Boston: Boston University, 1978.

Sears, D. O., Speer, L. K., & Hensler, C. P. Opposition to 'busing:' Self-interest or symbolic racism. Los Angeles: University of California at Los Angeles, 1976.

Taeuber, K., & Taeuber, A. F. *Negroes in cities: Residential segregation and neighborhood changes.* Chicago: Aldine, 1965.

Weidman, J. C. Resistance of white adults to the busing of school children. *Journal of Research and Development in Education*, Fall, 1975.

School Segregation and Residential Segregation

PREFATORY STATEMENT

GARY ORFIELD

The school desegregation cases of the 1970s brought the Supreme Court face to face with difficult problems of urban racial change. In dramatic contrast with the early southern cases, where one only needed to read the state code to find proof of unconstitutional action and where one could often repair the damage with a relatively simple and self-evident remedy, the Supreme Court now had to deal with complex social issues: How did the cities become segregated? How much difference did the segregationist acts of the local school boards make? What kind of remedy was technically feasible? What kind of a plan would work? Would the plan itself become a major force in the demographic change of the urban community? To what extent are the forces of segregation and ghettoization confined to individual areas and municipalities within a metropolitan area, and to what extent is any highly localized remedy a denial of social reality?

Many of these questions cannot be answered simply by reference to legal precedents or reliance on legal reasoning. They require some implicit or explicit theory of urban history, urban demography, and urban change, particularly in formulating remedies. The value and even the survival of school integration in a community depend in good measure on the adequacy of these basic assumptions.

Members of the Supreme Court began to show sharply divergent understandings of the nature of urban reality in a series of school decisions, beginning with the 5–4 decision in 1974 against metropolitan desegregation

GARY ORFIELD • Department of Political Science, University of Illinois, Urbana, Illinois 61801.

in Detroit, in *Milliken* v. *Bradley*.[1] By the time the court decided *Dayton Board of Education* v. *Brinkman*[2] and associated cases in 1977, it was apparent that there was at least one significant element on the court which believed that the precise extent of historic violations by local school officials must be demonstrated and that the remedy applied decades later should be limited to those exact problems. When the Supreme Court agreed to hear yet another case from Dayton and the Columbus, Ohio case (where Justice Rehnquist had suspended the implementation of a citywide desegregation plan days before school opened in 1978), it seemed likely that the court was moving toward some major new judgments about the nature of urban segregation.

During the preparation of the brief for the civil rights organizations involved in the litigation, it became apparent that the brief must deal with questions on the nature of urban change as well as the major legal arguments. Relatively late in the process, one of the attorneys, William Taylor of Catholic University Law School, asked James Loewen to prepare a draft research summary, and contacted Karl Taeuber and Gary Orfield about the possibility of submitting a broadly-based social science brief on the central questions.

We organized a meeting in Chicago the next week to discuss the issues. The participants in this drafting group were Edgar Epps and D. Garth Taylor of the University of Chicago, Reynolds Farley of the University of Michigan, Diana Pearce of the University of Illinois, James Loewen of the Center for National Policy Review, and myself. (Others were invited but could not come at the last moment. For a complete list of those who signed the statement, see the Appendix at the end of Chapter 10.) This group reached the basic conclusions about the structure of the document, the nature of the conclusions that could be tentatively or firmly sustained by existing research, and the questions on which social scientists had nothing of use to say. The job of fleshing out particular segments of the draft was assigned to individual members and less than a week was available for the job. Taeuber and Loewen assembled the segments and Taeuber mailed it immediately for signatures to a list of social scientists hastily prepared at the Chicago meeting. Those who received the document by special delivery then called in their decisions or were contacted by committee members by phone. The great rush in the entire process meant that many researchers who had made significant contributions and who may well have agreed with the document were not contacted. There was a very strict deadline for printing the statement for submission to the court.

The process of preparing the statement required intense interdisci-

---

[1] *Milliken* v. *Bradley*, 418 U.S. 717 (1974).
[2] *Dayton Board of Education* v. *Brinkman*, 433 U.S. 406 (1977).

plinary work on the policy consequences of existing research on urban racial change. The ideal academic process would have been a long series of drafts, criticisms, elaborate distinctions and qualifications, and eventual publication for a discerning scholarly audience. This would, of course, have been completely irrelevant to the Supreme Court's work. In addition, given the strong academic bias against interdisciplinary work, it would probably never have been done.

This statement was possible because of the existence of a group of researchers who had been continuously concerned about these issues for years, had immediate access to the research literature, and were sufficiently concerned about the development of workable remedies to respond immediately to the request. None of the drafters believe it to be a full and final statement on the issues. All, I am certain, share my belief that the effort shows clearly the need for much more research in this area. In spite of its limitations, however, I believe that it is the most useful effort to date to bridge the gap between the research community and policy makers on this very important set of issues. I hope that it may help to raise the level of policy discussion and provoke a more focused scholarly dialogue that will permit firmer conclusions from a more fully developed research literature in the future. An elemental and vastly complex problem like urban racial segregation can never be effectively dealt with until the nature and dynamics of its origin and continual spread is adequately understood.

School Segregation and Residential Segregation

A SOCIAL SCIENCE STATEMENT

The problem of school segregation and residential segregation in large cities is one of the major issues facing American society today. Courts, legislatures, public administrators, and concerned citizens have struggled to understand the origins of the problem, to assess legal and moral responsibility, and to devise appropriate and effective legal, legislative, and administrative responses. Although public acceptance of the principle of desegregation is at its highest point in our history,[1] there is remarkable dissensus and confusion about the legitimacy and effectiveness of many of the methods being used or considered to combat segregation. The issues are complex. Legal, factual, and political questions have become intertwined in the public debate. It is the purpose of this statement to identify certain of the factual issues that have been studied by social scientists, to summarize the knowledge that has resulted from these studies and has been reported in scholarly journals and books, and to comment on the limits of social science knowledge.

[1] "Over the past 25 years, the only period for which we have even moderately good data on public attitudes, there has been a consistent trend toward greater white acceptance of equality for Negroes, including greater acceptance of residential integration" (Bradburn, Sudman, & Gockel, 1970). In 1978, 13% of whites said they would move if a Black family moved next door, compared to 35% in 1967 and 45% in 1963 (American Institute of Public Opinion, 1978). Among northern White parents in 1963, 67% reported they would not object to sending their children to schools where half of the students were Black. This figure increased to 76% of the parents polled in 1970 and remained about the same through 1975 (American Institute of Public Opinion, 1976). An even higher proportion of White parents report no objections to sending their children to schools where "some" or "a few" of the pupils are Black. (See also Taylor, Sheatsley, & Greenley, 1978.) In the South, where the most school desegregation has occurred, the percentage of White parents saying they object to sending their children to schools where half of the students were Black fell from 83% (1959) to 38% sixteen years later (Orfield, 1978, p. 109).

This statement does not consider basic legal principles or goals for the nation. The signers of this statement cannot speak with any special authority on moral and legal issues. Some of the key issues, however, are factual issues, subject to social science analysis. Many aspects of the nature of urban development and the segregation of minority groups have been studied with care by numbers of independent social scientists. Much has been learned about urban history, urban politics, changing public attitudes, the changing character of race relations, the operation of urban housing markets, and the formation and spread of racial segregation in urban areas. The first section of this statement is a summary of the current state of knowledge on some of these issues. The next section describes the kinds of conclusions that social science can and cannot supply concerning causes and effects of specific policies and actions. The last section presents a brief review of accumulated social science knowledge on the probable stability and effectiveness of several types of remedies that have been tried in school desegregation efforts. This statement emphasizes findings on which there is broad scholarly agreement, and avoids issues about which the evidence to date does not permit reasonably clear conclusions to be drawn.[2]

THE CAUSES OF SCHOOL AND RESIDENTIAL SEGREGATION AND THE RELATIONS AMONG THEM

Residential segregation between White and Black Americans and other racial and ethnic minorities prevails in all large cities in the United States (Taeuber & Taeuber, 1965).[3] This segregation is attributable in important measure to the actions of public officials, including school authorities.

Although ethnic enclaves are a long-established feature of urban residential and commercial organization, the recent experience of Blacks

---

[2] Although this statement was prepared initially at the request of attorneys concerned with litigation concerning the Dayton and Columbus school systems, the evidence and conclusions herein stated refer to American urban areas generally. Some of the studies cited include Dayton and Columbus in their data base and some do not. Not all the signers of this statement purport to have studied either city.

[3] An index of residential segregation calculated from census data on the numbers of White and non-White households on each city block has a theoretical range from zero (no segregation) to 100 (complete segregation). Indexes for 109 large American cities varied from 64 (Sacramento) to 98 (Miami) in 1960, and averaged about 86. Other minority groups were also residentially segregated. Updates based on the 1970 Census show a continuation of the pattern, with an average White–non-White segregation index for the same 109 cities of 81 (Sørensen, Taeuber, & Hollingsworth, 1975). Viewed from a metropolitan rather than central-city perspective, racial segregation increased in many urban areas during the 1960s (van Valey, Roof, & Wilcox, 1977).

and Hispanic minorities in American cities has been far different than the historical experiences of persons of European descent. Some first- and second-generation European immigrants were discriminated against and were subject to restrictions on the housing they could obtain. Nevertheless, their degree of residential segregation declined rapidly from the peak levels attained during periods of rapid immigration, and those peak levels were never as high as the levels typical for Blacks and Hispanic minorities today (Lieberson, 1963; Taeuber, 1975). The ethnic enclave for Whites was temporary and, to a large extent, optional (Erbe, 1975), whereas for Blacks, Puerto Ricans, and other Hispanics, "segregation has been enduring and can, for the most part, be considered as involuntary" (Butler, 1977).

Every major study of the housing of Blacks and Whites in urban America has identified racial discrimination as a major explanation of the observed segregation (Commission on Race and Housing, 1958; DuBois, 1899; Myrdal, 1944; National Advisory Committee on Civil Disorders, 1968; U.S. Commission on Civil Rights, 1961; Weaver, 1948). A recent review listed many forms of racial discrimination practiced by governmental and private agencies and individuals within the housing industry (Taeuber, 1975). Nearly a decade after federal legislation outlawing many such practices and a Supreme Court decision rendering them all illegal, a government study revealed that such practices continued, but often in more subtle and covert forms (Pearce, 1976; U.S. Department of Housing and Urban Development, 1978).

Policies and practices of the federal government have been particularly important since the beginnings of major federal housing programs during the Depression.[4] The ghetto pattern created by deliberate policy has become far harder to alter than it was to create. The ghettos grew along with simultaneous pervasive discrimination and segregation in education, government employment, and provision of many government services. These became such fundamental features of American life that they were often taken for granted, viewed as "natural" forms of social organization.

A simple example will suggest the inertial resistance to change that has resulted from the history of racial discrimination in housing. Governmentally insured home mortgages spurred the widespread practice of low down-payments and long repayment terms. This brought home ownership within the reach of young middle-income families, and was an underlying

---

[4] Tens of millions of housing units have been built and occupied under federal government subsidy and insurance programs. The mass movement of White population to outlying urban and suburban developments and the growth of central area minority ghettos occurred during this period, guided by the explicit policies of discrimination written into government regulations and administrative practice. See Frieden and Morris (1968) pp. 127-131, and works cited in footnote 1.

facilitator of rapid White suburbanization during the last three decades. Most Blacks were excluded from the FHA and VA mortgage insurance programs, based upon, among other things, the assertion that: "if the children of people living in . . . an area are compelled to attend school with a majority or a considerable number of pupils representing a far lower level of society or an incompatible racial element, the neighborhood under consideration will prove far less stable and desirable than if this condition did not exist" (FHA, 1935). In the current period of persistent inflation, a much higher proportion of White families than of Black families has a growing equity in home ownership. Whatever gains Blacks may make relative to Whites in obtaining jobs and reasonable incomes, they will long lag far behind in wealth (Kain & Quigley, 1972; Orfield, 1977). Thus will past discriminatory practices of the FHA and other housing agencies continue for decades yet to come to exert an influence on the racial structure of the nation's metropolitan areas.

Not all the governmental discrimination that fostered residential segregation was practiced by housing agencies. Employment discrimination affected the earnings of Blacks and influenced their workplaces, and both of these effects constrained housing opportunities. Discrimination in the provision of public services, such as paved roads, frequent trash collection, and new schools, was standard practice in southern cities and common in northern cities. Thus, residential areas for Blacks were further demarcated and stigmatized. Racial discrimination was institutionalized throughout American society, and the resulting patterns of segregation in housing, schooling, employment, social life, and even political activity had many causes (Myrdal, 1944). Discriminatory practices and racial segregation in each aspect of life contribute to the maintenance and reinforcement of similar practices and segregatory outcomes in other aspects.

Education is a pervasive, governmentally organized activity that reaches into every community. The institutionalization of racially discriminatory practices throughout the public school system is a substantial cause as well as effect of society's other racial practices. Society's major institution for socializing the young, aside from the family, is the public school system. Most children are influenced greatly by their school experiences, not simply in formal academic learning but in developing a sense of self and knowledge and feelings about social life and behavior.

There is an interdependent relationship between school segregation and neighborhood segregation. Each reinforces the other. Policies that encourage development and continuation of overwhelmingly racially identifiable schools foster residential segregation. This residential segregation, in turn, fosters increased school segregation. The role of many governmental practices in the development and continuation of residential segregation has been documented repeatedly and summarized above. Several specific ways in which school policies and practices contribute to residential segregation may be delineated.

The racial composition of a school and its staff tends to stamp that identity on the surrounding neighborhood. In many urban areas, the attendance zone of a school defines the only effective boundary between "neighborhoods."[5] Homebuyers use school attendance zones as a guide in their selection of a residence. Realtors take particular pains to "sell" the school as they sell the home;[6] the school zone is listed in many newspaper classified advertisements for homes and often serves to identify the racial character of the "neighborhood."

In many American cities during the last 30–60 years, residential areas of predominant minority occupancy have greatly expanded. Often, an increasing Black or Hispanic population has moved into housing formerly occupied by (Anglo) Whites. This process of "racial succession" or "ghettoization" has been perceived as a relentless "natural" force, yet it is in fact governed by institutional policies and practices and is not at all inevitable (Taeuber & Taeuber, 1965). The process is a textbook example of a self-fulfilling prophecy. The expectation by Whites that an area will become Black leads them to take individual and collective actions that ensure the outcome. Housing market barriers against sale or rental to Blacks are reduced, panic selling tactics often stimulate White residents to leave, and potential White in-migrants from other parts of the city are steered away from the neighborhood because it is "turning" or "going."

Change in the racial identifiability of a school can influence the pace of change in racial composition in a "changing" residential area (Wolf, 1963). In contrast, a school with a stable racial mix connotes to nearby residents and potential in-movers that they will not be forsaken by school authorities. School policies can serve to "coalesce a neighborhood and generate confidence in its continued stability" (Vandell & Harrison, 1976, p. 13).

Even childless households are affected by the school and neighborhood racial labeling process. Residential location is a major factor in determining social status in America (Warner, 1949; cf. Berry *et al.* 1976; Guest & Weed, 1976; Loewen, 1971; Marston & Van Valey, 1979; Roof, 1979; Sennett, 1970). Many Whites who contemplate remaining in or entering an area where the school has an unusually large or increasing proportion of minority pupils or staff expect that such a school will be discriminated

[5] "No other boundary system within the city is as crucial to residential behavior as the system of attendance zones delineated by school authorities" (Taeuber, 1979, p. 164).

[6] Helper (1969) reports that school image and racial composition play the key role in labeling neighborhoods as undesirable: "People fear that the schools will become undesirable—this, say respondents, is the main reason why white people do not want Negroes to come into their area" (p. 80).

against by school officials. "As the proportion of disadvantaged students in the central cities has increased, there has been a simultaneous increase in what are known in the community as 'undesirable' schools, schools to which parents would prefer not to send their children" (Campbell & Meranto, 1975). These parents know what all citizens know: that Black Americans have less social status and power with which to persuade or coerce school authorities to meet their needs. This perception, that Black schools will be allowed to deteriorate, has historical justification (Campbell & Meranto, 1975). Whatever the objective circumstances, parents expect that children in schools perceived to be for minority children will receive inferior education. Many White parents are able to move or place their children in other schools (Crain & Weisman, 1972). Most Black parents are unable to avoid using identifiably Black schools. If all schools were interracial, Whites could not link racial composition to school quality, and neither could school authorities.

All discriminatory acts by school authorities that contribute to the racial identifiability of schools promote racially identifiable neighborhoods. Sometimes the effect is direct and obvious, as when the selection of school construction sites, the drawing of school boundaries, and/or the construction of additions are carefully undertaken to establish and preserve "White schools" and "Black schools." Sometimes the effect is less direct. In most school districts, minority teachers have, until very recently, rarely been assigned to schools with no minority pupils, and, in many large urban school districts, few minority teachers were employed. Had White pupils and parents regularly encountered Blacks in responsible, professional positions, and had minority pupils and parents seen White and Black professionals equally treated, the perpetuation of stereotypical attitudes and prejudicial habits of thought would have been significantly challenged (Taeuber, 1979).

A pervasive effect of this and certain other types of discriminatory school actions is upon the attitudes of the students who grow up experiencing such a system for a thousand hours a year. Participation in segregated institutions foments the development of prejudicial attitudes (Crain & Weisman, 1972). Participation in desegregated institutions, under benign conditions, can be a powerful force for breaking down prejudice (Festinger, 1958). "If in their own schooling they [parents] had been taught tolerance rather than intolerance many more of them would now be willing and even eager to seek out racially mixed rather than racially isolated residential areas" (Taeuber, 1979, p. 162).

Racially discriminatory pupil assignment policies tend to increase residential segregation in several ways. An open transfer policy is often manipulated by school authorities to encourage or permit Whites to flee schools that are becoming biracial, and to attend overwhelmingly White schools some distance away. The effect on residential patterns would appear to be to permit White families to remain in a biracial residential area. The larger effects are, however, segregative. First, because the children who transfer lose many of their neighborhood ties, the family finds it easier to move to the neighborhood around their new school or to a more remote White enclave. Second, because the sending school is now identified as "Black" or "changing," White families who might otherwise have moved into the area will be steered elsewhere and the area will become increasingly minority (Bradburn et al., 1970; Milgram, 1977; Molotch, 1972; Orfield, 1977).

When the elected officials and appointed professional leaders of a major societal institution (the public schools) establish or condone the operation of optional attendance zones in a discriminatory manner, this tells the users of the institution (students and their parents) and the general public that it is correct to view racial contact as a problem and to utilize institutional practices and policies in ways that avoid the problem. The effect on attitudes has both short-run and life-long effects that may affect so-called "private" choices in housing and other areas of life (Taeuber, 1979):

> The NORC study found that desegregated whites were more likely to have had a close black friend, to have had black friends visit their homes, and to be living in multiracial neighborhoods. It is believed that having had a close black friend relates directly to choice of residence in a multiracial area. This is also true for blacks. (Green, 1974, p. 251)[7]

The actions of school officials are part of a set of discriminatory actions by government agencies and other institutions. This web of institutional discrimination is the basic cause of school and residential segregation. Economic factors and personal choice are often considered as additional causes (Myrdal, 1944).

The assertion sometimes made that residential segregation results from racial differences in economic status rather than from racial discrimination is a curious one. Racial discrimination in employment and earnings is a major cause of racial differences in economic status, and racial discrimination in access to homeownership was cited above as a cause of racial differences in wealth. Racial discrimination in education in prior years is of course one of the causes of poorer job market outcomes for Black adults. It is not necessary to elaborate on these interlocking causes. The fact is that current racial economic differences have little effect on racial residential segregation. If economic variables alone determined where people lived, the rich of both races would live near one another and poor Blacks and poor

---

[7] NORC is the National Opinion Research Center. See also Weinberg, 1970, pp. 311–313, citing Pettigrew and NORC studies. Regarding Black choices, see Crain, 1971, p. 19. See also Bullough, 1969.

Whites would be close neighbors. Such is not the case. Well-to-do Blacks live in very different* areas than well-to-do Whites and poor Whites generally do not share their residential areas with poor Blacks (Taeuber, 1968; Taeuber & Taeuber, 1965). Nor can economic factors explain the general absence of Blacks from the suburbs. Studies of census data reveal that in most metropolitan areas the suburbs are open to Whites in all economic categories but are generally closed to Blacks, be they wealthy or impoverished (Farley, Bianchi, & Colasanto, 1979; Hermalin & Farly, 1967). If people were residentially distributed according to their income rather than their skin color, most urban neighborhoods would contain racially mixed populations.

Despite the civil rights legislation of the 1960s and numerous court orders that prohibit discriminatory employment practices, the incomes of Blacks continue to lag far behind those of Whites.[8] Improvements in the economic status of Blacks would allow more Blacks to upgrade their housing, but increased spending on housing would do little to alleviate racial residential segregation (Straszheim, 1974; Taeuber, 1968).

The personal choices of individuals must be considered in any explanation of racial residential segregation. In national and local survey studies, most Blacks express a preference for racially mixed neighborhoods for themselves and racially integrated schools for their children. For example, in a national study conducted in 1969, three-fourths of Black respondents wished to live in integrated neighborhoods while one in six expressed a preference for an all-Black area (Pettigrew, 1973). In Detroit, the proportion of Blacks who said they preferred racially mixed areas rose from 56% in 1968 to 83% in 1976 (Farley, Schuman, Biardi, Colasanto, & Hatchett, 1978). These preferences cannot be used to predict where Black families actually live, for they have had lifelong experience with discriminatory housing markets that offer little actual freedom of choice (Colosanto, 1978).

In the late nineteenth and early twentieth centuries, economic factors and personal preferences may have been important determinants of residential location of Blacks and European immigrants (Hershberg, Burstein, Erickson, Greenberg, & Yancey, 1979; Lieberson, 1963; Spear, 1967). As the number of Blacks increased, institutionalized Jim Crow practices developed and, for more than half a century, the Black residential patterns have diverged from those of the ethnic groups. The conclusions of a historical study of the development of the Negro ghetto in Chicago are exemplary of other historical studies:

> The most striking feature of Negro housing . . . was not the existence of slum conditions, but the difficulty of escaping the slum. European immigrants needed

---

[8] In 1977, Black men who worked full time for the entire year reported earnings about 69% as great as those of comparable White men. The average income of Black families was 57% as great as that of White families (U.S. Bureau of the Census, 1978).

only to prosper to be able to move to a more desirable neighborhood. Negroes, on the other hand, suffered from both economic deprivation and systematic racial discrimination. . . . The development of a physical ghetto in Chicago . . . was not the result chiefly of poverty, nor did Negroes cluster out of choice. The ghetto was primarily the product of white hostility. (Spear, 1967, p. 26)

Neither economic factors nor the preferences of Blacks for having some Black neighbors can be interpreted as current causes of residential segregation separate and distinct from discrimination. Neither income differences nor personal choice produce levels of racial residential segregation in hypothetical models that assume an absence of discrimination (Taeuber & Taeuber, 1965; Taylor *et al.*, 1978).

In this review of findings, frequent use has been made of the terms *cities* and *urban areas*. The usage has deliberately been loose. The concepts of a housing market, a labor market, and a commuting area all connote a broad territory. The effects of any action that alters residential patterns in a specific location are not felt solely in that location. The kinds of discriminatory actions reviewed earlier in this section, whether taken by school officials, other governmental officials, commercial or financial institutions, or other groups or persons, have effects that spread beyond the neighborhoods initially effected (Hawley, 1977; Taeuber, 1977).

In the 35 years since Myrdal's (1944) seminal study of America's racial problems was first published, American society has changed in many ways, and race relations have experienced profound transformations. Social scientists have published thousands of additional studies of various aspects of race relations. If there is a common theme emerging from this myriad of studies, it is continual reaffirmation of Myrdal's observation of a process of cumulative causation binding the separate threads of social life into a system. This review of research on a limited range of topics has shown that causes and effects of individual actions cannot be understood or evaluated apart from the broader social context in which they are imbedded. Residential segregation, school segregation, racial economic differences, housing preferences and neighborhood attitudes, discriminatory acts by school officials, and discrimination practiced by other governmental agencies are linked together in complex patterns of reciprocal causation and influence.

CONCLUSIONS SOCIAL SCIENCE CAN AND CANNOT SUPPLY

The previous section reported a brief summary of some of the conclusions that can be drawn from the writings of social scientists who have studied school segregation, housing segregation, and other aspects of race relations in twentieth-century American society. A few dozen articles, chapters, and books were cited, from the thousands that might be included in a comprehensive literature survey. The individual scholarly investigations utilized a variety of information sources—interviews with realtors, government documents, records of housing sales prices, census data, etc. The techniques for analyzing information were varied—historical interpretation, statistical analysis, logical testing of predictions from formal theories, etc. The common link is a laying out of evidence and mode of analysis so that other scholars can examine the basis for the conclusions drawn. Many social scientists agree that the conclusions reported above are reasonably well established. Of course, the evidence is stronger for some conclusions than for others, and the scientist is always open to altering conclusions on the basis of new evidence.

The principal conclusions reported in the first section concern relationships among discriminatory actions by educational agencies, school segregation, residential segregation, and other types of institutionalized racial discrimination. A pervasive pattern of interdependence within American urban areas was documented. In particular, it was concluded that segregative school policies are among the causes of urban racial residential segregation.

Some social scientists have been asked to refine these general conclusions and provide precise answers about specific causal relationships in particular places and times.[9] They have been asked how much effect discriminatory and segregative school policies had on residential segregation and what exactly was the reciprocal effect of that incremental residential segregation on school attendance patterns. Even more precision is requested in the question, what is the numerical effect on current school attendance patterns that results from direct and indirect effects of individual discriminatory actions taken in the past by school officials?

Social scientists cannot answer such questions with precision. The questions can be rephrased to call for stating what the present would be like if the past had differed in certain specified respects. This is reminiscent of the grand "what if" games of history. What if the South rather than the North had been victorious in 1865? Would the United States be one nation? When would slavery have ended? What role would Black labor have played in the industrialization of northern cities? Clearly, there is fascinating material here for historical speculation, but any answers, however well grounded on scholarship and logical reasoning, are inherently fictional. And the game loses all point if the question becomes too narrow: What would the racial composition of Atlanta and of Chicago be in 1980? History cannot be unreeled and reeled back differently.

[9] For an indication of the judicial context in which such questions have been posed, see Taeuber (1977).

The present state of empirical knowledge and models of social change does not permit precise specification of the effects of removing particular historical actions. Although many of the causes of segregated outcomes are known, this knowledge is not so thoroughly quantified as to permit precise estimates of the effects of specific discriminatory acts on general patterns of segregation. In addition, the knowledge that is available is incomplete. Many of the links between discrimination and segregation are only dimly perceived and not yet investigated carefully. The work of many specialists—economists, psychologists, sociologists, political scientists, geographers—cannot be integrated into a grand model. Even if each individual link were well understood, the model could not be used to crank out estimates without understanding how the entire set of relationships functions as a system.[10]

Social scientists studying real cities in a particular society and time period do not have available the techniques of experimental analysis for control of variables. There are a few hundred urban areas to be studied, and thousands of variables with which to describe them and differentiate one from another. The kinds of generalizations that are possible are limited in character. Historical reconstruction simply cannot quantify meaningfully what the racial distribution of pupils or residents would have been if particular school officials had acted differently. Delimiting the wrong that flowed from specific acts and righting the wrong are matters for jurisprudence, not social science.

KNOWLEDGE ABOUT THE DESEGREGATION PROCESS

Although most large urban school districts with substantial numbers of minority pupils enrolled have changed some of their practices as a result of Brown v. Board of Education[11] and subsequent court decisions, many have never implemented comprehensive desegregation plans. Of those that have implemented such plans, most of the activity has been in recent years. There has been relatively little opportunity for sustained study of the process of school desegregation in large urban areas. Nevertheless, the social science literature on school desegregation already numbers hundreds of articles and books.[12]

An early body of research on educational achievement utilized existing or only slightly modified standardized tests and assessment instruments. Many of these studies did not distinguish between racially mixed classrooms

---

[10] For an example of the inability to utilize certain formal models of the effects of prejudice and discrimination on racial segregation in the housing market, see Taylor (1968).

[11] Brown v. Board of Education, 347 U.S. 438 (1954).

[12] Weinberg (1970) lists 10,000 "selected entries."

or schools that resulted from specific desegregation efforts and those that occurred for other reasons. Most lacked a time dimension, investigating only the situation at the time of study, or assuming that desegregation was an event that occurred all at once. There is a virtual consensus, from a wide variety of studies conducted in this manner, that desegregation does not damage the educational achievement of White children (Coleman, Campbell, Hobson, McPartland, Mood, Weinfeld, & York, 1966; Jencks, Smith, Ackland, Bane, Cohen, Gintis, Heyns, & Michelson, 1972; St. John, 1975).[13]

The *Coleman Report* (1966) found limited but significant educational gains for minority children, which it attributed primarily to the placement of these children in more challenging educational settings dominated by students from families with more resources and stronger educational backgrounds. The *Report*, and a number of reanalyses of the national statistics on which it was based, found that the quality of the school was more important to poor children whereas family influences were more decisive for middle-class children.

Research in the 1970s has moved toward a view of desegregation as a process rather than as an event, a process which is very much influenced by the manner in which it is carried out. Segregation appears to be a deeply rooted problem. Years of quiet work within a physically desegregated school may be needed to attain the intended benefits (Forehand, Ragosta, & Lock, 1976; Orfield, 1975). Early experiences continue to influence later learning, and social and cultural patterns of race relations and cannot be altered rapidly and easily in the school when profound inequalities of income, employment and occupational status, educational background, and social status prevail in the society.

The positive effects of desegregation can be enhanced by strong leadership of the principal in the school, by training for teachers who need help in the readjustment, and by school rules that are perceived as fair by both White and minority children (Forehand & Ragosta, 1976). Efforts by teachers to explain racial issues and to assign students consciously to integrated work groups can have substantial positive effect (Cook, 1978; De Vries, Edwards, & Slaven, 1978; Slaven, forthcoming; Weigel, Wise, & Cook, 1975).

The importance of beginning integration at the onset of public schooling has long been noted. Young children have the smallest gap in academic achievement and the least developed racial stereotypes (Coleman, 1966; National Opinion Research Center, 1973). Integration becomes part of their concept of school from the beginning, not a drastic change. Federal officials

---

[13] There has also been some evidence of definite White gains in plans which combined desegregation with educational improvements (Pettigrew, Useem, Normad, & Smith, 1973; St. John, 1975).

report that there is seldom any difficulty associated with desegregating the earliest grades.[14] A review of scores of published studies of academic achievement shows that a large majority of the cases with first-grade desegregation bring positive educational results, yet later desegregation has little effect on Black pupil achievement scores (Crain & Mehard, 1979). A study of schools in the South showed that the more years of desegregation, the more positive were the results (Forehand *et al*, 1976; National Opinion Research Center, 1973). Pettigrew (1975) summarized the sociological theory and cited additional evidence. Empirical results and social theory buttress the commonsense observation that small children have not yet learned that race is supposed to matter, and, therefore, tend to act as if it does not.

Certain longer-run effects of school desegregation may occur outside the school. Few of these effects have yet been studied, but some evidence is beginning to accumulate. Students from integrated schools, for example, are more likely to succeed in strong colleges (Armor, 1972; Crain & Mehard, 1978). A retrospective study of Black adults found that those who reported attending integrated schools as children were more likely in later years to live in racially integrated neighborhoods (Crain & Weisman, 1972). Ultimately, studies of the long-run effects of desegregation may provide crucial evidence on the strength of the indirect effects of school discrimination that were cited in the first section. Already, there is limited evidence that school desegregation can spur stable residential desegregation (Braunscombe, 1977; Green, 1974; Orfield, 1977; Rossell, 1978; Taeuber, 1979).

Social scientists have played a central role in a vigorous political and scientific debate over the demographic and enrollment effects of implementing desegregation plans. As yet, there is little consensus over the terms of the debate, the appropriate measurement techniques and theoretical formulations, and the trustworthiness of various empirical results. Nevertheless, there seems to be an emerging consensus that certain types of desegregation actions are most likely to result in large declines in public school enrollment by White pupils. If a plan is limited to a small fraction of the system and produces schools with large minority enrollments surrounded by readily accessible White schools, there is likely to be great instability in White enrollments (Giles, 1978). A study of desegregation in large school districts across Florida showed that enrollment stability was aided by equalizing school racial compositions as much as possible (Giles, Gatlin, & Cataldo, 1976). A study of the experience in Charlotte–Mecklenburg showed that the exclusion of only a few schools produced some

---

[14] Report from Community Relations Service of the U.S. Department of Justice accompanying letter from Assistant Attorney General Ben Holman to Senators Edward Brooke and Jacob Javits, June 19, 1976, printed in *Congressional Record* (daily edition), June 26, 1976, pp. S10708-11.

residential instability (Lord, 1975, 1977). Limiting a desegregation plan to the immediate vicinity of the ghetto or barrio is likely to accelerate the process of ghetto expansion.

REFERENCES

Allport, G. W. *The nature of prejudice*. Garden City, N.Y.: Anchor, 1958.

American Institute of Public Opinion. *The Gallup Opinion Index*. Princeton, N.J.: American Institute of Public Opinion, February 1976.

American Institute of Public Opinion. *The Gallup Opinion Index*. Princeton, N.J.: American Institute of Public Opinion, November 1978.

Armor, D. J. The evidence on busing. *Public Interest*, 1972, *28*, 90–126.

Baron, H. M. Race and status in school spending. In S. Gale & E. G. Moore (Eds.), *The manipulated city*. Chicago: Maaroufa, 1975, 339–347.

Berry, B. J., Goodwin, C., Lake R., & Smith, K. Attitudes toward integration: The role of status in community response to racial change. In B. Schwartz (Ed.), *The changing face of the suburbs*. Chicago: University of Chicago Press, 1976, 221–264..

Berry, B. J., & Kasarda, J. D. *Contemporary urban ecology*. New York: Macmillan, 1977.

Bradburn, N. B., Sudman, S., & Gockel, G. L. *Integration in American neighborhoods*. Chicago: National Opinion Research Center Report #111-B, 1970.

Braunscombe, A. Times are a changing in Denver. *Denver Post*, May 1, 1977.

Bullough, B. L. *Social barriers to housing desegregation*. University of California at Los Angeles Graduate School of Business Administration, Special Report 2, 1969. (Processed)

Butler, E. W. *The urban crisis: Problems and prospects in America*. Santa Monica: Goodyear, 1977, p. 50.

Campbell, A. K., & Meranto, P. The metropolitan educational dilemma. In S. Gale & E. G. Moore (Eds.), *The manipulated city*. Chicago: Maaroufa, 1975, 305–318.

Colasanto, D. The prospects for racial integration in neighborhoods: An analysis of preferences in the Detroit metropolitan area. Doctoral dissertation, University of Michigan, 1978.

Coleman, J. S., Campbell, E. Q., Hobson, C. J., McPartland, J., Mood, A. M., Weinfeld, F. D., & York, R. L. *Equality of educational opportunity*. Washington, D.C.: Government Printing Office, 1966.

Commission on Race and Housing. *Where shall we live?* Berkeley; University of California Press, 1958.

Community Relations Service of the U.S. Department of Justice accompanying letter from Assistant Attorney General Ben Holman to Senators Edward Brooke and Jacob Javits, June 19, 1976, printed in *Congressional Record* (daily edition), June 26, 1976, pp. S10708-11.

Cook, S. W. Interpersonal and attitudinal outcomes in cooperating interracial groups. *Journal of Research and Development in Education*, 1978, *12*, 1, 97–113.

Crain, R. L. School integration and the academic achievement of Negroes. *Sociology of Education*, 1971, *44*, 19.

Crain R. L., & Mehard, R. E. High school racial composition and black college attendance. *Sociology of Education*, April 1978.

Crain, R. L., & Mehard, R. E. Desegregation and black achievement. *Law and Contemporary Problems*, forthcoming.

Crain, R. L., & Weisman, C. S. *Discrimination, personality, and achievement*. New York: Seminar, 1972.

DeVries, D. L., Edwards, K. J., & Slaven, R. F. Biracial learning teams and race relations in the classroom: Four field experiments using teams-games-tournament. *Journal of Educational Psychology*, 1978, *70* (3), 356–362.

DuBois, W. E. B. *The Philadelphia Negro*. Philadelphia: University of Pennsylvania Press, 1899.

Erbe, B. Race and socioeconomic segregation. *American Sociological Review*, 1975, *40*, 801–812.

Farley, R., Schuman, H., Biardi, S., Colasanto, D., & Hatchett, S.. Chocolate city, vanilla suburbs: Will the trends toward racially separate communities continue? *Social Science Research*, 1978, *7*, 319–344.

Farley, R., Bianchi, S., & Colasanto, D. Barriers to the racial integration of neighborhoods: The Detroit case. *Annals of the American Academy of Political and Social Science*, 1979, *441*, 97–113.

Festinger, L. *A theory of cognitive dissonance*. Evanston, Ill.: Row Peterson, 1957.

Forehand, G. A., & Ragosta, M. *A handbook for integrated schooling*. Washington, D.C.: Government Printing Office, 1976.

Forehand, G. A., Ragosta, M., & Rock, A. *Conditions and processes of effective school desegregation*. Princeton, N.J.: Educational Testing Service, 1976, pp. 217–230.

Frieden, B. J., & Morris, R. Eds. *Urban planning and social policy*. New York: Basic, 1968, pp. 127–131.

Giles, M. W. White enrollment stability and school desegregation: A two-level analysis. *American Sociological Review*, 1978, *43*.

Giles, M. W., Gatlin, H., & Cataldo, E. *Determinants of desegregation: Compliance/rejection behavior and policy alternatives*. Washington; D.C.: National Science Foundation, 1976.

Green, R. L. Northern school desegregation: Educational, legal and political issues. In C. W. Gordon (Ed.), *Uses of the Sociology of Education*. Chicago: University of Chicago Press, 1974, 251.

Guest, A., & Weed, J. Ethnic residential segregation. *American Journal of Sociology*, 1976, *81*, 1088–1111.

Hawley, A. H. *Human ecology*. New York: Ronald, 1950.

Helper, R. *Racial politics and practices of real estate brokers*. Minneapolis: University of Minnesota Press, 1969.

Hermalin, A. I., & Farley, R. The potential for residential segregation in cities and suburbs: Implications for the busing controversy. *American Sociological Review*, 1967, *38*(5), pp. 595–610.

Hershberg, T., Burnstein, A. N., Erickson, E. P., Greenberg, S., & Yancey, W. L. A tale of three cities: Blacks and immigrants in Philadelphia, 1850–1880, 1930 and 1970. *Annals of the American Academy of Political and Social Science*, 1979, *441*, 55–81.

Jencks, C., Smith, M., Ackland, H., Bane, M. J., Cohen, D., Gintis, H., Heyns, B., & Michelson, S. *Inequality: A reassessment of the effect of family and schooling in America*. New York: Basic, 1972.

Kain, J. F., & Quigley, J. M. Housing market discrimination, home ownership, and savings behavior. *American Economic Review*, 1972, *LXII*, 263–277.

Kentucky Commission on Human Rights. *Housing desegregation increases as schools desegregate in Jefferson County*. Louisville, Kentucky: Kentucky Commission on Human Rights, 1978.

Lieberson, S. *Ethnic patterns in American cities*. New York: Free Press of Glencoe, 1963.

Loewen, J. W. *The Mississippi Chinese: Between black and white*. Cambridge: Harvard University Press, 1971, 102–119.

Lord, J. D. School busing and white abandonment of public schools. *Southeastern Geographer*, 1975, *15*, 81–92.

Lord, J. D. School desegregation policy and intra-school district migration. *Social Science Quarterly*, 1977, *57*, 784–796.

Marston, W. G., & van Valey, T. L. The role of residential segregation in the assimilation process. *Annals*, 1979, *441*, 22–25.

Milgram, M. *Good neighborhood: The challenge of open housing*. New York: Norton, 1977.

Molotch, H. *Managed integration*. Los Angeles: University of California Press, 1972.

Myrdal, G. *An American dilemma*. New York: Harper, 1944.

National Opinion Research Center. *Southern schools: An evaluation of the effects of the emergency school assistance program and of school desegregation*. Chicago: National Opinion Research Center, 1973, 45–47, 79.

Orfield, G. How to make desegregation work: The adaptation of schools to their newly-integrated student bodies. *Law & Contemporary Problems*, 1975, *29*(2), 314.

Orfield, G. *Must we bus?* Washington, D.C.: Brookings Institution, 1978.

Pearce, D. *Black, white, and many shades of gray: Real estate brokers and their racial practices*. Unpublished doctoral dissertation, University of Michigan, 1976.

Pettigrew, T. A sociological view of the Post-*Bradley* era. *Wayne Law Review*, 1975, *21*, 813, 822.

Pettigrew, T. Attitudes on race and housing: A social-psychological view. In A. H. Hawley & V. P. Rock (Eds.), *Segregation in residential areas*. Washington, D.C.: National Academy of Sciences, 1973.

Pettigrew, T., Useem, E., Normand, C., & Smith, M. S. Busing: A review of "the evidence." In N. Mills (Ed.), *The great school bus controversy*. New York: Teachers College Press, 1973.

Roof, W. C. Race and residence. *Annals*, 1979, *441*, 7.

Rossell, C. *Assessing the unintended impacts of public policy: School desegregation and resegregation*. Washington, D.C.: National Institute of Education, 1978.

Sennett, R. The brutality of modern families. *Transaction*, 1970, 29037.

Slaven, R. E. Effects of biracial learning teams on cross-racial friendships. *Journal of Educational Psychology*, forthcoming.

Smith, M. B. Equality on educational opportunity: The basic findings reconsidered. In F. Mosteller & D. P. Moynihan (Eds.), *On equality of educational opportunity*. New York: Random, 1972.

Sorenson, A., Taeuber, K. E., & Hollingsworth, L. J. Indexes of racial residential segregation for 109 cities in the United States, 1940-1970. *Sociological Focus*, 1975, *8*, 125–142.

Spear, A. H. *Black Chicago: The making of a Negro ghetto, 1890-1920*. Chicago: University of Chicago Press, 1967.

St. John, N. H. *School desegregation: Outcomes for children*. New York: Wiley, 1975.

Straszheim, M. R. Racial discrimination in the urban housing market and its effect on black housing consumption. In G. M. von Furstenberg, Harrison, & Horowitz (Eds.), *Patterns of racial discrimination* (Vol. 1) *Housing*. Lexington, Mass.: Lexington Books, 1974.

Surgeon, G., Mayo, J., & Bogne, D. J. *Race relations in Chicago: Second survey, 1975*. Chicago: University of Chicago Family and Community Study Center, 1976, p. 158.

Taeuber, K. E. Demographic perspectives on housing and school segregation. *Wayne Law Review* 1975, *21*, 840–841.

Taeuber, K. E. Demographic perspectives on metropolitan school desegregation. In *School desegregation in metropolitan areas: Choices and prospects*. Washington, D.C.: National Institute of Education, 1977.

Taeuber, K. E. The effects of income redistribution on racial residential segregation. *Urban Affairs Quarterly*, 1968, *4*, 5–14.

Taeuber, K. E. Housing, schools, and incremental segregative effects. *Annals of the American Academy of Political and Social Science*, 1979, *441*, 164.

Taeuber, K. E., & Taeuber, A. F. *Negroes in cities*. Chicago: Aldine, 1965.

Taylor, D. G., Sheatsley, P. B., & Greeley, A. M. Attitudes toward desegregation. *Scientific American*, June 1978.

U. S. Bureau of the Census. *Current population report*. Series P–60, No. 116, July 1978.

U.S. Commission on Civil Rights, 1961 *Report*, VI, *Housing;* National Advisory Commission on Civil Disorders, *Report* (1968).

U.S. Department of Housing and Urban Development. Preliminary findings of the 1977 housing market practices survey of forty cities. Paper presented at the tenth anniversary conference of Title VIII of the Civil Rights Act, Washington, D.C., April 17–18, 1978.

Vandell, K. D., & Harrison, B. *Racial transition in neighborhoods.*Cambridge: Joint Center for Urban Studies, 1976, 13.

van Valey, T., Roof, W. C., & Wilcox, J. E. Trends in residential segregation: 1960–1970. *American Journal of Sociology*, 1977, *82*, 826–844.

Warner, W. L. *Social class in America.* Chicago: Science Research Associates, 1949, 151.

Weaver, R. *The Negro ghetto.* New York: Harcourt, Brace, 1948.

Weinberg, M. *Desegregation research: An appraisal* (2nd ed.). Bloomington, Ind.: Phi Delta Kappa, 1970, p. 88.

Weinberg, M. *The education of the minority child.* Chicago: Integrated Associates, 1970.

Wiegel, R., Wiser, P., & Cook, S. W. The impact of cooperative learning experiences on cross-ethnic relations and attitudes. *Journal of Social Issues*, 1975, *31*, 219–244.

Wolf, E. The tipping-point in racially changing neighborhoods. *Journal of the American Institute of Planners*, 1963, *29*.

APPENDIX

This statement was signed by Andrew Billingsley, Morgan State University; James E. Blackwell, University of Massachusetts; Ernst Borinski, Tougaloo College; Everett Cataldo, Cleveland State University; Kenneth B. Clark, City University of New York; Paul Courant, University of Michigan; Robert L. Crain, Rand Corporation; Robert A. Dentler, Boston University; G. Franklin Edwards, Howard University; Edgar G. Epps, University of Chicago; Reynolds Farley, University of Michigan; Joe R. Feagin, University of Texas; John Hope Franklin, University of Chicago; Eli Ginzberg, Columbia University; Robert L. Green, Michigan State University; Charles Grigg, Florida State University; Amos Hawley, University of North Carolina; Joyce A. Ladner, Hunter College; James W. Loewen, University of Vermont and Center for National Policy Review; Cora B. Marrett, University of Wisconsin; James M. McPartland, Johns Hopkins University; Dorothy K. Newman; Gary Orfield, University of Illinois; Thomas F. Pettigrew, Harvard University; Ray C. Rist, Cornell University; Christine H. Rossell, Boston University; Juliet Saltman, Kent State University; Julian Samora, University of Notre Dame; M. Brewster Smith, University of California; Michael J. Stolee, University of Wisconsin; D. Garth Taylor, National Opinion Research Center and University of Chicago; Karl E. Taeuber, University of Wisconsin; Phyllis A. Wallace, Massachusetts Institute of Technology; Robert C. Weaver, Hunter College; Robin W. Williams, Cornell University; Franklin D. Wilson, University of Wisconsin; and J. Milton Yinger, Oberlin College.

We appreciate the permission of the Center for National Policy Review to reprint this statement.

Implementing Desegregation in the School

Design and Redesign of the Desegregated School

PROBLEMS OF STATUS, POWER, AND CONFLICT

ELIZABETH G. COHEN

The chances of implementing and maintaining a truly integrated school, whether the goal is harmonious, interracial relations or improved, minority group academic performance are not, at this time, high.[1] This is not because such a successful school is, in principle, impossible. Rather we, as educational planners and researchers, are the victims of our own conventional and wishful thinking about the nature of the problems in this setting. We hear simplistic solutions recommended so often that they are accepted as truisms.

In a deep, intellectual sense, social scientists do not know what they are talking about when they speak of the desegregated situation. Desegregation does not represent a single phenomenon to be understood and manipulated with a single explanatory theory and a series of studies. The more I have studied the desegregated situation, the more I have come to understand that what happens to children inside a particular desegregated school is a product of changing sociohistorical forces which brought that particular school to the "desegregated" state, a product of the status and power rela-

---

[1] The point of view in this chapter is one of the social scientist faced with the realities of schools desegregated and continuing to be desegregated on legal grounds. I do not undertake to argue the legal issues or the desirability of goals of desegregation, i.e., increased social integration, the reduction of prejudice and the improvement of minority group achievement. I analyze the desegregated situation in terms of the internal processes which will increase the likelihood of attaining these goals. Obviously, there is no way to attain social integration without designing some desegregated experience.

ELIZABETH G. COHEN • Center for Educational Research, School of Education, Stanford University, Stanford, California 94305.

tions of minority to majority in the society and community, as well as a product of social and structural forces within the school. Relevant phenomena inside the desegregated school include the operation of status problems among the students, the power and authority relationships in the school as an organization; the social structure of the classrooms, and the norms for human relations held by students and staff for behavior in corridors and play areas.

Since sociology of education has not achieved a powerful understanding of these structural and social forces in schools in general, it is not surprising that social science does not know how to manipulate these forces to produce desired results in the desegregated situation. Common sense solutions stemming from admirable value positions like "educational equity" and "cultural pluralism" have proved to be insufficient to the task. Relatively simple panaceas like "cooperation" and "multicultural education" are not helping educational researchers to face squarely what must be understood if we are to progress beyond the pioneering work of Allport and Pettigrew on "equal status contact" (Allport, 1954; Pettigrew, 1967). Contemporary recommendations seem inadequate to me—and very possibly harmful. Each has a germ of truth; applied uniformly they can be positively mischievous.

In the first part of this chapter, I will take three currently popular recommendations and analyze them from a sociological point of view. Research evidence will be used to review what is known about the phenomenon. I could have chosen any number of other recommendations to illustrate my point. My basic argument in this section is that many of these recommendations lead to unanticipated and undesirable consequences because they are often necessary, but not sufficient conditions for desired changes. Very often social scientists have been fearful of facing the financial and organizational costs of the radical changes that will be necessary to achieve what the proponents of school desegregation desire.

The second part of the chapter will review what my colleagues and I have been able to learn about the treatment of status problems in the desegregated school. The problem of racial status cannot be distinguished from the problem of academic status in heterogeneous classrooms. Treatment of these problems requires fundamental shifts in the instructional practices of the classroom. Similarly, the problems of status cannot be disentangled from the problems of powerlessness of the minority student in the organizational context of the school. Status and power problems are not usually seen as distinctive; in my view they should be analyzed and treated separately in the desegregated setting. I will try in a final and third section to deal with the implications of this tangled web of phenomena for the practicalities of designing desegregated schools.

PART I

The Call for Cooperation

Much is heard nowadays about the benefits of a cooperative task structure for the desegregated classroom. This recommendation stems from Allport's (1954) early stress on the importance of interracial groups working for common goals as a means to reduce prejudice. Also important is the long history of laboratory work such as Deutsch's (1949) on the strong positive improvement in group affect of cooperative situations as compared to competitive situations.

Surely there could be nothing dangerous in such a recommendation. Much of my own experimental work with interracial situations has chosen to emphasize cooperative tasks. The problem is that simple interdependence in task structure and urging the children to be "cooperative" is not nearly enough.

Suppose teachers take this advice to heart and set up interracial interdependent task groups in the desegregated classrooms. They take care to set up a collective goal for the group and tell the students that they must function as a team. Rewards will only be given for the group product.

What will happen? No doubt many of the children will report enjoying the experience. There will be a marked increase in helping behavior in contrast to a competitive classroom. Sociometric choices will reveal a few more cross-racial friendship choices in the cooperative classroom. Examine closely what is going on in these groups; some are working rather well and some are experiencing ghastly interpersonal relations; some children will simply refuse to work with particular members of the class in the groups to which they have been assigned.

This is not the most worrisome aspect of what happens. If the goal in setting up these groups is to produce an equal status situation where prejudice will be reduced, and members of different races will learn what each other has to contribute, something is fundamentally wrong with the strategy. If a researcher videotaped each group's interaction and actually counted who was doing the task-related talking and who was influential in the group, he/she would probably find that the Whites were markedly more active and influential than the Blacks or Browns. Unfortunately, the status order of the small cooperative group often repeats the status order of the community and society outside the school. This will happen even if the task is nonacademic; it is quite irrational to believe that members of any particular race or social class have more to contribute to the group.

Is this what social scientists, policymakers, and educators had in mind for the outcome of cooperative interaction? In the literature, the goal is something called *equal status contact* capable of modifying racist stereotypes concerning the contribution of minorities to important tasks. If the minority students contribute little to the situation, they will only confirm these stereotypes in the minds of the majority children as well as in their own minds.

On what basis do I make this claim? Research has shown repeatedly that when a mixed status group works on a collective task, those who have higher social status will be more influential and powerful than those who have lower status (Berger, Cohen, & Zelditch, 1972; Webster & Driskell, 1978). There are several studies with groups of school children playing a game, requiring repeated decisions as a group. Results have yielded similar patterns of dominance by high status children for Black–White groups (Cohen, 1972), Chicano–Anglo groups (Rosenholtz & Cohen, in press), Indian–Anglo groups (Cook, 1974), and Israeli groups made up of Middle Eastern and Western Jews (Cohen & Sharan, 1977).

Turning to research on such cooperative groups in the schoolroom setting, the problem is not improved but compounded by the fact that minority students are often of a much lower social class background than the majority students. They are frequently behind the Whites in conventional academic skills. These differences in academic skills are highly salient to any group work in the classroom. If the task is right out of the ongoing curriculum, those who get the best marks in the subject will surely be seen as the most important and become the most influential in the cooperative work group.

In junior high school social studies classes (all Whites), Hoffman and Cohen (1972) found that those who were perceived to have higher academic ability were much more active and influential in cooperative task groups than those who were seen to have less academic ability. Similarly, in fifth- and sixth-grade classrooms, Rosenholtz (in press) found that those children who were ranked higher in reading ability by their classmates clearly dominated those who were ranked lower in reading ability (also all-White task groups). This was the case even though the criterion tasks in both these studies were games which did not demand reading or other academic skills. Thus, even in a segregated, all-White class, the children with higher academic status are likely to dominate those with lower academic status in cooperative tasks in the classroom.

Is it any wonder then, that the experimental treatment by Weigel, Wiser, and Cook (1975) of cooperative interracial learning groups in English classes failed to bring about any changes in intergroup attitudes? In experimental classrooms in junior and senior high classes, cooperative groups were formed to carry on the regular learning over a semester. Groups competed with one another for rewards allocated according to success in group learning. There were traditional control classrooms where teachers stressed individual assignments and rewards. The only positive results were greater respect and liking on the part of Whites for Mexican-American classmates in the experimental as compared to the control classrooms. Also, teachers reported less cross-ethnic conflict and higher proportions of cross-ethnic helping in the cooperative classrooms. White students' respect and liking for Blacks did not show improvement, nor did the sentiments expressed by the minority students themselves show any differences between treatments. A survey on interracial attitudes administered to students in the homes three months after the end of the classroom experience showed no differences between classrooms.

Although there were no systematic observations of group interaction by the researchers, one can well imagine that much of it consisted of the superior students (middle-class Whites) helping out the Mexican-Americans on their English lessons. What attitude toward the disadvantaged minority group would that experience be likely to change? More likely, attitudes about Black and Brown intellectual incompetence so endemic to American society would be reinforced.

Slavin (1977) has also conducted a series of classroom experiments in the desegregated setting in which cooperative interracial teams work for points as a team on learning conventional curriculum materials. In order not to penalize the teams for members who are academic low-achievers, Slavin gives points to team members relative to performance in their own achievement division. In other words, a team member earns points for his or her team by doing well in comparison to members of his or her own achievement division. In many of these classrooms, it is made explicit that team members should work with each other so as to improve each member's standing. Slavin finds positive effects on learning test scores for Blacks but not for Whites. There is also an increase in peer liking in this situation.

Before adopting Slavin's technique because it accomplishes that longed-for minority group achievement improvement, it is necessary to examine the costs in terms of goals of learning to work with other racial group members on an equal-status basis. This treatment has emphasized the intellectual stratification of the classroom with its use of achievement divisions. No doubt the treatment has increased the time on learning tasks on the part of minority students who may ordinarily spend much of their classroom time disengaged or working on unprofitable seatwork. But the group experience has also acted so as to confirm the White students' belief in the Black students' lack of intellectual competence.

Do I then advocate a return to old-fashioned competition for the desegregated classroom? No, there is every reason to believe that competition will aggravate the effects of status differences in the classroom (Had, 1972). The problem with the single-minded advocacy of cooperative task structure is the failure to realize that it is a worthwhile but not a sufficient change for the achievement of the major goals of desegregation. One must stop and decide which goals one is trying to maximize and at what cost to other possible goals. One must have an explanatory framework to understand what is happening to the members of cooperative task groups in a classroom. Because cooperation is recommended for the school and not for a summer camp, one must realize that the social structure of the classroom has powerful ways to influence students other than through the task structure. There are status and power structures, the nature of the content of classroom tasks, and the teacher's evaluation system, to name a few, which have powerful impact on the way students feel about themselves and each other. One cannot lightheartedly advocate the manipulation of one feature of this social system while ignoring what happens to other parts of the system.

Interracial Friendships Will Encourage Minority Academic Achievement

From the earliest discussions of the desegregated situation, it has been assumed that the production and development of interracial friendship was a major goal—and a legitimate measure of the "success" of integration. This much is obvious from the research literature in the frequent use of the sociometric measures of friendship as the criterion of successful integration. In an early, highly influential review of evidence as to the effects of desegregation, Katz (1964) argued that friendliness on the part of the White majority group might be helpful to incoming Black students in two ways: (1) acceptance by the dominant racial group in the classroom might reduce social threat and raise self-confidence, and (2) acceptance by achievement-oriented peers might increase their influence as role models and lead to adoption of their norms.

It is time for us to reexamine the assumptions behind the stress on the encouragement of interracial friendship. Let us look at a desegregated school with relatively high probabilities of cross-race friendship choice in comparison to one with lower levels. The research literature would immediately suggest that the first school provides more in-classroom contact than the second school (Patchen, 1977b). Here is the germ of truth concerning the stress on friendship—schools where there is formal and informal resegregation within their walls will not produce high levels of interracial friendship. Contact is a necessary, but by no means sufficient condition for the growth of student friendship (Hallinan, 1978). Schofield (1978) reviews the studies using observation of interracial interaction in desegregated schools. She states that the only finding which emerges consistently from these studies is that students interact more with others of their own group than would be expected if race were not an important grouping criterion. In some schools, resegregation is almost total. The level of observed interracial interaction is typically quite low.

If one is interested in social integration, it is probably more important to ask directly about tracking and in-classroom contact than it is to ask about cross-race contact or friendship. Especially important is a close examination of seating, grouping, and activity patterns. Some mixed-race classrooms use seating patterns which segregate races through ability grouping. Other mixed race classrooms allow the students to sit where they want, often producing a state of voluntary segregation. These techniques should be avoided, at minimum, if one is trying to produce social integration.

But what about Katz's early argument? Will promoting interracial friendship also encourage minority achievement? Research has been subject to two alternative interpretations. It could be that friendship with the majority group encourages achievement for minority students. Or, alternatively, it could be that high-achieving minority students are popular with their majority classmates (perhaps because they are in the same reading group).

In a study of 34 interracial classrooms, Lewis and St. John (1974) found that high academic performance contributed significantly to the popularity of White and Black children among students of both races. When the data were analyzed with achievement of minority students as a dependent variable, popularity with Whites was a significant contributor to improved achievement levels of Blacks. Even with the use of many important control variables, this study could not rule out the possibility that the causal flow moves from achievement to popularity rather than the other way around. In Gerard and Miller's (1975) definitive study on this subject, students were actually followed over time into the desegregated schools in Riverside, California. From pre- to postdesegregation, they found no effect of acceptance by Anglos on the achievement of low-achieving minority children. For initially higher-achieving minority children there was a drop in achievement for those who were not accepted by Anglos and no change in achievement for those who were. Among high school students with previous achievement and IQ controlled, Patchen, Davidson, Hyman, and Brown (1977a) found no correlation between friendly interracial contact and grades.

Even if researchers were able to document that under some conditions having White friends leads to improved achievement, it is necessary to examine what this causal chain would mean for the minority students. The idea that minority students who manage to make themselves acceptable to majority students, and thus are able to be successful by the school's formal criterion of grades, may imply cultural assimilation. A school where it is impossible for students to remain culturally and socially distinct and yet succeed by the school's criteria is a school which insists that the minority children become more like majority children before they will be labeled as successful.

Iadicola's (1977) analysis of friendship, achievement, and ethnic group orientation among Mexican-American students suggests the importance of a reexamination of promotion of intergroup friendship in a much less "desirable" light.[2] Iadicola measured ethnic in-group orientation among 211 elementary school boys and girls of Mexican-American background. Mexican-American girls with an ethnic out-group orientation were more likely to be accepted by Anglo classmates as a seatmate. Acceptance by Anglo peers in turn predicted academic grade point average. These results were interpreted as showing that the "price" of good performance for the Mexican-American girl is the giving up of ethnic identity and assimilation to the Anglo peer group. For the male, ethnic out-group orientation was not related to peer acceptance. However Mexican-American males with a strong in-group orientation received markedly lower grades.

If the price of good grades is the development of an out-group ethnic orientation, the designers of desegregated situations must rethink whether they are trying to produce a "melting pot" through the mechanism of school integration or a school where cultural pride and identity may be maintained and academic achievement maximized. This line of thought certainly puts the promotion of intergroup friendship and its use as a criteria of successful social integration in a different, more complex, and not so uniformly favorable light.

Katz's original argument turns out, upon further thinking and research, to contain another problem. The argument implies that the opposite of friendship choice in the classroom is social threat. Study of the desegregated situation reveals that these are not two ends of a single dimension. Aggressive, conflictful, and threatening interaction does not typically take place in classrooms at all. Rather, these conflicts occur in corridors, locker rooms, and toilets—away from the watchful eye of supervising adults. Patchen et al. (1977b) found that the report of friendly contact was uncorrelated with the reports of unfriendly contact.

The Stanford Equalization Project study of school climate finds a strong correlation between the report of incidents with racial overtones and

---

[2] The extent of in-group orientation was measured by the number of photographs of clearly identifiable Mexican-American versus Anglo children that a child chose as "kindest," "happiest," "strongest," "gets best grades," "most like himself or herself," "one he or she would like to be," and "one he or she would like to have as a friend." Mexican-American children who consistently chose Anglo pictures first on these criteria received a high "out-group orientation" score. Acceptance by Anglo peers was measured by the extent to which each of these children were chosen by their Anglo classmates as a student whom they would like to sit next to.

the report of any kind of aggressive behavior. The occurrence of interracial conflict may or may not have any meaning with respect to specific problems in relations between the races. In many schools, it may be a product of the generally lower-class and aggressive norms for human relations that govern the informal world of the students.

All this suggests a reexamination of friendship as a goal for treatment of the desegregated situation. The desired end-state for the integrated school is not, after all, universal love and brotherhood. A more reasonable goal for the desegregation process is some social integration and a lack of overt conflict whereby different racial and ethnic group members, given an objective important to both, can trust each other and listen to each other sufficiently well to complete the task at hand, whether it be a vocational task, an educational task, or a political task.

A Desirable Proportion of Minority Students

The optimal proportion of minority students for the desegregated situation has been a thorny practical and legal issue. Policymakers have not faced up to the sociopsychological consequences for the minority child of one of the favorite recommendations of desegregation plans. Frequently, the decision is to make each desegregated school reflect the proportions of the minority population in the area in general; this is often around 20%. Although satisfactory from some kind of formal equity point of view, those who are concerned with the internal functioning of desegregated schools should feel compelled to examine carefully what this means in terms of the experience of the minority student. In a class of Anglo students, 20% of a school often turns out to be two or three dark faces. Furthermore, it is hard to make an argument for a minority principal or the hiring of minority teachers when there are so few minority students. Basically, the power and authority structure of the school experiences no particular pressure to change with this relatively minor shift in population composition.

Rist (1978) has effectively portrayed the consequences of such a desegregation plan in Portland, Oregon, through a microethnographic study, *The Invisible Children*. He described the feelings of alienation and incompetence experienced by the handful of lower social class Black children put into an achievement-oriented White school. Well-meaning teachers struggled to understand the bizarre behavior of the newcomers as they all pretended, on the instructions of the principal, that they were "color blind."

Putting minority children in such an utterly powerless position in a White-dominated organizational structure and a White-dominated informal friendship structure, makes the production of equal status behavior or even academic improvement extraordinarily difficult. If the position of the minority student in the school reflects a powerlessness in the larger society, I would argue that it is much harder to produce almost any of the desired end-states for the integrated school.

The problem of power and authority in the organization of the school is often taken into account by simply counting Blacks, Browns, and Whites among the adults. Of course, it is usually the case that the principal is White; so are most of the teachers; but the teachers' aides and the adult in charge of discipline are Black or Brown, along with the counselor, the community liaison worker, and the bilingual education or special education teacher. Do we think that the children don't realize who is in charge? I am always amazed at the way adults deceive themselves about the shrewdness of organizational perceptions of children.

In a study of ethnic relations in a number of desegregated schools, Iadicola (1979) found a strong correlation between a cluster of variables such as percentage of minority students and racial composition of faculty and administration, and the extent to which students with higher social status dominate minority students in task groups. In schools where there are more minorities in the student body and in the faculty and administration, the tendency of Anglos to be more influential and active than minority students in interethnic relationships is markedly reduced. These results are highly suggestive of the effect of power in the organizational context, in inhibiting minority participation in classroom groups.

The issue to be considered is not so much the arithmetic proportion of minority students; the critical issue is one of powerlessness in the formal organization of the school and in the formal world of the students. If the minority student sees in the school situation that there are very few persons like him/her in positions of power and authority, he/she may feel powerless in respect to majority ethnic group classmates. Likewise, the majority student, seeing White teachers directing and supervising Black and Brown teacher aides may conclude it is only right and proper for Whites to tell Blacks and Browns what to do. If the experience of desegregation only confirms the relationship of powerful to powerless in intergroup relations, the goals of integration have not been achieved.

PART II

The questions I have raised in the first section of this chapter are serious; they are not academic questions with which practitioners feel they know how to cope. Rather, they are much like the question of teachers and administrators I have known who are struggling to make school desegregation work: What can I offer in the way of a constructive approach to the desegregated setting?

The first step to constructing powerful interventions is to analyze several of the phenomena in the desegregated setting; next, theoretical explanations for the operation of these different phenomena are necessary. I (Cohen, 1975) have argued elsewhere that without a systematic theoretical framework, one cannot resolve conflicting research results or develop interventions applicable to a variety of field settings.

Let us start with the basic phenomenon of status generalization, a problem highly pertinent to the desegregated school because of the mixture of students from different social classes and because of the sharp differences in academic status within many desegregated classrooms. *Status generalization* is the technical term for the self-fulfilling prophecies described above, whereby children who are White or children who are seen as better readers come to dominate minority children and/or poorer readers in collective task groups. *Expectation States Theory* provides a useful explanation of how this phenomenon operates.

Even if a collective task group in the classroom is working on a task that does not require reading, those perceived to have better reading ability are more likely to be active and influential than those who are perceived to have lower reading ability. What is the explanation for this self-fulfilling prophecy? According to Expectation States Theory, this is a process of status generalization. Reading ability is a specific status characteristic carrying with it a set of social evaluations: it is better to be a good reader than a poor reader; associated with being a good reader are expectations for competence. When a collective task setting forces the participants to evaluate each other's contributions to the task, the expectations for competence and incompetence attached to one's reading ability *spread* into the new situation and become the basis for expecting competence and incompetence on the new task. It is this process of generalization—the tendency of people to use available status information about each other in organizing new and unknown situations, which produces the observable differences in the new situation. Those who are expected to be more competent in the new situation are more active and, thus, become more influential than those who are expected to be incompetent. Because everyone in the situation holds expectations for self and for the other members, behavior is not a product of individual differences but a product of these invisible expectations held by everyone in the group.

This, in nontechnical terms, is the theoretical explanation offered by Expectation States Theory (Berger *et al.*, 1972; Berger & Fisek, 1974) for the basic status phenomenon. In the desegregated classroom, there is more than one status characteristic leading to low expectations for competence on the part of minority children with poor reading skills. In addition to reading, which is referred to as a *specific status characteristic*, there is race, called by the theory a *diffuse status characteristic*. Even if the children do not know each other and do not come from the same classroom, expectations based on differences in race become the basis for self-fulfilling prophecies whereby the Whites are more active and influential than the Blacks on the very same criterion task used in the studies of reading ability (Cohen, 1972).

Diffuse status characteristics, such as race or sex, differ from specific status characteristics such as reading ability only in that there are a set of general expectations attached to the high and low states of a diffuse status characteristic. Stemming from the culture, these are general expectations for competence and incompetence over a wide variety of situations. Men are generally expected to be more competent than women; Whites are often believed to be more intelligent then Blacks. These sexist and racist beliefs become activated in new situations and spread to new tasks where there is no rational reason to believe that men or Whites should be more competent. Webster and Driskell (1978) give an excellent summary of the current state of this theory.

There are several features of this theory which are frequently misunderstood. One important aspect of the theory is that it deals with expectations a person holds for him/herself *as well as* expectations held by others for that person. We are not just dealing with expectations a person holds for him/herself. In trying to prevent or modify status generalization, it is not sufficient to treat the person who holds low expectations for self—the other members of the group must be treated as well (Cohen & Roper, 1972).

Another, often misunderstood feature of the theory has to do with the conditions under which the phenomenon is said to take place—these are called *scope conditions* of the theory. These are sufficient conditions for the process of status generalization to take place. They include the condition that the group is actively involved in a task which implies a collective orientation—one where it is legitimate and necessary to consider every individual's ideas. *Status generalization* takes place when there is a mixed status group. This is important because the theory makes no predictions for how low status persons will behave in a segregated situation. The inhibited and uninfluential behavior is not an inherent characteristic of the low status individual but is activated by the mixed status situation.

Status Generalization in the Desegregated Classroom

In order to make the best use of this theoretical framework, it is essential to analyze the operation of status generalization in a desegregated classroom. If minority students are in the low state of the diffuse status characteristic of race and also are in the low state of the specific status characteristic of reading or academic ability, we have a dual basis for low general expectations for competence on the part of some Black and Brown students. These students are likely to be inactive, withdrawn, and unwilling to attempt new tasks; or they may attempt to gain attention by disruptive behavior. In theoretical terms, the classroom is a multicharacteristic situation; when the minority racial groups are also several years behind the majority group in reading achievement, the stage is set for status generalization, resulting in confirmation of ideas held concerning intellectual incompetence of people of color in American society.

The classroom, however, is not the same as the laboratory situation which brings people together who have not known each other previously. Academic status differences are produced by the ongoing social structure of the classroom and by previous and present evaluations students have received in academic competence. Furthermore, classrooms differ as to how strongly they reinforce a unidimensional rank ordering on academic ability, whereby children rank order themselves and each other as "smart" to "dumb" on a single dimension of intelligence/academic ability.

Two dimensions of traditional classroom organization—task and evaluation—combine to produce a strong shared perception of a single rank order based on academic ability. Classroom task structure can produce the perception that there is only one important intellectual ability, and that one's reading ability is a valid index of that ability. Conventional classroom task structure does this in two important ways. First, curriculum activities repeatedly require the same basic skills in all content areas, and, therefore, present a narrowly consistent picture of a student's academic capabilities. Specifically, reading skills are made the prerequisite of success in all other academic subjects. Better readers, therefore, outperform poorer readers in each content area, thereby providing uniformity in grades across subject areas. Second, there are no viable alternative conceptions of ability available to students in the traditional classroom. Music and art are given little emphasis; there are few intellectual tasks presented where students who are not accomplished readers can excel on other intellectual dimensions such as reasoning, decision making, observational acuity, or the generation of creative new ideas.

The unitary curriculum alone is not sufficient to produce academic status orders. If children do not perceive themselves, in a consensual way, as widely different in ability, then academic status orders cannot form. By supplying public performance information, the evaluation structure of the classroom makes it possible for children to interpret their performance comparatively. In the traditional classroom, the teacher is the dominant source of evaluation; whole-class recitation or ability groups with stable membership are the most common teaching techniques. In whole-class recitation, the teacher's evaluation of answers as right or wrong automatically become public knowledge. In ability groups, the label constitutes a public evaluation of competence which children invariably understand regardless of the teacher's attempt to hide the label. A third source of shared knowledge on competence are the formal grades allocated to students on report cards and tests. Many teachers are constantly making easily comparable evaluations in the form of grades or numbers on homework assignments and tests.

In the Status Equalization Project we have a shorthand term for such traditional classrooms: *single ability classrooms*. In the single ability classroom, there is likely to be a high degree of consensus on rank order on reading ability. Rosenholtz and Wilson (in press) correlated an index of the single ability classroom features just described with the degree of agreement children and teachers showed with each other on rankings on reading ability of each child in a class; there was significant positive correlation.

When the desegregated classroom resembles a single ability classroom, the strong operation of status effects based on reading rank makes achievement of equal status conditions almost impossible. In an ethnographic study of a desegregated school, Schofield and Sagar (1979) found a great emphasis on conventional academic goals which helped to make academic achievement an extremely salient dimension for interpersonal evaluation, even for students who were not at the top of their class. Many of the teachers in this school used ability groups which turned out to be highly correlated with race. They observed considerable competitive behavior in which students revealed that they thought many children quite incapable of doing better work. When a Black child did show high performance, he had to prove himself to every new member of the class. The children in the bottom ability group were subject not only to being seen as "dumb" but there were moral connotations of being on the bottom of the academic status order, i.e., the authors cite a classroom interchange where the poor student is called a "dumb bum." Schofield and Sagar (1979) conclude that personal characteristics in this classroom setting are conducive to the confirmation of traditional stereotypes and to the development of unequal status relationships; these academic differences are a real barrier to the development of positive intergroup relations. Also, Rist's (1978) extensive observation of minority children who were poor performers in classrooms fitting the definition of a single ability classroom, showed repeated withdrawal, refusal to settle down to work, and aggressive behavior such as poking at other children and stealing pencils.

Simpson (1977) characterized unidimensional versus multidimensional classrooms along much the same dimension we have just described. Examinations of racially integrated classrooms varying along this dimension revealed that in unidimensional classrooms, the teachers rated Blacks and Chicanos as having greater performance deficits than did teachers who ran multidimensional classrooms.

In review, bringing together children of different ethnic backgrounds who also are at different levels of basic skills achievement in a class where academic ability is narrowly defined, and where achievement differences are emphasized produces severe status problems. Black and Chicano students who are poorer readers will receive frequent evaluations telling them they are less able than their Anglo counterparts; this will certainly discourage effort on their part while confirming racial stereotypes held by the Whites.

Modifying Expectations for Competence

We have been able to show good success in treating single characteristic status problems in the laboratory and in the classroom. Using Expectation States Theory, my co-workers and I (Cohen & Roper, 1972) have inferred a variety of treatments that modify unwanted dominance of high status members in a mixed status group. The earliest treatment was *expectation training*, developed for interracial groups of junior high age boys. Expectation training has been carried out in a variety of settings and with several different tasks; the basic principle is that the low status child becomes a teacher of the high status child on a challenging new task such as building a two transistor radio or carrying on a brief conversation in the Malay language. Theoretically, we are assigning to the low status member competence on two new abilities—knowing how to carry out the task and knowing how to teach it to someone else. These expectations for competence combine with those stemming from race as a diffuse status characteristic. The net result is equal status behavior on a new criterion task, i.e., the high status members no longer show an expectancy advantage over the low status members. The White student has an experience of Black competence and has played a subordinate role as student of a Black teacher.[3]

If a status treatment is successful, one should be able to observe equal status behavior. This is behavior in the interracial group setting such that one cannot predict by the social or academic status of the individual how active and influential he or she will be in carrying out a collective task. Throughout the research program, we have used the same criterion measure for the measurement of equal status behavior. This is a game, called Shoot-the-Moon, which may be played by two or four people, evenly divided between high and low status participants. The group must make successive decisions as a team as to which way they will proceed on the paths on the board. They must reach the moon in 14 turns or less while earning as many points as possible. After the group decides on a path, the host experimenter rolls a die determining how many spaces they will advance. The number of

[3] Expectation training has also been shown to be effective for Indian-Anglo groups in Canada (Cook, 1974) and for groups in Israel made up of Middle Eastern and Western Jews (Cohen & Sharan, 1977).

points earned is totaled for the group from the values on the spaces on which the playing piece lands. From videotapes of the group interaction, we can determine activity rates of each player and how influential each person is in deciding which way the group goes.

Expectation training was carried out originally on Black–White groups of boys under controlled conditions (Cohen & Roper, 1972). Subsequently, we ran a lengthier version of the treatment at an experimental summer school, the Center for Interracial Cooperation, in Oakland, California in 1972. One week of expectation training was followed by four weeks of curriculum experience in racially integrated classrooms.

The curricula did not call for conventional academic skills although they were intellectually challenging. One set of activities was learning how to make movies as part of a team. The other was a social studies curriculum focusing on the subject of observation and teaching the students how to distinguish between fact and inference. Learning took place through active group tasks such as an "archeological dig." Evaluation was of the group product. Very often the small interracial group could not accomplish its aim without the contribution of each member. There was great stress on the norms of cooperation. Interracial teams taught each classroom.

Expectation training was successful in producing equal status behavior on the standard criterion task for both male and female classrooms after the first week of treatment. After the curriculum experience (at the end of five weeks), a second set of behavioral measures on the group task yielded some Black dominance in the boys' classrooms and equal status behavior in the girls' classrooms. The results for boys were felt to reflect the social dominance of the Black males in this free-ranging summer school program (Cohen, Katz, & Lohman, 1976).

The organizational structure of the summer school included a Black and a White co-principal and Blacks in research and teaching positions. Thus, students had many chances to see Blacks (primarily male) in positions of organizational authority. The significance of this field experiment lies in its demonstration of the robust and long-lasting effects on interracial interaction of expectation training under two sets of special conditions: (1) the curriculum and classroom procedures do not allow the construction of a status order based on academic ability in conventional schools skills; and (2) the organizational context shared power and authority between Blacks and Whites.

Expectation training has many similarities to Aaronson's (1978) "jigsaw" technique, a classroom method whereby each member of the group learns some academic material and is responsible for teaching it to his/her group members. The group is responsible for learning all the materials taught by each member. They are tested for learning as individuals. Using this technique, Lucker, Rosenfield, and Sikes (1976) show small, but statistically significant, learning gains (56% correct responses in experimental groups versus 49.7% correct responses in control classrooms) for Blacks only.

We have gained experience in these techniques of producing special competence in low status children and placing them in a teacher role. There are several very serious precautions that must be taken into consideration. It is essential that the child in the teacher role not be allowed to undertake a public display until he or she has reached a criterion level of competence. This takes a different amount of time with different individuals. Lockheed and Harris (1977) found that if boys were exposed to girls who behaved incompetently in the role of teacher, boys showed marked dominance over other girls in task groups—more so than untreated boys.

To have each child reach a criterion level of competence is a challenging goal, probably impossible to achieve in ordinary classroom settings. Studies of status problems in classrooms using the jigsaw technique would probably find that in groups where the minority children are successful in their role as teacher, there is an increase in their task engagement and their learning as well as a modification of the expectations held for their competence by themselves and by the other members of the group. Where the student who ordinarily holds a position of low academic competence fails in his or her role as teacher, we would expect none of these desirable effects. Thus, we would say the favorable effects of the treatment would be weakened by detrimental effects in some groups.

Multiple Ability Treatments

An alternative treatment at the Center for Interracial Cooperation also produced long-lasting equal status behavior for the boys' classrooms. This treatment consisted of an initial week of small, interracial groups experiencing a variety of challenging new tasks under the careful supervision of an interracial team. The tasks were engineered so that children experienced a fair degree of success and were protected by the adult supervising each small group from failure and from opportunities for invidious comparisons. Cooperative norms were stressed.

This unexpected success led to a creation of an alternative treatment to expectation training. After one week of treatment, the interracial groups of boys showed equal status behavior. After four more weeks of the cooperative curriculum (not requiring conventional academic skills) the group behavior still fit the equal status pattern. Stulac (1975) reasoned that the success of this alternative treatment lay in the creation of a variety of new skills or abilities at the new tasks in the first week of the field experiment. The evaluations children made of themselves and each other during that first week led to a mixed set of expectations for competence. Children varied a good deal as to which task they liked best. The structure of the classroom in the first week never met the task conditions for self-fulfilling prophecies. Thus, the students did not assign competence expectations on the new tasks to self and other on the basis of race. Competence expectations were not formed on the basis of reading ability, because reading was not a prerequisite for success at the tasks.

Stulac (1975) was able to show in a laboratory experiment with White children who differed in perceived reading ability, that she could produce equal status behavior by exposing the children to a new "multiple ability" task where they were told that many different abilities would contribute to success on the task. No one person was expected to be good on all abilities; everyone was expected to be good on at least one ability.

Rosenholtz (in press) adapted this treatment to the practical realities of the classroom in a one week multi-ability curriculum. The curriculum was originally tested in all-White classrooms with a sharp socioeconomic difference among the children. In the week that followed the curriculum, mixed academic status groups were formed to play the standard criterion task game. The pattern was not one of equal status behavior, but the degree of dominance by better readers was significantly reduced in comparison to groups run from untreated classrooms.

Subsequent to this success in an all-White setting,[4] the Status Equalization Project undertook to test the effectiveness of the multiple ability curriculum in producing equal status behavior in ongoing desegregated classrooms in three elementary schools. A specially trained, interracial team visited classrooms selected for the experimental treatment for one hour a day during one week. The Rosenholtz Multiple Abilities Curriculum (in press) is calculated to allow children to form evaluations of themselves and other on three new abilities: visual thinking, intuitive thinking, and reasoning. Each of these new abilities is introduced by a brief film picturing an interracial cast of actors, both children and adults, using the particular ability in solving real-life problems. The children are then placed in groups which are mixed as to reading ability, race, and sex. They experience a series of tasks, representing examples of the ability under consideration. These tasks are deliberately designed so that no one person can dominate the group, and everyone can function satisfactorily. Each group has an adult supervising the interaction, and the adult stresses the norms of cooperation and equal participation. On each of the abilities, some children feel themselves exceptionally good, while the others feel "about average." These self-evaluations are measured on a questionnaire just after the curriculum is completed. The formation of these new expectations for competence based on the abilities occurs because the group interaction never allows self-fulfill-

[4] This ongoing Status Equalization Project is being carried out at Stanford by the author and James Deslonde under the National Institute of Education Contract NIE–400–76–0059.

ing prophecies to take place and because the tasks and skills chosen were such that children who are seen as poor readers by their classmates often turn out to be outstanding in one of the skills or tasks. This curriculum is a prototype of permanent changes we hypothesize will be necessary in the desegregated classroom.

From the outset, the Status Equalization Project staff realized that they had taken on an extraordinarily ambitious task in trying to modify expectations based on racial and academic status in ongoing classrooms by a one-week curriculum. The classrooms in the three desegregated schools were far more academically heterogeneous than the classes of the successful Rosenholtz study. Furthermore, there were multiple status characteristics working against us—both academic status and race. As expected, these two characteristics turned out to be highly correlated. In the largest school, with a 56% Black population, each student ranked all other students of his/her own sex in the class on how good they were at reading. Of the three lowest-ranking readers for each classroom–sex group (using average reading rank attributed to each child), 84 were Black and 31 were White. Of the three best readers, 28 were Black and 70 were White. Thus, in many classrooms there was a double basis for low expectations for competence on the part of Black students perceived as poor readers. Despite this strong relationship, the lowest academic status children were not necessarily minority students in every classroom.

Variation in the ongoing social structure of classrooms presented a serious complication for this study. Theoretically, we have argued that single ability classrooms will produce a very strong academic status order. According to detailed studies of the teachers' instructional patterns and classroom social structure the year before the treatment, we found that some resembled single ability classrooms. They made much use of large group instruction, used little individualization and highly competitive evaluation techniques. However, as we suspected, there was immense variation between classrooms as to how well they fit this model. Many of the teachers were using individualization in some form; a few were utilizing systematic student conferences for detailed individualized feedback rather than competitive marking and grading. Only a very few classrooms were using tasks calling upon other intellectual abilities such as role playing, manipulative games and puzzles, or creative story telling. Since we expected that ongoing classroom social structure would have a strong impact on the strength of the status order, it was not clear whether we would be able to disentangle the effects of a one-week curriculum from its interaction with the characteristics of the particular classroom. Foreseeing this problem, we stratified classrooms according to the teachers' typical instructional pattern and assigned classrooms randomly to treatment from within strata.

To measure the effects of the interventions, we selected pairs of children from the treated and untreated classrooms. All these pairs were distinguished by percieved rank in reading ability, with one member perceived as "high" rank and the other perceived as "low." Some pairs were Black students; others had high readers who were White and low readers who were Black. Sex and perceived social power were controlled. Close friends were never paired. The pairs played the standard criterion task-game at several videotaping stations set up in the school.

Preliminary results of this experiment illustrate strong interaction between treatment and the ongoing social structure of the classroom; there are also marked differences between results in the three schools. We appear to be more successful in the school where Blacks are predominant numerically and socially; here there are many Blacks in positions of adult authority. In other words, when we examine the behavior of a Black student who is perceived to be a lower-ranking reader in interaction on our standard criterion task (treated classrooms), we are more likely to find equal status behavior in the 56% Black school. In addition, there are big differences in the success of treatment according to the particular classroom. At least one of the control classrooms in the 56% Black school does not appear to have needed treatment at all. Some classrooms resembling the single ability model appear highly resistant to treatment, at least a treatment of one week's duration. Finally, at least in the 56% Black school, we appear to be more successful in treating academic status problems among Black children who differ by reading rank than in treating groups where we have to contend with both racial and reading rank differences.

Power in the Organizational Context

Over the years of working with status treatments in interracial settings, I have begun to suspect that the ability of members of one race to direct the behavior of the members of another status group, in the organizational context of the school, has much to do with the dominance of high status over low status children in the small group setting. If the organizational context speaks to Anglo dominance, then we may be doomed to failure in producing equal status behavior. *Power* is here defined as the control of one person or a group of persons over the behavior of another person or group. When power differences are formalized, the ability to direct and control the behavior of others becomes a legitimate right assigned to the superior position in the authority system of the organization or institution. The operation of formal and informal power is really outside the scope of Expectation States Theory. Where they overlap, a powerless member of the group will behave in a way that is indistinguishable from a member of the group who has very low expectations for competence. The difference between status and power is not directly observable; presumably, if a status characteristic is operating, the person is quiet because he thinks he is not competent to make a contribution. In the case of powerlessness, he is quiet because he does not think he can control events in the group and because he may be fearful of being negatively sanctioned by more powerful group members if he becomes assertive. The more powerful members of the group think it is only right and proper to tell the powerless members of the group what to do.

Under natural social conditions, it is very frequently the case that those with low social status are also powerless. However, there are settings in which status and power do not go together. For example, in the 56% Black school just described, Blacks were powerful in the formal organizational context. In addition, Black children were often picked as the most powerful by classmates in the informal social relationships of the students. Despite this power in the school setting, Blacks were much more likely to have low academic status than Whites.

The study already cited by Iadicola (1979) suggests that dominance by Whites in the small group situation is correlated with the numerical and organizational dominance of Whites in the organizational context. A number of the studies of interracial groups based on Expectation States Theory have indicated interaction between the ideological and organizational version of "Black Power" and treatment of status problems. Newby (1974) found that those Black children who scored high on an ideological measure of race consciousness were less susceptible to White influence than Black children who scored low on this measure. In one of the earliest successful treatments for status generalization, Lohman (1970) worked in two school settings. In one school, the Black children were socially dominant; they also comprised a substantial proportion of the student body. In the other school, they were a smaller minority and the context was White middle class. The untreated interracial groups in the two schools showed similar patterns of White activity and influence rates, both showing a marked expectancy advantage for the Whites. In treated groups, differences between the school settings emerged. In the "Black turf" school, treated groups showed sharp Black dominance. In the other school, treated groups showed a pattern of equal status behavior.

For many years, we puzzled about this curious interaction of status treatment and organizational context. We returned to this finding when trying to interpret the first failure of expectation training in an experiment with Chicano and Anglo groups. We speculated that this failure was brought about by the experimental staffing pattern, which for the first time, was dominated by a White administrator with Chicanos in the subordinate role of trainers of the children. In a subsequent experiment, Robbins (1977) showed that expectation training was unsuccessful in a White-dominated organizational context. When, in a contrasting treatment condition, Robbins had a pair of administrators, one Chicano and one Anglo, run expectation training, and when this pair modeled equal status behavior for the children, he was able to produce equal status behavior in Chicano–Anglo groups.

Implications of the Power Dimension

From the above, it seems clear to me that it will be more difficult to produce equal status behavior in the desegregated schools when the proportion of any particular minority group is small and when the minority group is not well represented in positions of organizational authority.

Academic status is probably most difficult to treat in a context where the academically low status students are also powerless as a racial or ethnic minority group. In the study just cited, Lohman (1970) was able to treat the Black–White diffuse status characteristic in the school setting, but these were students from different classrooms and did not know what the other person's academic status was. Robbins (1977) showed that it is very difficult to treat the Chicano–Anglo status characteristic without manipulating the organizational context. Finally, the most recent attempt to treat academic status in the desegregated setting reveals marked interaction of the success of the status treatment with the organizational context of the school.[5]

PART III

I have tried to communicate my sense of humility about the complexity of the desegregated situation and the difficulties of producing change. The goal we want is *equal status* conditions which will have the effect of reducing stereotypes and teaching heretofore isolated groups in society how to work together. Equally strong is the desire to improve the performance of economically depressed minorities in academic skills. Educators and policymakers hope to achieve these goals through the medium of desegregated schools.

I do not think social scientists will develop effective ways to reach these goals without dealing with the separate phenomena involved: the status problems, the power problems, and the problems of the human relations climate in the schools as a whole. These are different phenomena, and they must be understood with different conceptualizations and treated by different sets of rules. When we are forced to deal with all of them at once, we face the further scientific difficulty of understanding how they affect each other. For example, I have argued in this chapter that power phenomena can invalidate status treatments.

[5] The treatment was less successful in the two schools where the largest racial group was White and where there were only a few Blacks or Browns in positions of authority.

What can I say of the practical implications of this discussion in the meantime? Before this research is anywhere near completed, desegregated schools will continue to be planned and practitioners will continue to work very hard to ameliorate many of the problems discussed. I list below six recommendations which follow from the analysis of multiple phenomena in the desegregated school.

1. Optimal Social Class of Desegregated Schools. Combining racial groups with similar levels of academic achievement makes it much easier to produce equal status relationships. Reasoning from the evidence of successful status treatments such as expectation training, where Whites experience competence in Black and Brown peers, expectations based on race alone become modified with the experience of new competence displayed in the interaction. The result is equal status behavior.

Classroom research evidence provides some support for this recommendation. In their study of interracial classrooms, Lewis and St. John (1974) found that the smaller the social class differential between racial groups, the less race served as a basis for friendship choice. Stulac (1976), in her microethnographic study of a naturally integrated school in a surburban area, where Chicanos, Blacks, and Whites all lived in modest housing tracts, found that racial group was not a salient dimension of interpersonal evaluation either in judging academic competence or in choice of friends. The school population was homogeneous, socioeconomically and academically; parents were all striving to move up from poorer backgrounds to surburban home ownership and middle class status. When such similar social class groups are combined, there is greater academic homogeneity and, thus, the desegregated school represents the "equal status conditions" which Allport's (1954) early work recommends for the reduction of prejudice.

2. Changing Instructional Practice in Academically Heterogeneous Classrooms. Because minority groups are of lower social class than majority groups in this country, obviously many desegregated schools will turn out to have minority students who come from much poorer economic backgrounds. These will be academically heterogeneous classrooms. We have described this setting as the most challenging of all in which to produce equal status behavior. This setting has the potential of confirming stereotypes and depressing expectations for academic competence on the part of the minority child.

I am recommending fundamental shifts in the nature of instruction and the social structure of these classrooms. These classrooms must, in effect, become multi-ability classrooms, not in a one-week treatment, but as a result of permanent changes in the methods of teaching. A multi-ability classroom is one in which there are many dimensions of intellectual competence. No individual is likely to be rated highly on all these dimensions. Each individual is likely to be rated highly on at least one dimension.

Thus, there are no students who are generally expected to be incompetent at new tasks and no students who are generally expected to be superior regardless of the nature of the task. In a multi-ability classroom, one's skill in reading represents only one important competence; it is not an index of general expectations for success at all classroom tasks.

Individualization, properly implemented, is a useful and theoretically suitable technique for these academically heterogeneous classrooms. When a subject matter is broken down into small skills and objectives and temporary groups are formed on the basis of mastery of each of these skills, the same children are not uniformly successful at mastering skills at an accelerated pace. Thus, a subject area such as reading is perceived as a task involving multiple abilities with inconsistent evaluations for each student. In addition, if the teacher uses multiple media in assignment of tasks, so that a student receives an assignment in the media where he has been more successful, individuals have an increased chance of attaining success.

In the intensive study of instruction in desegregated classrooms carried out by the Status Equalization Projects, we often found teachers who assigned tasks on an individualized basis in math and reading and who kept individualized records. However, many teachers failed to carry out an individualized system of feedback where each student learned of their progress on mastering objectives on a strictly private basis. Instead, they used a public and standardized evaluation system undoing all the work of individualization; they unwittingly translated the variety of tasks into a single dimension of success to failure. The project staff also observed many teachers who thought they were carrying out a highly individualized program, but who were actually giving out a variety of seatwork paper-and-pencil tasks. Students who could barely read were merely being kept busy with routine tasks either insufficiently challenging or far too difficult.

How many discussions of desegregation are realistic about the technical and financial problems of supporting teachers in carrying out a fully individualized program in the basic skills? Individualization, meeting the requirements of a multi-ability classroom, is unlikely to be carried out by an isolated teacher. Such systems are found in academically heterogeneous urban classrooms where teachers work very closely with aides, or specialists, or other teachers on teams (Intili, 1977). Extra technical assistance for teachers, extra staff, and time for meeting implies additional cost as well as the administrative skill of the principal in making sure that the staff is working closely together on instructional problems.

In addition to individualized programs in the basic skills, a multi-ability classroom can be created through careful use of group work in subject areas such as social studies and science. If the task of the group does not make reading or computation a prerequisite for success, and if the teacher defines the multiple skills or abilities involved in the task (for example, creative thinking, sharp observational skills, hypothesis making, or meticulous data collection), different children will find that they are evaluated as excellent on different abilities. It is possible and practical for teachers to adapt available social studies and science curricula along these lines.

In the Status Equalization Project, we have found small, cooperative group work a useful tool in working with teachers to implement the multiple ability classroom. Students must be taught skills for working in groups; these do not develop naturally or automatically. With proper training for shared participation and good listening behavior, much can be done to avert self-fulfilling prophecies based on perceived differences in reading ability (Morris, 1977). Group work allows for successful participation, improved affect and for peer evaluation of skills independent of teacher evaluation. Under these conditions, children of different academic and social status can and do make important contributions to the group, thus helping to destroy a single rank order based on a unidimensional conception of ability.

3. Trying to Treat Powerlessness. We know the least about the problem of powerlessness. Yet, it seems imperative to examine this dimension in the desegregated school and to attempt some treatment. Marlaine Lockheed argues in her recent work on leadership with elementary school boys and girls that if girls are given leadership opportunities in the classroom, both boys and girls will be less likely to see leadership as a male prerogative.[6] Her work on sex has many parallels to the work on interracial classrooms; leadership opportunities in American classrooms are typically given to high performing White males. Following Lockheed, in working with teachers on group work procedures, the Status Equalization Project staff made use of a group facilitator role. It was the job of the group facilitator to make sure that the group stayed on task and that everyone participated. Systematic observation data revealed that minority students who were ranked as poor readers were very successful in the leadership role of group facilitator when training was provided. If the leader has such a legitimate role, understood by all members of the group, we may be able to produce a genuine sense of "empowerment" on the part of girls and minority students in the classroom. This proposition remains untested at the present writing.

Adults in the desegregated setting need to see their behavior as an extremely important model for the students. If the children see Whites always directing Blacks and Browns as to what to do, they will evidently conclude that it is correct for them to behave in the same way. In some schools, children may simply never see interracial interaction among the

[6] M. Lockheed, research in progress. This research is briefly described in an article, "Fifth Grade Study Finds Boys View Girls as Smart but Not as Leaders: Girls Agree." Educational Testing Service Developments, Vol. XXV, No. 2, 1978.

staff. I would suppose that, in those cases, they learn to avoid each other. If, on the contrary, they see equal-status problem-solving behavior modeled by interracial pairs or groups of adults, it will help to produce equal status behavior among the children. For this reason, team teaching with interracial pairs could have a highly desirable effect.

4. *Avoiding Small Minority Representation.* Desegregation guidelines that call for spreading around the minority population so that they comprise only a few members of each classroom should be reexamined. It may prove impossible to treat the powerlessness that results from this situation. Especially if the minority student is achieving at a lower level in basic skills, the problems of producing equal status behavior or academic improvement are immense.

5. *Treating the Norms for Human Relations in the Whole Desegregated School.* I have argued for a careful and separate examination of aggressive and threatening relations in the desegregated school—quite separately from the issue of promoting interracial friendship. Aggressive interracial behavior may turn out in a given school, not to be a product of interracial relations, but a product of the general social class in the school and the failure of the faculty and administration to develop and implement policies concerning how students should treat each other outside of classrooms. Threatening and assaultive behavior have no place in any school, let alone in a desegregated school. However, this behavior may be part of a larger pattern of violence in the school which is open to misinterpretation as racial conflict. In schools like these, teachers are reluctant to supervise halls and playgrounds; the principal takes no firm action to deal with the problem.

One of the integrated schools we studied showed an excellent climate of human relations. The children were far less likely to report aggressive and threatening behavior in this school than in any other school ever surveyed.[7] This was no accident; the principal and faculty have worked consistently for several years toward improving this climate. They have introduced and maintained exemplary instructional treatments stressing positive means of solving interpersonal problems. Children have a clear idea of how they are supposed to treat each other on school grounds; one can see them instructing newcomers in these norms for human relations. Teachers and principal are highly visible and model the desired behavior. Instead of allowing students to fashion their own norms for interpersonal behavior, these norms become a subject of instruction and policy, firmly and fairly enforced throughout the school.

Although such a climate is obviously highly desirable for the desegregated school, it should be clear that the achievement of this goal will not

---

[7] The measuring instrument was the Multicultural Social Climate Scale developed by James Deslonde.

treat the status and power problems discussed above. However, a most undesirable climate might certainly undo much positive classroom experience and confirm stereotypes about aggressive behavior from lower class minority groups.

 6. *Integrated Learning Experience as a Separate School Program.* Conventional desegregation plans that simply dictate that there shall be a maximum mixing of the races in the composition of each school as a remedy for social isolation are not likely to produce equal status conditions. Nor are such plans likely to produce marked academic achievement on the part of the minorities. It is not, in principle, impossible to treat these problems; however, the task is expensive and difficult, especially if the desegregated population must experience a total school program in the conventional context.

 An alternative desegregation plan in the face of these difficulties is the creation of a specific set of educational experiences designed to teach children that members of other racial and ethnic groups do indeed have important contributions to make on intellectually demanding tasks. We do know how to create equal status behavior in a group setting focusing on challenging, creative tasks. If we do not have to contend simultaneously with remediating the basic skills, the creation of equal status behavior is not an impractical goal. Neither is it impractical to design a learning situation in the area of social studies and science that will show dramatic learning gains in the area of social studies and science, provided these subjects are taught as multi-ability tasks, and the learning outcomes are measured in a suitable fashion. The field experiment at the Center for Interracial Cooperation described above showed the practicality of this design.

 This alternative plan for desegregation was actually proposed by the Los Angeles Board of Education to Judge Egly in the recent desegregation case in the city.[8] The board proposed to set up a specialized learning center[9] to which students and their teachers from various segregated schools would come. These experiences were designed for grades 4, 5, and 6 for one-third of each year. The curriculum had a multicultural, a social studies, and a science emphasis. The staff was to be made up of specially qualified and enthusiastic teachers. Classroom teachers, accompanying their students, would be able to see for themselves how differently their charges behaved in a social situation which encourages participation, ideas, and creativity. They would have been able to see how it was done, to ask questions, and to bring back ideas to their own classrooms. Basic skills were to be taught in the neighborhood school, along with bilingual education.

 Although this plan was rejected by Judge Egly, it continues to make sense in terms of the research and theory reviewed here. If equal effort were

[8] *Crawford* v. *Board of Education of the City of Los Angeles,* 30485, 17 (1976).
[9] Plan for the Integration of Pupils in the Los Angeles School District, Vol. II, Component 3.

put into the improvement of basic skills teaching in those neighborhood schools showing poor mastery of basic skills objectives, by the time the population reached junior high school, fewer students would be reading well below grade level. With a more homogeneous academic population at the junior high level and considerable experience with successful social and intellectual integration, a thorough desegregation plan becomes more feasible.

PART IV

The Future

Social scientists have come a long way in understanding inequity in the school setting in 25 years. It is now clear that in desegregating schools, many were attempting to make the schools repair the most basic problems of inequity in American society. Unfortunately, the schools are not the most powerful of institutions in the society; even if social scientists and educators were able to produce equity in the schools, the balance of power and status in the outside society would probably remain the same.

If, as social scientists, we face this difficulty honestly, we need not counsel despair. We have also learned in the intervening 25 years since *Brown* v. *Board of Education*[10] that it is possible to structure situations so that we can produce equal status behavior. Many classrooms and schools have demonstrated that they are successful in teaching conventional academic skills to poor, minority students (Brookover, 1978). Although it is unlikely that schools can solve the problems of society, they need not be faithful mirrors of the inequities of society. With the sharpened diagnostic and analytical tools in our possession, there is much that can be done in the deliberate design of desegregated situations moving toward an equal status model. We, as social scientists and educators, still have a tremendous amount of work to do in attaining these goals.

REFERENCES

Allport, G. W. *The nature of prejudice*. Reading, Mass. Addison-Wesley, 1954.
Aronson, E. *The jigsaw classroom*. Beverly Hills, Calif.: Sage, 1978.
Berger, J., & Fisek, M. A generalization of the theory of status characteristics and expectation states. In B. Berger *et al.* (Eds.), Expectations status theory: A theoretical research program. Cambridge, Mass.: Winthrop, 1974, 163–205.

---

[10] *Brown* v. *Topeka Board of Education*, 347 U.S. 483 (1954).

Berger, J., Cohen B., & Zelditch, M., Jr. Status conceptions and social interactions. *American Sociological Review*, 1972, *37*, 241-255.

Cohen, E. Interracial interaction disability. *Human Relations*, 1972, *25*, 9-24.

Cohen, E. The effects of desegregation on race relations. *Law and Contemporary Problems*, Part II. School of Law, Duke University, Vol XXXIX, Spring, 1975, 271-299, No. 2.

Cohen, E., & Roper, S. Modification of interracial interaction disability: An application of status characteristic theory. *American Sociological Review*, December, 1972, *37*, 6.

Cohen, E., & Sharan, S. *Modifying status relations in Israel youth: An application of expectations states theory*. Paper presented at the annual meeting of AERA, New York, 1977.

Cohen, E., Katz, M., & Lohman, M. Center for interracial cooperation: A field experiment. *Sociology of Education*, 1976, *49*.

Cook, T. *Producing equal status interaction between Indian and white boys in British Columbia: An application of expectation training*. Unpublished doctoral dissertation, Stanford University, 1974.

Deutsch, M. A theory of cooperation and competition. *Human Relations*, 1949, *2*, 129–152.

Gerard, H., & Miller, N. *School desegregation: A long-range study*. New York: Plenum, 1975.

Had, A. *Effects of status and task outcome structures upon observable power and prestige order of small-task oriented groups*. Unpublished doctoral dissertation, Stanford University, 1972.

Hallinan, M. T. *The peer influence process: A reconceptualization*. Paper presented for N.I.E. Conference on Organizational Variables and Student Outcomes, San Diego, January 1978.

Hoffman, D., & Cohen, E. *An exploratory study to determine the effects of generalized performance expectations upon activity and influence of students engaged in a group simulation game*. Paper presented at AERA, Chicago, April 1972.

Iadicola, P. *Desegregation as a model of assimilation*. Paper presented at ASA, Chicago, August 1977.

Iadicola, P. *Schooling and social power: A presentation of a Weberian conflict model of the school*. Unpublished doctoral dissertation, University of California, Riverside, 1979.

Intili, J. *Structural conditions in the school that facilitate reflective decision making*. Unpublished doctoral dissertation, Stanford University, 1977.

Katz, I. Review of evidence relating to effects of desegregation on the intellectual performance of negroes. *American Psychological Association*, 1964, 19, 381–389.

Lewis, R., & St. John, N. Contribution of cross-racial friendship to minority group achievement in desegregated classrooms. *Sociometry*, 1974, *37*, 79–91.

Lockheed, M., & Harris, A. *Modifying status orders in mixed sex groups of fourth and fifth grade children: An application of expectation states theory*. Paper presented at the American Sociological Association, Chicago, August 1977.

Lohman, M. *Changing a racial status ordering by means of role modeling*. Unpublished doctoral dissertation, Stanford Unversity, 1970.

Lucker, G., Rosenfield, D., Sikes, J., & Aronson, E. Performance in the interdependent classroom: A field study. *American Educational Research Journal*, 1976, *13*, 115–123.

Morris, R. *A normative intervention to equalize participation in task-oriented groups*. Unpublished doctoral dissertation, Stanford University, 1977.

Newby, R. *The effect of racial consciousness of black youth on white influence in small groups*. Unpublished doctoral dissertation, Stanford University, 1974.

Patchen, M., Davidson, J., Hyman, G., & Brown, W. *Class racial composition, friendliness of interracial contact and student performance*. Paper presented at the American Sociological Association, Chicago, Illinois, 1977. (a)

Patchen, M., Davidson, J. P., Hyman, G., & Brown, W. R. Determinants of students' interracial behavior and opinion change. *Sociology of Education*, 1977, *50*, 55–75. (b)

Pettigrew, T. Social evaluation theory: Convergences and applications. In D. Levine (Ed.), *Nebraska Symposium on Motivation*, Vol. 15. Lincoln: University of Nebraska Press, 1967.

Rist, R. *The invisible children: School integration in American society*. Cambridge: Harvard University Press, 1978.

Robbins, A. *Fostering equal-status interaction through the establishment of consistent staff behaviors and appropriate situational norms*. Paper presented at the annual meeting of the American Educational Association, New York, 1977.

Rosenholtz, S. J. Treating problems of academic status. In J. Berger & M. Zelditch, Jr. (Eds.), *Status, attributions, and justice*. New York: Elsevier, in press.

Rosenholtz, S. J., & Cohen, E. Status in the eye of the beholder. In J. Berger & M. Zelditch, Jr. (Eds.), *Status, attributions, and justice*. New York: Elsevier, in press.

Rosenholtz, S. J., & Wilson, B. The effect of classroom structure on shared perceptions of ability. *American Educational Research Journal*, in press.

Schofield, J. W. School desegregation and intergroup relations. In D. Bar-Tal & L. Saxe (Eds.), *Social psychology of education: Theory and research*. Washington, D.C.: Hemisphere, 1978.

Schofield, J. W., & Sagar, A. The social context of learning in an interracial school. In R. Rist (Ed.), *Desegregated schools: Appraisals of an American experiment*. New York: Academic, 1979.

Simpson, C. *Classroom structure and the reality of ability differences*. Paper presented at the annual meeting of Pacific Sociological Association, March 1977.

Slavin, R. *Student teams and achievement divisions: Effects on academic performance, mutual attraction and attitudes*. Report No. 233, Center for Social Organizations of Schools, Johns Hopkins University, Baltimore, Md., August, 1977.

Stulac, J. *The self-fulfilling prophecy: Modifying the effects of a unidimensional perception of academic competence in task-oriented groups*. Unpublished doctoral dissertation, Stanford University, 1975.

Stulac, J. Field studies in urban desegregated school: Interim report. Far West Laboratory, San Francisco, Calif., 1976.

Webster, M., & Driskell, J. E. Status generalization: A review and some new data. *American Sociological Review*, 1978, *43*, 220–236.

Weigel, R., Wiser, P., & Cook, E. The impact of cooperative learning experiences on cross ethnic relations and attitudes. *Journal of Social Issues*, 1975, *31*, 1, 219–245.

12

Building Effective Multiethnic Schools

EVOLVING MODELS AND PARADIGMS

JANE R. MERCER, PETER IADICOLA, AND HELEN MOORE

During the 25 years since *Brown* v *Board of Education* (1954),[1] research concerning school desegregation has evolved through three basic paradigms. Studies during the early period were primarily atheoretical, impact studies. These were followed by a variety of studies based on deficit models and psychologistic hypotheses. More recently, interest has shifted to models which describe the interpersonal processes and the social structural characteristics of the school as a social system and relate system characteristics to educational outcomes.

ATHEORETICAL, IMPACT STUDIES

St. John (1975) and the National Institute of Education (1976) have published complete summaries of the major studies of the effects of school

[1] *Brown* v. *Board of Education of Topeka*, 347 U.S. 483 (1954).

JANE R. MERCER, PETER IADICOLA, AND HELEN MOORE • Program for Research in Integrated Multiethnic Education, University of California, Riverside, California 92502. The data in this chapter have been collected under the auspices of the following grants: United States Office of Education, OEC-9-73-0137. Under the provisions of Title IV, Section 403, of Public Law 88-352, The Civil Rights Acts of 1964: National Institute of Mental Health, Department of Health, Education, and Welfare, Grant No. MH26607-01,02,03. The work presented and reported herein does not necessarily reflect the position or policy of the funding agencies and no official endorsement should be inferred.

desegregation which were conducted during the early period. Most of these studies are either cross-sectional surveys or simple before-and-after research designs which attempt to measure the impact of school desegregation on a variety of student outcomes: academic achievement, self-concept, racial prejudice, educational and occupational aspirations, and so forth. A few have some type of comparison group. They are, for the most part, action research uninformed by theory. "Propositions derived from legal, philosophical, educational, or political opinion have been tested by social science methods" (St. John, 1975, p. 87).

In addition to serious problems concerning the internal validity of such studies (Campbell & Stanley, 1963), they are based on a highly simplistic concept of school desegregation which views it as a single, global treatment which will result in a consistent and measurable pattern of outcomes. Not surprisingly, the findings from such studies have been ambiguous and contradictory. They have done little to provide a solid basis for the accumulation of a systematic body of knowledge and they have been of little value in informing public policy. In retrospect, we must agree with Glazer (1975) when he notes:

> How simple and simple-minded our understanding of that question has been. . . . There was no reason to believe that desegregation alone—the achieving of some statistical mix of children of different races—would raise the educational achievement of black children, enhance their self image, or improve race relations. Indeed, the evidence to date demonstrates that to expect a clear result from *one* change in a situation, without considering everything else that is crucially important in children's lives, was naive. (p. vi)

DEFICIT MODELS AND PSYCHOLOGICAL HYPOTHESES

When simple impact studies found no solid evidence that school desegregation *per se* resulted in significant and predictable changes in students, some investigators refocused attention on locating the culprits. If desegregation does not produce the anticipated results, then it must be because of deficiencies in the actors. Three general hypotheses were explored: deficiencies in minority children, deficiencies in minority families, and deficiencies in teachers.

Deficiencies in Minority Children

In the late 1960s, Jensen (1969) and Eysenck (1971) revived the hypothesis that minority chidren have less "innate ability" than majority children and/or have a different type of "intelligence" that allows them to perform adequately on rote learning tasks but prevents all but a favored few from performing adequately on tasks that require abstract reasoning. The policy implications of such hypotheses are, of course, profound. It would follow that money spent on conpensatory educational programs would be regarded as wasted since the programs would be expected to have limited effect. Efforts at school desegregation would be futile since no significant changes would be expected in the performance of minority students. Indeed, the failure of the early desegregation studies to demonstrate important, measurable change could be explained readily as evidence of supposed deficiencies in minority children. Carried to its logical conclusion, such a position would argue for separate schools in which minority children would receive educational programs geared to their type of "intelligence" (Jensen, 1971).

It is beyond the scope of this paper to review the lengthy controversy over the proper interpretation of scores on so-called "intelligence" tests. (Mercer, 1971, 1972, 1973, 1974, 1977, 1978–1979; Mercer & Brown, 1973; Deutsch & Brown, 1964). Suffice it to say that the use of deficit models which explain differences in human behavior on the basis of presumed defects in minority groups have far-reaching political implications. Thus, it comes as no surprise that deficit models and the tests used to measure supposed "deficits" are being debated in the courts within the adversary process (*Larry P.* v. *W. Riles*, 1971;[2] *Diana* v. *California State Board of Education*, 1969[3]). Recent federal legislation (*Public Law 94–142*, 1975[4]) mandates that tests used in assessing children for programs for the handicapped which place children in special education programs and tracks which assume that the child has limited learning potential shall be racially and culturally nondiscriminatory. Although the battle over the proper use of tests in the public schools is not ordinarily perceived as an aspect of school desegregation, that dispute is fundamentally concerned with the use of deficit models and its resolution will surely influence social policy in the arena of desegregation.

Deficiencies in Minority Families

A long line of social research studies has used deficits models in studying minority families. Findings from studies conducted in the 1940s (Davis, 1948; Davis & Havighurst, 1946) were reinforced by interpretations of findings from the report on *Equality of Educational Opportunity* (Coleman, Campbell, Hobson, McPartland, Mood, Weinfeld, & York, 1966). Armor

---

[2] *Larry P.* v. *W. Riles*. Civil Action No. C 71 2270: United States District Court, Northern District of California: filed, 1971.
[3] *Diana* v. *California State Board of Education*. Civil Action No. C–70 37 RFP, United States District Court, Northern District of California (1969).
[4] *Public Law 94–142. Education for All Handicapped Children Act of 1975.*

(1972) reanalyzed the data from the study and confirmed the original conclusion. Using 6th grade verbal achievement as the dependent variable, he concluded that 80% of the achievement variance for the nation as a whole could be accounted for by community and family background characteristics. School factors had little weight.

Other studies had investigated a variety of family characteristics. Some of the more influential studies linked the following family characteristics to school achievement: socioeconomic status (SES) (Bloom, Whiteman, & Deutsch, 1965; Goldstein, 1967; Sewell, Haller, & Strauss, 1957; Sewell & Hauser, 1976; Whiteman, Brown, & Deutsch, 1967; Whiteman & Deutsch, 1968; Wilson, 1963), amount and type of verbal and linguistic interaction in the family (Bernstein, 1969; Jensen, 1968), family size and family structure (Whiteman & Deutsch, 1968), type of parental interaction with children (Hess & Shipman, 1966; Marans & Lourie, 1967; Pavenstedt, 1965; Tulkin & Kagan, 1972; Wortis, Bardach, Cutler, Rue, & Freedman, 1963), parental educational aspirations for their children (Rosen, 1956; Rosen & D'Andrade, 1959; Strodtbeck, 1964), and biological damage due to poor prenatal and health care (Pasamanick & Knobloch, 1958). Jencks (1972) analyzed data from several studies and concluded that family background characteristics (socioeconomic status and educational level) had much more influence on educational attainment than cognitive skills as measured by tests or qualitative differences between schools. He concluded that schools should be evaluated "in terms of their immediate effects on teachers and students" and that "equity seems to require that every family have a free choice as to which school its children attend" (pp. 256–257). In short, family deficit models lead to essentially the same policy implications as models based on supposed deficits in minority children, i.e., school desegregation is futile since the schools have little impact on achievement of minority children relative to the influence of the family. Hence, social policy should concentrate on modifying socialization practices in minority families and intervening in early childhood rather than focusing on school desegregation (Bereiter, 1968; Gordon, 1968; Gray & Klaus, 1965; Karnes, Teska, Hodgins, & Badger, 1970; Schaefer, 1972; Stendler-Lavatelli, 1968; Weikart & Lambier, 1968).

Deficiencies in Teachers

Becker (1952) was among the first to describe the lower academic expectations of teachers working with minority students, their difficulties in dealing with student discipline, and their rejection of the students' behavior as offensive and "morally unacceptable". Harvey and Slatin (1975) and Hollingshead (1949) found social class to be a central variable in determining educational outcomes and participation in school activities. Silberman

(1964) focused attention on racial and social class biases in the behavior of teachers, and Gottlieb (1964) reported that White teachers had more negative perceptions of Black students than did Black teachers. More recently, Rist (1970) found discriminatory grouping, verbal interaction, and disciplinary practices in a case study of a desegregated elementary school and related these variables to the race, socioeconomic status, and academic performance of students. Jackson and Cosca (1974) observed that teachers in 494 ethnically mixed classrooms engaged in significantly fewer positive interactions with Hispanic students than with non-Hispanic students, such as praise, acceptance of student's ideas, and questioning. They concluded that teachers are unprepared to deal with ethnic and cultural differences. Johnson, Gerard, and Miller (1975) came to similar conclusions in their study of teacher influences in desegregated classrooms and suggest that teacher ethnic attitudes and differential teaching standards mediate success or failure for the children involved. Weinberg (1977) summarizes a series of studies which report generally negative teacher perceptions of minority children.

It is not difficult to demonstrate that teachers have more negative perceptions and lower educational and occupational expectations for minority than for majority children. In a study of 56 desegregated elementary schools in California, third- and sixth-grade teachers were asked to rate each child in their classes on a series of semantic differential, five point ratings using bipolar adjectives. These ratings factored into three distinct factors: student competence, student sociability, and student social conformity. The 3,479 White children were rated as significantly more competent than the 2,213 Black and 1,222 Hispanic children ($p < .001$), i.e., more intelligent, more able to concentrate, more organized, more persevering, and having better memories. White children were also rated as most sociable ($p < .001$), that is, more extroverted, colorful, friendly, cheerful, and warm. Both Hispanic and White children were rated as significantly ($p < .001$) more socially conforming than Black children, that is, more obedient, cooperative, patient, kind, and easy to discipline. Teachers also had significantly higher educational and occupational expectations for White than for either Black or Hispanic students ($p < .001$) (Mercer, Coleman, & Harloe, 1974). We have replicated these findings several times on other samples of students and teachers in desegregated schools.

There is little doubt that teachers have lower expectations and more negative perceptions of minority students than majority students, but what does that finding mean? If we conclude that teachers are prejudiced, that they have preconceived opinions or judgments held in disregard of facts that contradict them, then the social policy conclusion is that programs need to be initiated to modify teachers' prejudices. Such is the conclusion usually drawn from such findings. However, Sewell and Hauser (1976) concluded that race and socioeconomic level were not significantly biasing factors in teachers' evaluations of students when the student's actual performance had been taken into account. If this is the case for teachers in desegregated schools, then the policy implications are quite different. A model which hypothesizes deficiencies in teachers would not be appropriate.

Because the teacher deficit model has been the basis for spending large amounts of money on attitude change programs, cultural awareness efforts, and technical assistance through in-service educational programs for teachers in desegregated districts under Title IV of the Civil Rights Act, we decided to examine the assumptions of that model empirically.

Design of the Study of Teacher Prejudice

Questions Addressed in the Study. The study addressed three questions: Do teachers have more negative perceptions of minority students than of majority students? Do teachers behave more negatively toward minority students than toward majority students as reported by the students themselves? When measures of student performance based on academic achievement measures and peer sociometrics are taken into account, do teacher perceptions of minority students reflect socioeconomic and/or racial or ethnic bias?

Samples. Two samples of sixth-grade and one of eigth-grade students and their teachers were studied. The 1973 sixth-grade sample consisted of a stratified random sample of approximately 1,330 students of each of the three ethnic/racial groups from among 8,000 students enrolled in 135 elementary schools in eight desegregated school districts in California and Washington. The ethnic identity of each student and the occupational level of the student's family, using an SES category scale ranging from "welfare or unemployed" to "professional" was reported by the student's teacher. Teachers were instructed to omit the occupational rating if they were uncertain about their information. However, most teachers were able to provide the information for all their students.

The 1977, sixth-grade sample consisted of 154 White, 117 Hispanic, and 77 Black students attending 13 schools in four California school districts. The schools were selected from a larger pool of 174 elementary schools, so that 7 schools were among those having the most favorable educational outcomes and 6 schools were among those having the least favorable outcomes. Students in each ethnic group were selected randomly from the sixth-grade enrollment. Of the students and parents selected for the sample, 96% agreed to participate. Again, teachers reported the ethnic identity of each student and parental occupational level. Because family interviews were also conducted in this smaller study, information on ethnic identity and occupation was subsequently verified by the parents. Occupations were coded using the Duncan Socioeconomic Index (Reiss, 1961), which yields scores ranging from 0–99.

The eighth-grade sample was studied in 1973. Questionnaires were administered to all students in 209 classrooms in 19 junior high schools in four west coast school districts. A sample of 109 White, 100 Hispanic, and 111 Black students was selected, randomly, from among those students for whom there was complete data. Each student reported his or her own ethnic group and the occupation of his or her mother and/or father. Occupations were coded using the Duncan Socioeconomic Index (Reiss, 1961) which yields scores ranging from 0–99.

Measures. Each student took a vocabulary test based on selected items from standardized tests appropriate for his or her grade level. In addition, sixth-grade students completed a peer sociometric in which they reported how often they wanted to do things with each of the other students in the class: always, sometimes, or never. A student's score is the average of the choices received from all other members of the student's class. Scores can range from 0–2 on each individual rating. No sociometrics were administered to eighth-grade students. Students in the eighth-grade sample and in the 1977 sixth-grade sample were also asked questions concerning the types of negative sanctions they had received during the school year, such as being kicked out of class, being sent to the principal's office, or being suspended. Data on negative sanctions was not collected from the 1973 sixth-grade sample.

The teacher of each student completed a series of 18 semantic differential ratings for each student, the same set of ratings described above (Mercer *et al.*, 1974). The reliabilities for these ratings are .86 and higher. *Competence* included the following adjective pairs: intelligent–dull minded, quick–slow, able to concentrate–subject to distraction, organized–disorganized, good memory–poor memory, and persevering–quitting. *Sociability* included extroversion–introversion, sociable–unsociable, warm–cool, colorful–colorless, friendly–aloof, and cheerful–morose. *Social Conformity* included kind–cruel, obedient–disobedient, prone to anger–not prone to anger, easy to discipline–difficult to discipline, cooperative–obstructive, and patient–impatient. Each rating was scored from 1–5 and total scores on each scale can range from 6–30 points.

In addition to the semantic differentials, each teacher reported how much schooling he or she expected the student to complete, and the level of occupation he or she anticipated the student would achieve as an adult. These were five category ratings. The two ratings were summed to produce a single index on which total scores can range from 2–10.

Findings. Table I presents an analysis of variance across ethnic group comparing the SES, peer sociometric scores, and word knowledge scores for students in the three samples. White students come from significantly higher

Table I. Analysis of Variance across Ethnic Group on Pupil Characteristics in Three Samples

Sample	Socioeconomic			Peer sociometric			Word knowledge		
	M	*SD*	Sig.	*M*	*SD*	Sig.	*M*	*SD*	Sig.
1973, 6th grade									
White (*N* = 1342)	3.0	1.5		.74	.27		30.2	10.5	
Hispanic (*N* = 1332)	1.7	1.1	.001[abc]	.77	.27	.001[bc]	21.7	9.5	.001[ab]
Black (*N* = 1333)	1.8	1.3		.73	.24		20.9	9.1	
1977, 6th grade									
White (*N* = 117–151)	47.9	29.0		.76	.31		30.9	10.2	
Hispanic (*N* = 91–114)	19.3	19.6	.001[abc]	.83	.33	NS	23.1	8.9	.001[ab]
Black (*N* = 57–68)	31.4[c]	28.2		.74	.36		23.5	9.4	
1973, 8th grade									
White (*N* = 116)	45.5	23.8					51.0	24.7	
Hispanic (*N* = 101)	26.9	19.0	.001[ab]		no data		38.2	22.8	.01[abc]
Black (*N* = 111)	31.7	23.2					34.9	20.7	

[a] White–Black differences, $p < .05$.
[b] White–Hispanic differences, $p < .05$.
[c] Black–Hispanic differences, $p < .05$.

socioeconomic levels than Black and Hispanic students in all three samples ($p < .05$). Black students come from higher socioeconomic levels than Hispanic students in all three samples, but the differences reach statistical significance only in the two sixth-grade samples. Hispanic students receive significantly higher peer sociometric ratings in the 1973, sixth-grade sample ($p < .05$) but there are no reliable differences in ratings for the 1977 sixth-grade sample. On word knowledge, White students score significantly higher than both Black and Hispanic students ($p < .05$) in all three samples. Hispanic students do better than Black students in the 1973, eighth-grade sample but there are no reliable differences in word knowledge for these groups in the sixth grade.

Table II presents an analysis of variance across ethnic group for teacher perceptions of the competence, sociability, and social conformity of students and their educational and occupational expectations for students. It also presents data on student report of having received negative sanctions from the school. Teachers rate White students as more competent than Black students in all three samples and as more competent than Hispanic students in the sixth-grade samples. They have significantly lower expectations for the occupational and educational futures of Hispanic children than for White in all three samples and lower expectations for Hispanic children than Black in two samples. White students are consistently rated higher

Table II. Analysis of Variance across Ethnic Group for Teacher Perceptions and Behavior toward Three Samples

Sample	Teacher rating competence			Teacher occupational educational expectations			Teacher rating sociability			Teacher rating social conformity			Student report of negative sanctions		
	M	SD	Sig.	M	SD	Sig.	M	SD	Sig.	M	SD	Sig.	M	SD	Sig.
1973, 6th grade															
White (N = 1342)	21.2	5.8	.001^{ab}	6.6	2.4	.001^{ab}	22.1	4.6	.05^c	22.5	5.5	.001^c		no data	
Hispanic (N = 1332)	20.1	5.5		5.4	2.1		21.8	4.5		22.5	5.7				
Black (N = 1333)	18.4	5.8		5.3	2.3		22.3	4.8		19.9	6.1				
1977, 6th grade															
White (N = 132–154)	21.4	5.9	.01^{ab}	6.6	2.4	.001^{bc}	22.2	5.1	.002^{ac}	22.2	5.7	.001^c	2.5	2.4	
Hispanic (N = 106–117)	19.1	5.0		4.9	2.1		21.7	4.9		21.4	6.3	NS	3.1	2.6	.05
Black (N = 62–74)	19.5	5.9		6.1	2.5		24.3	4.0		20.7	6.0		3.1	2.4	
1973, 8th grade															
White (N = 109)	22.2	5.8	.01^{ac}	6.6	2.2	.01^{bc}	22.8	4.3	.01^{ac}	23.4	4.9	.05^{ac}	.9	1.5	.02^{ab}
Hispanic (N = 100)	21.0	5.5		5.6	2.0		22.2	4.1		22.8	5.6		1.3	1.9	
Black (N = 111)	19.4	6.0		5.8	2.4		23.4	4.6		21.6	6.0		1.6	2.1	

[a] White–Black differences, p < .05.
[b] White–Hispanic differences, p < .05.
[c] Black–Hispanic differences, p < .05.

than Black, but differences are statistically reliable only in the 1973, sixth-grade samples. Blacks are rated higher than Hispanics in two samples.

Black students are consistently rated higher on sociability than either White or Hispanic students and the differences are statistically significant in all cases except the comparison with White students in the 1973, sixth-grade sample. On the other hand, teachers perceive Black students as lowest in social conformity, but differences are statistically reliable only in the eighth-grade sample and between Hispanic and Black students in the 1973, sixth-grade sample. Both Hispanic and Black students report more negative sanctions than White students in the two samples for which we have data.

Do teachers have more negative perceptions of minority students than majority students? The answer is mixed. In our three samples teachers do perceive minority students as less competent and have lower expectations for minority students than for White students. They also see Black students as more difficult to discipline, but the differences are not uniformly reliable. Minority students also report more negative sanctions. However, the highest ratings on sociability consistently go to Black students. Hence, teachers are not uniformly negative toward minority students, as much of the earlier literature would imply, but differentiate their evaluations depending upon the attribute being rated.

Because Black and Hispanic students' performance on the word knowledge tests is consistently lower than that of White students, it is possible that lower teacher ratings on competence and lower teacher expectations for minority students simply reflect their actual performance. In order to determine what weight, if any, the student's actual scholarship as measured by the word knowledge test and actual sociability, and as measured by the peer sociometric, have on teacher evaluations, we did a series of multiple regression analyses. The student's ethnic group, SES, word knowledge score, and peer sociometric score were treated as independent variables and the various ratings by teachers were treated as the dependent variables. Table III presents the findings for teacher rating of competence and teacher occupational and educational expectations. The analysis was done separately for the Black–White samples and the Hispanic–White samples in each of the studies. Minority group was coded 1 and majority group coded 0.

Table III presents the multiple correlations between the independent variables and teachers' perceptions and the percentage of the variance explained by the combined independent variables. The beta coefficients for each independent variable can be interpreted as the relative contribution of that variable to the teachers' evaluations when all independent variables are considered simultaneously. Five aspects of the table should be noted:

1. Ethnic group, SES, and word knowledge predict relatively little of the variance in teachers' evaluations of eighth-grade students. The

Table III. Factors Explaining the Variance in Teacher Perceptions of Academic Competence and Educational and Occupational Expectations for Students in Three Samples

Dependent variable	Ethnic groups	Sample	R	Percentage variance explained	Beta coefficients			
					Ethnic group	SES	Word knowledge	Peer sociometric
Teacher rating competence	Black–White	6th grade, 1973	.60[a]	36.5	NS	.15[a]	.47[a]	.18[a]
		6th grade, 1977	.71[a]	50.0	NS	.18[b]	.50[a]	.28[a]
		8th grade, 1973	.26[b]	7.0	−.22[b]	NS	NS	no data
	Hispanic–White	6th grade, 1973	.53[a]	28.3	.11[a]	.15[a]	.41[a]	.21[a]
		6th grade, 1977	.65[a]	42.5	NS	NS	.50[a]	.23[a]
		8th grade, 1973	.19	3.6	NS	NS	NS	no data
Teacher educational occupational, expectations	Black–White	6th grade, 1973	.68[a]	46.0	.06[a]	.35[a]	.43[a]	.14[a]
		6th grade, 1977	.70[a]	49.5	NS	.26[a]	.49[a]	.24[a]
		8th grade, 1973	.19	3.4	NS	NS	NS	no data
	Hispanic–White	6th grade, 1973	.64[a]	41.1	NS	.35[a]	.38[a]	.15[a]
		6th grade, 1977	.70[a]	49.0	NS	.19[b]	.50[a]	.15[b]
		8th grade, 1973	.28[b]	7.7	NS	.17[c]	NS	no data

[a] $p < .001$.
[b] $p < .01$.
[c] $p < .05$.

multiple correlation coefficients are small, and only two are statistically significant. On the other hand, the multiple correlation coefficients are very high for sixth-grade students, accounting for between 28.3–50% of the variance in teachers' evaluations. It appears that teachers are more responsive to the individual characteristics of students in the elementary school than in the junior high school.

2. Word knowledge, a measure of the student's actual knowledge of English vocabulary, has the greatest weight in predicting the evaluations of elementary school teachers. Thus, the student's academic performance is the most important of the variables in determining the teacher's perception of his or her competence and future educational and occupational prospects.

3. How the student is rated by his or her peers is a consistent factor in teacher evaluations. Those given higher ratings by their peers are seen as more competent and as having better chances for educational and occupational achievement.

4. The student's SES also makes a statistically reliable contribution to teacher evaluations in all but one of the analyses. Teachers view students from higher socioeconomic levels as having brighter futures and greater competence.

5. Ethnic group is *not* an important predictor of teachers' ratings. Its contribution is statistically reliable in only 2 of the 8 analyses for sixth-grade students and even in those 2 cases, the contribution is relatively minor.

Table IV presents similar analyses for teacher's ratings of a student's sociability and social conformity and for the student's own report of negative sanctions. Looking first at ratings of sociability, student characteristics are not significant predictors of teacher ratings for the eighth grade but are predictive for the sixth grade. However, the multiple correlations are much lower than those in Table III. How a student is rated by his or her peers is the most important factor in teacher perceptions, with word knowledge and SES making some contribution in the 1973 sixth-grade sample. Ethnic group makes a significant contribution in the Black–White analyses. Black students are rated *higher* in sociability.

Social conformity ratings cannot be predicted for eighth-grade students but are significantly correlated with student characteristics in the sixth grade. Being popular with one's peers and scoring high on word knowledge are the major components of teachers' evaluations. SES makes a minor contribution in the 1973 sixth-grade samples, as does ethnic group. Black students are rated as less conforming, and Hispanic students as more conforming relative to White students.

A student's own report of negative sanctions is correlated significantly

Table IV. Factors Explaining the Variance in Teacher Perceptions of Sociability and Social Conformity and Student Report of Negative Sanctions Received in Three Samples

Dependent variable	Ethnic groups	Sample	R	Percentage variance explained	Beta coefficients			
					Ethnic group	SES	Word knowledge	Peer sociometric
Teacher rating sociability	Black–White	6th grade, 1973	.28^a	7.7	.11^a	.11^a	.11^a	.19^a
		6th grade, 1977	.35^a	12.5	.16^c	NS	NS	.32^a
		8th grade, 1973	.13	1.6	NS	NS	NS	no data
	Hispanic–White	6th grade, 1973	.28^a	8.0	NS	.11^a	.22^a	.08^a
		6th grade, 1977	.21	4.4	NS	NS	NS	.18^c
		8th grade, 1973	.08	.6	NS	NS	NS	no data
Teacher rating social conformity	Black–White	6th grade, 1973	.34^a	11.6	−.11^a	.08^b	.16^a	.16^a
		6th grade, 1977	.36^a	13.2	NS	NS	NS	.25^b
		8th grade, 1973	.17	2.9	−.16^c	NS	NS	no data
	Hispanic–White	6th grade, 1973	.24^a	5.6	.06^b	.06^b	.12^a	.17^a
		6th grade, 1977	.31^b	9.4	NS	NS	.21^c	NS
		8th grade, 1973	.07	.5	NS	NS	NS	no data
Student report negative sanctions	Black–White	6th grade, 1977	.42^a	17.9	NS	NS	−.35^a	NS
		8th grade, 1973	.24^b	5.6	.18^c	NS	NS	no data
	Hispanic–White	6th grade, 1977	.35^a	12.1	NS	NS	−.32^a	NS
		8th grade, 1973	.30^a	9.0	NS	NS	−.29^a	no data

^{a} $p < .001$.
^{b} $p < .01$.
^{c} $p < .05$.

with that student's characteristics in all four samples for which we had data. In three samples, word knowledge accounts for practically all the variance. Being Black is the only significant variable in the eighth-grade sample.

Conclusions. The findings from three samples of students attending desegregated public schools give little support to the teacher deficit model. Being Hispanic is not a significant factor in teacher evaluations. The two vectors that were reliable statistically were small but positive. Being Black is also a relatively minor factor in teacher ratings. In a total of 14 analyses, being Black had a negative vector 4 times, a positive vector 3 times, and no significant impact 7 times. All the beta coefficients were relatively small. SES is a more salient factor than ethnic group, but neither of these status characteristics are as crucial in teacher evaluations as the student's academic performance and relationship with peers.

Cohen and Roper (1972) theorize that a critical factor producing inter-racial interaction disability in the schools is the almost exclusive emphasis on academic achievement in establishing the rank order of status among students. Our findings tend to confirm that hypothesis. Word knowledge was the most powerful predictor not only of teacher evaluations of competence and future educational and occupational prospects, but was almost the sole predictor of which students would receive negative sanctions.

INTERPERSONAL MODELS AND SOCIAL STRUCTURAL PARADIGMS

At the close of her review of desegregation studies, St. John (1975) concludes that desegregation is a multifaceted process which can be simultaneously beneficial and harmful in its effects, depending upon the extent to which the staff in the school is able to implement an integrated educational experience. She suggests that future research should test theoretically grounded propositions and give greater emphasis to social status factors within the schools. In line with that recommendation, we have been working from a conceptual model which is based on previous research and which permits the development of theoretically grounded propositions that can be tested and that can have implications for social policy.

The Status Equalization Model

The basic theoretical framework is a status equalization model that borrows heavily from the work of Allport (1954), Cohen and Roper (1972), Cohen (1972, 1973), Katz and Cohen (1962), Lohman (1972), and Berger,

Cohen, and Zelditch (1972). Allport (1954) concluded that prejudice could be

> reduced by equal status contact between majority and minority groups in the pursuit of common goals. The effect is greatly enhanced if the contact is sanctioned by institutional support (i.e., by law, custom, or local atmosphere), and if it is of a sort that leads to the perception of common interests and common humanity between members of the two groups. (p. 267)
>
> Contact in a hierarchical social system, or between people who equally lack status (poor whites and poor Negroes), or contacts between individuals who perceive one another as threats, are harmful rather than helpful. . . . To be maximally effective, contact and acquaintance programs should lead to a sense of equality in social status, should occur in ordinary purposeful pursuits, avoid artificiality, and if possible enjoy the sanction of the community in which they occur. . . . While it may help somewhat to place members of different ethnic groups side by side on a job, the gain is greater if these members regard themselves as part of a team. . . . Once again we see how important it is to abolish segregation before optimum conditions of contact and acquaintance can occur. (pp 453–454)

A re-reading of Allport (1954) would have prepared researchers for the contradictory findings from the early atheoretical impact studies. Simply bringing members of different racial or ethnic groups together does not guarantee any particular set of outcomes. From his work, we can draw the following propositions concerning the probable effect of group contact in desegregated schools:

1. Contact among students, staff, and parents of equal status in desegregated schools will reduce racial/ethnic prejudice whereas unequal status contacts will increase prejudice.
2. Equal status contacts will be enhanced if (a) equal status contact is sanctioned by a strong, explicit school policy; (b) if students, staff, and parents of various racial/ethnic groups work together as members of teams in the ordinary, purposeful pursuits of the school; (c) if the school program emphasizes the common interests and common humanity of persons of all racial/ethnic groups through multicultural programs; (d) if contacts take place in a nonhierarchical social system which is nonthreatening for all groups.

More recent empirical and theoretical work has found that achieving status contacts among persons of different racial/ethnic origins is complicated by factors not foreseen in Allport's (1954) earlier model. Katz (1967–1968) found that Blacks in biracial work groups matched on measured intelligence displayed marked social inhibition and subordination to White partners, made fewer proposals, accepted contributions of Whites uncritically, and talked more to Whites than other Blacks. Similar findings were reported in over a dozen other investigations between 1950 and 1960 (Berger *et al*, 1972). Cohen, Lohman, Hall, Lucero, and Roper (1970) reported similar responses in biracial student groups in which White students had higher initiation rates and were more influential than Blacks.

This diverse literature on status organizing processes has been generalized into a single theoretical framework by Berger *et al.* (1972) around the central concept of *diffuse status characteristics*. A diffuse status characteristic: (1) is differentially valued in society; (2) is associated with a set of specific abilities which are perceived as accompanying that status; and (3) arouses general expectations as to the competence or incompetence of persons holding that status. Race, age, and sex are examples of diffuse status characteristics because they fulfill all three aspects of the definition. Persons of differing races, ages, and sexes are valued differentially in society, are perceived as having specific abilities or disabilities, and these perceptions arouse general expectations as to the relative competence of individuals. The theory then specifies that diffuse status characteristics will be activated and will tend to organize the social interaction in the performance of a new task: (1) when the task is valued and individuals are task-focused and collectively oriented; (2) when the individual is perceived as having the status characteristic and the attributes associated with that status; (3) when the group task is one which can be judged as having a successful or unsuccessful outcome, and members are motivated to succeed; and (4) when the task is a collective one in which other's behavior is taken into account. Under these conditions, there will be a general expectation on the part of both low and high status subjects that the high status group will demonstrate superior competence *if* there is no other social basis of discrimination and *if* there has been no previous demonstration that the general expectation does not hold in this particular instance.

Applying this theoretical model to the desegregated school, we would theorize that the diffuse status characteristic of racial/ethnic groups would lead to the general expectation on the part of teachers and of students of both minority and majority groups, that White students would have superior competence. This expectation would lead to an interaction chain in which teachers and students of both groups would expect the minority student to participate at a lower level in quality and quantity to defer to White suggestions, and so forth. This cycle of rank order status differentiation is especially potent in the school setting in which the primary dimension for allocating status is academic performance. The process results in what Cohen (1972) has termed "interracial interaction disability."

Cohen (1973) reports a series of experiments designed to prevent the activation of the diffuse status characteristic of race in student interactions by training Black students in the task of assembling a radio *and* having the Black students then teach the White students the task. She found that the expectations of *both* groups, Black and White, must be modified, otherwise the diffuse status characteristic will be activated, and Black students will continue to play a subordinate role even though they are, in fact, more competent at the task than White students. This finding is particularly significant in relation to school desegregation, for it indicates that attempts to increase the competence of minority students in isolation from majority students are not likely to succeed. "One must also treat the expectations for his performance held by the high status member" (Cohen & Roper, 1972, p. 656).

In a subsequent experiment conducted with Black and White students enrolled for a four-week session, the experimenters attempted to avoid the development of a single rank order of status based on academic ability and the competitive system of individual accountability by eliminating grades and teacher evaluations of individual performance and replacing them with evaluations of the collective performance of small groups. In addition, 33 Black students were given preliminary training on four new tasks which they later taught to 33 White students. Teachers were organized into racially balanced teams and the balance of power and authority between races was maintained throughout. They concluded that five elements of the classroom were critical in developing equal status relationships: (1) student participation in racially mixed groups; (2) experience of success in these groups; (3) strong, explicit norms for interracial cooperation; (4) elimination of teacher evaluation of individuals and individual competition in favor of evaluation of group products and cooperative learning; and (5) the presence of adult role models exemplifying a balance of power and authority between races. Lohman (1972) extended the series of studies by developing a procedure in which a Black male college student served as a role model for Black boys and found that the students who had experienced the Black role model had significantly higher rates of initiating behavior in racially mixed groups and higher rates of influence.

Katz (1967-1968) comes to seven major hypotheses after reviewing the literature. (1) Desegregated situations in which Whites are numerically predominant and have superior power and/or are hostile to minority students will increase social threat and anxiety resulting in impaired performance for minority students. (2) White teacher and White student friendliness to minority students in desegregated schools will increase minority motivation toward scholastic achievement. (3) Since studies indicate that the strength of motivation is at a maximum when the probability of success is .50, achievement motivation for minority students will decline if the academic standards in a desegregated school are substantially higher than those encountered previously and the student is subject to the threat of failure. (4) Direct competition with Whites arouses a fear of failure and loss of confidence which would have a depressing effect on the performance of minority students, especially on verbal-symbolic and perceptual-motor tasks. (5) A minority student's vulnerability to stress will be greatest in those schools in which White students predominate because minority students will not have the supportive effect of members of the same group. (6) The prospect of *successful* competition against a White peer and approval of a White authority figure has greater incentive strength for the minority student than the prospect of successful competition against a minority peer and approval of a minority authority figure. (7) Test situations are most stressful when the comparison group is White, the test administrator is White, and the minority student is told that the test measures "intelligence."

An Integrated Status Equalization Model

Figure 1 presents, schematically, a status equalization model which attempts to integrate the findings and hypotheses from earlier work. There are four classes of variables in the model: contextual variables, educational process variables, equal status contact, and educational outcomes. Both the contextual variables and educational process variables are, to some extent, amenable to policy interventions. Figure 1 presents a path diagram of the hypothesized relationships among the four sets of variables. All variables have been described so that the hypothesized direct and indirect vectors would be positive.

The Contextual Variables

Racial/Ethnic Balance. If the racial/ethnic balance is approximately equal, we would hypothesize that the relative power of the student groups within the school would tend to be equal. Therefore, status equalization processes would be easier to implement within the structure of the school program, and hence, ethnic balance would have an indirect effect on both equal status contacts and educational outcomes through educational processes. In addition, we would hypothesize that it would have a direct effect on equal status contacts and an indirect effect on educational outcomes through equal status contacts. Finally, we would anticipate that ethnic balance would have direct effects on educational outcomes, especially for minority students.

Socioeconomic Status (SES). Large discrepancies in the SES of students from different ethnic/racial groups, especially when the majority students were from the higher socioeconomic levels, would tend to create greater status discrepancies in the school, greater discrepancies in social power, and greater discrepancies in academic performance. This would tend to create the hierarchical statuses which Allport (1954) noted were deleterious to equal status contacts. Hence, we would hypothesize that relatively more equal SES across ethnic groups would have an indirect effect on

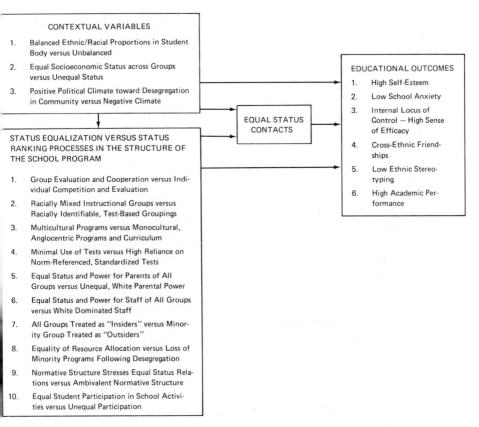

Figure 1. Path diagram of hypothesized relationships among contextual variables, educational process variables, equal status contacts, and educational outcomes in desegregated school.

educational outcomes through facilitating status equalization processes in the school program and through creating more equal status contacts. In addition, it would impact directly on educational outcomes.

Community Normative Climate. Allport (1954) emphasizes the importance of a strong normative structure favoring cooperation and equality. Although the political climate of the community being served by the desegregated school is beyond the direct control of social policy, it will influence to some extent what happens in the school because students will bring to the school attitudes, preconceptions, and behaviors learned in the community. Community norms will influence directly the ease with which the school will be able to implement status equalization practices and the extent to which students in the school are likely to engage in equal status contacts, thus indirectly influencing educational outcomes. We hypothesize there will also be some direct effects on educational outcomes which are not mediated through other variables.

Status Equalization versus Status Ranking Processes

The ten status equalization processes in Figure 1 attempt to translate directly into the educational setting the variables which previous research has shown to be related to equal status contacts and/or to particular educational outcomes. We theorize that these status ranking processes are endemic in American public schools. Because they vary only slightly from school to school, we anticipate that there will be relatively little between school variance in the extent to which these processes are operating. For this reason, the usual survey study which attempts to isolate crucial factors by explaining between school variance will have difficulty tracking the link between these processes and educational outcomes for minority students.

Our overall hypothesis is that these ten status ranking processes are institutional mechanisms by which the rank order of status in the larger society is replicated within each public school and helps to perpetuate the inferior social status of persons from minority racial and ethnic backgrounds from generation to generation. We hypothesize that the processes are additive. Their effect is likely to be exacerbated in the desegregated school and could account for ambiguous findings in earlier studies. Furthermore, they could work at cross-purposes so that a positive vector could be canceled by a negative vector, resulting in no measurable effect on educational outcomes. Hence, the interpersonal processes and the social structure of the desegregated school will need to be consciously modified if there are to be positive outcomes for minority students.

Group Evaluation and Cooperation versus Individual Competition. The traditional school relies heavily upon individual evaluation and rewards which encourage competitive relations among students in the classroom. Academic grades, awards, and teacher approval are bestowed on those who achieve individually rather than to those who assist each other in the learning process. Katz (1967-1968) cites an extensive literature on the debilitating effect which direct competition, especially with Whites, has on the performance of minority persons. Cohen and Roper (1972) found that elimination of individual evaluations and individual competition in favor of cooperative learning was an important factor in producing equality in biracial interaction. We hypothesize that decreasing individual competition in favor of cooperative arrangements will have an indirect effect on educational outcomes through enhancing equal status contacts as well as have direct, positive effects through raising self-esteem, lowering school anxiety, giving students a greater sense of efficacy, nurturing cross-ethnic friendships, reducing ethnic stereotyping, and improving academic performance.

Racially Mixed Instructional Groupings. When classroom groupings are based on test performance and/or academic skills in the standard curriculum, there is a direct replication in the school of the rank order of status in the larger society. Tracking and "homogeneous" grouping, when used in the desegregated school, operate to resegregate students along racial/ethnic lines with minority students being assigned to the "slow" tracks and majority students being assigned to the "accelerated" programs. Although "ability" grouping is widely practiced in schools, there is clear evidence that the practice has a negative effect on low-achieving students and evidence regarding its effectiveness for "superior" groups is inconclusive (Findley & Bryan, 1970). One of Cohen and Roper's (1972) most important findings was that organizing students into cooperative, racially-mixed teams was an important factor in eliminating interracial interaction disability. We hypothesize that racially heterogeneous instructional groupings will have a direct effect on equal status contacts and both direct and indirect effects on educational outcomes.

Multicultural Progams. Monocultural, anglocentric educational programs are traditional in public schools. They derive from a long history in which the public schools were the primary mechanism for socializing immigrant children to conform to the expectations of a society dominated by Anglo-American institutions and values (Karier, Violas, & Spring, 1973; Katz, 1971). The first California statute governing public education required that all instruction be in English. Until recently, it was commom practice for Hispanic students to be reprimanded for speaking Spanish on school grounds in California. According to a recent survey by the United States Civil Rights Commission (1972), the use of Spanish is discouraged in 30% of the elementary schools in Arizona, 13% in California, 16% in Colorado, 30% in New Mexico, and 66% in Texas. Only 4.3% of the Southwest's elementary schools and 7.3% of the secondary schools include Mexican-American history in their curriculum. The omission of Black history and the achievements of other American minorities from standard texts is now generally recognized as a violation of cultural democracy in a pluralistic society. Based on Allport's (1954) findings, we hypothesize that multicultural programs will increase students' sense of their common humanity and have a direct effect upon equal status contracts as well as both direct and indirect effects on educational outcomes.

Minimal Use of Standardized Testing. When public schools use norm-referenced tests of intelligence, aptitude, or achievement to assess and label and classify public school students, a disproportionately large number of children of non-Anglo heritage are labeled as subnormal and mentally retarded (Mercer, 1973). Because norm-referenced tests are constructed to test the student's knowledge of Anglo-American society and do not take cultural background into account, the labeling process recreates the rank order of status in the larger society by labeling majority as more intelligent than minority students. Thus, norm-referenced, standardized tests legitimate the diffuse status characteristics associated with racial/ethnic groups. They serve the latent functions of preserving the superordinate position of majority children, discrediting non-Anglo cultural traditions, and provide the schools with a mechanism for "cooling out" minority parents who criticize the schools by convincing them that defects in the family or the child are responsible for low educational achievement, not the school (Mercer, 1974). Katz (1967-1968) also reported that test situations are most stressful for minority students when they are being compared to majority students, the test administrator is White, and the test is purportedly measuring their intelligence. It is our hypothesis that minimal use of norm-referenced tests will have a direct effect on equal status contacts and both direct and indirect effects on such educational outcomes as self-esteem, school anxiety, sense of efficacy, and academic performance.

Equal Status and Power for Parents of All Groups. Parent power is a dimension of the school environment that is seldom analyzed systematically. However, the importance of adult role models (Lohman, 1972) prompts us to include it as a critical component in achieving equal status relationships among the students in a desegregated school. If the adult power structure in which minority parents participate in the school community mirrors that of the larger society, we hypothesize that interracial interaction disabilities are likely to increase for minority students. If, on the other hand, minority parents participate fully in the power structure of the school, students will have adult models of cooperation and mutual respect. We theorize that the dimension of parent power will directly influence equal status contacts among students as well as have both indirect and direct effects on self-esteem, school anxiety, sense of efficacy, cross-ethnic friendships, ethnic stereotyping, and possibly academic performance.

Equal Status and Power for Staff of All Groups. Frequently, desegregated schools have many fewer minority teachers and administrators than majority teachers and administrators. The schools in the samples reported in Table I through IV had an average of 2% Hispanic and 12% Black teachers. All but a handful of administrators were White males. Paraprofessionals, cafeteria workers, and custodians were mainly Hispanic or Black. Thus, the student in the desegregated school learns through observation that Whites hold higher status than Blacks or Hispanics. Entwisle and Webster (1973, 1974) report a series of studies of the affect of the status characteristics of adults on the ability of the adult to raise a child's expectations for his own performance at schoollike tasks. Based on hundreds of children in both segregated and desegregated schools, they found students performed better, faster, and more effectively when the adult administering reinforcement was of the same race as their own. As reported earlier, Cohen and Roper (1972) concluded that adult role models exemplifying a balance of power and authority was a significant factor in eliminating interracial interaction disability in their experimental summer program. We hypothesize that a multiethnic staff of equal status and power to the White staff will have a positive impact on equal status contacts among students and will directly and indirectly influence educational outcomes such as self-esteem, school anxiety, and ethnic stereotyping.

All Groups Treated As "Insiders". When school desegregation is accomplished by busing, it is not uncommon for teachers and students to perceive the "bused students" as a special category of outsiders. The role of the outsider is further emphasized if only neighborhood students are able to participate in after-school activities, and a one-way busing program transports minority students into predominantly majority neighborhood schools. Cross-busing distributes the burden more equitably across groups. Although there is no research literature that addresses this issue specifically, our observations of desegregated schools lead us to hypothesize that the "insider–outsider" differentiation made between "our" children and the "bused" children by teachers and students alike increases status inequalities, especially when minority students are being bused into majority neighborhoods. We hypothesize that it will have a direct effect on equal status contacts in the school and both indirect and direct effects on other education outcomes.

Equality of Resource Allocation. A primary concern of many minority parents, especially those with children in bilingual and bicultural programs, is that special programs designed to meet the particular needs of their children will be eliminated following desegregation. Although most public schools have music teachers, art teachers, speech therapists, and a wide variety of special resources for majority students, it is only recently that schools have begun to develop the kinds of programs and resources required to meet the specific needs of minority children. When school desegregation distributes minority students throughout the system so that individual schools lack sufficient numbers of students from particular groups to justify continuation of such programs, they are likely to be eliminated. We hypothesize that there will be a direct relationship between the presence of resources and programs designed to meet the needs of minority students and educational outcomes.

Normative Structure Stresses Equal Status Relations. Both Allport (1954) and Cohen and Roper (1972) report that explicit norms which support equal status contacts among students, parents, and teachers of all ethnic and racial groups are a significant factor in achieving equal status contacts. When the principal of a school favors either minority or majority students in enforcing the behavioral code, the normative structure is undermined and the situation is likely to precipitate interethnic hostilities

(Mercer, 1968). We hypothesize that equal status norms will have a direct effect on equal status contacts and influence educational outcomes both directly and indirectly.

Equal Student Participation in School Activities. The United States Commission on Civil Rights (1971) found that Mexican-American students in five southwestern states did not participate in extracurricular activities at the same rate as majority students, even when they comprised a majority of the school enrollment. When Mexican-American students were a minority in the school, their representation was lowest in those activities having the greatest prestige and influence. The tendency of majority students to hold positions of greatest power and prestige would undermine equal status relations. We hypothesize that the dimension of student power is related directly to equal status relations and effects educational outcomes.

CONCLUSION

We believe that the time has come to move away from atheoretical attempts to measure the impact of desegregation. That approach assumes a simple set of linear effects that cannot explain the complexities of the real world of the school. Models that assume deficits in students and their families pose serious value dilemmas in a pluralistic society and lead to questionable public policies of either educational segregation or highly ethnocentric attempts to socialize minority groups to the values, beliefs, and life style of the politically dominant group. Teacher deficit models do not hold up when tested empirically and are likely to lead to superficial interventions in which teachers are blamed for institutional processes beyond their control. The status equalization model would provide a framework for developing and testing theoretically grounded propositions concerning educational processes in the public schools that would be amenable to public policy.

REFERENCES

Allport, G. W. *The nature of prejudice.* Reading, Mass.: Addison-Wesley, 1954.

Armor, D. J. School and family effects on black and white achievement. In F. Mosteller & D. P. Moynihan (Eds.), *On equality of educational opportunity.* New York: Vintage, 1972.

Becker, H. S. Social class variations in the teacher–pupil relationship. *Journal of Educational Sociology,* 1952, *25,* 451–465.

Bereiter, C. A non-psychological approach to early compensatory education. In M. Deutsch, I. Katz, & A. Jensen (Eds.), *Social class, race, and psychological development.* New York: Holt, Rinehart & Winston, 1968.

Berger, J., Cohen, B. P., & Zelditch, J. Status characteristics and social interaction. *American Sociological Review*, 1972, *37*, 241–255.

Bernstein, B. Language and social class. *British Journal of Sociology*, 1960, *11*, 271–276.

Bloom, R., Whiteman, M., & Deutsch, M. Race and social class as separate factors related to social environment. *American Journal of Sociology*, 1965, *LXX*, 471–476.

Campbell, D. T., & Stanley, J. C. *Experimental and quasi-experimental designs for research*. Chicago: Rand McNally, 1963.

Cohen, E. G. Interracial interaction disability. *Human Relations*, 1972, *25*, 9–24.

Cohen, E. G. Modifying the effects of social structure. *American Behavioral Scientist*, 1973, *16*, 861–878.

Cohen, E. G., & Roper, S. S. Modification of interracial interaction disability: An application of status characteristic theory. *American Sociological Review*, 1972, 37, 643–657.

Cohen, E. G., Lohman, M., Hall, K., Lucero, D., & Roper, S. Expectation training I: Altering the effects of a racial status characteristic. *Technical Report No. 1*, Stanford, California: School of Education, 1970.

Coleman, J. S., Campbell, E. Q., Hobson, C. J., McPartland, J., Mood, A. M., Weinfeld, F. D., & York, R. L. *Report on equality of educational opportunity*. U. S. Office of Education, Department of Health, Education, and Welfare, Washington, D. C.: U. S. Government Printing Office, 1966.

Davis, W. A. *Social-class influences upon learning*. Cambridge, Mass.: Harvard University Press, 1948.

Davis, W. A., & Havighurst, R. J. Social-class and color differences in childrearing. *American Sociological Review*, 1946, *11*, 698–710.

Deutsch, M., & Brown, B. Social influences in negro–white intelligence differences. *Journal of Social Issues*, 1964, 24–35.

Entwisle, D. R., & Webster, M. Status factors in expectation raising. *Sociology of Education*, 1973, 115–126.

Entwisle, D., & Webster, M. Expectations in mixed racial groups. *Sociology of Education*, 1974, 301–318.

Eysenck, H. J. *The IQ argument: Race, intelligence, and education*. New York: Library Press, 1971.

Findley, W. G., & Bryan, M. M. *Ability grouping: 1970*. Center for Educational Improvement, College of Education, University of Georgia, Athens, Georgia, 1970.

Glazer, N. Foreward. In N. H. St. John (Ed.), *School desegregation: Outcomes for children*. New York: Wiley, 1975.

Goldstein, B. *Low income youth in urban areas*. New York: Holt, Rinehart & Winston, 1967.

Gottlieb, D. Teaching and students: The views of negro and white teachers. *Sociology of Education*, 1964.

Gordon, E. W. Programs of compensatory education. In M. Deutsch, I. Katz, & A. Jensen (Eds.), *Social class, race, and psychological development*. New York: Holt, Rinehart & Winston, 1968.

Gray, S. W., & Klaus, R. A. An experimental preschool program for culturally deprived children. *Child Development*, 1965, *36*, 887–898.

Gray, S. W., & Klaus, R. A. The early training project: A seventh year report. *Child Development*, 1970, *41*, 909–924.

Harvey, D. G., & Slatin, G. T. The relationship between the child's SES and teacher's expectations: A test of the middle class bias hypothesis. *Social Forces*, 1975, *54*, 1–13.

Hess, R. D., & Shipman, V. Early experience and the socialization of cognitive modes in children. *Child Development*, 1966, *34*, 869–886.

Hollingshead, A. B. *Elmtown's youth*. New York: Wiley, 1949.

Jackson, G., & Cosca, C. The inequality of educational opportunity in the southwest: An observational study of ethnically mixed classrooms. *American Educational Research Journal,* 1974, *11,* 219–229.

Jencks, C. *Inequality: A reassessment of the effect of family and schooling in America.* New York: Basic, 1972.

Jensen, A. Social class and verbal learning. In M. Deutsch, I. Katz, & A. Jensen (Eds.), *Social class, race, and psychological development.* New York: Holt, Rinehart & Winston, 1968.

Jensen, A. R. How much can we boost IQ and scholastic achievement? *Harvard Educational Review,* 1969, *39,* 1–123.

Jensen, A. R. Do schools cheat minority children? *Educational Research,* 1971, *14,* 3–28.

Johnson, E. B., Gerard, H. B., & Miller, N. Teacher influences in the desegregated classroom. In H. B. Gerard & N. Miller (Eds.), *School desegregation.* New York: Plenum, 1975.

Karier, C. J., Violas, P., & Spring, J. *Roots of crisis: American education in the twentieth century.* Chicago: Rand McNally, 1973.

Karnes, M. B., Teska, J. A., Hodgins, A. S., & Badger, E. D. Educational intervention at home by mothers of disadvantaged infants. *Child Development,* 1970, *41,* 925–935.

Katz, M. B. *Class, bureaucracy and schools: The illusion of educational change in America.* New York: Praeger, 1971.

Katz, I. Desegregation or integration in public schools: The policy implications of research. *Integrated Education,* 1967–1968.

Katz, I., & Cohen, M. The effects of training Negroes upon cooperative problem solving in biracial teams. *Journal of Abnormal and Social Psychology,* 1962, *64,* 319–325.

Lohman, M. Changing a racial status ordering: Some implications for integration efforts. *Education and Urban Society,* 1972, *4,* 383–402.

Marans, A. E., & Lourie, R. Hypotheses regarding the effects of child-rearing patterns on the disadvantaged child. In J. Hellmuth (Ed.), *Disadvantaged child (Vol 1).* New York: Brunner/Mazel, 1967.

Mercer, J. R. Issues and dilemmas in school desegregation: A case study. *Proceedings of the 17th western regional conference on testing problems.* Educational Testing Service, San Francisco, 1968.

Mercer, J. R. Institutionalized anglocentrism: Labeling mental retardates in the public schools. In P. Orleans & W. Russell (Eds.), *Race, change, and urban society: Urban affairs annual review* (Vol. 5). Los Angeles: Sage, 1971.

Mercer, J. R. Who is normal? Two perspectives on mild mental retardation. In E. G. Jaco (Ed.), *Patients, physicians and illness* (rev. ed.). Glencoe, Ill.: Free Press, 1972.

Mercer, J. R. *Labeling the mentally retarded.* Berkeley: University of California Press, 1973.

Mercer, J. R. A policy statement on assessment procedures and the rights of children. *Harvard Educational Review,* 1974, *44,* 125–141.

Mercer, J. R. Test "validity," "bias," and "fairness:" An analysis from the perspective of the sociology of knowledge. *Interchange,* 1978–1979, *9,* 1–16.

Mercer, J. R. *System of multicultural pluralistic assessment: Technical and conceptual manual.* New York: Psychological Corporation, 1979.

Mercer, J. R., & Brown, W. C. Racial differences in IQ: Fact or artifact? In C. Senna (Ed.), *The fallacy of IQ.* New York: Third Press, 1973.

Mercer, J. R., Coleman, M., & Harloe, J. Racial/ethnic segregation and desegregation in American public education. In W. Gordon (Ed.), *Uses of the sociology of education: The 73rd yearbook of the national society for the study of education* (Vol. 2). Chicago: University of Chicago Press, 1974.

National Institute of Education. *The desegregation literature: A critical appraisal.* U.S. Department of Health, Education, and Welfare. Washington, D.C. 20208, July 1976.

Pasamanick, B., & Knobloch, H. The contribution of some organic factors to school retardation in Negro children. *Journal of Negro Education,* 1958, *27,* 4–9.

Pavenstedt, E. A comparison of the child-rearing environment of upper-lower and very low-lower class families. *American Journal of Orthopsychiatry*, 1965, *35*, 89–98.

Reiss, A. J. *Occupations and social status*. New York: Free Press, 1961.

Rist, R. C. Student social class and teacher expectations: The self-fulfilling prophecies in ghetto education. *Harvard Educational Review*, 1970, *40*, 411–451.

Rosen, B. C. The achievement syndrome: A psychocultural dimension of social stratification. *American Sociological Review*, 1956, *21*, 203–211.

Rosen, B. C., & D'Andrade, R. The psychological origins of achievement motivation. *Sociometry*, 1959, *22*, 185–218.

St. John, N. H. *School desegregation: Outcomes for children*. New York: Wiley, 1975.

Schaefer, E. S. Parents as educators: Evidence from cross-sectional, longitudinal and intervention research. *The young child: Reviews of research* (Vol. 2). Washington, D.C.: National Association for the Education of Young Children, 1972.

Sewell, W., & Hauser, R. Causes and consequences of higher education: Models of the status attainment process. In W. Sewell (Ed.), *Schooling and achievement in American society*. New York: Academic, 1976.

Sewell, W., Haller, A. O., & Strauss, M. A. Social status and educational and occupational aspiration. *American Sociological Review*, 1957, *22*, 67–73.

Silberman, C. *Crisis in black and white*. New York: Random House, 1964.

Stendler-Lavatelli, E. B. Environmental intervention in infancy and childhood. In M. Deutsch, I. Katz, & A. Jensen (Eds.), *Social class, race, and psychological development*. New York: Holt, Rinehart, & Winston, 1968.

Strodtbeck, F. L. The hidden curriculum of the middle class home. In C. W. Hunnicutt (Ed.), *Urban education and cultural deprivation*. Syracuse, N.Y.: Syracuse University Press, 1964.

Tulkin, S. R., & Kagan, J. Mother–child interaction in the first year of life. *Child Development*, 1972, *43*, 31–41.

United States Commission on Civil Rights. *The unfinished education: Outcomes for minorities in the five southwestern states*. Mexican-American Education Series, Report II. Washington, D.C.: U.S. Government Printing Office, 1971.

United States Commission on Civil Rights. *The excluded student: Educational practices affecting Mexican-Americans in the southwest*. Mexican-American Education Series, Report III. Washington, D.C.: U.S. Government Printing Office, 1972.

Weikart, D., & Lambie, D. Preschool intervention through a home teaching program. In J. Hellmuth (Ed.), *Disadvantaged Child* (Vol. 2). New York: Brunner/Mazel, 1968.

Weinberg, M. *Minority students: A research appraisal*. Department of Health, Education, and Welfare, Washington, D.C.: U.S. Government Printing Office, 1977.

Whiteman, M., Brown, B., & Deutsch, M. Some effects of social class and race on children's language and intellectual abilities. In M. Deutsch (Ed.), *The disadvantaged child*. New York: Basic, 1967.

Whiteman, M., & Deutsch, M. Social disadvantage as related to intellective and language development. In M. Deutsch, I. Katz, & A. Jensen (Eds.), *Social class, race, and psychological development*. New York: Holt, Rinehart, & Winston, 1968.

Wilson, A. B. Social stratification and academic achievement. In A. H. Passow (Ed.), *Education in depressed areas*. New York: Teachers College Press, 1963.

Wortis, H., Bardach, J. L., Cutler, R., Rue, R., & Freedman, A. Child-rearing practices in a low socioeconomic group. *Pediatrics*, 1963, *32*, 298–311.

13

Making School Desegregation Work

Norman Miller

INTRODUCTION

The first section of this chapter contains a set of principles about school desegregation. In preparing them, I (Miller, 1977) specifically attempted to construct a set of guidelines that would appeal broadly to social scientists and at the same time reflect current evidence and research related to school desegregation. Over 25 outstanding social scientists, including several past presidents of the American Psychological Association and the American Sociological Association, endorsed them. All had established their reputation for work in desegregation and/or closely related areas such as prejudice, interpersonal relations, and social mobility. Subsequently, these principles were submitted by the Los Angeles City Board of Education to the court of Judge Paul Eagly as part of their second desegregation plan. I prepared them after the court had rejected the first plan submitted by the Los Angeles Board of Education, hoping they would not only educate the court, but also influence the school board and the district in their preparation of a new plan. In later sections of the chapter I discuss in detail recent data that bear on a notion which is the cornerstone for much theorizing about how school desegregation produces academic benefit for minority children, namely, the lateral transmission of values hypothesis. Finally, I discuss briefly some alternate classroom and educational strategies for desegregation.

NORMAN MILLER • Department of Psychology, University of Southern California, Los Angeles, California 90007. Preparation of this chapter was facilitated by support from National Institute of Mental Health grant MH 26094; Norman Miller, Principal Investigator.

er the *Crawford*[1] decision of the California Supreme Court, the Los Angeles School District was required to produce a desegregation plan that provides its students with an "integrated learning experience." The ultimate goal is to eliminate the harms to minority students that flow from the maintenance of segregated schools. *Crawford*, like most court decisions, does not define desegregation, or specify particular remedies for segregated schools. It specifies only that a district must make meaningful progress toward *alleviating* racial isolation. It also specifically directs attention to the long-term effects of a desegregation program. At the same time, in its willingness to accept a plan that is "reasonable and feasible," it recognizes the need to balance costs of various sorts—financial and educational—when devising a desegregation plan.

The principles below bear on the design of a desegregation program that is most likely to meet the goals of *Crawford*. Although *Crawford* does not specifically state or define the harms of segregation, I assume they share substantial overlap with those explicitly and implicitly recognized by *Brown*[2] in the 1954 Supreme Court decision. Consequently, attention must be directed toward alleviating racial isolation, enabling minority students to achieve as high a level of academic achievement as White students, improving intergroup relations, and positively affecting the self-concepts of children in the district.

Two facts hindering the effectiveness of any desegregation program need to be made clear at the outset. They are important because they specify two constraints, neither financial nor logistical, that set the stage for the principles to be enumerated below.

First, it is very difficult to devise and implement a desegregation plan that will meet these goals. A dispassionate review of the desegregation literature makes this quite apparent (Armor, 1972; Clement, Eisenhart, & Wood, 1976; Cohen, 1975; Crain, Armor, Christen, King, McLaughlin, Sumner, Thomas, & Vanecko, 1974; Gerard & Miller, 1975; Kurtz, 1975; Mercer, 1973; O'Reilly & Solomon, 1976; Pettigrew, Useem, Normand, & Smith, 1973; Purl & Dawson, 1973; Stephan, 1978; St. John, 1975; Weinberg, 1977). Simply distributing students in each school in proportion to their frequency in the district as a whole, without simultaneous initiation of numerous other programs, is very unlikely to provide a desirable kind of integrated learning experience, or to improve academic achievement of minority children, their self-concepts, or intergroup relations. Glazer (1975), Cohen (1975), Amir (1976), and Kirp (1976) reflect the more realistic, if not

---

[1] *Crawford* v. *Board of Education of Los Angeles*, 30485, 17 C. 3d (1976) 280-310.
[2] *Brown* v. *Topeka Board of Education*, 347 U.S. 483 (1954).

pessimistic, outlook for desegregation programs that has been forced upon us by existing data. Glazer asserts, "There was no reason to believe that desegregation alone—the achieving of some statistical mix of children of different races—would raise the educational achievement of Black children and hence their self-image, or improve race relations." In accord with Gerard and Miller (1975), he asserts that such an assumption "was naive." Cohen (1975) states:

> Perhaps courts and other decision makers would come to realize that trying to change the status order of an entire society by superficial change in the racial composition of an organization which traditionally has reflected faithfully the power and status order in society at large is not an easy thing to do either politically or practically. (p. 299)

Amir (1976) concurs. After reviewing over 250 studies concerned with intergroup contact and prejudice, he seriously questions

> whether increasing ethnic contact in school is the ultimate tool in improving the attitudes and the ethnic relations between the children. . . . The question can be raised whether such contact necessitates the deeper, more involved interactions that are sometimes referred to as "true integration." . . . However, social planning can make the difference of whether one will like it, just accept it, or even fight against it. (pp. 293–294)

After reviewing the history of the San Francisco desegregation case, Kirp (1976) turns to consider its consequences:

> The kind of education that children in San Francisco and elsewhere presently receive is shaped by the reality of court-ordered desegregation. Yet those who achieved this "victory" have not been involved with the immensely more complicated business of providing an intelligent, humane, integrated educational program in racially and socioeconomically heterogeneous schools. It is tempting, but unhelpful and simplistic to label such behavior as irresponsible. The point, rather, is to inquire how desegregation might be made to work in the light of that sobering history. . . . (p. 606–607)

Therefore, desegregation programs that attend more pointedly and carefully to all the dimensions relevant to providing and maintaining an integrated learning experience must be tried. Second, in Los Angeles, as well as other major cities, the percentage of White children in the district is steadily decreasing. This remains true regardless of whether or not one agrees with arguments suggesting that desegregation may increase the rate of White loss. Much debate has centered around the thesis of *White flight*. There is no debate, however, about a separate, independent, demographic trend in the United States—the steady departure of Whites from the central city. Coleman, Kelly, and Moore (1975) state:

> The emerging problem with regard to school desegregation is the problem of segregation between central city and suburbs; and in addition, that current means

by which schools are being desegregated are intensifying that problem, rather than reducing it. The emerging problem of school desegregation in large cities is the problem of metropolitan area residential segregation, Black central cities, and White suburbs, *brought about by loss of Whites from the central cities*. This loss is intensified by extensive school desegregation in those central cities, but in cities with high proportions of Blacks and predominantly White suburbs, it proceeds at a relatively rapid rate with or without desegregation. (Emphasis added; pp. 79–80)

Pettigrew and Green (1976), despite their ceaseless criticism of Coleman's thesis regarding desegregation and White flight, state in specific reference to this quote that "most specialists would agree with the basic thrust of this conclusion" (p. 21).

Examination of metropolitan areas in the United States shows that the percentage of Blacks living in the central city has remained relatively stable in recent years: 77.4% in 1950; 79.5% in 1960; 79.4% in 1969. This means, of course, that the percentage of Blacks outside the central city (but in the metropolitan area) also remained steady at just over 20%. On the other hand, the data for Whites show a quite different picture. Whereas for Whites the percentage living in the central city in 1950 was 56.6%, by 1960 it had shifted down to 47.9%, and by 1969 was down to 40%. At the same time, the total number of both Blacks and Whites living in metropolitan areas was increasing. Blacks increased from 8.4 million in 1950 to over 15.5 million by 1969; similarly, the Whites increased from approximately 80 million in 1950 to almost 120 million by 1969.

Any imaginable desegregation program depends on the continued existence of White children in the district. Therefore, a good desegregation plan must include features that will reduce or reverse the trend of decreasing White enrollments. This is particularly true for districts in which the percentage of White students is already below 40% or districts in which "metropolitan plans" are legally, politically, or logistically infeasible.

In the sections to follow, principles will be organized around three major points, each of which is critical to the maximization of long-term benefits from a desegregation program: (1) The desegregation program must be educationally sound and enable schools to continue to fulfill their educational obligation; (2) interracial contacts must occur under circumstances that are likely to promote positive intergroup relations and create an appreciation of diverse cultures; (3) the long-run success of any desegregation plan rests on its ability to create and maintain community acceptance. A lack of community acceptance will reduce its chances of achieving long-term benefits. Although, for the purposes of presentation, each principle is listed separately, they form a complex interdependent system in which each influences the others. This interdependence must be kept in mind when developing any desegregation plan.

Educational Obligations

The evidence from past research on school desegregation shows that, to date, desegregation plans have not produced dramatic benefits to minority children. It argues for a skeptical view and suggests that much care needs to be given to a variety of factors that contribute to the success or failure of desegregation in any particular education setting. It suggests a need to devise and test new desegregation strategies and procedures, to implement innovations carefully, to evaluate their results systematically, and to modify them responsively.

The Integrity of the Educational Program Must Be Maintained or Improved

Schools find it difficult to educate the poor successfully, regardless of their race or ethnic background. Whatever the reason, educators as a whole need to know a good deal more about how to teach these children effectively. One could argue that if this is the case, there is little reason to hesitate about implementing massive districtwide desegregation programs. According to this line of thought, if education for the poor is typically ineffective, one need not be concerned about the possibility of additional loss in educational quality as a consequence of the desegregation plan. Several considerations argue strongly against this view. *Crawford* (1976) specifies that desegregation is a means to an end. Effective education for all is one of the ends. The means must not be distorted into the end. Both minority and White parents alike strongly value education (Gerard & Miller, 1975). Among an array of various social goals, Blacks rank "good education" second, a ranking positioned only below that of "more employment opportunities" and one that is noticeably higher than that given to it by Whites (Wilson, 1970). Education has been viewed historically as the key to social mobility.[3] The *Crawford* decisions itself regards education explicitly

---

[3] This is not to deny the importance of Jencks's (Jencks, 1973; Jencks, Smith, Acland, Bane, Cohen, Gintis, Heyns, & Michelson, 1972) analyses showing the modest contribution of education to earnings in the United States. However, in a recent study of inequality in six American communities, Curtis and Jackson (1977) argued that education does have important functions. Although alienation, feelings of powerlessness, and a distrust of the government have been known to characterize those with low incomes in the United States, their work suggests that a lack of education may play an important role, separate from low income, in creating this distrust in a stable normative system. In other words, solving problems of income inequality would not remove this alienation. "The barely literate in a highly literate society is especially cut off from participation in social life" (p. 326). To put this somewhat differently, Jencks argues that the ties between income and either education or occupation are so tenuous that equalizing the population with respect to education or occupa-

as the avenue to occupational and social mobility:

> Indeed as we emphasized in *Serrano*, the "fundamental" nature of the right to an
> equal education derives in large part from the crucial role that education plays,
> "preserving an individual's opportunity to compete successfully in the economic
> marketplace, despite a disadvantaged background. . . . [T]he public schools of
> this state are the bright hope for entry of the poor and oppressed into the
> mainstream of American society." (*Crawford* v. *Board of Education*, 1976,
> p. 297)

Moreover, there are, indeed, instances in which particular schools have been relatively successful in educating the poor (Edmonds, 1976; Mercer, 1975; Orfield, 1975). Given the public desire for quality education and the fact that such concern constitutes part of the initial impetus for school desegregation, the design of desegregation plans must insure that instruction along the basic educational dimensions—learning to read, write, perform basic mathematical computations, to speak clearly, to be informed, and to think abstractly—not be impaired.

Desegregation Plans Should Be Innovative and Flexible

Since previous approaches to desegregation have not been demonstrably successful, new procedures need to be tried. To take a specific problem as an example, most proponents of desegregation stress the

---

tion would do little to equalize the distribution of income. Consequently, Jencks suggests that the best way to equalize the distribution of income is through more direct means of redistribution. Curtis and Jackson, however, argue that "ties between income and many aspects of life style are so tenuous that equalization of income would produce very little change in many current patterns of behavior and attitudes." In other words, redistribution of income would not enable those who are now poor to attain the level and feeling of cultural participation that those with more income currently experience. Increased education, they contend, would produce this effect.

At the same time, it is important to point out that Jencks *et al.* (1972), Blau and Duncan (1967), Duncan, Featherman, and Duncan (1972), and Sewell and his associates (Sewell & Haller, 1969; Sewell, Haller, & Ohlendorf, 1970; Sewell & Hauser, 1975) all show that education has a substantial relation to occupational attainment. Further, all these studies also show a strong relation between fathers' education (and also mothers' where reported) and sons' occupation. This literature suggests that educational attainment can contribute importantly to equalizing social-occupational status between minorities and Whites. The issue is complicated somewhat by the fact that equal levels of educational attainment do not reflect equal levels of educational achievement. As Porter (1974), Portes and Wilson (1976), DeBord, Griffen, and Clark (1977), Kerckoff and Campbell (1977), and others have noted, the tie between educational achievement and attainment is much stronger for White students than for minority students. For the latter, educational aspirations or motivation are seen as more importantly contributing to eventual educational attainment than past educational achievement *per se*. Although school desegregation has been thought to contribute positively to both these factors—motivation and scholastic achievement—these gains are not the consistent rule.

importance of scholastic achievement norms within the school or classroom. Particularly in cities such as Los Angeles, where White children are numerically a minority, peer group norms emphasizing Black or Mexican-American solidarity may emerge in desegregated schools and create special problems. Triggered by perceptions of average achievement differences, minority students may adopt the characteristic lower-class ideology found among lower-class Whites as well as other racial-ethnic groups. This ideology, which emphasizes anti-sissy, anti-teacher's pet, pro-tough attitudes, may make the studious minority student feel like a traitor to his peers in the minority group. Techniques to minimize the emergence and influence of such norms need to be developed and tested.

Taking another example, little is known about those specific teacher characteristics that make for effective education (Boocock, 1966; Hanushek, 1971; Crain et al., 1974, Vol. 1, p. 57). As will be argued later, this is particularly true for the desegregated setting.

Problems like these suggest that programs should "start small" in order to provide ample planning and development time (Crain et al., 1974, Vol. 2, p. 41). They suggest that a variety of different procedures should be explored simultaneously. The long-term goal of providing an effective integrated learning experience for as many children as possible rests on achieving success in the initial stages.

The Components of Desegregation Plans Must Be Evaluated; Instructional and Administrative Staff Must Be Held Accountable

No plan can be modified effectively without adequate evaluation of its effects and its impact on students, communities, staff, and administration. Evaluation must not only provide information on the extent to which a plan is achieving its aims, but must also provide information on how to modify its ingredients so as to increase future effectiveness. For meaningful evaluation to occur, those responsible for it should have some independence from the district, and their employment should not depend upon the outcome of the evaluation.

Evaluation itself, however, is of no value unless the information it produces is used. The information it provides must enable staff and administration to be held accountable to the community and to the school board. It must elicit changes. Those principals and teachers who produce tangible, observable improvements on basic educational dimensions and do so in conjunction with an integrated learning experience must receive tangible recognition. Those who do not must be induced and encouraged to change their behavior. When such a policy is implemented with resolve, children will benefit educationally. Steps to elicit the active cooperation teachers and principals in implementing a program of educational ɔuntability warrant high priority.

Maximizing Beneficial Interracial Contact

Desegregation Plans Should Explicitly Implement the Conditions for Favorable Contact

The social science literature specifies a number of prerequisites for maximizing the likelihood of improved intergroup relations when interethnic contact occurs.

The status of the members of the interacting ethnic groups should be approximately equal (Allport, 1954; Amir, 1976; Pettigrew, 1971). Although schools have no immediate power to eradicate the average socioeconomic differences that separate Whites from Blacks and Browns, they can take two steps toward providing equal status contact. They can organize intergroup contact around tasks or curriculum segments that are most likely to minimize the existing inequalities in status and to maximize opportunities to establish equalities and similarities between the interacting children. Additionally, by selection or by training, they can provide teachers for integrated learning experiences who behave with equality toward the children of the various racial-ethnic backgrounds.

Steps must be taken to create positive perceptions of the respective groups as a result of the contact. Again, teachers play a critical role. White and minority children will be inclined to model their behavior on that of the teacher. Teachers need to receive accurate feedback about the extent to which they are indeed creating a setting in which this positive modeling can have favorable consequences. Such feedback must be designed to increase their likelihood of changing their behavior rather than prodding them to act defensively and reducing the future likelihood of change on their part. The same concerns apply to principals and other administrators as well, since they, in many instances, seem to set the "climate" of the schools they supervise (Orfield, 1975).

The activities in the contact situation should require interdependence among children of differing racial-ethnic backgrounds. Further, the tasks should require cooperation toward superordinate or common goals rather than separate or independent goals for each student (Aronson, 1975; Cohen, 1975; Cook, 1969; Johnson & Johnson, 1975; Sherif, 1966; Sherif, Harvey, White, Hood, & Sherif, 1961; Sherif & Sherif, 1953). This is not meant to imply a reduction or curtailment of individualized instruction, but rather to emphasize the use of cooperative learning, group grading, or other group products in the contact setting.

The psychological climate of the classroom peer group has impact on students' academic achievement. Particularly important peer group factors are norms stressing academic achievement (Pettigrew, 1971) as well as help-fulness and emotional support (Schmuck, 1968). Childrens' acceptance of one another as friends across racial-ethnic boundaries is particularly important if White scholastic achievement norms are to have impact on minority students (Gerard & Miller, 1975; Lewis & St. John, 1974; Schmuck, 1968). Students' academic performance is associated with their feelings about themselves (Weber, Cook, & Campbell, 1971) and relations with classmates influence these self-appraisals.

Lastly, the contact must not be ephemeral, but must have some continuation or duration on a day-to-day basis in order to provide an opportunity for impact.

Harmful situations are those in which the contact either increases the competition between students differing in racial-ethnic background, produces unpleasant or tension-laden interaction, lowers the prestige or status of one group relative to another, or emphasizes moral and ethnic standards on the part of one group that are objectionable to the other (Amir, 1976). Again, teachers and principals have an important role in avoiding them.

Desegregation Plans Should Minimize the Adverse Effects of the Achievement Gap

True performance differences between minority students and Whites exist on the average for most standardized measures of academic achievement (Coleman, Campbell, Hobson, McPartland, Mood, Weinfeld, & York, 1966; Gerard & Miller, 1975). These differences cause problems. They help to substantiate and maintain stereotypes that depict the White child as "smarter" than the minority child. The inevitable social comparison of "own performance" to "others' performance" confirms prior stereotypic characteristics of the racial-ethnic groups, which, in turn, acts to reduce the academic motivation of the minority student. This has been noted by Clarke and Campbell (1955), Cohen (1975), Gerard and Miller (1975), Katz (1968), and others. Amir (1976) specifically recommends attempting to equalize the task performance status of the respective groups if other important dimensions of inequality naturally occur (e.g., socioeconomic differences). Cohen and Roper (1973) show that explicit training on the relevant task dimension, when given beforehand to minority students, can act to break this "stereotype-performance" cycle if it is coordinated with procedures to disrupt the typical dominance by White students over their minority peers in their social interaction with each other.

It is, therefore, a good idea to structure intergroup contact around some aspect of the curriculum that does not explicitly emphasize reading and mathematics, since these are the academic performance dimensions on which the average performance levels of Whites and minority students are most likely to differ. Instead, intergroup contact situations structured around a social studies or science program during the elementary or junior high school years (Aronson, 1975) provide the flexibility to make these performance differences in math and reading less salient. At the same time, the complexities of race relations in the United States should be addressed directly within the context of social studies programs. An increased awareness of real differences between racial-ethnic groups and their role in prejudicial attitudes (Campbell, 1967) should be beneficial (Glock, Wuthnow, Pilliavin, & Spencer, 1975).

Use of Criterion-Referenced Testing Should Be Expanded

The use of criterion-referenced testing, in coordination with specific curriculum plans, should operate to help minimize or counter the cyclic reaction between the academic achievement gap and racial-ethnic stereotypes mentioned above. Criterion-referenced testing emphasizes the acquisition of specific knowledge regarding the particular curriculum module that is being taught. More traditional, standardized achievement testing is norm-referenced. It compares the performance of an individual child to the norms established by the test developer. Frequently, these norms are based on performance of an entirely or predominantly White sample. The existing achievement gap between minority and White children means that minority children almost inevitably perform poorly compared to Whites. Criterion-referenced tests minimize intergroup competition and, to some extent, ameliorate the almost inevitable "put down" that the minority child experiences from norm-referenced tests. Criterion-referenced testing goes hand in hand with individualized instruction—a teaching strategy that attempts to assess a child's current level of skills for the purpose of tailoring instruction to it. Whereas norm-referenced testing invidiously acts to label the minority child as inferior and creates expectations on the part of teacher and child that interfere with learning (and thereby maintains his subordinate or inferior position), criterion-referenced testing may, to some extent, minimize these debilitating labeling effects.[4]

---

[4] Another feature of most standardized norm-referenced tests that adds to this problem is that they measure the acquisition of knowledge more abstractly and rely more heavily on proper use and knowledge of grammatical and other "English language" skills. The "bidialectical thesis" contends that Blacks (as well as Mexican-American and other non-English speaking students) use a language structure that differs from standard American English (Baratz & Baratz, 1970; Cazden, 1966; Labov, 1969; Stewart 1964; Torrey, 1970; Williams, 1970). Consequently, the standardized achievement test further penalizes the minority student by being less culture fair. Again, this is not to argue against the mastery of English by minority students, but instead, to avoid the debilitating motivational effects of the labeling process that flow from such testing.

The point here is not to mislead children or prevent them from knowing about their true performance levels. A realistic view of one's abilities is healthy. Instead, criterion-referenced testing, along with the teaching style and attitudes that seem to dovetail with it, is more likely to disrupt the cycle linking labeling, self-denigration, motivational malaise, and continued academic inferiority. Criterion-referenced testing, by itself, cannot cure the academic achievement gap, but it can help create a climate where teachers can provide continual positive reinforcement for whatever progress a particular child is making instead of habitually reiterating his failure to meet a middle-class White standard of performance.

If criterion-referenced testing procedures cannot be implemented throughout an entire district, they should, at minimum, be used in the contact situation.

Multicultural Curricula and Programs Should Be Coordinated with Interracial Contact

Many minority parents feel that schools with a monocultural emphasis do not meet the needs of their children. The benefit of interracial contact will be enhanced by coordinating a multicultural curriculum program with it. A multicultural program can help create the conditions of equal status contact by raising minority self-esteem (Arciniega, n.d.). Additionally, the presence of a multicultural program meshes nicely with a contact situation structured around social studies. In contrast, a monocultural emphasis implicitly relegates minority culture, language, and custom to an inferior status.

To implement a multicultural program is a serious and substantial undertaking. It requires, at each grade level, the development of new curriculum models and materials for all phases of the educational program. In addition, it requires that teachers be trained carefully, not only in terms of how to use such materials, but also in regard to their attitudes and approach to students.

Desegregation Plans Should Rely on Voluntary Action and Choice as Extensively as Possible

Choice and voluntary behavior produces commitment and favorable attitudes (Brehm & Cohen, 1962; Festinger, 1957; Gerard, 1965; Kiesler, 1971; Zimbardo, 1969). Restricting choice and freedom can produce resistance and negative attitudes (Amir, 1976; Brehm, 1966). Even when a person initially likes to do something, when forced to do it he comes to dislike it (Brehm, 1972). By allowing or inducing students and their families to participate voluntarily in a desegregation program, they will be more committed to making it work and will feel greater personal responsibility toward it than those on whom it is forced. At the same time, this does not argue against the use of both negative and positive incentives to help induce voluntary action.

Although these principles regarding choice and commitment are powerful and well documented, they can easily be distorted and misused to support evasion and inaction. In asserting their importance, they must not be misconstrued as an excuse for evading desegregation.

Desegregation Plans Should Include Programs to Increase the Multiracial Composition of the Teaching and Administrative Staff

It is a good idea for minority children to see minority adults in positions of authority for two reasons. First, it makes it easier to create equal status contact in desegregated learning settings. Second, it may raise the aspirations of minority children. This principle can be extended to include teacher aides as well.

Teacher Selection and Preparation Must Precede the Implementation of Desegregation Plans

Teacher behavior is crucial. Crain *et al.* (1974) see "the behavior of teachers to be the most important factor in the school." Rosenthal and Jacobson (1968) demonstrated dramatically the effects that teacher expectations can have on student performance. Although Gerard and Miller (1975) found no overall improvement in the academic performance of minority students following desegregation, this net result reflected two opposing tendencies—an improvement among those minority students in the classes of less biased teachers and an impairment for those in the classes of biased teachers. Weiner, Frieze, Kukla, Reed, Rest, and Rosenbaum (1971) suggest that teacher attitudes toward children who exhibit poor academic performance may be a key factor leading them to develop self-defeating attitudes. Brophy and Good (1974), in their careful review of the research on teacher–student relationships, conclude that "teacher expectations have the potential for affecting student achievement both directly, by affecting the amount that the student learns, and indirectly, by affecting his motivation to learn" (p. 118).

Although years of educational research have revealed relatively little about the characteristics of effective teachers or the particular behaviors involved in effective teaching (Brophy & Good, 1974; Dunkin & Biddle, 1974; Rosenshine, 1971), two factors appear important: teacher warmth (Heim, 1973) and a structured classroom environment (Solomon & Kendall, 1976; Sowell, 1964) do seem to help students from low socioeconomic status (SES) backgrounds. In addition, teachers need feedback about their teaching behavior once they have been selected and trained. Rollins, McCandless, Thompson, and Brassell (1974) show that teachers who have been trained to rely very heavily on positive reinforcement techniques produce better student outcomes in inner-city schools than do other teachers. Brophy and Good (1974, p. 291) conclude that most teachers are willing to change their behavior "if given specific feedback that they can perceive as relevant and credible." They attribute inappropriate teaching "to lack of awareness in the teacher rather than the deliberate carelessness or inability to change."

A desegregation program is likely to add to the problems of the teachers. Typically, it increases the heterogeneity among the academic performance levels of the children in a class. A racial-ethnic mix close to 50% White and 50% minority, particularly when, as is typically the case, the White students are more middle class than the minority children, maximizes such heterogeneity. The drastic difference between the outcome of the desegregation programs in Riverside, California, and those of Pasadena and Inglewood, California, may reflect such differences in heterogeneity. In the latter two cases, the educational outcomes were bad (Kurtz, 1975); in the former, they were not (Gerard & Miller, 1975). These contrasting outcomes can probably be traced to the differences in percentage of minority students in the classroom. A sixth grade teacher facing a 50–50 distribution, with minority students reading at a grade level of 3.5 on the average and Whites reading on a sixth grade level, would have to abandon or drastically alter her previously prepared lesson plans. She might well have to work out new teaching strategies that seem appropriate for this new situation. On the other hand, a teacher in Riverside, usually having only four or five minority students in her class, might continue to find it feasible to use previously developed lesson plans, teaching at the level developed for her more middle-class White classrooms. In contrast to the Pasadena or Inglewood teacher, the result would be a higher level of demand and expectation and a higher level of subsequent academic performance by all students in the latter situation. This discussion emphasizes the need to prepare teachers for the increased heterogeneity of performance in the desegregated classroom.

The teacher also serves as an important authority figure or model to the students in her classroom. Her example defines the types of behaviors that are appropriate and inappropriate. Interestingly, in classrooms where teachers do not expect minority students to do poorly, the White children in the classroom are more accepting toward them and less likely to use race as a basis for friendship or social interaction (Gerard & Miller, 1975).

Community Acceptance of the Desegregation Plan

Community acceptance of a desegregation program makes it effective. Children bring parental and family attitudes to the desegregated classroom setting. Furthermore, community involvement and commitment to schools, as indexed by the ratio of school taxes to community wealth, is related to children's academic performance (Bureau of School Programs Evaluation, 1972). "Citizens support for the school system and tolerance among races are necessary to the survival of a pluralistic urban society" (Crain *et al.*, 1974 p. 40, Vol. 1).

Decentralized Decision-Making That Includes the Community Will Enhance Acceptance of the Desegregation Plan

A large social psychological literature demonstrates the powerful effects of choice and voluntary action upon commitment to the attitudes represented by the action. Thus, to the extent that a desegregation plan involves the community in decentralized decision-making about the form or type of desegregation program that is to be implemented, both parents and children will be more committed to it and will approach it with more positive attitudes (Chesler, Guskin, Sanchez, Shaevitz, & Smith, 1974; Crain *et al.*, 1974, Vol. 1, pp. 37, 54; Likert, 1967). St. John (1975) states:

> Desegregation, as symbol of equality affirmed and powerlessness denied, should increase Black sense of control and White appreciation of Democracy *provided* it is achieved through individual and self-determination and is freely chosen by the families involved, and provided Black parents share in the control of school policies. (p. 107)

Elsewhere (p. 121) she states: "families should be given circumscribed choice among schools that differ in educational philosophy as well as in location and racial ratio." Parental and community involvement in the decision-making can also help to prevent the community polarization that can in the long run undermine the success of the schools and of any desegregation plan by dooming budget appropriations, bond issues, and tax overrides.

Still another benefit to be derived from involving parents, particularly minority parents, in the decision-making about a desegregation plan relates again to modeling effects and the indirect transmission of attitudes. Educators universally acknowledge the difficulty of involving working-class parents of all racial-ethnic backgrounds in the activities and programs of the schools. They believe parents' involvement is educationally beneficial. If they play a role in decision-making and maintain contact with the school, parents will indirectly convey to their children the fact that schools are indeed important. In other words, parental involvement will enhance student interest.

Long-Term Success in Providing District Children with an Integrated Learning Experience Depends on Initial Success

The success of the program as perceived by the community will contribute to the acceptance of the desegregation plan and to the benefits that ensue from community acceptance. Plans should, therefore, be implemented initially on a small enough scale so that available resources can be concentrated and observable benefits will occur. Parents, especially Whites, are opposed to having children spend long periods on buses for the purposes of desegregation. Such attitudes are often expressed in terms of a concern for loss of instructional time. For this reason, it would be important that the desegregation plan be perceived as educationally sound—as fundamentally improving the capacity of the schools in the district to educate their children. Periodic monitoring and evaluation of program impact, when translated into successful modifications of the plan, will snowball to enhance community acceptance.

This principle should not be invoked as a justification for delaying or avoiding desegregation. Rather, it reflects the view that desegregation can produce educational and social benefits only when appropriate technologies for day-to-day application have been developed for classroom use. It also reflects the view that community support and participation can be mobilized more readily for programs that have been shown to produce demonstrable benefit.

Extensive and Effective Communication about the Desegregation Plan
Will Facilitate Acceptance

Community members must understand the plan before it is initially implemented and must remain aware of how it is functioning if they are to maintain interest in it and support it. This takes effective communication.

A Desegregation Plan That Preserves Existing Bilingual Programs Will Be
More Acceptable to Non-English Speaking Ethnic Groups

Another factor that should contribute to community acceptance in a district with a substantial proportion of children of Mexican-American or other ethnic heritage is the explicit attempt to include in the desegregation plan provisions that preserve existing bilingual programs. Although research addressing the educational effectiveness of such programs as yet presents no clear picture, it is both evident and understandable that they are important to the Mexican-American (Arciniega, n.d.) as well as other ethnic communities.

The proponents of bilingual programs differ in their reasons for supporting them. One group, emphasizing cultural pluralism, stresses the inherent value of the Mexican-American culture and the necessity of teaching it in order to develop self-esteem in the Mexican-American child. Another group, emphasizing cultural assimilation, supports these programs as vehicles to enable the Spanish-speaking child to learn despite the fact that he has not yet mastered English. Although important differences in educational philosophy separate these views, *both* nevertheless advocate bilingual programs. Learning about the heritage and values of Mexican-American culture as well as the language itself, it is hoped, will also produce skills and abilities that will enable the Mexican-American child to participate in American culture more fully.[5] At the same time, non-Mexican-American children can also benefit educationally from the presence of multicultural programs that contain bilingual components.

Public Commitment to School Desegregation by School Authorities As Well As by Other Public Officials Will Facilitate Community Acceptance of a Desegregation Plan

Vigorous public commitment to desegregation on the part of school and other officials will discourage organized community resistance to desegregation. These community leaders serve as models to parents and children. Their open and irrevocable commitment augments community acceptance (Kirby & Crain, 1974; Van der Zanden, 1972).

SOURCES OF DIFFICULTY IN DEVELOPING PRINCIPLES FOR EFFECTIVE DESEGREGATION

Although these principles received widespread acceptance and, as stated earlier, were explicitly written so as to elicit it, reservations about virtually any one of them can be raised. This is the case not merely because social scientists, like other people, differ in their values. More importantly, we lack clear empirical resolution to our questions, which to me, is by far the more important reason for maintaining a stance of caution and skepticism.

In part, this uncertainty is due to the characteristics of school desegregation research. It is not that there are too few studies upon which to base conclusions. Rather, too many of the studies are poor in conception, design, analysis, and interpretation. Further, most view the implementation of a desegregation program as a unitary experimental treatment, ignoring that it is qualitatively a multidimensional one. In this respect, school desegregation is similar to most other applied social programs that are studied by social scientists. The program to be evaluated is not only a complex amalgam of specific variables, it also typically contains systemlike

---

[5] Although the bearing of pluralistic versus assimilationist positions on multicultural school programs applies in principle to the Black child as well, these concerns have not affected school policy to the same degree that they have in regard to the Mexican-American, Puerto Rican, or Chinese-American child.

feedback effects among its various components. This situation stands in vivid contrast to the scientific aspiration of manipulating a conceptually distinct variable, namely, one that has discriminant validity, and observing its subsequent causal effect on a dependent measure of interest. Its consequence is that when a program of evaluation has been completed, one can rarely specify why it was or was not successful. Moreover, if it was indeed successful, one has little certainty that if implemented again, at another time or place, it would yield a similar outcome.

The issue is further complicated by the previously implied fact that school desegregation, as do many social reforms, addresses a multidimensional rather than a singular goal. Unfortunately, procedures that may function ideally to remedy problems with respect to academic achievement may not be ideal for raising the self-concept of minority children or improving intergroup attitudes and social relations. Indeed, since the school day is finite in time, educational resources directed toward one goal must often necessarily mean less attention to another.

The Lateral Transmission of Values Hypothesis

Having stated some general difficulties, I will examine in greater detail one of the cornerstones upon which social science theorizing about desegregation rests, namely, the hypothesis of *lateral transmission of values*.

The Model

This hypothesis, which is more correctly viewed as a theoretical model of the process by which desegregation produces educational benefit, contains a number of distinct components. It suggests that: (1) a specific set of values facilitate achievement; (2) many, if not most White, middle-class children possess these values, whereas most lower-class and minority children do not; (3) interracial mixing of minority children into classrooms that have a numerical preponderance of middle-class White children, and consequently, also have a White, middle-class norm structure, causes minority children to internalize these achievement-related values; and (4) in conjunction with the higher achievement level that is normative in the middle-class school, as minority children adopt these values, their academic achievement improves.

The logic behind this process is deeply rooted in experimental social psychology. The notions of (1) specific values facilitating achievement (e.g., Douvan, 1958; McClelland, 1961; Strodtbeck, 1958); (2) social influence processes resulting in the norms of the majority being passed onto the minority (e.g., Asch, 1952; Deutsch & Gerard, 1955; Sherif, 1935); and (3) performance levels being responsive, within limits, to standards (e.g.,

Atkinson, 1964), have all been well documented. Further evidence suggests a greater prevalence of achievement-related values in White children than in minority children (e.g., Mussen, 1953). The substantial evidence supporting the notions which comprise the lateral transmission of values hypothesis, led social scientists who have studied school desegregation to interpret their findings in terms of value transmission, despite the fact that other interpretive alternatives were, in fact, available (Coleman *et al.*, 1966; Crain & Weisman, 1972).

The *value* dimensions in the lateral transmission of values hypothesis presumably can bring about academic achievement change in two different ways. First, they can directly exert normative influence on achievement: when these values are predominant in a social setting, if people behave in ways that are consistent with them, they will exhibit greater achievement. An alternative view argues that sustained exposure to these new values causes one to internalize them and change one's personality. This, in turn, produces changes in achievement. This latter sequence, which can be drawn more clearly from the social psychology literature cited earlier, appears to be the one implied by Coleman *et al.* (1966) and by Crain and Weisman (1972). Taking as an example a specific aspect of achievement motivation—locus of control—they emphasize that minority children in desegregated classrooms exhibit a greater tendency to perceive themselves as controlling their own environment than do their agemates in segregated schools.

Regardless of one's preference between the two versions of the model suggested above, there seem to be two additional variables that mediate value transmission: First, unless minority children are accepted by their White peers, value transmission seems unlikely to occur. Support for this proposition is provided by the U.S. Commission on Civil Rights (1967), which found scholastic achievement of Black children to be related to (1) lack of racial tension in their school setting; (2) having a close friend who is White; and (3) a high percentage of White students in the classroom. Therefore, peer acceptance occupies a pivotal position in the transmission of values hypothesis.

Second, teachers may contribute directly to normative influence effects in the classroom. That is, their own values are an additional source of salient influence. However, insofar as (1) teachers in White schools hold basic educational values that do not substantially differ from those held by teachers in minority schools; and (2) differences in teacher's expectations for children tend to affect ongoing classroom processes but not their scholastic outcomes (Brophy & Good, 1974), this latter source of influence might be seen as somewhat less important.

To summarize, the lateral transmission of values hypothesis follows logically from previous research and provides a plausible model of the effects of school desegregation upon academic achievement. It proposes that values mediate the relation between children's background and their scholastic performance. Given that middle-class White children are numerically preponderant in the classroom, the values of minority children can presumably be changed by (a) favorable interracial contact which causes (b) minority children to acquire the values of the White children, and *may* in turn (c) lead to change in personality structure of the minority children, but in any event will (d) result in higher achievement by minority children. Thus, in this model, acceptance by their White classmates is critical for improvement in the academic performance of minority children.

Evidence

The findings of Gerard and Miller (1975) must be considered disappointing to anyone advocating a lateral transmission of values approach to desegregation. Riverside voluntarily implemented a desegregation program backed by community support; further, the percentage of minority children in Riverside was 20%, a proportion presumably beneficial for school desegregation (e.g., U.S. Commission on Civil Rights, 1967). Given these and other factors (see Hendrick, 1968), Riverside should have provided a good environment both for producing successful desegregation and for examining the lateral transmission of values hypothesis.

Despite the promotive environment that seemingly existed, there was no positive effect of desegregation on achievement test scores for minority children, although the achievement scores of White children were not adversely affected. The predesegregation scholastic achievement deficits that characterized minority children were not made up, but continued to increase as grade-in-school increased. Desegregation produced a decrease in the class grades of the minority children and an improvement in those of White children. This stemmed from two facts: since White children on the average perform at a higher scholastic level than do minority children, the desegregated classrooms contained a wider range in children's performance levels. At the same time, teachers typically employ a consistent standard when they grade their students, assigning approximately the same number of A's, B's, etc., from one year to the next. This grade normalization consequently resulted in poorer grades for the minority students and better grades for the White students.

The achievement results, however, do not in and of themselves constitute disconfirmation of the lateral transmission of values hypothesis. Despite the general lack of academic benefit following desegregation, it was still possible that those few minority students who did in fact improve academically were those who had been accepted and did adopt the values of the White children. Analyses of the personality measures, however, show simply no support whatsoever for the lateral transmission of values hypothesis. Although some personality changes among minority children may be interpreted as consistent with it, these effects were so minimal and so inconsistent that they preclude the possibility that personality importantly predicts achievement or mediates academic benefit. Any impact of White children on minority children, "is most assuredly not mediated by changes in basic personality structures" (Miller, 1975, p. 302). Reanalyses of the Riverside data using "causal model" approaches (Maruyama, 1977; McGarvey, 1977), clearly reaffirm this conclusion. Recently, a large-scale study of school desegregation in Israel (Minkovich, Davis, & Bashi, 1977) similarly fails to provide substantial support for this personality mediational version of the lateral transmission of values.

Consistent with the version of the lateral transmission of values hypothesis that postulates direct normative influence, however, minority children accepted by Whites did, in fact, perform better than their peers who were not accepted (see Gerard, Jackson, & Conolley, 1975). Nevertheless, several considerations temper this result. First, interracial acceptance was, in fact, low. Therefore, any benefits of positive cross-racial interaction would necessarily be restricted to a small number of minority students. Second, consistent with the preceding reasoning, the positive relation between acceptance and achievement was due primarily to differences in acceptance among those minority children who had been high achievers in the segregated classrooms. Third, interracial acceptance resulted at best in maintaining past achievement levels, not improving them. The most important point, however, is that although the results are consistent with direct normative influence, they are not conclusive. Gerard *et al.*'s (1975) analyses do not speak on the causal direction of the relation between a minority child's popularity and his academic performance.

Subsequently, two dissertations using a maximum likelihood structural equation approach to these data (cf. Joreskog, 1970) sought to test path analytic causal models (McGarvey, 1977; Maruyama, 1977). Maruyama, examining cross-sectional data from the data set, found that in the pre-desegregation year the peer acceptance of White children was positively related to the evaluations they received from teachers and parents and to their achievement. His evaluation of the causal processes seemed to indicate that peer acceptance did mediate the favorable effect of adult evaluations on achievement. Additionally, the Black child's acceptance by White peers was directly related to achievement, as in the predesegregation all-minority classroom. McGarvey (1977) addressed the issue more directly. Rather than comparing static cross-sectional models of pre- and postdesegregation data, he tested a longitudinal model. When Whites were considered apart from minorities, academic ability caused popularity in the postdesegregation year. This effect was not primarily mediated by increases in the child's popularity prior to desegregation (as was the case among minorities); pre-desegregation academic ability made a causally independent contribution to postdesegregation popularity. This was not the case for minority children, whose academic ability alone was not enough to gain them popularity in the desegregated setting. In a similar vein, Blanchard, Weigel and Cook (1975) found that the competence of Blacks interacted with situational factors to affect the liking ratings received by them, whereas competence alone affected the ratings of liking received by Whites.

These findings provide little support for a view that puts peer acceptance as an antecedent of the minority child's academic achievement in the predominantly White classroom. Additionally, they force us to reconsider the results obtained by Maruyama (1977). With the advantage of retrospective wisdom, it can now be seen that Maruyama's findings, based as they were on static cross-sectional analyses, found support for the normative influence model only because, prior to testing the model, he specified the direction of the relation between acceptance and academic achievement to be in accord with it. Given McGarvey's (1977) results, in which the causal relation between variables is specified by the temporal design rather than by intuition or prior theorizing, Maruyama's positive path should be reversed to show (in accord with McGarvey) that it is academic ability which leads to acceptance.

To my knowledge, Lewis and St. John (1974) provide the only other test of the normative influence model. They, too, focus on the relation between popularity and academic achievement of Black students in the desegregated classroom. Drawing from the findings of the U.S. Commission on Civil Rights (1967) cited earlier, they, too, argued that the academic success of Black students would be contingent upon peer acceptance. They proposed a path model with SES and percentage of White students as background variables external to the model; either past grade point average (GPA) or IQ (Otis group administered test) and popularity with Whites as intervening variables; and present GPA or reading achievement as the criteria.

Although their data could perhaps be fitted as readily to other models, Lewis and St. John (1974) did seem to find support for the normative influence model with a data base that provided a temporal design. Popularity was related to GPA, though not to reading achievement. In light of these findings, Lewis and St. John suggested that "the social process that best explains the beneficial effect of acceptance by White peers on Black achievement is probably the lateral transmission of achievement-oriented norms and/or skills" (p. 89). More recently, however, Maruyama and Miller (1978) reanalyzed these same data, again using a structural equation approach to the data analysis (Joreskog, 1970). These latter procedures are superior to path analysis procedures in that they treat specific measures as indicators of the latent theoretical variables, thereby taking a more sensible approach with regard to measurement error and reliability. They also contain procedures for testing the goodness of fit of the specific model to the data. Reanalysis failed to confirm Lewis and St. John's view that the popularity or acceptance of minority children by their classmates subsequently produces scholastic achievement gains. Instead, it supported the opposite causal sequence; peer acceptance was the result, not the cause of good academic performance.

At this stage, existing research now appears to offer little if any support for either version of the lateral transmission of values hypothesis, at least as it applies to achievement test scores or grades. In part, the failure to find unambiguous support for a causal relation between peer acceptance and academic achievement in the desegregated setting may reflect the fact that sociometric choices and interracial contact are so strongly constrained within racial-ethnic boundaries among both minority and White child alike (Gerard et al., 1975; Stephan & Rosenfield, 1978) and further, that the influence of race on these preferences seems to increase if not remain constant after desegregation (Gerard & Miller, 1975; Rosenberg & Simmons, 1971; Schofield, 1975; Silverman & Shaw, 1973; Stephan, 1978). In Rosenberg and Simmons's (1971) examination of integrated schools, sociometric measures showed as much as 96% of third choices for friend by Black students to be within-race choices. Even in a school setting that probably came as close as is possible to meeting Allport's (1954) or Cook's (1969) criteria for beneficial interracial contact, Schofield and Sagar (1977) found little decrease in the extent to which race determined social interaction patterns among children in a middle school. If the desegregated school setting is indeed so strongly characterized by an absence of interracial contact and interaction, there is little opportunity for normative influence to operate. To put it somewhat differently, if the friendship choices and social interactions of Black children were entirely restricted to other Black children, it would be logically impossible to find a relation between acceptance by their White classmates and scholastic performance.

Reconsideration of the Model's Relevance to the School Setting

The preceding presentation and discussion of data suggest the need for some reexamination of the circumstances under which normative influence occurs. Indeed, one might well question why theorists had such expectations in the first place. What are the circumstances under which persons accept group norms and behave in accordance with them? More specifically, what circumstances would lead minority children to adopt norms that support scholastic achievement?

Although the answers to such questions have received considerable if tangential attention in discussions of the circumstances necessary for beneficial interracial contact (Allport, 1954; Amir, 1976; Cook, 1969; Schofield, 1978), important considerations have not been addressed. First, when school desegregation experiences are compared to the classic laboratory studies that demonstrate powerful normative influence effects (e.g., Asch, 1952; Sherif, 1935), they differ in a number of important ways. Since group members in laboratory studies were typically strangers, the only dimension on which participants could evaluate each other was in terms of the task at hand. In other words, for any given subject there was no ambiguity about which particular dimension of behavior others would use to appraise him. Additionally, participants were typically all highly co-oriented; they were college students, all brought into a strange laboratory to participate in a novel scientific experiment; they shared a common fate in a strange setting. Moreover, in most of the laboratory research, the groups of students lacked any organized social structure based upon a prior history of social interaction.

A second concern is whether minority children are aware of an existence of higher scholastic standards in the desegregated classroom. There is scant data on this issue, and what little there is presents a mixed picture. The fact that minority children receive lower grades when they move to the desegregated classroom (Singer, Gerard, & Redfearn, 1975) certainly sets the stage for such an awareness. And Schofield, Shaeffer, and Hopkins (1977) do report an awareness by minority students of tougher standards in the desegregated classroom. On the other hand, Singer *et al.* (1975) also found that minority students in the classes of teachers who employ a double standard, and thereby tend to resist lowering the grades of the minority children as they join the desegregated classroom, are the ones most likely to show academic improvement on standardized achievement tests. In other words, academic benefit is most likely to be found among those with lessened opportunity for directly noticing that academic standards in the desegregated classroom are higher than those they had previously experienced.

A third problem centers on the extent to which minority children view the internalization of or adherence to prevailing scholastic norms as instrumental for their acceptance by the White minority. Not only must White students make their own acceptance of minority children and their friendship toward them contingent upon the minority child's adoption of White scholastic achievement norms, but additionally, minority children must perceive that their acceptance by White classmates is indeed contingent upon adopting such norms. It is doubtful whether either of these contingencies occurs consistently in desegregated classrooms. In the normal classroom, it is not even certain that the overt behavior which supposedly reflects the internalization of scholastic achievement norms, namely, good scholastic performance, does in fact strongly influence children's friendship choices—either within racial-ethnic groups or between them. Neither is it clear that children would or could verbalize such norms as being important in their friendship selection. Since the acceptance of minority children often operates within the confines of the playground setting rather than the schoolwork situation (Gerard *et al.*, 1975), it seems likely that any perceived contingency between their own behavior or characteristics and their subsequent acceptance by White classmates is not likely to center upon their own scholastic achievement behavior. Instead, it seems more likely that socioeconomic similarity, common interests, teacher behavior, and a variety of other factors will operate to influence friendship patterns.

Fourth, minority children differ from middle-class White children along a number of dimensions: racial-ethnic background, cultural background, occasionally language, and other factors linked to the social class disparity between them. Such sources of differing co-orientations must act to interfere with norm transmission and acceptance, particularly when there are sufficient numbers of minority students to constitute a subgroup and provide a social support system distinct from that of the middle-class White students. Working in concert with this, in most desegregated classrooms, the children from each racial-ethnic group were a part of a prior social structure; they had roles and friendship ties within that structure as it existed in the predesegregation classroom.

In early desegregation cases, the courts seemed to lean toward imposing a redistribution of students in which the proportion of minority students in any one school would equal their relative proportion throughout the district. Although this definition of desegregation seems logical and straightforward, it would not uniformly make sense according to the lateral transmission of values hypothesis, which requires that Whites be numerically preponderant in the classroom. In cities like Los Angeles, where less than one third of the students are Whites, proportional redistribution would leave Whites as a distinct minority in every classroom. On the other hand, if, as argued above, the normative influence model is not in fact the vehicle for academic benefit to minority children, desegregation plans that leave Whites as a numerical minority in the classroom need not be rejected. Most likely, however, is the possibility that a mixed strategy will make most sense. Whereas the percentage of Whites in the class may not in fact affect minority academic performance, it apparently does affect the motivation of minority students to attend college (Crain & Mahard, 1978; Falk, 1978). If such motivation develops primarily in high school, it would be desirable to devote careful attention to maintaining a White majority in as many desegregated high schools as possible within a district.

The point of the preceding discussion is not to challenge the validity of normative influence as a social psychological principle. Rather, it is to inject a note of caution; I no longer share the optimism of some researchers who seem to view beneficial normative influence processes as likely to occur in any classroom having a majority of students who possess achievement-related values. As desegregation programs are normally implemented, they contain many features that work against beneficial cross-racial normative influence upon minority academic performance. Unless teachers and principals interject into the classroom specific procedures that are designed to overcome the problems described above, little optimism for beneficial normative influence effects is warranted.

Strategies of Classroom Intervention

If peer acceptance plays such an important role in the theorizing about beneficial desegregation effects, and if cross-race acceptance is so infrequent, it becomes important to examine other factors that affect a White child's prejudice against minority children. Likewise, since reciprocity of "liking" plays such an important role in attraction and friendship, it becomes equally important to examine minority prejudice.

Augmenting Cognitive Complexity

Westman and Miller (1978) selected children who exhibited an extreme increase or decrease in prejudice following desegregation. Prejudice was measured by children's responses to an ethnic pictures test, in which degrees of in- and outgroup acceptance and rejection are reflected in the preference ranks assigned by the White, Mexican-American, and Black children to same- and other-sex facial color pictures of children from these three racial groups.

Using this index, children who tend to distinctly and exclusively prefer the pictures of those who belong to their own racial-ethnic group can be compared to those whose preferences are less influenced by race. A detailed analysis of the correlates of this outgroup prejudice shows that prejudice among children is related to their intelligence. Children whose post-desegregation prejudice decreased had higher IQ scores than did children whose prejudice increased, although this difference was not manifested on scholastic achievement tests or on classroom grades. Similarly, differentiation between children whose prejudice increased and those whose prejudice decreased was pronounced in teacher's ratings; the less prejudiced children were rated more favorably. Finally, those whose prejudice decreased as desegregation continued received more sociometric nominations as school-work partners.

This result for schoolwork popularity can be seen as consistent with those for intelligence and for teacher ratings: the child with greater intellectual ability is less prejudiced, receives more favorable ratings from the teacher, and is sociometrically more popular on the schoolwork criterion, which is perhaps most directly relevant to the arena of intelligence and achievement. One explanation for these results, as previously implied, is that rejection *by* others leads to a rejection *of* others, in this case members of the outgroup. Of course, the causal direction could be reversed, such that *being* prejudiced makes one less desirable in the eyes of others and thus leads to rejection (nonacceptance) by them. As Westman and Miller (1978) note, however, the failure to find differences between prejudiced and unprejudiced children on the play partner and seating partner sociometric popularity indicators appears to weaken this latter interpretation to the extent that the difference in popularity was specific to the "schoolwork situation."

Since no meaningful or consistent differences between children whose prejudice increased and those whose prejudice decreased were found on an array of personality measures (including self-attitudes, self-esteem, and anxiety), these results give no support to a view that sees prejudice as a form of displaced hostility stemming from the self-hatred that underlies low self-esteem, high anxiety, and a sense of rejection by others. Instead, they support the cognitive sophistication interpretation suggested by Glock *et al.* (1975). This latter view, emphasizing the role of cognitive complexity, sophistication, and cynicism in curtailing the development of prejudice, builds upon an earlier discussion of stereotypes which emphasizes their substantial basis in truth (Campbell, 1956, 1967). Prejudice, as well as representing an explanation of group difference via completion of self-fulfilling prophecies, more fundamentally rests on the perception that true group differences do exist. Cognitive sophistication promotes immunity to prejudice by enabling one to deal more effectively with the truth component of stereotypes. It enables one to discriminate between relative versus absolute differences, to curtail their overgeneralization, and by increasing one's understanding of how such differences arise, to resist prejudicial responses to them.

Of course, we do not know what these correlational data mean with regard to a remedy for prejudice. Will classroom procedures designed to augment children's cognitive complexity make them more accepting of outgroup members? If so, exactly what procedures will be effective? Will multicultural educational materials enhance the ability of children to take another's perspective (Aronson, Bridgeman, & Geffner, 1978) and thereby reduce their prejudice? Or instead, do Westman and Miller's (1978) data primarily reflect differences in Level II intelligence that are primarily hereditary in origin (Jensen, 1969) and, therefore, largely immutable? At present, we simply do not know.

Altering Status Hierarchies

Cohen (1975) advocates a remedial procedure designed to alter status configurations. She notes that when Black and White students interact, the Whites typically assume a dominance that interferes with the development of positive interracial attitudes. This dominance fundamentally arises from the disparity in academic ability that characteristically exists between minority and White students. To remedy this problem, she proposes, prior to interracial contact, special training for minority students that provides them with a level of expertise for the task at hand which will exceed that which the White students possess. This strategy proves to disrupt White dominance effectively in a laboratory setting in which Black students received specialized training about transistor radios before interacting with Whites. Her procedures, however, do not appear to have widespread potential for newly desegregated schools. There, the particular dimensions along which pretraining and development of minority student's expertise is required are the very dimensions for which desegregation itself is imposed as a remedy—namely, basic academic skills. At present, educators have achieved relatively little success in closing the academic achievement gap that exists between minority and White students. Although a successful elimination of it might indeed dramatically facilitate the development of positive cross-racial attitudes, the intractability of the academic achievement gap suggests that a hidden millenialism lies in Cohen's approach to interracial acceptance.

Another alternative, of course, is to structure contacts between minority and White students around segments of the school curriculum that do not strongly engage dimensions along which there are such average disparities in performance levels, e.g., the arts, athletics, and perhaps social studies. This approach also seems to lack feasibility, however, in that the courts have viewed identifiable minority schools as the problem requiring a remedy. Bringing children together for only part of their academic programs, whether at midsites or in home schools, would still leave minority schools readily identifiable as such.

Introducing Cooperative Learning Procedures

As mentioned earlier in this chapter, a number of researchers have developed cooperative learning procedures for classroom use which address more directly the goals of school desegregation. Some focus explicitly upon academic performance, whereas others seem aimed primarily at improving intergroup relations within the learning context. At least five distinct groups of researchers are currently engaged in implementing and evaluating outcomes of various cooperative learning techniques: Aronson and his colleagues (see Aronson *et al.*, 1978), Cook and his associates (see Weigel, Wiser, & Cook, 1972), the Johnsons (Johnson & Johnson 1974), the Sharans (Sharan & Sharan, 1976); and Slavin and his predecessors (see DeVries & Slavin, 1978).

Each has developed cooperative procedures that contain features which distinguish it from others, yet all implicitly impose principles that work to enhance interracial attraction and friendship. First, they restructure the classroom setting so as to increase substantially the amount of interracial interaction in the classroom. Second, although the reward structures they employ differ along several dimensions, they all tend to reinforce explicit positive behaviors on the part of children toward their classmates: helping, attending and listening to, rooting for, commiserating with, depending upon, etc. More importantly, these behaviors are reinforced across as well as within racial-ethnic boundaries. Third, by their very nature, they tend to make explicit a norm structure that endorses interracial cooperation.

Although some combination or integration of these separate research efforts is called for, yet lacking, a fairly positive picture emerges. Outcomes are not always consistent, but cooperative learning experiences have had salutory effects on a wide range of children's outcomes, including achievement, individual psychological health, and interpersonal and interethnic acceptance, trust, and liking (cf. Johnson & Johnson, 1974).

Whereas the lateral transmission of values hypothesis places peer acceptance as causally antecedent to minority scholastic improvement, it seems likely that cooperative learning procedures exert an independent and direct influence upon each of these variables. In other words, though they contain features that should work to enhance intergroup acceptance, it seems likely that their effects upon learning are not mediated by changes in cross-racial social relationships and attitudes. Instead, it seems likely that when they do produce scholastic improvement, it stems from direct increases in motivation as a result of peer interest and/or because their use forces the teacher to restructure classroom activities and thereby results in more time being spent actively in learning activities.

Although it is too soon to view cooperative learning as a panacea for both educational ineffectiveness and interracial intolerance, it does seem to offer more promise than does a reliance upon the passive and indirect influence process that lies at the heart of the lateral transmission of values hypothesis—an influence process which, in its dependence upon a level of intergroup interaction and acceptance that does not often seem to empirically emerge, seems doomed to failure.

ADDITIONAL CONCERNS THAT BEAR ON POLICY

Before concluding this chapter, a number of additional points warrant some discussion. In most cases in which a desegregation program emerges from court litigation, the plaintiffs press for proportional redistribution of minority students. Among various desegregation alternatives, this procedure provides the most extensive or thoroughgoing mixing of students. Although some social scientists have argued that White flight is not a serious consideration and should not deter the imposition of extensive mandatory desegregation, it seems clear that in large metropolitan centers the outflow of Whites from the inner city is exacerbated by this type of mandatory desegregation plan (Armor, 1978). In Los Angeles, district figures in the first year of their current plan reveal staggering White losses in schools involved in its mandatory aspects. As reported in the *Los Angeles Times* (January 29, 1979), for those grades that participate (4–8) the loss is 46% (compared to 24% for grades not in the plan). For the two junior high school years the loss from these same schools is 62%. These percentages are to be contrasted with base rate losses due to declining birth rates and normal outmigration that were under 10%. Given that less than one-third of all students are Whites, insistence upon meaningful desegregation of all identifiable urban minority schools is either an unrealistic flight of fancy or political fodder for a perceived political constituency. Nevertheless, preference for this strategy persists among minority leaders even in instances where it results in such very substantial loss of Whites from the district and thereby ultimately results in less opportunity for minority students to have contact with White children than would have been the case if some other desegregation strategy had been chosen.

Has minority leadership simply been misled by their social science advisors? Do the dynamics of conflict resolution, as it operates within the legal arena, require more polarized stands than would be necessary within some other bargaining or negotiating context? Or, does such persistence require that we reconsider whether the goals of minority leadership do indeed parallel those I cited earlier (p. 310) as implicit in *Brown* and *Crawford*? Have the specific goals of improving educational achievement and interracial attitudes become less important than the more symbolic achievement of immediately maximizing interracial contact *per se*, irrespective of its long-range costs, and imposing as extensive a restructuring of the school system as possible?

I suspect that minority legal leadership *has* in fact been led to believe that desegregation *per se* is beneficial, largely because some reviewers of the literature continue to hold this view. Weinberg, a professor of history and the editor of *Integrated Education*, has followed the desegregation literature for many years, diligently accumulating bibliographies, and attempting to summarize its voluminous findings. His prodesegregation stand is well known as a result of these monumental efforts. Since he readily acknowledges that it is beyond his scope to evaluate systematically and critically the methodology and approach used in the various studies of desegregation that he reviews, it is fair to assume that his overall conclusions rest in part on the current evaluations of those more expert in these matters. In this regard, his writings are particularly interesting, showing as they most recently do, a rather dramatic change in opinion. As recently as 1975, he concluded that desegregation has a positive effect on achievement levels for Blacks with no harmful effect for Whites (Weinberg, 1975). Yet by 1977, in a very substantial review prepared for the National Institute of Education (NIE), he, too, shifted to a different position, one that followed closely on the heels of a slightly earlier review, also prepared for NIE, in which Clement et al. (1976) concluded that the "findings from the desegregation research to date suggest that social race mixing alone has little consistent effect on Black–White outcomes" (p. 47). Taking, if anything, an even more pessimistic view, Weinberg (1977) stated:

> [I]n the early 1960's many proponents of desegregation declared that overcoming segregation and deprivation required no more than attendance of Black and White children in one school. *Today, the same contention is seen more properly as a prescription for failure.* . . . The relationship between education and integration bears far more explication than it has thus far received. A disjunction between the two is often assumed by both partisans of and antagonists to integration. *Nothing in the research evidence supports such a view.* (p. 331; emphasis added)

Nevertheless, despite a consensus among most reviewers of desegregation research that buttresses Weinberg's most recent position, a number of other visible social science spokesmen have taken positions that continue to provide support for the stance taken by Black legal leadership (Crain & Mahard, 1978; Pettigrew et al., 1973). Similarly, others, such as Pettigrew and Green (1976), Mercer and Scout (1974), and Rossell (1975–1976) have argued that fears of White flight are unwarranted. Given this source of empirical confusion, it must be easy for those representing the plaintiffs in desegregation litigation to assume that any statement of reservation about desegregation only proves that bigots continue to invade the social sciences.

At the same time, however, I suspect that Black legal leadership is also responsive to concerns other than the consensus of social science research. Political concerns must require that attention be directed to the symbolic goals as well. Were evidence to show proportional desegregation to produce a clear educational detriment to Blacks, the effect of the ensuing conflict with symbolic goals upon Black legal stands would be revealing. To the external observer, it appears as if school desegregation, a policy that *Brown* viewed as the means, has curiously been converted into the end.

If instead, specific educational and interpersonal goals are to remain paramount, if may well be important for educators and community members to specify clearly their priorities among them. For instance, procedures that improve most effectively the academic achievement of minority students may not be ideal ones for developing positive interracial attitudes. To take a specific example, the Teams Games Tournament cooperative learning procedures developed by DeVries and Edwards (1974) seem to hold substantial educational promise for minority children (Slavin, 1978). Yet, as noted by Sharan (1978), these procedures at the same time sharply delineate the disparities in children's academic performance within the class and act to make them constantly aware of their respective status differences. By concretizing these status differences, racial stereotypes about intelligence, reflecting as they do the average differences that exist between minority and White academic performance, are likely to become more entrenched. They will reinforce existing patterns of dominance in social interaction which, organized as they tend to be around racial-ethnic lines (Cohen, 1975), interfere with the development of positive cross-racial attitudes. Thus, a particularly effective procedure for achieving one goal may exacerbate problems that exist with respect to another.

I do not think that social science can tell us which goal is more important—improvement in the academic performance of minority children or amelioration of interracial relations. The point that needs to be made is that in some instances educators must make a choice rather than pretend that each specific program will solve all problems simultaneously. Where possible, parents should know the emphasis of this or that school and be allowed to make their own choice. In those instances where choice must be made, my own preference leans clearly toward maximizing academic benefit. In part, this preference reflects my belief that academic disparities lie at the core of other difficulties. For instance, if there is any preponderant direction of causal effect between anxiety and academic performance, it is in the direction of the anxiety being the consequence rather than the cause of scholastic achievement (Calsyn & Kenny, 1977; McGarvey & Miller, 1978). Similarly, although I do not mean to imply that by eliminating average differences in academic performance we will largely succeed in eliminating within-race friendship preferences, I do agree with Cohen (1975) that it will set the stage for implementing other constructive efforts.

In my earlier discussion of the normative influence model (pp. 325–331), attention was properly focused on what proportion of White children is sufficient. There is another concern, however, for which existing research provides little guidance. Often, desegregation plans, in redistributing children throughout the district, embed a very small number of students into a class that very predominantly contains children of another racial-ethnic group. In the more typical extreme instance, one or two Black children might be assigned to an otherwise all-White class. (Yet, as previously noted, in many very large urban school districts, a proportional redistribution of students could also result in classrooms containing only a very few White children.) What are the psychological effects of being the only Black girl in an otherwise all-White class? Does a lack of peers from one's own racial-ethnic group adversely affect social development, academic performance, or self-concepts? Although little research bears on the answer, the fact that some experts recommend a minimum of 20% minority students in desegregated classrooms may reflect expectations of adverse effects for children who lack the social support of same-race peers.

If such isolation does indeed impose a psychological burden on children, it must naturally occur for literally thousands of children who belong to racial-ethnic groups whose numbers within any given community are insufficient to provide a social support system wherever needed in classrooms. This same problem undoubtedly occurs in many communities for children of some religious denominations. Perhaps in such cases, all that can be hoped for is a sensitive teacher. The issue here, however, is whether a needed social reform—school desegregation—should be imposed in a form that deliberately creates such circumstances. Clearly, we need research on this issue. Should such isolation create social problems for children, responsive sensitivity to it could be incorporated easily into desegregation plans.

As previously noted, in most of the larger urban school districts of the country, White students are numerically in the minority. The well-established realities of the demographic trends in our large cities (Farley, 1975; Taeuber, 1975) suggest that this direction of racial imbalance will continue. Thus, in many of these large cities (e.g., New York, Los Angeles, San Francisco) concerns about race relations, at least at the level of day-to-day social interactions, do not focus primarily on Whites, but instead, center on relations among minority groups. Despite these demographic realities, however, court-imposed solutions typically focus only upon the relation between minority groups and Whites and not on restructuring the contacts and the relations that minority groups of differing racial-ethnic background have with each other. Surely a more intelligent application of desegregation policy would bend toward responsiveness to these demographic realities and the problems in social relations that emerge from them. The reason for this problem, of course, is that the courts are concerned with redressing inequality in educational opportunity and, whereas a case for such inequality has been made in the comparison of Blacks with Whites, litigation has not pursued the question of whether differential opportunity exists among minority groups.

Courts, as well as districts, know that educational programs require resources. In the past, considerable increases in district revenues were associated with the initiation of desegregation programs. For instance, as reported by Sullivan (1977), Berkeley, California spent an amount on teacher inservice predesegregation preparation which equaled 20% of its total predesegregation budget. Today, in an era of tax revolt and increasing distrust of "big government," the likelihood of substantial increases in school budgets is slim. Therefore, money spent transporting students is money that cannot be spent educating them. If all of a district's budgetary lattitude is diverted into its transportation efforts, the goals of desegregation are unlikely to be achieved. Particularly in cities like Los Angeles, where accidents of history, politics, and geography have created a district over 60 miles in length, with travel times that put the majority of inner-city minority schools beyond reach of White schools at its periphery, desegregation plans that include lengthwise traversal lack cost-effectiveness.

Although the prospects for metropolitan desegregation plans have dimmed, they hold the only promise for overcoming the consequences of White migration from the inner city. A court-ordered mandatory desegregation plan, however, will provide no immediate solution; the political realities are long and costly litigation, as adjacent suburban communities seek to exempt themselves.

Voluntary metropolitan plans may provide more immediate relief provided that attractive incentives for the adjacent suburban districts can be found. Voucher systems, in which for each transferred student the state awards the receiving school the dollar allocation formerly provided to the sending school, may be sufficiently attractive to some predominantly White districts facing enrollment losses from declining White birthrates and consequential school closings and overstaffing. Tacking on additional dollar amounts for each incoming minority student would "sweeten the pot" but may lack legal practicality in California, where the Serrano[6] decision seeks to equate across districts the dollar amount spent per pupil. Attempts to equate travel burdens for minority and White students will create additional problems for voluntary metropolitan plans. Particularly within the confines of Serrano, it will be difficult to find effective incentives to encourage parents in predominantly White districts to bus their students to inner-city minority schools.

If any single concluding point can be distilled from the preceding comments, it must be one that is founded upon the modesty of what we know. It must recognize that situations differ and that no single desegregation strategy, such as mandatory reassignment of students so as to reproduce district proportions of racial-ethnic groups within each grade level of all schools, can be urged intelligently.

In our large cities, where White flight in combination with existing

---

[6] Serrano v. Priest, 5 Cal. 3d. 584, 603; 96 Cal. Reporter, 601, 615, 487; P 2d. 1241, 1255 (1971).

demographic trends of White exodus leave insufficient numbers of White students to desegregate meaningfully inner-city minority schools, until voluntary metropolitan plans can be effectively implemented other means must be found to improve education in these schools: (1) Consideration should be given to the possibility of exempting those minority schools that have functioned most effectively prior to desegregation. (2) Since level of teacher training is one of the few input variables shown to effect educational outcomes (Heim, 1973), the teachers assigned to inner-city schools should be those with the the highest educational attainment. Additionally, it might make sense to apportion money to provide extra financial incentives for master teachers who are willing to teach in ghetto schools. (3) Although the means of achieving it are not well understood, some school principals can convert an ineffective ghetto school into one with high morale and strong academic performance. Inevitably, however, such persons are soon assigned to higher administrative posts, leaving the school to dwindle down to its former level of mediocrity. In an effort to disrupt this most typical but frustrating policy, districts should offer special incentives to principals and teachers who do produce demonstrable improvements in inner-city schools. (4) Experimentation with promising new educational procedures, such as cooperative learning teams, should be directed toward these schools. Frequently, innovative procedures and new techniques reach these schools last.

In conclusion, I want to reiterate that the purpose of school desegregation is not to desegregate schools; rather, it is to do something of educational and psychological benefit for children, particularly minority children. The major function of the schools is to educate.

ACKNOWLEDGMENT

I wish to thank William Miller for assistance in preparing this chapter.

REFERENCES

Allport, G. W. *The nature of prejudice*. Reading, Mass.: Addison-Wesley, 1954.
Amir, Y. The role of intergroup contact in change of prejudice and ethnic relations. In P. A. Katz (Ed.), *Towards the elimination of racism*. New York: Pergamon, 1976.
Arciniega, T. A. Problems and issues in preparing teachers of bicultural Chicano youngsters. Institute for Cultural Pluralism, San Diego State University (undated).
Armor, D. J. The evidence on busing. *The Public Interest*, Summer 1972, *28*, 90–126.
Armor, D. J. *White flight, demographic transition, and the future of school desegregation*. Rand Corporation, 1978.
Aronson, E. Busing and racial tension—The jigsaw route to learning and liking. *Psychology Today*, Feb. 1975, 43–50.

Aronson, E., Bridgeman, D. L., & Geffner, R. Interdependent interactions and prosocial behavior. *Journal of Research and Development in Education*, 1978, *12*, 16–27.

Asch, S. E. *Social psychology*. Englewood Cliffs, N.J.: Prentice-Hall, 1952.

Atkinson, J. W. *An introduction to motivation*. Princeton, N.J.: Van Nostrand, 1964.

Baratz, S. S., & Baratz, J. C. Early childhood intervention: The social science base of institutional racism. *Harvard Educational Review*, 1970, *40*, 29–50.

Blanchard, F. A., Weigel, R. H., & Cook, S. W. The effect of relative competence of group members upon interpersonal attraction in cooperating inter-racial groups. *Journal of Personality and Social Psychology*, 1975, *32*, 519–530.

Blau, P. M., & Duncan, O. D. *The American occupational structure*. New York: Wiley, 1967.

Boocock, L. S. Toward a sociology of learning: A selective review of existing research. *Sociology of Education*, 1966, *39*, 1–45.

Brehm, J. W. *A theory of psychological reactance*. New York: Academic, 1966.

Brehm, J. W. *Responses to loss of freedom: A theory of psychological reactance*. Morristown, N.J.: General Learning, 1972.

Brehm, J. W., & Cohen, A. R. *Explorations in cognitive dissonance*. New York: Wiley, 1962.

Brophy, J. E., & Good, T. L. *Teacher-student relationships: Causes and consequences*. New York: Holt, Rinehart and Winston, 1974.

Bureau of School Programs Evaluation. *Variables related to student performance and resource allocation decisions at the school district level*. Albany, N.Y.: State Education Department, June 1972.

Calsyn, R. J., & Kenny, D. A. Self-concept of ability and perceived evaluations of others: Cause or effect of academic achievement? *Journal of Educational Psychology*, 1977, *69*, 136–145.

Campbell, D. T. Enhancement of contrast as a composite habit. *Journal of Abnormal and Social Psychology*, 1956, *53*, 350–353.

Campbell, D. T. Stereotypes and the perception of group differences. *American Psychologist*, 1967, *22*, 817–829.

Cazden, C. Subcultural differences in child language—An interdisciplinary review. *Merrill–Palmer Quarterly*, 1966, *12*, 185–219.

Chesler, M., Guskin, A., Sanchez, D., Shaevitz, M., & Smith, W. *Desegregation/integration: Planning for school change*. Washington, D.C.: National Education Association of the United States, 1974.

Clarke, R. B., & Campbell, D. T. A demonstration of bias in estimates of Negro ability. *The Journal of Abnormal and Social Psychology*, 1955, *51*, 585–588.

Clement, D. C., Eisenhart, M., & Wood, J. W. School desegregation and educational inequality—Trends in the literature, 1960–1975. In *The desegregation literature—A critical appraisal*. Washington, D.C.: U.S. Department of Health, Education, and Welfare, 1976.

Cohen, E. G. The effects of desegregation on race relations. *Law and Contemporary Problems*, 1975, *39*, 271–299.

Cohen, E. G., & Roper, S. Modification of interracial interaction disability: An application of status characteristic theory. *American Sociological Review*, 1973, *37*, 643.

Coleman, J. S., Campbell, E. Q., Hobson, C. J., McPartland, J., Mood, A. M., Weinfeld, F. D., & York, R. L. *Equality of educational opportunity*. Washington, D.C.: Office of Education, U.S. Government Printing Office, 1966.

Coleman, J. S., Kelly, S. D., & Moore, J. A. *Recent trends in school integration*. Paper presented at the Annual Meeting of the American Educational Research Association, Washington, D.C., April 1975.

Cook, S.W. Motives in a conceptual analysis of attitude-related behavior. In D. Levine (Ed.), *Nebraska Symposium on Motivation, 1969*. Lincoln: University of Nebraska Press, 1969.

Cook, S. W. Interpersonal and attitudinal outcomes in cooperating interracial groups. *Journal of Research and Development in Education*, 1978, *12*, 97–113.

Crain, R. L., & Mahard, R. L. *Desegregation and black achievement*. Institute of Policy Sciences and Public Affairs. Durham, N.C.: Duke University, 1977.

Crain, R. L., & Mahard, R. E. School racial composition and black college attendance and achievement test performance. *Sociology of Education*. 1978, *51*, 81–101.

Crain, R. L., & Weisman, C. S. *Discrimination, personality, and achievement: A survey of northern blacks*. New York: Seminar, 1972.

Crain, R. L., Armor, D., Christen, F. G., King, N. M., McLaughlin, M. W., Sumner, G. C., Thomas, M. A., & Vanecko, J. J. *Design for a national study of school desegregation* (R–1516/1–USCCR). Santa Monica, Calif.: Rand, 1974.

Curtis, R. F., & Jackson, E. F. *Inequality in American communities*. New York: Academic, 1977.

DeBord, L. W., Griffin, L., & Clark, M. Race and sex influences in the schooling processes of rural and small town youth. *Sociology of Education*, 1977, *50*, 85–102.

Deutsch, M., & Gerard, H. G. A study of normative and informational social influence upon individual judgment. *Journal of Abnormal and Social Psychology*, 1955, *51*, 629–636.

DeVries, D. L., & Edwards, K. Student teams and learning games: Their effects on cross-race and cross-sex interaction. *Journal of Educational Psychology*, 1974, *66*, 741–749.

DeVries, D. L., & Slavin, R. E. Teams-Games-Tournaments (TGT): Review of ten classroom experiments. *Journal of Research and Development in Education*, 1978, *12*, 28–38.

Douvan, E. Social status and success strivings. In J. W. Atkinson (Ed.), *Motives in fantasy, action, and society*. New York: Van Nostrand, 1958, pp. 509–517.

Duncan, O. D., Featherman, D. L., & Duncan, B. *Socioeconomic background and achievement*. New York: Seminar, 1972.

Dunkin, M., & Biddle, B. *The study of teaching*. New York: Holt, Rinehart & Winston, 1974.

Edmonds, R. R. Search for effective schools: The identification and analysis of the schools that are instructionally effective for poor children. Unpublished manuscript, Harvard University, 1976.

Falk, W. School desegregation and the educational attainment process: Some results from rural Texas schools. *Sociology of Education*, 1978, *51*, 282–288.

Farley, R. Residential segregation and its implications for school integration. *Law and Contemporary Problems*, 1975, *39*, 164–193.

Festinger, L. A. *A theory of cognitive dissonance*. Stanford, Calif.: Stanford University Press, 1957.

Gerard, H. B. Deviation, conformity and commitment. In I. D. Steiner & M. Fishbein (Eds.), *Current studies in social psychology*. New York: Holt, Rinehart and Winston, 1965.

Gerard, H. B., & Miller, N. *School desegregation*, New York: Plenum, 1975.

Gerard, H. B., Jackson, T. D., & Conolley, E. S. Social contact in the desegregated classroom. In H. B. Gerard & N. Miller, *School desegregation*. New York: Plenum, 1975.

Glazer, N. Foreward. In N. H. St. John, *School desegregation: Outcomes for children*. New York: Wiley, 1975.

Glock, C., Wuthnow, B., Pilliavin, J., & Spencer, M. *Adolescent prejudice*. New York: Harper & Row, 1975.

Hanushek, E. Teacher characteristics and gains in student achievement: Estimation using microdata. *American Economic Review*, 1971, *61*, 280–288.

Heim, J. J. *What research says about improving student performance*. Albany: The University of the State of New York, The State Education Department, Bureau of School Programs Evaluation, March 1973.

Hendrick, I. G. The development of a school integration plan in Riverside, California: A history and perspective. Unpublished manuscript, State McAteer Project Number M7-14, September 1968.

Jencks, C. Inequality in retrospect. *Harvard Educational Review*, 1973, *43*, 138-164.

Jencks, C., Smith, M., Acland, H., Bane, M. J., Cohen, D., Gintis, H., Heyns, N., & Michelson, S. *Inequality a reassessment of the effect of family and schooling in America.* New York: Basic, 1972.

Jensen, A. R. How much can we boost IQ and scholastic achievement? *Harvard Educational Review*, 1969, *39*, 1-123.

Johnson, D. W., & Johnson, R. T. Instructional goal structure: Cooperative, competitive or individualistic. *Review of Educational Research*, 1974, *44*, 213-240.

Johnson, D. W., & Johnson, R. *Learning together and alone—Cooperation, competition, and individualization.* Englewood Cliffs, N.J.: Prentice-Hall, 1975.

Joreskog, K. G. A general method for analysis of covariance structures. *Biometrika*, 1970, *57*, 239-251.

Katz, I. Factors influencing Negro performance in the desegregated school. In M. Deutsch, I. Katz, & A. R. Jensen (Eds.), *Social class, race and psychological development.* New York: Holt, Rinehart and Winston, 1968.

Kerckhoff, A. C., & Campbell, R. T. Black–white differences in the educational attainment process. *Sociology of Education*, 1977, *50*, 15-27.

Kiesler, C. A. *The psychology of commitment: Experiments linking behavior to belief.* New York: Academic, 1971.

Kirby, D. J., & Crain, R. L., The functions of conflict: School desegregation in 91 cities. *Social Science Quarterly*, 1974, *55*, 478-492.

Kirp, D. L. Race, politics, and the courts: School desegregation in San Francisco. *Harvard Educational Review*, 1976, *46*, 572-611.

Kurtz, H. The educational and demographic consequences of four years of school desegregation in the Pasadena Unified School District. Pasadena, California: Pasadena Unified School District, 1975.

Labov, W. The logic of nonstandard dialect. In J. Alatis (Ed.), *School of languages and linguistics monograph series, No. 22.* Washington, D.C.: Georgetown University, 1969.

Lewis, R., & St. John, N. Contribution of cross-racial friendship to minority group achievement in desegregated classrooms. *Sociometry*, 1974, *37*, 79-91.

Likert, R. *The human organization.* New York: McGraw-Hill, 1967.

McClelland, D. C. *The achieving society.* Princeton, N.J.: Van Nostrand, 1961.

McGarvey, W. E. *Longitudinal factors in school desegregation.* Unpublished doctoral dissertation, University of Southern California, 1977.

McGarvey, W. E., & Miller, N. Causal relations among personality variables and academic achievement: A cross-lagged panel analysis. Unpublished manuscript, 1978.

Maruyama, G. *A causal-model analysis of variables related to primary school achievement.* Unpublished doctoral dissertation, University of Southern California, 1977.

Mercer, J. R. Evaluating integrated elementary education. Unpublished manuscript, University of California, Riverside, 1973.

Mercer, J. R. Student mental health in desegregated schools. Unpublished grant proposal, University of California, Riverside, 1975.

Mercer, J. R., & Scout, T. The relationship between school desegregation and changes in the racial composition of California School Districts, 1966-73. Unpublished manuscript, 1974.

Miller, N. Summary and conclusions. In H. B. Gerard & N. Miller, *School desegregation.* New York: Plenum, 1975.

Miller, N. *Principles relevant to successful school desegregation.* SSRI Research Report, Social Science Research Institute, University of Southern California, 1977.

Minkovich, A., Davis, D., & Bashi, J. *An evaluation study of Israeli elementary schools.* Hebrew University School of Education, Jerusalem, June 1977.

Mussen, P. H. Differences between the TAT responses of Negro and White boys. *Journal of Consulting Psychology*, 1953, *17*, 373–376.

O'Reilly, R. P., & Solomon, D. School, classroom and individual influences on the outcomes of school desegregation. Unpublished research proposal, Department of Research and Evaluation, Montgomery County Public Schools, Rockville, Maryland, 1976.

Orfield, G. How to make desegregation work: The adaptation of schools to their newly integrated student bodies. *Law and Contemporary Problems*, 1975, *39*, 314–340.

Pettigrew, T. F. *Racially separate or together?* New York: McGraw-Hill, 1971.

Pettigrew, T. F., & Green, R. L. School desegregation in large cities: A critique of the Coleman "White Flight" thesis. *Harvard Educational Review*, 1976, *46*, 1–53.

Pettigrew, T. F., Useem, E. L., Normand, C., & Smith, M. Busing: A review of "the evidence." *Public Interest*, 1973, *30*, 88–118.

Porter, J. N. Race socialization, and mobility in educational and early occupational attainment. *American Sociological Review*, 1974, *39*, 303–316.

Portes, A., & Wilson, K. L. Black–white differences in educational attainment. *American Sociological Review*, 1976, *41*, 414–431.

Purl, M. C., & Dawson, J. A longitudinal and cross-sectional study of the achievement of black and Spanish-surnamed students in desegregated elementary and secondary schools. Unpublished manuscript, Riverside Unified School District, Riverside, Calif. 1973.

Rollins, H. A., McCandless, B. R., Thompson, M., & Brassell, W. R. Project success environment: An extended application of contingency management in inner-city schools. *Journal of Educational Psychology*, 1974, *66*, 167–178.

Rosenberg, M., & Simmons, R. G. *Black and white self-esteem: The urban school child.* Washington, D.C.: American Sociological Association, 1971.

Rossell, C. School desegregation and white flight. *Political Science Quarterly*, 1975–1976, *90*, 675–695.

Rosenshine, B. *Teaching behaviours and student achievement.* London: NFER, 1971.

Rosenthal, R., & Jacobson, L. *Pygmalion in the classroom: Teacher expectation and pupils' intellectual development.* New York: Holt, Rinehart and Winston, 1968.

Schmuck, R. A. Helping teachers improve classroom group processes. *Journal of Applied Behavioral Science*, 1968, *4*, 401–435.

Schofield, J. W. *To be or not to be (black).* Paper presented at the Annual Convention of the American Psychological Association, Chicago, September 1975.

Schofield, J. W. School desegregation and intergroup relations. In D. Bar-Tal & L. Saxe (Eds.), *Social psychology of education: Theory and research.* Washington, D.C.: Hemisphere, 1978.

Schofield, J. W., & Sagar, H. A. Peer interaction patterns in an integrated middle school. *Sociometry*, 1977, *40*, 130–138.

Sewell, W. H., & Hauser, R. M. *Education, occupation, and earnings: Achievement in the early career.* New York: Academic, 1975.

Sewell, W. H., Haller, A. O., & Portes, A. The educational and early occupational attainment process. *American Sociological Review*, 1969, *34*, 82–92.

Sewell, W. H., Haller, A. O., & Ohlendorf, G. W. The educational and early occupational status attainment process: Replication and revision. *American Sociological Review*, 1970, *35*, 1014–1027.

Sharan, S. Cooperative learning in small groups: A review of methods and effects on achievement, attitudes and race/ethnic relations. Unpublished manuscript, 1978.

Sharan, S., & Sharan, Y. *Small group teaching.* Englewood Cliffs, N.J.: Educational Technology, 1976.

Sherif, M. A study of some social factors in perception. *Archives of Psychology*, 1935, *27*, No. 187.

Sherif, M. *In common predicament: Social psychology of intergroup conflict and cooperation.* Boston: Houghton-Mifflin, 1966.

Sherif, M., & Sherif, C. W. *Groups in harmony and tension.* New York: Harper, 1953.

Sherif, M., & Sherif, C. W. *Reference groups: Exploration into conformity and deviation of adolescents.* New York: Harper, 1964.

Sherif, M., Harvey, O. J., White, B. J., Hood, W. R., & Sherif, C. W. *Intergroup conflict and cooperation: The Robber's Cave experiment.* Norman, Okl.: Institute of Group Relations, University of Oklahoma, 1961.

Silverman, I., & Shaw, M. E. Effects of sudden mass desegregation on interracial interaction and attitudes in one southern city. *Journal of Social Issues*, 1973, *29*, 133–142.

Singer, H., Gerard, H. B., & Redfearn, D. Achievement. In H. B. Gerard & N. Miller, *School desegregation.* New York: Plenum, 1975.

Slavin, R. E. Student teams and achievement divisions. *Journal of Research and Development in Education*, 1978, *12*, 39–49.

Solomon, D., & Kendall, A. J. *Final Report: Individual characteristics and children's performance in varied educational settings.* Rockville, Md.: Montgomery County Public Schools, 1976.

Sowell, T. Patterns of black excellence. *The Public Interest*, 1976, *43*, 26–58.

Stephan, W. G. School desegregation: An evaluation of predictions made in *Brown v. Board of Education. Psychological Bulletin*, 1978, *85*, 217–238.

Stephan, W. G., & Rosenfield, D. The effects of desegregation on race relations and self-esteem. *Journal of Educational Psychology*, 1978, *70*, 670–679.

Stewart, W. Urban Negro speech: Sociolinguistic factors affecting English teaching. In R. Shuy (Ed.), *Social dialects and language learning.* Champaign, Ill.: NCTE, 1964.

St. John, N. H. *School desegregation:* Outcomes for children. New York: Wiley, 1975.

Strodtbeck, F. L., *Family interaction, values and achievement.* In D. C. McClelland, A. L. Baldwin, U. Bronfenbrenner, & F. L. Strodtbeck (Eds.), *Talent and Society.* New York: Van Nostrand, 1958, pp. 135.

Sullivan, N. Personal communication, Aug. 1977.

Taeuber, K. E. Racial segregation: The persisting dilemma. *Annals*, 1975, *422*, 87–96.

Torrey, J. W. Illiteracy in the ghetto. *Harvard Educational Review*, 1970, *40*, 253–259.

United States Commission on Civil Rights. *Racial isolation in the public schools.* Washington, D.C.: U.S. Government Printing Office, 1967.

Van der Zanden, J. W. *American minority relations* (3rd ed.). New York: Ronald, 1972.

Weber, S. J., Cook, T. D., & Campbell, D. T. *The effect of school integration on the academic self-concept of public school students.* Paper presented at the Midwestern Psychological Association meetings, Detroit, May 1971.

Weigel, R. H., Wiser, P. L., & Cook, S. W. The impact of cooperative learning experiences on cross-ethnic relations and attitudes. *Journal of Social Issues*, 1972, *28*, 1–19.

Weinberg, M. The relationship between school desegregation and academic achievement: A review of the research. *Law and Contemporary Problems*, 1975, *39*, 240–270.

Weinberg, M. *Minority students: A research appraisal.* Washington, D.C.: National Institute of Education, U.S. Government Printing Office, 1977.

Weiner, B., Frieze, I., Kukla, A., Reed, L., Rest, S., & Rosenbaum, R. M. *Perceiving the causes of success and failure.* New York: General Learning, Module Series, 1971.

Westman, G., & Miller, N. Concomitants of outgroup prejudice in desegregated elementary school children. SSRI Research Report, Social Science Research Institute, University of Southern California, 1978.

Williams, F. *Language and poverty.* Chicago: Markham, 1970.

Wilson, W. Rank order of discrimination and its relevance to civil rights priorities. *Journal of Personality and Social Psychology*, 1970, *15*, 188–224.

Zimbardo, P. G. *The cognitive control of motivation: The consequences of choice and dissonance*. Glenview, Ill.: Scott, Foresman, 1969.

Index